BRAVE HEARTS

Indian Women of the Plains

Joseph Agonito

TWODOT®

GUILFORD. CONNECTICUT
HELENA. MONTANA

A · TWODOT® · BOOK

An imprint and registered trademark of The Rowman & Littlefield Publishing Group, Inc.
4501 Forbes Blvd., Ste. 200
Lanham, MD 20706
www.rowman.com

Distributed by NATIONAL BOOK NETWORK

British Library Cataloguing-in-Publication Information available

Library of Congress Cataloging-in-Publication Data
Names: Agonito, Joseph, author.
Title: Brave hearts : Indian women of the Plains / Joseph Agonito.
Description: Guilford, Connecticut : TwoDot, [2017] | Includes bibliographical references and index.
Identifiers: LCCN 2016012458 (print) | LCCN 2016035338 (ebook) | ISBN 9781493019052 (hardcover : alk. paper) | ISBN 9781493019069 (ebook)
Subjects: LCSH: Indian women—Great Plains—Biography. | Indians of North America—Great Plains—Biography.
Classification: LCC E78.G73 A37 2017 (print) | LCC E78.G73 (ebook) | DDC 920.0092/97078—dc23
LC record available at https://lccn.loc.gov/2016012458

ISBN 978-1-4930-5249-3 (paper : alk. paper)

CONTENTS

CONTENTS

PREFACE

Some years ago I published *Lakota Portraits: Lives of the Legendary Plains People*, a series of biographical sketches that illuminated the course of Lakota history from their earliest times to the present. In researching *Lakota Portraits* it became clear that given the nature of the historical literature, the book would center largely, though not exclusively, on the accomplishment of men—as hunters, warriors, civil chiefs, and spiritual leaders. I did include some women in *Lakota Portraits*, but I always wanted to do more in telling the fascinating life stories of Plains Indian women from the many tribes—nomadic and horticultural—that lived on the Great Plains. *Brave Hearts: Indian Women of the Plains* is that book.

There are, of course, fine studies of Plains Indian women. Marla N. Powers's *Oglala Women: Myth, Ritual, and Reality* and Virginia Bergman Peters's *Women of the Earth Lodges: Tribal Life on the Plains* come to mind—but these excellent books are more analytical or descriptive than biographical in nature. Nancy M. Peterson's *Walking in Two Worlds: Mixed-Blood Indian Women Seeking Their Path* employs the biographical approach in telling the story of a special group of biracial Indian women, including some from the Great Plains. But there is no single study that portrays through a series of biographical portraits the rich diversity of Plains Indian women from the major nomadic and horticulture tribes in the nineteenth and twentieth centuries, which is the central focus of *Brave Hearts: Indian Women of the Plains*.

My decision to tell the story of Plains Indian women through a biographical approach influenced the methodology I had to follow. The first question was simply who to include? The study, out of necessity, had to be selective. It could not include all Plains Indian women for whom there existed some sort of documentary record. There would have to be a sufficient body of material that permitted the telling of a woman's life story—though with Plains Indian women there was often less documentation than with famous men, so it became necessary to mine every conceivable source of information, which is noted in the text and bibliography.

Above all, I wanted the book to represent the rich diversity of Plains Indian women, who lived extraordinary lives: hunters and warriors, women who led traditional lives within their nomadic or horticulture tribes, women who transitioned between the old days and the world of the reservation, women who were biracial struggling to live in two worlds, educated women who challenged white dominance over their culture and land, and modern reservation women who fought to retain their tribal identity while adapting to an intrusive white world. I decided to break ground by including two remarkable persons who would not ordinarily be included in a book on Plains Indian women: Cynthia Ann Parker, who had been captured as a young girl and after many years of living with the Comanches considered herself a member of the tribe; and Osh Tisch, a Crow batée, who having been born a male decided at a very young age to live her life fully as a woman.

I have written *Brave Hearts: Indian Women of the Plains* for a general audience, but the work is grounded in the best historical literature. I have cited my major sources in the text and in the detailed bibliographies that buttress each chapter. Accordingly, there are few footnotes. Sometimes the footnotes document a point in the text, sometimes they reference a special source that proved indispensable for understanding the character, and sometimes they seek to reconcile differing accounts in the oral tradition.

Although the work of a researcher/writer is sometimes a lonely endeavor, I have been surrounded these past few years with rich companions: the fascinating women who grace these pages. I am grateful to the women who shared their life stories with Euro-Americans—Kate Bighead, Iron Teeth, Pretty Shield, Buffalo Bird Woman, and Sanapia—and I am likewise grateful to these same Euro-American men, such as Dr. Thomas B. Marquis, Frank Linderman, Gilbert Wilson, and David E. Jones, who realized the importance of collecting these stories for the historical record. I am grateful to those women—Susette La Flesche, Josephine Waggoner, Zitkala-Ša, and Mary Brave Bird—who studied, sometimes painfully, in American schools and acquired a command of the English language, which they then used to tell their own life stories and those of their people from an Indian perspective. The legion of Native and Euro-American historians who have researched and written about Plains Indian women are too numerous to mention here, though they are all listed in the text and bibliography.

Although I conducted most of the research and writing for *Brave Hearts: Indian Women of the Plains* in upstate New York—far from the West—I have traveled across the Great Plains a number of times. I was always struck by the beauty and grandeur of the landscape and can appreciate why the loss of their ancestral lands and way of life pained many of the women in this study.

I have visited over time many places that were special to some of the women in this book: the Knife River villages of the Mandan and Hidatsa, so important to the early life of Buffalo Bird Woman; the Little Bighorn Battle site, where Buffalo Calf Road fought Custer, an incident reported by Kate Bighead in her memoir; Fort Robinson, where Iron Teeth suffered imprisonment and the loss of her beloved son; the Wounded Knee cemetery at Pine Ridge, where Lost Bird began her tragic life and which is now her final resting place, and where, many years later during the takeover of Wounded Knee in 1973, Mary Brave Bird gave birth to her son. I hope that the grandeur of the Great Plains and the special nature of these historic sites inform this narrative.

CHAPTER 1

Woman Chief: Leader of Her People

The young girl who would one day become a skilled hunter, a fierce warrior, and a prominent chief of a Crow band was born a member of the Gros Ventre of the Prairie. Though she was captured by the Crows in 1816 when she just ten years old, there is no record of her birth name among the Gros Ventre or her childhood name among the Crows.

Like so many female captives, she was adopted by a Crow family, but the young girl made no effort to assist the women of the lodge in domestic pursuits. She preferred to shoot at birds while practicing her skill with the bow and arrow, to learn to ride the family's horses, and to guard those horses. In time she learned to handle a gun. Tall and strong, she rivaled most young men in riding horses and killing game. Mounted on her buffalo pony, she could kill four or five buffalo in the chase and without assistance cut up the meat, which she then loaded on her packhorses. Even on foot she killed deer and bighorn sheep, which she butchered and carried home on her back. Her adoptive father encouraged her in these pursuits.

Despite these "manly" activities, she continued to dress as a woman. Edwin Denig, the longtime fur trader at Fort Union on the Upper Missouri who knew Woman Chief for some twelve years, said that she was "tolerably good looking" but for some reason (perhaps she was such a strong figure) she did not attract much attention from Crow men. Woman Chief, who was not given this name until much later in her life, went her own, single way. When her adoptive, widowed father died, she assumed responsibility for his lodge and family.

As a young woman, she counted her first coup in battle in an unexpected way. She was with a small band of Crows encamped near a trading post when a Blackfoot war party attacked their lodges. Several men were killed and the survivors fled with their horses into the fort for protection. The enemy, camped outside of rifle range, signaled that they wanted to speak to someone in the fort. No white trader or Crow warrior was foolish enough to venture outside the fort; none, except the young woman. When she

1

Shoshone female catching a horse, painting by Alfred Jacob Miller, 1837

appeared outside the fort, a group of Blackfeet warriors, sensing an easy tar-get, charged the lone figure. She urged them to stop, but one of them fired a shot at her. In response, she fired her pistol, killing a warrior. The stunned Blackfeet watched as she quickly shot two more with arrows. Reinforced, the enraged warriors charged the woman, who swiftly escaped to the safety of the fort, where whites and Crows shouted praise of her bravery.

Her small band composed songs celebrating the young woman's bravery, and soon her daring deed against the Blackfeet was known throughout Crow country. She was now a warrior woman. A year later she led her first war party against the Blackfeet, attacking their camp at night and running off with seventy horses. The Blackfeet followed, and in the ensuing fight, the young woman killed and scalped one of her enemies. A second Blackfoot was wounded in the fight, and Woman Chief counted coup by being the first to strike the fallen warrior and take his gun. The Crows returned victorious with Blackfeet horses and two scalps.

Over time the young woman led further raiding parties against her people's enemies, always returning victorious with horses and scalps. Proud of their warrior woman, the Crows composed songs celebrating her brave deeds. In time the elders invited her to attend the council of chiefs and warriors, where she took her place among the chiefs, ranking third in a band of one hundred and sixty lodges. They gave her the honored name of Woman Chief.

In the following years she continued her life as a hunter and warrior, but the domestic chores of keeping a lodge seemed increasingly ill-suited to her newfound status. She needed help in tending her many horses and in preparing buffalo hides for trading purposes at the nearby forts. So, she did the unexpected: she took a "wife" in the traditional Crow way by offering the bride's family traditional gifts. In time Woman Chief took three more wives to help with keeping her prosperous lodge. What sexual relationship, if any, Woman Chief had with her wives remains a mystery. Edwin Denig, who wrote the first sketch of Woman Chief, offered only a tantalizing comment when he marveled at Crow country where some "males [the berdache] assume the dress and perform the duties of females while women turn men and mate with their own sex!" For a writer who should have known more about Woman Chief's private life, he said, unfortunately, very little.

The only other European who met Woman Chief was Rudolph Friederich Kurz, a Swiss artist and explorer. Denig introduced the two at Fort Union. Kurz called her "the famous Absaroka amazon." In a journal entry dated October 27, 1851, Kurz left an invaluable description of Woman Chief: "She looked neither savage nor warlike. On the contrary, as I entered the room she sat with her hands in her lap, folded, as when one prays. She is about 45 years old; appears modest in manners and good natured rather than quick to quarrel."

Woman Chief had presented Denig a scalp that she had taken from a Blackfoot warrior. Denig gave the scalp as a gift to Kurz, who was so excited that he forgot to paint a portrait of Woman Chief, missing a splendid moment to capture a likeness of one of the most remarkable women in Crow history. It would not come again, as Woman Chief died a few years later in a most tragic way.

The Treaty of Fort Laramie in 1851, which had established tribal boundaries, opened up the possibilities of peace among the Northern Plains tribes. The Gros Ventres of the Prairie, for instance, sent friendly messages to their enemies, the Assiniboines and the Crows, and invited them to visit. The Assiniboines accepted the invitation. They were well received by the Gros Ventre, who gave them horses as presents. Woman Chief, a long-time warrior, decided to play the role of peacemaker. She planned to visit the Gros Ventres and reach a peace between the tribe of her birth and her adoptive tribe, the Crows. Many of her old friends—Indian and white fur traders—tried to dissuade her from this dangerous journey as her military exploits against the Gros Ventres were too well known. But Woman Chief, perhaps overly confident in her abilities, persisted. Accompanied by four Crow warriors, she traveled north of the Missouri, where she met a large party of Gros Ventres returning home from a trading expedition at Fort Union. Woman Chief boldly approached the group; she spoke to them in their own language and smoked the pipe with them. As they made their way to the main camp, some of the party discovered that this woman was one of their most hated enemies. They shot her and the four Crow warriors in cold blood.

Denig was saddened by the death of this remarkable woman who, for so many years, had conducted herself with distinction in all things, and who had achieved a measure of fame, honor, riches, standing, and influence that no woman had ever achieved among the Crows.

CHAPTER 2

Osh Tisch: Becoming a Woman

Osh Tisch, which in the Crow language loosely translates as "Finds Them and Kills Them," was the most famous (and, perhaps, the last surviving) batée that ever lived among the Crows. The Crow batée was a man who, for deeply personal or religious reasons, assumed the dress, occupation, manner, and sexual behavior of the female sex, thereby creating a change in gender status.[1]

Osh Tisch's remarkable career spanned the transition from the old nomadic life to the harsh realities of the reservation. Born in 1854, Osh Tisch (there is no record of his/her birth name) was a member of the Mountain Crows. Osh Tisch was born a boy, but during an interview Osh Tisch gave late in her life to retired General Hugh L. Scott, she stated that from infancy she felt destined to live life as a girl and not as a boy. At the time of this interview in 1919, Osh Tisch, who was then around sixty-five years old, was known by white people at the agency by her more common (and perhaps derisive) name, "Woman Jim."

Scott found "Woman Jim" at her home on the Crow Reservation near St. Xavier on the Big Horn River, wearing a calico dress with her hair combed in a woman's fashion. Familiar with the historical literature on the "berdache" tradition—that is, men who lived as women—Scott pressed Woman Jim if she had been pressured to live like a woman by some medicine man or because she had had a spiritual dream or vision when young. Woman Jim replied categorically: "No. Didn't I [already] tell you—that is my road? I have done it ever since I can remember because I want to do it. My Father and Mother did not like it. They used to whip me, take away my girl's clothes and put boy's clothes on me but I threw them away—and got girl's clothes and dolls to play with." Woman Jim gave the same answer when

---

1   The Europeans referred to such men as "berdaches," a term that Native Americans dislike. I prefer to use the Crow term for such persons as Osh Tisch, which has been rendered over time as "boté," "baté," and "badé." When citing Crow or Euro-American observers, I use the term they employ; but, in all other cases, I use the term "batée," which is how the most recent Crow dictionary spells the word.

Osh Tisch (Finds Them and Kills Them) posing in her elaborate burial dress, 1928 COURTESY OF MUSEUM OF THE AMERICAN INDIAN, HEYE FOUNDATION, NEW YORK CITY. PHOTOGRAPHED BY CROW AGENT, C. H. ASBURY

Scott asked if other batées were inspired by a spirit or vision: "No," Woman Jim replied, "it was just natural, they were born that way."

While some anthropologists viewed the male "berdache" as a person who chose to live life as a woman, others, most notably Walter L. Williams and Sabine Lang, reject the concept of the "berdache" as a "transexual woman." They argue that the "berdache" was androgynous—a gender mixing of masculine and feminine, in effect, a "third gender." But this was not true for Osh Tisch, who suffered no gender ambivalence. Osh Tisch decided from an early age that she was destined to live her life as a woman, and Crow traditionalists accepted her gender transformation.

Osh Tisch came of age in the glory days of the Crows in the mid-nineteenth century as they hunted buffalo and fought their enemies to preserve their beautiful land in the Powder River country in Montana. By early adulthood Osh Tisch had become a respected batée. She was not alone. Prince Maximilian, a German explorer who visited the Northern Plains in the mid-1830s, noted the many "berdaches" who lived among the Crows, as did Edwin Thompson Denig, a fur trader who wrote an early account of the Crow nation. Lieutenant Hugh L. Scott, who lived among the Crows for a few weeks in the summer of 1877, noted that he counted five or six males wearing women's clothes but did not pay it much attention at the time. A. B. Holder, an agency physician at Crow Agency in the 1880s, who knew Osh Tisch personally, also said that there were five "berdaches" living at the Crow Agency at that time.

The Crow batées lived in close relationship with one another, and as Holder pointed out, they also maintained a special "fellowship" with other "berdaches" among the Northern Plains tribes. Even though the Crow batées spent considerable time with women, they pitched their lodges together in the camp and lived as a distinct group. Thomas Yellowtail, a prominent Crow elder, told anthropologist Walter L. Williams that the Crow "badés" called each other "sister" and recognized Osh Tisch as their leader.

The Crow batées, free from the obligations that came from bearing and raising children, devoted themselves to women's work. They excelled in all aspects of domesticity: they were experts in sewing, beading, and tanning hides; they butchered animals and proved the most efficient cooks; their tipis were the largest and the best looking; and they were highly regarded for their many charitable acts.

A. B. Holder provided the earliest description of OshTisch. He referred to the "berdache" with the Crow word "boté," which he defined as "not man, not woman." Though the doctor disdained the boté's sexual lifestyle, he found Osh Tisch a "splendidly formed fellow, of prepossessing face, in perfect health, active in movement, and happy in disposition." For a small sum, the doctor persuaded a reluctant Osh Tisch to submit to a thorough physical exam.

Dr. Holder noted that Osh Tisch was thirty-three years old and that he (Holder did not use the female pronoun in referring to Osh Tisch) had dressed like a woman since the age of five. Osh Tisch was five feet eight inches in height and weighed one hundred and fifty-eight pounds, with a frank, intelligent, and beardless face. Holder commented that Osh Tisch was dressed that day in typical female attire. His hair measured at least twenty-four inches long and was parted (like a female) in the center and allowed to hang loose in two masses behind the shoulders. Holder removed OshTisch's dress and found his skin smooth and free from hair on the legs, arms, breast, or armpits; but, as the doctor pointed out, this was not unusual for Indian men or women. Osh Tisch's breasts were small, as usually found in the male.

Dr. Holder then proceeded to the most "interesting" part of the examination, the sexual organs. Before the examination began, Osh Tisch secured a promise from the doctor that he would not reveal anything about the exam to the agent or any member of the tribe. When Osh Tisch removed his dress, Holder could see nothing since "he threw his thighs together as to completely conceal his organs." When Holder finally persuaded Osh Tisch to open his thighs, it became clear that he showed perfectly normal male organs. After the examination was completed, Osh Tisch told the physician that no one had seen his genital organs since childhood and that he hid his sexual organs even from the women with whom he long associated.

Osh Tisch denied that he ever had sex with a female; in fact, Holder noted that Osh Tisch "lived for two years as the female party to a marital partnership with a well-known male Indian." Osh Tisch was not a homosexual, which is how some Euro-Americans defined the "berdache." Unfortunately, even the recent *A Dictionary of Everyday Crow* described the batée as "homosexual, gay," a concession to modern, not historical Crow, sensibilities. Though the sexual relationship between a batée and a typical man is anatomically "same sex," that is not how traditional Crows perceived the relationship. As Dr. Holder wisely pointed out, Osh Tisch was the female partner in the relationship, and the male partner understood that he was having sex with a transformed woman.[2]

For some unexplainable reason Osh Tisch assumed the role of a warrior for a day in the summer of 1876. General George Crook sent some runners to the Crow Agency to recruit scouts for his campaign against the Lakotas and Cheyennes. One hundred and seventy-five warriors signed up for the fight against their traditional enemies. In the crowd of men, which included

---

2   Sabine Lang, *Men as Women, Women as Men: Changing Gender in Native American Cultures*, Austin: University of Texas Press, 1998, pp. 206–212, made a compelling case that such a sexual relationship was not homosexual because the parties were of different genders.

the war leader Plenty Coup, there were two remarkable women characters: Osh Tisch and The Other Magpie.

In the 1930s Pretty Shield, an elderly Crow woman, told her fascinating life story to Frank Linderman, a Montana frontiersman and journalist. It was Pretty Shield who revealed, perhaps for the first time, the role Finds Them and Kills Them (Pretty Shield and Linderman referred to Osh Tisch by the English rendering of her name) and The Other Magpie played in the fight against the Lakotas that took place on Rosebud Creek in Montana on June 17, 1876.

Pretty Shield saw the Crow scouts leave the village to join General Crook's blue-coat soldiers and described how Finds Them and Kills Them "looked like a man, and yet she wore woman's clothes; and she had the heart of a woman. Besides, she did a woman's work. She was not a man, and not yet a woman." While recognizing the special nature of the batée, Pretty Shield respected the womanly side of Finds Them and Kills Them by always referring to "her" with feminine pronouns.

The Other Magpie rode a "black horse" armed only with a coup stick. She "wore a stuffed woodpecker on her head, and her forehead was painted yellow." Pretty Shield said that she was a "wild one who had no man of her own. She was both bad and brave . . . and she was pretty." The Other Magpie went to war seeking revenge for her brother who had been killed by the Lakotas.

During the fight at the Rosebud, these two women fought bravely, expecting death at the hands of the enemy. For this reason, Finds Them and Kills Them changed into men's clothing before the fighting began. Pretty Shield explained Finds Them and Kills Them's reasoning: "so that if killed the Lacota would not laugh at her, lying there with a woman's clothes on her. She did not want the Lacota to believe that she was a Crow man hiding in a woman's dress."

The two women counted coup that day. At one point in the fight, Bull Snake fell from his horse, badly wounded. Finds Them and Kills Them rode to his defense, firing her gun at the advancing Lakotas. The Other Magpie rode around her two comrades "singing her war song and waving her coup stick" against the enemy. When the Lakotas charged them, The Other Magpie "rode straight at them, waving her coup stick." So strong was her "medicine" that day that the Lakota warriors turned and rode away. Bull Snake was saved.

For a second time, The Other Magpie rode straight at the Lakotas with only her coup stick and "spat at them." She mocked the enemy by calling out: "See, my spit is my arrow[s]." Finds Them and Kills Them rode behind and shot an enemy warrior. The Other Magpie took his scalp.

Pretty Shield watched with excitement as the scouts returned to the village while The Other Magpie and Finds Them and Kills Them continued to look after the wounded Bull Snake. The Other Magpie waved with pride the enemy scalp she had taken in the fight. Pretty Shield was "proud of these two women, even the wild one, because she was brave."

The Other Magpie, who fought so bravely, regrettably disappeared from the historical record. Finds Them and Kills Them, who earned her name from the brave role she played in the Rosebud fight, would live on during the reservation era, subject to harassment from Indian agents and missionaries because of the life she had chosen so many years earlier.

Indian agents at the Crow Agency tried to control Crow sexual practices and gender relations. They were particularly hard on Osh Tisch and the few remaining batées. Joe Medicine Crow, tribal elder and historian, told the anthropologist Walter L. Williams the story of how one of the Indian agents in the 1890s tried to change the "badé." "He tried to interfere with Osh Tisch, who was the most respected badé. The agent incarcerated the badés, cut off their hair, made them wear men's clothing. He forced them to do manual labor, planting . . . trees. The people here were so upset that Chief Plenty Eagle came into Crow Agency, and told [the agent] to leave the reservation. It was a tragedy trying to change them. [The agent] was crazy."

Thanks to the intervention of Chief Plenty Eagle, Osh Tisch may have enjoyed a brief respite, but the harassment resumed during the superintendence of Evan W. Estep, the agent from 1914 to 1917. Lillian Bullshows, an elderly Crow woman who personally knew Osh Tisch (whom she called Ohchiish), recounted this story late in her life. Estep, "a hot-tempered fellow," had the Indian police drag Osh Tisch into his office. The agent angrily told Osh Tisch that he was a man and should stop dressing and acting like a woman. Friends warned Chief Plenty Coup, who rushed to protect Osh Tisch, who was "crying" outside the agent's office. Plenty Coup warned the agent that if he didn't stop harassing Osh Tisch, he would be driven from his office "within two hours." Plenty Coup defended Osh Tisch's lifestyle: "In her youth, she don't go for the men [men's way]—she dress like a woman and still she's dressed—I want it that way. She's kind to people, she's

Crow Osh Tisch in a beautiful dress holding a mirror, with her female companion, most likely The Other Magpie, a Crow warrior woman, who fought alongside Osh Tisch at the Rosebud fight, June 17, 1876, circa 1877–1878 PHOTOGRAPHED BY JOHN H. FOUCH. COURTESY OF DR. JAMES S. BRUST

good-natured, she goes to dances and takes part in every activity." Faced with such opposition, the agent relented and told the "crying" Osh Tisch that she could continue to dress like a woman. Lillian Bullshows concluded her colorful account by saying that Plenty Coup was "a good man" but that Estep was "no good."

Osh Tisch survived the agent's hostility, but it did not end there. In 1902 the Crows invited the Reverend William Petzold, a young Baptist minister, to come to Crow Agency and set up a day school for the children. Along with the school came Petzold's version of Christianity. Thomas Yellowtail, a Crow tribal elder, shared with anthropologist Walter Williams what then happened: "When the Baptist missionary Peltotz [sic] arrived in 1903, he condemned our traditions, including the badé. He told congregation members to stay away from Osh Tisch and the other badés. He continued to condemn Osh Tisch until his death in the late 1920s. This may be the reason why no others took up the badé role after Osh Tisch died."

Despite the hostility of the agent and the missionary, Osh Tisch did not alter her domestic lifestyle or lose status among the traditional Crows in the last years of her life as witnessed by the distinguished chiefs who defended her from the hostility of Indian agents. During these years Osh Tisch built a home near St. Xavier on land that she was allotted in the 1880s. Occasionally, members of her family lived at her homestead. Exploring census returns for these years, historian Will Roscoe, who has spent years studying the "berdache" tradition, found out that Osh Tisch was listed as head of a family, which consisted of a brother, niece, and nephew, along with other adults and children. By 1891, however, Osh Tisch was living alone with a three-year-old boy named Brings Horses Well Known, listed as an "adopted" child. This was not unusual since berdaches were known to take in orphans. But, a few years later, the same child is listed as an adopted daughter. Roscoe speculates that Finds Them and Kills Them was raising a "berdache child."

Osh Tisch continued to maintain a wide range of friends (some were most likely "berdaches") on and off the reservation. She had her own horses and buggy, so she traveled freely wherever she wanted, often visiting the Nez Perce in Idaho, with whom she traded for grass bags—an Indian basket woven from vegetal fibers. She sold one of these Nez Perce grass bags to the wife of agent Samuel G. Reynolds. Their daughter, Carolyn Reynolds Riebeth, later wrote that she found "Maracota [Woman] Jim" a "friendly person" and "good-natured." The young Lillian Bullshows, who knew Osh Tisch during this same period, said on more than one occasion in her memoirs that Osh Tisch was "good-natured," a "nice person."

General Scott shared the same feelings as Carolyn Reynolds and Lillian Bullshows when he spent some time with "Woman Jim" (as he called Osh Tisch) in August 1919. Scott remarked favorably on Osh Tisch's womanly ways: "She was most jolly, had a simple air of complete satisfaction with herself, perfectly unconscious of anything abnormal. . . . One could not resist liking her for her frank, simple, jolly manner and evident truthfulness."

When Scott met Woman Jim, she was recovering from a severe case of blood poisoning. Thinking that she was going to die, she showed Scott with great pride her finely designed burial dress: "a dark blue woman's dress with abalone shell ornaments." Some years later the Indian agent at Crow Agency sent Scott a photograph of Woman Jim (whom the agent clearly identified as Finds Them and Kills Them) wearing her burial dress. Woman Jim parted with Scott in a friendly way, presenting him with a Nez Perce grass bag, saying, "You have come a long way—I give you this."

Osh Tisch lived her last days in the traditional way at Crow Agency. She continued to excel in the domestic crafts, even exhibiting her work beyond the agency. Once famous for sewing buffalo hides for the tipi, she turned in new directions, winning awards at county fairs for her bedspreads and traditional Crow foods.

She traveled to various sites on the reservation to take part in the traditional dances. Osh Tisch especially liked the ancient Beaver Dance, where she sang her special songs. On such occasions she would wear her prized beaded men's leggings, but she also adorned her person with earrings, bracelets, and perfumed scents.

Lillian Bullshows remembered the many times Osh Tisch visited her parents' home to enjoy her mother's good cooking and to relax by playing cards. Osh Tisch often spent the night. She called Lillian's mother "sister" and teased Lillian's father (as one would a brother-in-law). Lillian said that Osh Tisch was also a good cook, remembering that she baked biscuits while singing Beaver Dance songs. Lillian and her younger brother enjoyed Osh Tisch's visits because she often brought them some oranges and apples and candy. Even at that young age, Lillian knew that Osh Tisch was a man. Though she dressed like a woman, acted like a woman, and talked like a woman, Lillian remembered that she had a "cracked voice" that was that of a man. But Lillian never said anything to question Osh Tisch's persona. When anthropologist Robert H. Lowie visited the Crow Agency in 1907, he met Osh Tisch. Lowie was also struck by the quality of Osh Tisch's voice. "Dressed as a woman," Lowie reported, "he might have passed for one except for his affectedly *piping* [italics mine] voice."

In the last year of her life, Osh Tisch took sick and ended up in the hospital. Lillian Bullshows visited her, noting that Osh Tisch looked pale. She asked, "All right, are you feeling better?" Osh Tisch replied: "Yes, some better." Lillian left when Osh Tisch got up to go to the bathroom, promising to visit again, though she never did. She did not know if Osh Tisch ever left the hospital. "After that," Lillian said, "I never see him. That's the last time I ever talked to him."

Osh Tisch died on January 2, 1929, at the age of seventy-five. Since the age of five when she cast off boy's clothes, Osh Tisch boldly lived her life as a Crow woman. Faithful to her inner calling, she remained, in good and bad times, true to herself and all others.

CHAPTER 3

Running Eagle:
Brave-Hearted Woman

An old saying among the Blackfeet Indians of the Northern Plains, "Men for the war trail, women for the home lodge," did not apply to Running Eagle, a remarkable warrior woman whose military exploits were legendary among her people. Generations of Blackfeet women revered the extraordinary life of this woman, and some even tried to follow her brave example. Born Brown Weasel Woman, probably in the early part of the nineteenth century, she was a member of the Piegan tribe of the Blackfoot Nation. She was the eldest child of five, her father was a prominent warrior, and her mother was a traditional lodge keeper.

From an early age she expressed a desire for a more active life than was expected for a Blackfoot girl. Around the age of ten or twelve, she asked her father to make a set of bow and arrows so that she could practice shooting and become skilled with the weapon. Over time, as she grew tall and strong, her father indulged the young woman by taking her out to hunt buffalo, which she easily brought down with her bow.

On one of these hunts, Brown Weasel Woman proved her courage. After father and daughter had a successful hunt, they were returning to their home village, their horses loaded with meat. Suddenly an enemy war party attacked, shooting her father off his horse. Brown Weasel Woman, at a distance ahead of her father, quickly unloaded the meat from her horse and raced back to save her father. He jumped on her horse and they escaped to the safety of their village. Some spoke with pride of her brave deed; others were not so happy, fearing the bad influence her exploits could have on other young girls destined for the lodge.

Brown Weasel Woman may have desired the more exciting, masculine lifestyle of the warrior and the hunter, but the illness of her mother forced her to care for the lodge and her young siblings. She did the job well, but without pleasure. She had no boyfriends and took no interest in the marriage plans of her friends.[1]

The young woman's life changed suddenly. Her warrior father died in combat against the Crows and her sick mother died soon after. She seized the moment to realize her dream of following men's ways—hunting and fighting against her people's enemies. She found a widow to care for the lodge and her young siblings.

Looking for a way to prove herself a warrior, she followed at a distance a war party trying to recover some horses stolen by the Crows. She was armed with her father's gun and dressed for the fight. When discovered, the leader of the war party threatened her but she refused to leave. Even when he threatened to call off the raid if she persisted, Brown Weasel Woman boldly replied, "You can return if you want to; I will go on by myself." A cousin, with whom she had hunted, intervened and said that he would be responsible for the young woman.

The war party then continued its journey. After several days on the trail, the warriors discovered the Crow camp, and under cover of darkness, they located the Crow horse herd. Brown Weasel Woman, with her cousin, captured eleven horses. As the Blackfeet left with their captured horses, their enemy mounted a pursuit. Some distance from the Crows, the war party rested. Brown Weasel Woman stood guard on a high hill, when she spotted two Crows heading for the captured herd. She charged, shot the lead Crow, and grabbed his rifle to fire at the second Crow, who fled the scene. Brown Weasel Woman had saved the herd. One of her fellow warriors scalped the dead enemy, giving her the scalp. She had avenged the death of her father.

When the war party returned home, some praised her coup; others questioned the place of a woman on the war trail. Beverly Hungry Wolf, who interviewed elderly Blackfeet women (including her mother and grandmother) for the story of Brown Weasel Woman, which she narrated in *The Ways of My Grandmothers*, declared that this was a decisive moment for the young woman. The elders instructed Brown Weasel Woman to seek a vision

---

1   Some aspects of Running Eagle's life are controversial. Did she ever marry? James Willard Schultz, who lived among the Blackfeet Indians for a long time, insisted in his memoir, *Blackfeet and Buffalo*, that Running Eagle was a "virgin woman." But historian John Ewers, in his essay "Deadlier Than the Male," *American Heritage*, XVI (June 1965), 10–13, claimed that elderly Blackfeet warriors had told him that the young Running Eagle had married and that her husband died in a raid against the Crows. It was only then that she prayed to the Sun for revenge. She received a powerful vision, but, in return, promised that she would never take another lover.

Running Eagle knelt and aimed her gun at the Crow enemy. SKETCH BY JAMES WILLARD SCHULTZ IN *RUNNING EAGLE: THE WARRIOR GIRL*, 1919

to guide her on the correct path to follow. She fasted and prayed for four nights, and the Powers Above granted her a vision—the spiritual power she needed to lead a warrior's life. As she interpreted her dream vision, the Sun demanded that she never marry or take a lover.[2]

After her vision Brown Weasel Woman joined a war party that journeyed west of the Rockies to raid the horse herds of the Kalispell tribe. She did not wear a buckskin dress; instead, she dressed as a warrior with leggings, shirt, and breech cloth. She still had her father's rifle, along with a fine rawhide war shield.

The war party struck a Kalispell village, killing a number of the enemy and capturing more than six hundred horses. In the thick of the fight, two Kalispell arrows struck Brown Weasel Woman's shield.

---

2 Weasel Tail, an elderly Blackfoot, disagreed with the timing of this event. Weasel Tail told the historian John Ewers that the young woman went on her vision quest after the death of her husband as a way of obtaining power to avenge his death. In any case, Weasel Tail agreed with Beverly Hungry Wolf that in return for her power vision, the Sun demanded that the young woman never marry again or even take a lover.

When the war party returned home, Brown Weasel Woman celebrated the victory alongside the male warriors. She was allowed to share her war exploits, which the people applauded with "drum beats and war whoops." Lone Walker, the head chief, gave her a singular honor, renaming her Running Eagle, the ancient name of several famous warriors. The Brave Society of young warriors invited her to become a member.

Evidently her "masculine" pursuits did not frighten away all men, for some still wanted Running Eagle as a wife. But she refused them all, claiming she had vowed to the Sun never to marry. Running Eagle had no desire to give up her warrior's lifestyle and maintain a man's lodge.

Over time her status as a warrior rose among her people, and Running Eagle even led war parties against the enemy. White Grass, a prominent Piegan band chief, declared that he had joined a war party against the Nez Perce, led by Running Eagle. Discovered en route by a large group of Nez Perce, the Blackfeet quickly dug foxholes for protection. As leader of the group, Running Eagle placed her foxhole in the front. Before the fight she took out her medicine bag containing two feathers attached to a flat disk of brass, tied it to her hair, and sang her war song. Running Eagle killed the first Nez Perce who charged. Inspired by her bravery, the Blackfeet drove off the Nez Perce without suffering a single casualty.

Sometime around 1850 Running Eagle's legendary life as a warrior woman came to a dramatic end in an attack against the Flathead Indians. It was, as often the case, a revenge raid in retaliation for Flathead invasion of Blackfoot country. Running Eagle led the large Blackfoot war party. After an initial exchange of long-range gunfire, Running Eagle ordered a charge against the enemy village. In deadly hand–to-hand combat with knives and war clubs, Running Eagle was in the thick of the fight.

Somewhere in the melee a Flathead warrior struck a mortal blow with his war club, killing the legendary warrior woman.[3] Running Eagle died a warrior on the battlefield defending her people, but she lived on in the hearts and minds of the Blackfeet. Over time there were some Blackfeet

---

3   Even in death, there was no end to controversy. Weasel Tail told John Ewers a different version of Running Eagle's death that was more prosaic. The Flathead Indians tired of this bold woman coming into their villages and stealing horses, so they set a trap for her. On the night of her death, Running Eagle boldly snuck into the Flathead village, where the Flatheads lay in wait. When they sighted the intruder, they called out to her, but she could make no response since she did not understand the Flathead language. Realizing that she was a stranger, they shot her on sight. According to Weasel Tail, Running Eagle died because she had broken her vow to the Sun by falling in love with a handsome member of the war party.

women—Lance Woman and Otter Woman—who tried to live their lives like Running Eagle. James Willard Schultz told their stories in *Blackfeet and Buffalo*. But Lance Woman and Otter Woman were no Running Eagle. Faced with the dangers of war, real or imagined, they chose the comfort of home and family. They lacked Running Eagle's vision, her devotion to her vow, her desire to protect the people from their enemies, and her strength and bravery in the face of death. Truly, there was only one Running Eagle, warrior woman of the Piegan tribe.

CHAPTER 4

Buffalo Calf Road: Warrior Woman

On a fine June day in Montana, a young Northern Cheyenne woman by the colorful name of Buffalo Calf Road emerged from the shadows of history to make her mark as an outstanding warrior woman. Her life was like a meteorite passing through the heavens, brilliant but short-lived. Before that June day her history remains obscure, as it was for many Plains Indian women. This much is known. She was in her early twenties, married to a mercurial warrior named Black Coyote, with one daughter around four years old. But many questions remain unanswered: Who were her parents? When and where was she born? She was likely a Southern Cheyenne, but if so, when did she come to the Northern Plains? And how did she meet Black Coyote, with whom she had an intense and devoted relationship?[1]

Buffalo Calf Road's public life began on June 16, 1876, when Cheyenne scouts rode into the Cheyenne/Lakota camps on Reno Creek warning the people that they had sighted many blue-coat soldiers and their Indian scouts on the Rosebud. The Indians did not know that the summer campaign of the Great Sioux War had begun. They did not know that the soldiers—one thousand strong and backed by some three hundred Crow and Shoshoni scouts—were led by one of the army's best Indian fighters, General George Crook. They did not know that Crook's advance was part of a grand plan by the United States Army—a multiprong attack to find, defeat, and force the so-called "hostile" Lakotas and Cheyennes out of the Powder River country and onto the Great Sioux Reservation. For now it was enough to know that soldiers were in their country threatening their people.

The young warriors decided to rush out and confront the soldiers before an attack on their villages could harm women, children, and the aged. Young Two Moons set out that night for the Rosebud, some twenty-five miles away, with about two hundred brave-hearted Lakota and Cheyenne warriors.

---

1   For a search to uncover what little is known about this famous warrior woman, see Rosemary Agonito and Joseph Agonito, "Resurrecting History's Forgotten Women: A Case Study from the Cheyenne Indians," *Frontiers: A Journal of Women Studies*, VI (Fall 1981), 8–16.

Other warriors followed Crazy Horse and the elder Two Moons. In an odd twist, Buffalo Calf Road joined Young Two Moons's warriors along with her husband, Black Coyote, and her brother Comes In Sight, who had come from the Southern Cheyenne Reservation in Indian Territory to visit his sister. There had been some brave Cheyenne women who fought in defense of their people when attacked by the enemy, but few had ever ridden so boldly with the men as Buffalo Calf Road did that day.

When Young Two Moons's party arrived in the morning hours, the fight had already begun. Pausing on a high hill overlooking the valley of the Rosebud, they could see the blue-coat soldiers pursuing some hard-pressed Cheyennes who were fleeing up the hill, their ponies wounded and exhausted. Young Two Moons's warriors did not hesitate; they charged down the hill, pushing back the soldiers. Buffalo Calf Road, riding a gray horse and armed with her six-shooter, charged with the men. She was dressed that day in her finest clothing: an elk-tooth dress with her waist encircled by a broad, decorated leather belt, a shell choker around her neck, and long shell earrings dangling from her pierced earlobes.

During that long, hot day, fighting took place in fragmented groups along an extended front. It was a day marked by charge and countercharge. Wooden Leg, a prominent Cheyenne warrior who took part in the fight, described the action that day: "Until the sun went far toward the west there were charges back and forth. Our Indians fought and ran away, fought and ran away. The soldiers and their Indian scouts did the same. Sometimes we chased them, sometimes they chased us." In the tumult of battle, it's not likely that many noticed the two "women" fighting together alongside the Crows: The Other Magpie, a young warrior woman probably close to Buffalo Calf Road's age, and Osh Tisch, the batée who chose, for a day, to fight as a warrior against his people's enemies.

During a lull in the fight, Buffalo Calf Road followed some warriors to the top of a high bluff, probably to rest their horses. From here she could look down into the valley where the fighting raged. She spotted her brother Comes In Sight, easily distinguished by the long war bonnet he wore in battle, bravely "run" the enemy lines. Suddenly his horse crashed headfirst to the ground. Comes In Sight landed on his feet and ran in a zigzag line to escape the bullets chasing him. Shoshoni scouts charged the downed enemy for an easy kill.

John Stands in Timber, the longtime historian of the Northern Cheyennes, described what happened next. Without hesitation Buffalo Calf Road

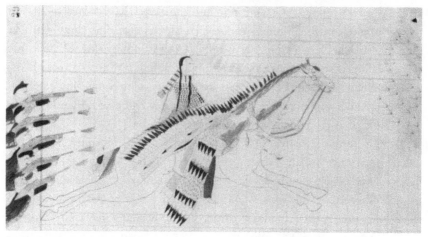

Buffalo Calf Road saving her brother Comes In Sight at the Battle of the Rosebud, June 17, 1876
COURTESY OF THE NATIONAL ANTHROPOLOGICAL ARCHIVES, SMITHSONIAN, 57,161-A. A LEDGER-BOOK SKETCH BY CHEYENNE ARTIST SPOTTED WOLF, CIRCA 1889

spurred her horse to a run down the valley floor, heading straight for her brother. In the midst of flying bullets, she turned her horse sharply, pausing for an instant as Comes In Sight grabbed her saddle with one hand and clutched the horse's neck with the other. With her brother hanging on the side of her horse, his war bonnet blowing in the wind and his rifle dangling from his arm, Buffalo Calf Road dashed back to the safety of the bluff. The warriors shouted praise for her brave deed.

After fighting bravely all day and inflicting casualties on the soldiers, the war leaders called off the fight. Exhausted warriors withdrew from the field, satisfied that they had prevented the blue-coat soldiers from attacking their villages. In fact, they had caused enough casualties that General Crook withdrew to his home base, where he remained inactive for some time. His Crow and Shoshoni scouts left for their home villages.

The great camp broke up the next morning in search of good grass and water for their large horse herds and fresh meat for their people. The Lakotas and the Cheyennes settled along the Greasy Grass River (called the Little Bighorn by whites)—the largest encampment ever on the Northern Plains, with one thousand lodges, over six thousand people, and some fifteen hundred warriors. The great camp stretched one and a half miles along the river, with the Cheyenne camp at its northern end.

After a period of mourning the warriors who died in the Rosebud fight, the people celebrated their victory over the soldiers. Everywhere stories of bravery were told. But the most popular (certainly for the Cheyennes) was the tale of Buffalo Calf Road's bravery in saving her brother's life. From this time forward, the Cheyennes would refer to the fight at the Rosebud as "The Battle Where the Girl Saved Her Brother." When the celebrating ended, Buffalo Calf Road returned to her lodge with her husband, Black Coyote, and her young daughter, where she resumed her chores as a Cheyenne wife and mother.

But her domestic work was sharply interrupted on June 25, 1876 ("bloody Sunday" as some call it), when Lieutenant Colonel George Armstrong Custer led the Seventh Cavalry against the Indians massed on the Little Bighorn River. (The warriors at the Little Bighorn did not know that Custer, or "Long Hair" as they called him, was leading the soldiers until sometime after the fight.) Custer had no real idea of the size and layout of the great encampment, though he had been warned by his Crow scouts of its magnitude. He also badly underestimated the number of warriors and their renewed confidence and determination given the Rosebud battle.

Custer did not make the first charge; he left that to the inexperienced Major Reno who, with only 125 soldiers and a few Arikara scouts, attacked the southern end of the camp—that place of honor belonging to Sitting Bull's Hunkpapas. Custer planned to strike the northern end of the camp in order to catch the "hostiles" in a classic pincer movement.

Having crossed the river, Major Reno's soldiers fired into the village but they never reached it. Gall, the great Hunkpapa Lakota warrior and Sitting Bull's chief lieutenant, led several hundred warriors to counterattack the soldiers, forcing them into the trees along the river. Crazy Horse arrived on the scene late but took part in the hand-to-hand fighting as Reno led his men out of the tree line to recross the river to safety. Some Cheyenne warriors from the northern end of the village arrived in time to fight Reno, but Black Coyote and Buffalo Calf Road did not engage in this fight. That would come against Custer.

While the Reno fight raged, Custer moved along the north side of the river looking for a safe place to cross. He never made it to the river. A small group of well-armed Cheyenne and Lakota warriors held the soldiers back. Heavy reenforcement came after Reno was defeated as the warriors doubled back to deal with the cavalry soldiers they spotted on the high ridges across the river. Gall led one contingent of Hunkpapa warriors who crossed the river at Medicine Tail Coulee; Crazy Horse's Oglala and Cheyenne warriors crossed the river at Deep Coulee.

Kate Bighead, the Northern Cheyenne woman who roamed over the battlefield to observe the fighting, noted the presence of Buffalo Calf Road in the fight. The young warrior woman, along with her husband and brother, joined forces with Gall as he moved up the ford to attack the horse-soldiers on the ridge. Comes In Sight, along with Yellow Nose and Contrary Belly, bravely charged the soldier lines. Black Coyote, like many warriors, dismounted and moved steadily along the gulches, firing at the soldiers. Buffalo Calf Road stayed on her horse and shot at the soldiers on the ridge with her trusted revolver. Once again, she demonstrated bravery in battle. When a young Cheyenne warrior boldly charged the soldier line, his horse was killed. Buffalo Calf Road flew to the doomed boy. She was prepared to give him her horse when Kate Bighead shouted that Cheyenne women had captured some of the soldiers' runaway horses down near the river. Buffalo Calf Road took the young boy on her horse and dashed to the river. Leaving the boy safely behind, she returned to the fighting until the last of Custer's men lay dead. After the fight the Cheyennes remembered her brave deed by bestowing on her the honorary name Brave Woman.

The battle over, the great encampment broke up. Word had come of more soldiers advancing in search for revenge. To escape more easily from the soldiers and to search for grass for their ponies and buffalo meat for their people, the Indians broke into smaller tribal groups.

Chief Dull Knife took a large following deep into the Bighorn Mountains, where he located camp on a swift stream far up the Powder River. Buffalo Calf Road and Black Coyote joined Dull Knife's secluded village with the hope that they could quietly resume their lives. Buffalo Calf Road was pregnant with her second child.

But the peace of the village was shattered on November 25, 1876, when Colonel Ranald Mackenzie, who commanded General Crook's strike force, suddenly attacked and destroyed the village. Some forty Cheyenne men, women, and children lay dead, with more wounded. With almost no food or blankets, the survivors fled in bitter subzero cold and a raging snowstorm that lasted for days. Many babies froze to death, eleven the first night alone. Buffalo Calf Road protected her small daughter and unborn child against the cold and hunger as best she could. At last the desperate Cheyennes found shelter with Crazy Horse's Oglalas, who shared what little they had.

For a brief time tribal leaders thought they could hold on. Crazy Horse even felt bold enough to lead Lakota and Cheyenne warriors to challenge Colonel Nelson Miles's infantry at the recently established Fort Keogh on the Tongue River. He tried to lure the soldiers into a trap away from the fort as the pugnacious Miles accepted the challenge. On that bitterly cold day, Miles's infantry pursued Crazy Horse's warriors into Wolf Mountain, where they sometimes fought hand to hand. But the fighters' exhaustion, the bitter cold, and a blinding snowstorm brought an end to hostilities. Although they fought bravely, the warriors failed to drive the soldiers from their country.

By late January unity among the tribes began to unravel. Sitting Bull and Gall decided to take their people to Canada. Crazy Horse wanted to fight on, but even Crazy Horse could see his people were tired, cold, hungry, and ill. Many of the Lakota and Cheyenne chiefs began to doubt the wisdom of continued struggle, and they listened to the peace envoys that Miles and Crook sent to the camps with soothing words: they would be well treated and subject to no punishment other than surrendering their horses and guns. Two Moons led his people to Fort Keogh; Little Wolf and Dull Knife led their people to Fort Robinson.

But some refused to surrender and go to the reservation. Buffalo Calf Road and her husband and child stayed out with a small band of thirty-four under the war-chief Last Bull, intent on living in the old way as long as they could. Wooden Leg, who joined the group, described the last days. For several weeks they struggled to survive, hunting on the lean ground along the Powder and Tongue Rivers. During this desperate period, Buffalo Calf Road gave birth to a boy. Now there were thirty-five in the band. Many-Colored Braids's wife helped to deliver the child and look after the young mother, cutting the umbilical cord and saving it to be encased in a sacred beaded turtle pouch. When they broke camp, Buffalo Calf Road and the baby were carried on a travois, and the women helped to take down and set up her tipi.

By early summer Last Bull's hungry band still struggled to survive. They had too few hunters to provide the band with meat and skins. The people were hungry, their clothes worn, and their lodges thin. They received reports from agency Indians that if they came in they could settle at Red Cloud Agency, where they would be well treated with plenty of food and clothing.

So, with heavy hearts, they decided to "surrender" at Fort Robinson and rejoin their Cheyenne relatives already there. On reaching the fort, they were greeted by Lieutenant W. P. Clark ("White Hat"), who welcomed them in fluent sign language, telling them they must surrender their horses and guns. Black Coyote refused to surrender his gun, and when three Lakota scouts approached, he aimed his gun at them. Last Bull intervened, pushing the gun aside. "Don't shoot. You are crazy." He warned Black Coyote that he would get them all killed. Lieutenant Clark motioned the three scouts to leave. Black Coyote relented, "then quieted down" and gave his gun to Last Bull.

Finally, Buffalo Calf Road and her husband and children were settled on the hated reservation. But they were there less than a week when orders came from the blue-coat officers that the Cheyennes were to pack and begin the long journey to Indian Territory (present-day Oklahoma), where they would rejoin their southern brethren. A few of their own chiefs supported the move, but as Wooden Leg noted, most Cheyennes were unhappy about relocating and felt betrayed by the false promises of the whites who told them that if they stopped fighting and turned in their guns and horses they could settle at Red Cloud Agency.

The Cheyennes left Fort Robinson on May 28, 1877. The move south took seventy long days. The nearly one thousand Cheyennes who made the journey were treated well by the soldiers on the march south. They reached the Southern Cheyenne Agency in Indian Territory in late summer. Captivity in the south sat hard with Buffalo Calf Road and her people. The land was alien, the climate hot and humid. There was little food since they could not hunt off the reservation. Families began to disintegrate, and diseases such as measles and malarial fever caused illness and death.

Finally, Little Wolf and Dull Knife, the two "old man" chiefs, decided that they had had enough and determined to save their people by returning north to their beloved country despite the threat of the agent that the army would pursue and kill them. On September 9, 1878, 287 Cheyennes fled the reservation under cover of darkness. They were headed home to the Yellowstone country, some 1,500 miles north. Mostly on foot, they labored northward, pursued relentlessly by the army. When, at last, they crossed the Platte River in Nebraska, the band split in two. Dull Knife, looking at the desperate people, decided to seek shelter at the nearby Red Cloud Agency.

Little Wolf decided that safety lay in the continued northward journey to the Yellowstone. He found temporary shelter at Lost Chokecherry Creek in the remote Sandhills of Nebraska.

The place was well hidden from the army, but Black Coyote's small group found him there. For some unknown reason Black Coyote and Buffalo Calf Road and their two children left the southern agency some days after Little Wolf and Dull Knife's departure. Somehow they tracked Little Wolf to the Sandhills. By this time Dull Knife's band had been captured and imprisoned at Fort Robinson.

Buffalo Calf Road and Black Coyote spent some peaceful time that winter at Lost Chokecherry, but it did not last. Little Wolf urged his followers, once again, to take up their journey to the Yellowstone country. As the band approached the Little Missouri River, outside the Black Hills, trouble erupted for the young couple. Black Coyote got into a heated argument with Black Crane, one of the older Cheyenne chiefs, for reasons that are not entirely clear. Black Crane struck Black Coyote with his riding whip; perhaps he even threatened the young warrior with his knife. In a rage Black Coyote shot the old man and exchanged fire with Black Crane's son, who ran to avenge his father. Black Coyote was slightly wounded in the arm.

Little Wolf, following Cheyenne custom, sent the "murderer" into exile. Buffalo Calf Road, with the two children, left with Black Coyote, as did Black Coyote's mother and his two warrior friends, Mad Hearted Wolf and Whetstone.

Shortly after this deadly incident, Little Wolf and his band resumed their flight, reaching the Powder River country in southeast Montana by late March, where they were "captured" by the soldiers and brought to Fort Keogh.

Black Coyote's small band of exiles struggled to survive in the wilderness. At one point they came upon two soldiers working on a telegraph line: Black Coyote killed one and wounded the second. The army tracked down the "killers" in mid-April, taking three men to Fort Keogh and charging them with murder. The three warriors languished in a jail awaiting their fate. The women and children were reunited with Little Wolf's band camped outside the fort.

By June it was all over for the ill-starred lovers. Buffalo Calf Road, the warrior woman who had fought so bravely against the soldiers in defense of her people, caught the dreaded white-man's disease, diphtheria. Despite the care of a Cheyenne medicine woman and the white doctor from the fort, Buffalo Calf Road died. The Cheyennes mourned the passing of their "Brave Woman," burying her high in the rocks above the Yellowstone River.

Black Coyote went into despair when he heard the sad news, deciding that he would not die at the hands of the white man. His two fellow warriors agreed; they would take their own lives instead. First one warrior hanged himself; then the second. When the jailer arrived in the morning, he found the two men lying lifeless on the floor; the third man, Black Coyote, was still hanging in the air, a leather strap around his neck attached to an iron rod above the door.

Inseparable in life and battle, Buffalo Calf Road and Black Coyote died tragically, symbols of the end of the fight to preserve the old nomadic way of life.

CHAPTER 5

Kate Bighead: Wartime Reporter

When Dr. Thomas B. Marquis interviewed Kate Bighead in 1926, she was an elderly grandmother living a quiet, circumscribed life at Lame Deer, the Northern Cheyenne Reservation in Montana.[1] That was not always the case. For the first thirty years of her life, Kate Bighead (known by her birth name as Antelope Woman) followed her people as they roamed freely over the Great Plains, living a nomadic, buffalo-hunting, tipi-dwelling lifestyle. Cheyenne women were widely known for their beauty and their virtue; Cheyenne warriors were respected by their friends, feared by their enemies.

Kate Bighead told Marquis little about her life as a young woman during the nomadic years, except to say that she was born near the North Platte River in 1847, spending her early years among the Southern Cheyennes, nor did she tell him anything about her life at Lame Deer, the reservation in Montana, where she later lived for some forty years. Certainly she could have since Marquis was eager to record the daily life of women. When, for instance, Marquis interviewed Iron Teeth at Lame Deer, the elderly Cheyenne woman freely shared her domestic life during the nomadic and reservation years. The difference in the two accounts may have been that during the most turbulent years of the 1860s and the 1870s, when the Cheyennes struggled against American westward expansion, Kate Bighead was still single at twenty-nine; Iron Teeth had been long married, with five children. Without a husband and children, Kate Bighead was not involved with domesticity in the same way as Iron Teeth. As a single woman, Kate had greater freedom to observe the larger world exploding around her. She seemed never to have gotten past the excitement and tragedy of this period.

When she recounted her life story to Marquis, Kate Bighead limited it mainly to those years when the Cheyenne people fought to preserve their way of life against intruding white settlers and soldiers. Her interest in the

---

1   Kate Bighead, "She Watched Custer's Last Battle," in *Custer on the Little Bighorn*, compiled and edited by Thomas B. Marquis, Lodi, CA: Dr. Marquis Custer Publications, 1980, is the primary source for this chapter.

Kate Bighead with grandchild Mary White Horse, 1926 COURTESY OF THE BUFFALO BILL CENTER OF THE WEST, CODY, WYOMING, PN.165.1.79. PHOTOGRAPHED BY THOMAS B. MARQUIS

military exploits of men made her different from other women. As she explained to Marquis, "I had seen [many] battles in past times. I always liked to watch the men fighting. Not many women did that, and I often was teased on account of it." Perhaps Kate Bighead found the life of men—who hunted and went off to war—more exciting than the everyday life of women.

During these troubled but exciting years, Kate witnessed the many battles her people fought with the blue-coat soldiers and she came to know, in however limited a way, famous Indians and white soldiers. But Kate was always an observer, and a keen one at that, rather than a participant like the warrior-woman Buffalo Calf Road, who fought in some of the very fights that Kate observed from a distance.

Kate Bighead was living in Black Kettle's village on the Washita River (Indian Territory, later the state of Oklahoma) in November 1868 when Lieutenant Colonel George Armstrong Custer's Seventh Cavalry attacked the camp. It was a cold, snowy morning when the fight began. Kate jumped from her bed and, barefooted, ran for her life. Black Kettle was killed, along with women and children. The soldiers took captive many other women and children, including Kate's cousin Meotzi (whom Custer called Monahsetah), burning the tipis and property left behind as people fled for their lives.

The survivors of the Washita attack fled westward and established a camp on the Red River in Texas. Kate Bighead was there with her people when Custer, accompanied by her cousin Meotzi, found the Southern Cheyennes again, although this time there was no fighting. Custer smoked the peace pipe and promised never to fight the Cheyennes again.

Kate Bighead saw Custer (whom the Cheyennes called *Hi-es-tzie*, meaning "Long Hair") many times during those days. One day Kate took a good look at him: "He had a large nose, deep-set eyes, and light-red hair that was long and wavy. He was wearing a buckskin suit and a big white hat." A young, twenty-two-year-old woman at the time, Kate confessed that she "admired him" and "all of the Indian women talked of him as being a fine-looking man," even though the soldier-chief had destroyed their village at the Washita. On many occasions Kate saw her cousin Meotzi ride alongside Long Hair. Strangely, Kate did not disapprove of the love affair between Meotzi and Custer.

Eventually, the Southern Cheyennes came in to their reservation in Indian Territory, but Kate did not stay long. She joined her brothers White

Bull and White Moon as they relocated to Red Cloud Agency in the north, remaining at the agency until trouble broke out over the discovery of gold in the Black Hills in 1874–1875. Kate Bighead and her brothers then went to live with the Northern Cheyennes and the Lakotas in the buffalo-rich Powder River country in Wyoming and Montana that had been set aside for the nontreaty Lakotas who did not want to come in to the Great Sioux Reservation as provided in the 1868 Fort Laramie Treaty. One day Indian runners came to tell the Powder River Indians that they had to relocate to the reservation by January 31, 1876, or be declared "hostiles" by the army. Many Indians refused to leave their hunting grounds.

The winter of 1876 was brutally cold. Kate Bighead and her brothers camped with Old Bear's Northern Cheyennes on the west side of the Powder River. Suddenly, in the early morning hours on March 17, 1876, blue-coat soldiers attacked the village. Once again Kate Bighead had to flee for her life, leaving behind her precious property, which was destroyed by the soldiers. After days of wandering, the Cheyennes reached the safety of Crazy Horse's Oglala village, where they were given food and shelter. War had come once again to the people.

The two tribes linked up for safety with Sitting Bull's powerful Hunkpapas. As spring came on, they were joined in time by kin from other Lakota tribes: Sans Arcs, Brulés, and Miniconjou. The large tribal assembly moved freely across the plains in search of fresh grass for their numerous ponies and buffalo meat for the people. By mid-June they were camped on Reno Creek, near the Little Bighorn River. Resting there for some days, the men killed buffalo and the women tanned skins and preserved the meat.

Suddenly, scouts brought news that soldiers were advancing down the Rosebud toward their village. Hundreds of Cheyenne and Lakota warriors rushed to meet the soldiers. Kate noted that Buffalo Calf Road (whom she calls Calf Trail Woman) fought alongside the warriors—the only Cheyenne/Lakota woman to do so. In the fight on the Rosebud that day (June 17, 1876), the warriors inflicted enough damage that the enemy was forced to retreat.

The great village moved the next morning down the Little Bighorn River, always in search of grass and game. "There were more Indians in those six camps," Kate said, "than I ever saw together anywhere else." By June 24 they were camped near the mouth of the Little Bighorn, planning to spend only one night there and then to cross over into the Bighorn River valley to hunt the large antelope herds that scouts had sighted. They were not looking for or even expecting a fight with the soldiers, but that's what they got.

The next morning Kate Bighead went with an Oglala woman to visit some friends among the Miniconjous, who were located near the Hunkpapa village, where Sitting Bull's people guarded the southern entrance to the great encampment. Kate remembered that the day was hot, with no clouds in the sky. Finding her Miniconjou friends bathing in the river, she and her Oglala friend joined them. Others—men, women, and children—played in the water as some boys were fishing. "All of us," Kate said, "were having a good time. It was somewhere past the middle of the forenoon. Nobody was thinking of any battle coming."

Soon two Lakota boys came running toward the bathers, shouting, "Soldiers are coming!" The Indians did not know at the time that these horse-soldiers belonged to Lieutenant George Armstrong Custer's famous Seventh Cavalry and that the attack against the Hunkpapa village was led by Major Marcus Reno—the first round in the battle of the Little Bighorn.

Hearing the shooting, Kate and her friends hid in the brush for safety. They heard old men calling the young warriors to battle. In response, young men were "singing their war songs as they answered the call." The women stared from their hiding place and saw "throngs of Sioux men on horses" racing to the trees near the river just south of the Hunkpapa camp where the soldiers had fled after the warriors broke their line. Kate caught glimpses of soldiers fleeing the woods to seek high ground across the river, warriors in pursuit, shooting and beating the soldiers as they fled.

Kate bolted from her hiding place and ran back to the Cheyenne camp, more than one mile away. As she raced through the Indian camps, Kate noticed everywhere great excitement. Women were bringing war horses from the herds; old men were helping young warriors dress and paint themselves for battle. Other women quickly took down their tipis, loading packhorses with their possessions. Still others carried heavy burdens and many left with nothing but their children. Kate saw one Lakota woman "jumping up and down [in one spot] and screaming, because she could not find her little son."

Horses kicked up clouds of dust as warriors rushed to the fighting at the Hunkpapa camp. By the time Kate neared her own village, she could see many warriors riding back to the camps. She mistakenly thought they had been beaten and were running away, but they had returned from the Reno fight to challenge a second group of soldiers advancing across the river. Kate then spotted the soldiers on a high ridge across the river, nearly opposite the Cheyenne camp. A few Indians held them off at the river crossing. Kate did not know at the time that this second troop was led by the soldier-chief whom the Cheyennes called Long Hair.

As more and more Indians crossed Deep Ravine to head off the soldiers, Kate became very excited. "Let me have a horse," she begged her older brother, White Bull. She wanted to watch the fight but, more importantly, she wanted to "sing strongheart songs" for her nephew Noisy Walking, White Bull's son. Noisy Walking, only eighteen years old, was one of five Cheyenne suicide boys who had pledged their lives for victory. Kate was very close to her nephew, and he expected her to be there. She was told that Noisy Walking had wrapped a red scarf about his neck so that his aunt could recognize him in battle.

Kate crossed the river and followed up the coulee where the warriors had gone. She encircled the field of battle, keeping herself out of fire-range while looking for her nephew. When she reached the southern side, she noted that many Oglala and Cheyenne warriors, hiding in the deep gulches and behind the ridges, were engaging the soldiers from a distance, mainly with bows and arrows. Noisy Walking was in the deep gulch with his fellow Cheyenne warriors, although Kate did not know that he was there. Still, she sang her strongheart songs.

It was probably at this point in the encounter that Kate noticed Calf Trail Woman, armed with her six-shooter, firing at the soldiers. The warrior woman stayed on her pony all the time, following her husband, Black Coyote, who was one of the warriors creeping forward in the gulches to get closer to the soldiers on the ridge. At one moment in the fight, a young Cheyenne warrior who ventured too close to the soldier line lost his horse; Calf Trail Woman was about to give the warrior her horse but Kate yelled that there were captured ponies at the river, so Calf Trail Woman took the young man there on her pony. Then she returned to the fight.

The momentum of the fight changed when a band of mounted soldiers rode in a gallop down the broad coulee toward the river to dislodge the hiding warriors who threatened their unit. The warriors quickly withdrew to safer places in the ravine. Stopping short of the river, the soldiers dismounted and took a new position on a low ridge. With the soldiers so close, the war leaders encouraged their warriors to move forward and surround them. Lame White Man, a Cheyenne warrior, urged his men to rise up and be brave. Hundreds of warriors descended on the outnumbered soldiers. Noisy Walking, one of the suicide boys, was mortally wounded in this charge. The soldiers' horses, frightened by the tumult, broke loose and headed for the river to drink, leaving their riders alone on the ridge. Then Kate witnessed a shocking thing: one soldier shot himself, then another did, and another, with some soldiers shooting each other at point-blank range. The warriors looked on with some confusion and then charged the soldiers who remained.[2]

The warriors, taking guns and ammunition from the dead soldiers, pursued the retreating soldiers up the ridge in a northwest direction. Kate followed at a distance, witnessing a series of fights along the ridge. Warriors surrounded the outnumbered soldiers as horses fled, and some frightened soldiers shot themselves rather than be captured. Finally, Kate reached what would later be recognized as the "last stand." Hundreds of warriors surrounded the soldiers, many keeping safe behind the dead horses littering the field. Some younger warriors pushed dangerously close to count coup, and Kate saw a Sioux boy killed.

Finally, the firing from the soldiers stopped. The Indians rushed forward, thinking all were dead, but seven soldiers jumped up and ran toward the river, followed by hundreds of Indians. In the confusion Kate could not see what happened to these soldiers; later she learned that they all died at their own hands. She believed that "the Everywhere spirit made all of them go crazy and do this, in punishment for having attacked a peaceful camp."

As Kate watched the aftermath of the fight, she saw one dazed soldier sitting on the ground rubbing his head as if he did not know where he was. Three warriors seized the man, stretched him on his back, and cut off his head with a "sheath-knife." She saw other mutilated dead soldiers, some cut up by women mourning for their dead.

Kate did not know at the time that the soldier-chief killed at the Little Bighorn was Long Hair. That news came later. Kate also heard from her

---

2   Kate Bighead's account of soldiers committing suicide was shared by Wooden Leg, a Cheyenne warrior who fought in that battle. Their controversial statements have been questioned by scholars of the Little Bighorn. Richard G. Hardorff, compiler and editor of *Cheyenne Memories of the Custer Fight*, rejects the suicide theory. Hardorff thinks that Thomas Marquis, who communicated with Kate Bighead and Wooden Leg through sign language, may have misunderstood their explanation. Based on other Cheyenne and Lakota testimony, Hardorff is willing to admit that in the heat of the fight military discipline broke down and that some fearful soldiers behaved erratically, like "drunken" men shooting wildly in the air, but they were not drunk.

people in the south what happened to Custer after the fight. Two Southern Cheyenne women had been in the great Cheyenne camp at the Little Bighorn. After the fight, as they walked the battlefield, they recognized the dead body of the soldier-chief they called Long Hair. The two women had met Custer some years earlier after he destroyed Black Kettle's village on the Washita. There Custer had taken captives, one of whom was Kate Bighead's cousin, a beautiful young woman named Meotzi, whom many Cheyennes claimed became Custer's lover. So, when a Lakota warrior came to mutilate Custer's body, the women stopped him by claiming that Custer was a "relative." The warrior cut off only one joint of a finger. Still, the women could not leave Custer untouched. They remembered that after the Washita, Custer made peace with the Southern Cheyennes, promising never to fight them again. The chiefs warned Long Hair that he would be killed if he broke his promise. Perhaps he did not hear the chiefs; the two women then "pushed the point of a sewing awl into each of his ears, [deep] into his head." Perhaps, now, they thought, this would "improve his hearing."

Kate roamed the battlefield looking for her nephew until someone told her where Noisy Walking lay. Kate found him mortally wounded in a deep gulch, shot and stabbed several times. A young man ran to the village to call Noisy Walking's mother, who returned with a lodgepole travois. Noisy Walking died that night. The Cheyenne buried their dead in hillside caves away from the camp while the Lakotas left their dead warriors in burial tipis or on scaffolds, as was their custom.

On the second day, heralds rode about the camps warning people that more soldiers were coming up the Little Bighorn valley. The chiefs decided that there had been enough fighting, with too many young warriors dead, so they should leave. The women began to pack, and before sundown thousands of Indians with their large horse herds left the valley.

Soon the tribes separated, each searching for grass for its ponies and game for its hungry people. The Cheyennes went to the mouth of the Powder River, where they found a great deal of food hidden in holes left by the soldiers: bacon, beans, rice, sugar, coffee, crackers, dried apples and corn for the horses. Some months later when the Cheyennes realized that Long Hair had probably cached this food, Kate said that her people joked among themselves: "It is too bad we killed him, for it must have been him, our friend, who left all of the good food for the Cheyennes, his relatives."

Throughout the summer men hunted for buffalo and women tanned skins and stored meat. As winter approached, the Cheyennes, including Kate Bighead and her brothers, located their village far up the Powder River close to the Bighorn Mountains. Despite the remoteness of their site, the soldiers with their scouts found them on November 26, 1876, killing many warriors and destroying the village. Once again the people were forced to flee for their lives, and again they found shelter with Crazy Horse, who shared what little he had.

Still there was no peace. Colonel Nelson Miles had established a soldier fort, Fort Keogh, in the heart of the Powder River country. Crazy Horse's Oglala and Cheyenne warriors challenged the soldiers on a cold, wintry day in early January 1879, but the fight ended in a stalemate. The winter and constant warfare took its toll on the people. By spring many were prepared to listen to peace envoys sent by the army, promising fair treatment if they came in to the agencies. Two Moons took a large band to Fort Keogh (on April 22, 1877), which included Kate Bighead and White Moon, her younger brother. (White Bull, her older brother, who had gone in slightly earlier, became a scout for General Miles.) The war years had ended for Kate Bighead and the Northern Cheyennes.

In 1884 President Chester A. Arthur signed an executive order creating a small reservation for the Northern Cheyenne in southeastern Montana, known as Lame Deer. Kate Bighead would spend the remainder of her long life at Lame Deer, but she had, regrettably, little to say to Marquis about her life on the reservation. At some point Kate married, bearing a child named William Bighead, who became a Cheyenne policeman in the 1920s. By the time Marquis met Kate, she was an elderly grandmother.

Kate Bighead closed her interview with Marquis with a surprising statement, which reflected the fascination she held for those earlier, more exciting but troubled times. "Through almost sixty years," she exclaimed, "many a time I have thought of Hi-es-tzie [Long Hair] as the handsome man I saw in the South. And I often have wondered if, when I was riding among the dead [at the Little Bighorn] where he was lying, my pony may have kicked dirt upon his body."

CHAPTER 6

Iron Teeth: Strong-Willed Survivor

In 1926 Susan Iron Teeth was ninety-two years old, one of the few remaining survivors of the famous Northern Cheyenne flight from the Darlington Agency in Indian Territory to their homeland in Yellowstone country. She lived in a poor cabin some twenty miles from agency headquarters at Lame Deer, the Northern Cheyenne Reservation in Montana. Impoverished by reservation life, isolated from society, and living alone with a widowed daughter, Iron Teeth had little but her vivid memories, which she shared with agency physician Dr. Thomas B. Marquis, who recorded her long, troubled, heroic life story.[1]

Iron Teeth (whose Cheyenne name was Mah-i-ti-wo-nee-ni) was born in the Black Hills in 1834 in the "moon when the berries are ripe, in the last part of summer." Raised among the Cheyenne people, her father was Cheyenne, her mother Sioux.

Iron Teeth lived close to her grandmother, who shared with the girl the early history of her people. The grandmother, born in the 1700s, could remember when the Cheyenne people did not have many horses and relied on dogs for transporting their goods. In her early years, Iron Teeth remembered her people planting corn every year in the Black Hills. The Cheyennes had been farmers along the river bottoms in their early days in Minnesota and North Dakota, digging holes with sharpened sticks, dropping in kernels of corn. After the planting, people went out to hunt, returning in late summer to gather their crops. Unfortunately, the Pawnees and Arikaras often raided their fields.

---

1   Thomas Marquis published three versions of Iron Teeth's memoir: "Red Ripe's [Pipe's] Squaw," *Century Magazine*, June 1929; "Iron Teeth, A Cheyenne Old Woman," in Thomas B. Marquis's *The Cheyennes of Montana*; and "Iron Teeth, A Cheyenne Old Woman," in *Cheyenne and Sioux*, compiled and recorded by Thomas B. Marquis. John H. Monnett, who had reviewed all three versions for his essay on Iron Teeth, "'My heart has now become changed to softer feelings': A Northern Cheyenne Woman and Her Family Remember the Long Journey Home," *Montana, The Magazine of Western History*, 59 (Summer 2009), points out that the Iron Teeth narrative, which appeared in *Cheyenne and Sioux*, is "the most complete and faithful to the original [Marquis] diaries." It is the piece I used for this chapter.

Iron Teeth, at age 93, the oldest woman living among the Northern Cheyennes, circa 1927 COURTESY OF THE NATIONAL PARK SERVICE, LITTLE BIGHORN BATTLEFIELD NATIONAL MONUMENT, LIBI_00012_07524. PHOTOGRAPHED BY THOMAS B. MARQUIS

Iron Teeth remembered when raiding parties left for long journeys south to obtain horses by raid or trade. The men went on foot, carrying a lariat rope, bow and arrows, sheath-knife, dried meat, and extra moccasins. When Iron Teeth was six, she recalled her people, along with the Arapahos and Kiowas, trekking a long way south to meet with Comanches and Apaches for trade and peace talks. The Cheyennes and their allies traded guns and blankets to the southern tribes, who gave them, in return, many horses. As the Cheyennes obtained more horses, they gave up farming for a nomadic lifestyle of hunting the rich buffalo herds for meat and skins. In place of corn, they gathered wild foods growing on the plains: turnips, sweet potatoes, berries, and nuts.

Iron Teeth enjoyed an ordinary childhood, but her innocent playtime prepared her for the life of a Cheyenne woman. She and her friends built tipis for themselves and their dolls. Imitating their mothers, the girls hung little pieces of meat out to dry. Sometimes they played at moving camp. The boys helped by dragging willow baskets holding the girls' possessions; the girls rode stick horses, carrying the dolls on their backs.

Particularly fond of a doll that her mother made for her, Iron Teeth kept it in a rawhide satchel with its extra clothes and moccasins. But during a Pawnee raid on their village, she ran with the women and children, leaving the doll behind. For some time she "cried about the lost baby. At night, I dreamed about the enemy having scalped it and cut up its body."

At age ten Iron Teeth's father gave her a yearling colt to ride. Boys teased her by riding up close and lashing her colt to make it jump. "At first I was frightened, and [the boys] laughed at me. But soon I got used to it and after a little while I became a good rider." As she grew older, Iron Teeth like to "break horses." She and her sister would take a wild horse to a sandy place beside the river before trying to ride, and sometimes they led the wild horse out into deep water before mounting. Iron Teeth understood that "a horse cannot buck hard in deep water." Though thrown occasionally, she never suffered any serious injury.

There were lots of wild horses running loose on the Southern Plains. Iron Teeth always carried with her a "lariat rope made of spun and plaited buffalo hair" that she learned to throw as a young girl. One time, after she married, Iron Teeth was riding on the plains with her baby strapped to her back. She spotted some wild horses. Placing her baby on the ground in the cradleboard, she raced after the herd, catching two wild horses.

Iron Teeth was twenty-one when she married Red Pipe, but since Cheyenne women in those days did not change their name, she was still called Mah-i-ti-wo-nee-ni, Iron Teeth. The two were devoted to each other. Red Pipe never took another wife and she never knew another man. Iron Teeth would have five children with Red Pipe.

Loving and protecting her children like all good Cheyenne women, Iron Teeth demonstrated her love in simple ways. According to Cheyenne custom, young children rode in woven willow baskets hung between travois poles when traveling. Children often climbed out of the baskets to play along the way before climbing back in, but sometimes got lost. Iron Teeth always watched the baskets closely when traveling, even when no danger was apparent. She "enjoyed looking back and exchanging glances with exactly the right number of sparkling black eyes peeping up at me. One day, a pair of eyes was missing! I jumped from my working animal, mounted a led one, and hurried back along the line of travelers. My fright was changed to joy when I found my absent girl asleep with another woman's children in their basket."

Cheyenne women also looked after each other, especially those who were with child. Iron Teeth related a typical incident: Once, when the Cheyennes were fleeing from the Pawnees, Iron Teeth and another woman stayed behind to help a friend deliver her baby, hiding in the woods while the Pawnees passed by. They stayed two days after the baby came, then placed mother and baby on a travois covered with buffalo skin and made it safely back to the newly established Cheyenne village. The women continued to look after the new mother and her baby until she was strong enough to resume her domestic duties.

Although married with children, Iron Teeth engaged in activities that went beyond the domestic. She broke wild horses and hunted buffalo with her husband. Once, while chasing a small herd of buffalo, Red Pipe urged her to turn the herd uphill, which she did. As the buffalo slowed, Iron Teeth rode alongside and struck down some with her hatchet. An angry bull buffalo whirled and knocked down her pony. She fell, but Red Pipe drove away the angry animal and saved her life. Another time, alone and on foot, she roped a buffalo calf that dragged her across the prairie. But she held on and eventually led the animal back to camp. While the Cheyennes loved buffalo meat the best, they hunted elk, deer, antelope, and bighorn sheep. In lean times the Cheyennes hunted smaller game. Iron Teeth described in her memoir how she hunted beaver, skunk, prairie dogs, and chickens. She even caught turtles and fish in the streams.

Surrounded by hostile tribes, Cheyenne women learned to protect themselves and their families. On one journey two Shoshoni warriors rushed Iron Teeth. One Cheyenne called out, "They will capture Iron Teeth." But Iron Teeth had a gun and fired at the two Shoshoni, who fled the scene.

Iron Teeth admired strong women who fought to protect the people from their enemies as she had done against the Shoshoni. One time a band of Pawnees attacked a Cheyenne camp searching for coup and women captives. Comes Together was running away alone and on foot. A Pawnee warrior caught her. Comes Together pretended that she would go easily, then she "jerked her hatchet from her belt and struck him. His head was split wide open, and he fell dead." When her people gathered, she was "heralded as a brave woman. Young warriors led her on horseback about the camp and sang songs in her praise. . . . Her husband, White Frog, gave away all of his horses and robes and blankets, to show how proud he was of her."

The cold, snowy winter of 1866 found Red Pipe and Iron Teeth camped near the head of the Tongue River in Wyoming not far from Fort Phil Kearny, a fort the army built that year to protect emigrants traveling the newly established Bozeman Trail on their way to the goldfields in Montana. The Bozeman Trail, with its soldiers and gold miners, threatened the rich buffalo herds that roamed the Powder River country—land claimed by the Lakota and the Northern Cheyenne.

Red Cloud, the Oglala war leader, led a resistance movement that lay siege to the forts. On December 21, 1866, an Indian war party composed of Lakota and Cheyenne warriors ambushed and killed Captain William J. Fetterman and eighty-one soldiers outside Fort Phil Kearny. Shortly after the fight, Red Pipe came back to camp with news that the Indians "had killed a hundred of the soldiers at the fort." Where had Red Pipe been? Was he out hunting or had he taken part in the fight? Iron Teeth does not say. Upon hearing the good news, the Cheyennes "built big bonfires" to celebrate the victory.

After peace was later achieved (with the signing of the Fort Laramie Treaty in 1868), the fighting coalition broke in two. Many who signed the treaty eventually settled on the newly established Great Sioux Reservation—roughly all land in the Dakotas west of the Missouri River (including the sacred Black Hills). Those who refused to go onto the reservation chose to remain, by right of treaty, in the "unceded" territory in Powder River country. Red Pipe took his family to the reservation.

They remained there quietly for some time, taking no part in the tumultuous fighting between the soldiers and the Powder River "hostiles," which culminated in the defeat of Long Hair at the Little Bighorn. After receiving this startling news, Red Pipe made the fateful decision to rejoin his fellow Cheyennes in the Powder River country. Since Red Pipe and Iron Teeth were close to Dull Knife (also known as Morning Star), one of the four "old man" chiefs, it's likely they left the agency with his band and reached their Cheyenne relatives sometime in late July.

The tribes remained together throughout the summer and fall. Red Pipe, like most men, hunted buffalo, antelope, and deer; Iron Teeth, like most women, kept "busy tanning skins and storing up meat and berries for use during the winter." As winter approached, Dull Knife made camp on a small stream that flowed into the upper Powder River near the Bighorn Mountains. It seemed like a safe place. The "men did not want to fight. They wanted to be left alone so they might get food and skins [for] their families. They said that nobody would trouble us in this place so far away from other people." They were wrong.

Whites and Indians scouting for the army found the hidden village. On November 25, 1876, Colonel Ranald Mackenzie attacked the sleeping village. Warriors rushed out of their tipis to protect their families, but they were overwhelmed. Some forty Cheyennes—men, women, and children— were killed and many wounded. Dull Knife lost two sons in the fight; Little Wolf, the other "old man" chief, was wounded in the struggle. The soldiers seized 750 horses along with 1,000 buffalo robes and tons of buffalo meat, and then set fire to everything left in the village, leaving the Northern Cheyennes impoverished.

Iron Teeth ran away with her children, leaving behind her warm lodge and rich stores of food. Looking back as she fled, she could see Red Pipe and Gathering His Medicine, her older boy, fighting a rearguard action to protect their people. Red Pipe was on foot leading his horse so that he could more carefully aim at the soldiers. Suddenly Iron Teeth saw him fall, shot, his horse running away. She wanted to go back, but her two sons urged her to safety with the three girls. It was too late—Red Pipe, her beloved husband, was dead. Iron Teeth was now a forty-two-year-old widow with five children. For a long time after the death of her husband and the destruction of Dull Knife's village, Iron Teeth was "afraid of all white men soldiers," who she said "represented the most extreme cruelty."

"From the hilltops," she said, "we Cheyennes looked back and saw all of our lodges and everything in them being burned into nothing but smoke and ashes." The survivors fled through the deep mountain snow, most without horses. "We had no lodges," Iron Teeth remembered, "only a few blankets, and there was only a little dry meat food among us. Some died of wounds, many froze to death." After eleven days of trekking through the snow and winter cold, they reached the safety of Crazy Horse's Oglala village, where they were fed and sheltered.

But such relief was temporary. Winter was hard as the people suffered from cold and hunger and the soldiers stationed at Fort Keogh posed a constant threat. By late April 1877, the Northern Cheyennes, assured they would be treated well by the soldiers, decided to surrender. Two Moons's band (including Kate Bighead) came in to Fort Keogh; Dull Knife's band, including Iron Teeth and her children, came in to Fort Robinson, assuming that they would take up residency at the Red Cloud Agency. But the army ordered them to journey south and live with their kin at the Darlington Agency in Indian Territory.

Nearly one thousand Cheyennes left Fort Robinson on May 28, 1877, arriving seventy days later in a strange country so unlike the Northern Plains. Within a few months, many contracted malaria. Medical supplies were limited, food inadequate, and winter clothing in short supply. During the winter of 1877–1878, forty-one people died.

After a year Dull Knife and Little Wolf told the Indian agent that they were going home, back to the Northern Plains. Despite threats from the agent that the soldiers would bring them back by force if necessary, the two chiefs made preparations to leave. In the early morning darkness of September 10, 1878, some three hundred Northern Cheyennes slipped away from Darlington Agency. Iron Teeth and her five children joined the exodus.[2]

The journey north to the Yellowstone, some 1,500 miles mostly on foot, would take them through Indian Territory, Kansas, Nebraska, South Dakota, and eventually Montana. As predicted, the army pursued the fleeing Cheyennes. There were serious fights at Turkey Springs in Indian Territory and Punished Woman's Fork in Kansas. Iron Teeth said that some people, mostly Southern Cheyenne, "went back as soon as the bullets began to fly," but Gathering His Medicine told his mother they should push on to the north country—"that it was better to be killed [on the journey] than to go back and die slowly."

To stay ahead of the avenging soldiers, the chiefs pushed the people over great distances, often in the dead of night. Many suffered exhaustion and hunger. Throughout the journey Iron Teeth suffered from chills and fever. She had few provisions for her family. Like others, she had packed lightly, taking only what she could carry on her back, a few items of clothing, some pemmican, a revolver, and, most important, the elk-antler hide scraper Red Pipe had made for her as a wedding gift. (She had carried the hide scraper with her when she fled the soldiers attacking Dull Knife's village.) She had

---

2   John H. Monnett's *Tell Them We Are Going Home: The Odyssey of the Northern Cheyenne* is by far the best account of the Northern Cheyenne exodus and the Fort Robinson massacre. Monnett made extensive use of Iron Teeth's narrative.

no lodge. "Day after day," she told Marquis, "my daughters helped me at making willow branch shelters." She looked closely after her younger children, keeping "my youngest daughter strapped to my body, in front of me, on my horse. I led another horse carrying the next youngest daughter." The oldest daughter rode her own horse and the two sons always stayed behind to help in watching for soldiers.

Sometime in October, after they had crossed the Platte River in Nebraska, Little Wolf and Dull Knife decided to separate. Everyone was hungry and exhausted. Little Wolf decided that, despite their desperate condition, safety lay in continuing the journey to their home country, but first he would rest his people in an isolated place in the Nebraska Sandhills. Dull Knife thought the wisest course for his tired and hungry people was to seek shelter at the nearby Red Cloud Agency, now called Pine Ridge.

Iron Teeth and her family stayed with Dull Knife. As they neared the agency site, several members of Dull Knife's group decided to push ahead. Iron Teeth's younger son and oldest daughter joined the group, while Iron Teeth stayed behind with her two younger daughters and older son Gathering His Medicine. Many feared they would be killed by Indian scouts, but the small group went anyway and made it safely to Pine Ridge where they were protected by the Oglalas. They had made a wise decision.

As Dull Knife's larger group neared the agency, they were apprehended in late October by soldiers from Fort Robinson. Although Dull Knife expressed his desire to take his people to the agency site, the soldiers took them to the fort. At first the Northern Cheyennes were treated well, but then orders came from Washington that they must be returned to Indian Territory. Captain Henry Wessells, the commanding officer, tried, at first, to persuade the captives to return south, but the chiefs insisted that they would rather die than return to the hated Darlington Agency.

Failing to persuade the Cheyennes to return south, Captain Wessells locked most of the Cheyennes in a post barracks. Still they would not yield. So Wessells withheld fuel, then food, and finally water. Iron Teeth said that they went eleven days without food except for the few pieces of dried meat the women had hidden in their packs, and they went three days without water except for the frost they scraped from the windows. Finally, the warriors (forty-four men were of fighting age) decided to break out of the barracks. They were prepared to risk death rather than go south. The well-known Cheyenne ethnologist George Bird Grinnell quoted one warrior named Little Shield, who said, "Now, dress-up and put on your best clothing. We will all die together." Another warrior exclaimed: "It is true that we must die, but we will not die shut up here like dogs; we will die on the prairie; we will die fighting." The warriors had only a few rifles and eleven revolvers that the women had hidden either under the barracks' floorboards (which Iron Teeth had covered with her blanket) or on their persons, for they knew the soldiers would not search a woman.

Iron Teeth was prepared, like the other women in the barracks, to face death. She cut up her robe to make extra moccasins for herself and her children. She prepared a small pack with a few possessions; it contained her prized elk-bone hide scraper. She had concealed a revolver beneath her dress, which she gave to her twenty-two-year-old son, Gathering His Medicine, as he then took his place with the warriors.

The plan was to break out after the soldiers retired for the night. It was a bitterly cold night (January 9, 1879), with the temperature near zero and a half foot of snow on the ground. Unfortunately, the moon was full, so those fleeing would be visible in the moonlight. The bugler sounded taps around nine in the evening, and an hour later the warrior Little Shield broke a window and ripped out the outside boards. At the other window, Gathering His Medicine broke the pane with his revolver and others ripped out the boards. One by one, the Cheyennes jumped out the windows into the biting cold. Once outside, Gathering His Medicine took his youngest sister on his back while Iron Teeth ran with her second daughter.

Sleepy soldiers poured out of their barracks, firing wildly on the fleeing Cheyennes. "One of them," Iron Teeth exclaimed, "fired a gun almost at my face, but I was not harmed." Everyone headed for the White River, where they hurriedly took their first drink in days. Then they scattered in a hail of bullets from pursuing soldiers. Gathering His Medicine and his mother parted at the river as he ran with his sister on his back in one direction and she ran another way with her other daughter.

Iron Teeth made her way to the bluffs overlooking the fort, where she and her daughter crawled into a cave for safety. A man named Crooked Nose joined them. She could only imagine what happened to her son and young daughter. From her hiding place, Iron Teeth heard "lots of shooting." By early the next morning, the soldiers had killed twenty-six Cheyennes, fourteen men and twelve women and children. Four of the dead were good friends of Iron Teeth.

Iron Teeth never forgot the ordeal. "We stayed in the cave seven nights. . . . More snow kept falling, it was very cold, but we were afraid to build a fire. We nibbled at my small store of dry meat and ate snow for water. Each day we could hear horses and the voices of soldiers searching for Indians." For the next twelve days, Captain Wessells's soldiers hunted down the runaway Cheyennes. Starving and cold, some fought to the death while others surrendered.

After a week of misery hiding in the cave, Iron Teeth's position was discovered by an army captain who found her tracks going in and out of the cave. The captain called out that if they surrendered, he would treat them well. After the three cold and weary Cheyennes came out of the cave, soldiers took them back to Fort Robinson. Iron Teeth suffered from mild frostbite on her toes and fingers. The post surgeon told her to rub snow on the frozen parts, and after experiencing some pain and burning, she eventually recovered.

At the fort Iron Teeth searched anxiously for her son and young daughter among the survivors. Finally she found the little girl. Iron Teeth "asked her about her brother. It appeared the girl did not hear me, so I asked again. This time she burst out crying. Then I knew he had been killed." The girl told her mother that they hid that first night in a hole in the Hat Creek Bluffs. The next day they heard soldiers approach their hiding place. Gathering His Medicine feared they had been discovered, so he decided to save his sister's life. He said to her: "Lie down, and I will cover you with leaves and dirt. Then I will climb out and fight the soldiers. They will kill me, but they will think I am the only one here, and they will go away after I am dead. When they are gone, you can come out and hunt for our mother." After hiding the girl, Gathering His Medicine bravely jumped up and began to shoot at the soldiers with the revolver his mother had given him. The soldiers killed him on the spot. The next day they found the little girl wandering on the bluffs and carried her back safely to Fort Robinson, where she was reunited with her mother.

The worst was not yet over for Dull Knife's people. On January 22 Captain Wessells's troops located the last group of holdouts, some thirty-two Cheyennes—eighteen men and older boys and fourteen women and young children—led by the warrior-artist Little Finger Nail. They had decided to make their stand for freedom in a dry creek bed of Antelope Creek. Though surrounded on all sides by superior numbers and firepower, the Cheyenne warriors fought to the death. They killed four soldiers and wounded three in the fight, including Captain Wessells, who suffered a three-inch scalp wound. When the firing stopped, the soldiers found seventeen men dead in the pit, along with four women and two children. There were only nine survivors, some wounded. The soldiers searched for Dull Knife among the dead and wounded, but he was not there. Somehow Dull Knife and his immediate family made it to Pine Ridge, where his friends gave him shelter. Still, it was a bittersweet moment for Dull Knife; back in the high bluffs along the White River and Soldier Creek, Dull Knife lost two daughters and one son.

The recaptured Cheyennes were brought back to Fort Robinson, where they were kept under guard. They were given some coffee and crackers to eat and some shoes, socks, and blankets to keep warm. Without lodges to protect them against the cold, Iron Teeth said that she and her daughters collected "some cottonwood branches and built ourselves a kind of lodge. With the blankets given to us, this was the best place for sleeping I had been in for a week."

A few days later they were placed in a "prison house." Once again a soldier-chief came to talk and despite all that happened he wanted the Cheyennes to return south. "But we were mourning for our dead," exclaimed Iron Teeth, "and we had no ears for his words. Everybody said 'No, we will not go back there.'" After they refused once again to go south, Iron Teeth feared the soldiers would come into the prison and shoot them all—but they did not. Instead, a few days later they were all taken to Pine Ridge to live among Red Cloud's Oglala.

In November 1879 the Bureau of Indian Affairs (BIA) and the army permitted Dull Knife's people at Pine Ridge to rejoin their relatives at Fort Keogh. Two Moons and White Bull's bands had been camped at Fort Keogh since they surrendered in April 1876. They had never been forced south. Kate Bighead was part of this group.

Little Wolf's people were already there. After spending a quiet winter in the Nebraska Sandhills, Little Wolf continued his journey back to the Powder River country in early spring. They passed safely through the Black Hills into southeastern Montana where, on March 25, 1879, they were peacefully apprehended by soldiers and taken to Fort Keogh.

By this time the BIA and the army had relented in their opposition—the heroic march north and the desperate fighting by Dull Knife's band at Fort Robinson had won for the people their beloved homeland in the Powder River country. In 1884 the president of the United States established for the Northern Cheyenne the Tongue River Reservation in Montana.

For some reason Iron Teeth and her family remained behind at Pine Ridge, but in time she too relocated to the enlarged Northern Cheyenne Reservation. Little is known of her early years on the reservation. When Thomas B. Marquis met Iron Teeth in 1926, she was a ninety-two-year-old woman living out her last days in a poor, isolated log cabin in the hills with a widowed daughter who had no children. They lived on very little. Once a month an Indian policeman brought her some food: one quart of green coffee, one quart of sugar, a few pounds of flour, and a small quantity of baking powder. Iron Teeth was told that she could get more food if she went personally each month to the agency for her rations, but she argued that without any horse or wagon she could not travel such a long distance over the mountains to the agency headquarters twenty miles away. "It would be hard enough in summer," she told Marquis, "it is impossible in winter."

Iron Teeth did what she could to survive. Although old and partially blind, she chopped wood for her fire; she gathered chokeberries and service-berries, which she dried for winter; she did the same with the squashes and pumpkins that a missionary gave her. One time the same missionary gave her a dog who, unfortunately, barked at people who came to visit, so she killed the dog, ate some of the meat, and dried the rest for winter. Sometimes friends like Prairie Woman shared food with her; and when winter got too cold, Spotted Dog let her stay in his house to keep warm. Iron Teeth did not like depending on her friends; she faulted the Indian Bureau for not keeping its promise "to take care of the old Indians." She told Dr. Marquis that she once smoked; but she had stopped when she realized that "it was not good for the health, and it also cost too much money."

Although poor in material possessions, Iron Teeth possessed two objects that she treasured and carried with her throughout her long life. They were both made by Red Pipe: a sheath-knife, which every day "dangled" from her belt, and the elk-horn hide scraper. Speaking of her hide scraper, Iron Teeth explained to Marquis that "the Indian men of the old times commonly made this kind of present to their young wives." She explained that the scraper had a dual purpose: she used it for tanning hides and, by making notches on the bone for each of her five children, she kept a record of their ages. The precious gift had never been lost. "I was carrying it in my hands when my husband was killed on upper Powder River. It was tied to my saddle while we were in flight from Oklahoma. It was in my little pack when we broke out from the Fort Robinson prison." Some white people had offered her money for it, but though poor, such money never tempted her. She explained her reasoning to Marquis: "Red Pipe was the only husband I ever had. I am the only wife he ever had. Through more than fifty years I have been his widow. When I die, this gift from my husband will be buried with me."

When thinking of her husband and older son who had been killed in battle, Iron Teeth told Marquis that she "used to hate all white people, especially the soldiers. But my heart now has become changed to softer feelings. Some of the white people are good, maybe as good as Indians."

Still, Iron Teeth could not forget the old days. She concluded her talk with Marquis on a cold November day by remembering her son Gathering His Medicine. "Lots of times," she told Marquis, "as I sit here alone on the floor with my blanket wrapped about me, I lean forward and close my eyes and think of him standing up out of the pit and fighting the soldiers, knowing that he would be killed, but doing so that his little sister might get away to safety." And then she asked Marquis, "Don't you think he was a brave young man?" What answer could Marquis give other than yes!

In honoring her son, Iron Teeth was paying homage to all the Northern Cheyennes who risked their lives by fleeing from the Darlington Agency in Indian Territory back to their beloved Powder River country—but especially to the men, women, and children at Fort Robinson who, like Gathering His Medicine, died in defense of their freedom, their homeland, and their loved ones. As John H. Monnett said in his classic study of the Northern Cheyenne odyssey, the Fort Robinson martyrs "died with honor, and their sacrifice *is* remembered."

CHAPTER 7

Medicine Snake Woman:
Embracing the White World

In 1840 Chief Menestokos (Father of All Children), a Blood/Blackfoot from Canada, came to trade at Fort Union, the American Fur Company's largest fort on the Upper Missouri River. The chief brought with him his beautiful daughter, Natawista Iksana, best known as Medicine Snake Woman. She caught the eye of Alexander Culbertson, the fort's commander/bourgeois, who offered to marry her. He conducted the marital negotiations in the Indian way by presenting nine horses to the girl's older brother, Seen-From-Afar, who reciprocated by sending nine horses to Culbertson along with his young sister. Medicine Snake Woman was fifteen years old, Culbertson twice her age. She did not speak English, but Culbertson spoke her native tongue.[1]

It's likely that the marriage was, in the beginning, one of convenience, not true love, although in time deeper ties of affection developed between the two. For Culbertson, marriage with the daughter of a prominent chief of the Blood/Blackfoot nation of Canada gave the American Fur Company an entrée into the Canadian market. For Medicine Snake Woman, the marriage placed her family and tribe in an advantageous trading position with the man who ran Fort Union and, later, all of the American Fur Company's trading posts on the Upper Missouri River. The liberal gifts of ammunition and tobacco Alexander Culbertson made to members of the Blood/Blackfoot tribe helped to make Seen-From-Afar head chief of his tribe by 1855 and one of the wealthiest men of his generation.

During the years that Culbertson presided over Fort Union, Medicine Snake Woman remained constantly by her husband's side, serving as hostess,

---

1   For background on Culbertson's life in the fur trade, see Ray H. Mattison's "Alexander Culbertson," in Vol. 1, *The Mountain Men and the Fur Trade of the Far West*, edited by LeRoy R. Hafen. For an account of Medicine Snake Woman's life, see Mildred Walker Schemm's "The Major's Lady: Natawista," *Montana, the Magazine of Western History*, 2 (January 1952), 5–15, and Anne McDonald's "Mrs. Alexander Culbertson," *Contributions to the Historical Society of Montana*, 10, 243–246.

Medicine Snake Woman (Natawista Culbertson) COURTESY OF THE MONTANA HISTORICAL
SOCIETY RESEARCH CENTER, PHOTOGRAPH ARCHIVES, HELENA, MONTANA, CATALOG NUMBER 941-819

interpreter, and diplomat. Euro-American visitors to the fort spoke favorably of her beauty, her intelligence, and her strength of character.

John James Audubon, the famous naturalist, spent some time in the summer of 1843 at Fort Union, entertained by Alexander Culbertson and Medicine Snake Woman. Audubon was intrigued by this full-blood Indian woman who moved so easily between the native and white worlds. He wrote in his *Journal* a fascinating account of this young, vibrant, eighteen-year-old woman whom he called "Mrs. Culbertson" or the "princess."

Medicine Snake Woman's skill and energy when it came to physical activities impressed Audubon. One day the Culbertsons staged a horse race. Audubon was captivated by the women riders:

> *The* ladies *had their hair loose and flying in the breeze, and then mounted on horses with Indian saddles and trappings. Mrs. Culbertson and her maid rode astride like men, and all rode a furious race, under whip the whole way, for more than one mile on the prairie; and how amazed would have been any European lady, or some of our modern belles who boast their equestrian skills, at seeing the magnificent riding of this Indian princess—for that is Mrs. Culbertson's rank.*

Audubon could not help noting how attractive Medicine Snake Woman appeared in a "superb dress," her "magnificent black hair floating like a banner behind her." For her part Medicine Snake Woman was fascinated by Audubon's wildlife paintings. One day she presented him with six young mallards that she had caught swimming in the Missouri River. Audubon observed her in the water and noted with some awe that "she is a most expert and graceful swimmer, besides being capable of remaining under water a long time."

"Mrs. Culbertson" excelled as well in the domestic arts. Audubon observed her careful work: She made a parfleche, a carrying case made from rawhide, which she decorated with color-dyed porcupine quills and the feathers of a golden eagle. He also noted that Medicine Snake Woman knew how to survive in the wilderness. At one point Alexander Culbertson escorted Audubon's party as they made their way up the Missouri River by boat. Medicine Snake Woman, by now with a young child, joined the group. Along the way they were overtaken by a sudden, violent windstorm. Everyone left the shaky boat for safety on land. "Mrs. Culbertson, with her child in her arms, made for the willows, and had a shelter for her babe in a few minutes."

But then this remarkable woman surprised him. Audubon wanted to save the head of a dead buffalo for study, but neglected to tell "Mrs. Culbertson," who "had its skull broken open to enjoy its brains. Handsome, and really courteous and refined in many ways, I cannot reconcile to myself the fact that she partakes of raw animal food with such evident relish." Audubon had forgotten, at least for the moment, that this young, dynamic woman he so admired was a full-blood Indian woman, and in her culture many delicate parts of the buffalo, such as the brain, liver, kidney, and bone marrow, were considered a delicacy.

Around 1845 Culbertson (at the command of the American Fur Company) moved farther up the Missouri to tap the rich fur trade with the native tribes of northern Montana and lower Canada. By 1848 Culbertson established Fort Benton, which came in time to supplant Fort Union in importance in the fur trade. During these years Medicine Snake Woman gave birth to four children: Jack, Nancy, Julia, and Fannie. Nancy, born in 1848, tragically drowned in the Missouri River. The surviving children were sent east to be educated in convents or military school.

On Christmas night in 1850, Major Culbertson gave a ball to celebrate the completion of his new house inside the stockade. A huge fire warmed the big room as guests danced to the music of a fiddle. Some sang songs in French. There was punch and liquor and food for all the invited guests: Medicine Snake Woman's relatives, army officers, hunters, fur trappers and their Indian wives, post clerks, and interpreters. At one point Culbertson called for quiet to make an announcement: The new fort was officially named Fort Benton (in honor of Senator Thomas Benton from Missouri). Hands clapped in celebration as the music began again and the major took his place on the dance floor with his "lithe little wife," dressed in a full red silk skirt that had come from St. Louis, with a silver cross hanging from her neck. The music rang throughout the fort, and some stranger approaching from a distance could take some comfort from that lonely speck of light in the cold night coming from the banks of the Missouri.

Fort Benton, although far up the Missouri River, continued to welcome distinguished guests. Rudolph Friederich Kurz, a Swiss artist, arrived at Fort Benton in October 1851 and attended a ball at the fort sponsored by Major Culbertson. He was favorably impressed with Medicine Snake Woman and wrote about her in his *Journal*: "His Indian wife in her ball-gown fringed and valanced according to European mode, looked extra-ordinarily well. She has much presence, grace, and animation for a full-blooded Indian." Kurz considered her a beautiful woman, and he would have painted her portrait but, unfortunately, "she had her long, lustrous black hair cut short" to honor the death of her younger brother killed by an Assiniboine Indian. Medicine Snake Woman had not forgotten the mourning traditions of her people. "She would be," Kurz said, "an excellent model for a Venus ideal woman of a primitive race: a perfect little wife."

In 1853 the Congress of the United States entrusted Isaac I. Stevens, the newly appointed governor of the Washington Territory, with the task of finding the best route for a transcontinental railroad from the Mississippi to the Pacific. Stevens's survey route would take him into the heart of dangerous Blackfoot country; fearing for the safety of his exploration party, Stevens decided to employ Alexander Culbertson as an intermediary. Culbertson was known for his knowledge of the country and the native tribes; but equally important to Stevens was the fact that Culbertson "had married a full-blooded Blackfoot woman."

Stevens met the couple for the first time at Fort Union. He was impressed with "Mrs. Culbertson, who had fully adopted the manners, costume and deportment of the whites, and who, by her refinement, presents the most striking illustration of the high civilization which these tribes of the interior are capable of attaining." Stevens found the couple apprehensive about the reception the Americans would receive from the Blackfeet; any untoward act could lead to hostilities. Culbertson decided, for safety's sake, to leave his wife back at Fort Union while the survey party worked its way upriver to Fort Benton, but Medicine Snake Woman insisted that she would make the journey: "My people are a good people, but they are jealous and vindictive. I am afraid that they and the whites will not understand each other; but if I go, I may be able to explain things to them, and soothe them if they should be irritated. I know there is great danger; but, my husband, where you go, I will go, and where you die I die."

Stevens soon recognized the value of Mrs. Culbertson's presence. "She was in constant intercourse with the Indians," Stevens reported, "and inspired them with perfect confidence. . . . She heard all that the Indians said, and reported it through her husband to me." Stevens found Indian men and women gathered around Mrs. Culbertson as she regaled them with funny stories about the strange behavior of white people, especially the ladies of St. Louis. On a more serious note, Medicine Snake Woman probably helped to persuade Little Dog, her cousin, to bring the Canadian Blackfeet chiefs to Fort Benton to counsel with Stevens. In his report to Washington, Stevens recognized that Mrs. Culbertson "rendered the highest service to the expedition, a service which demands this public acknowledgement." The irony in this whole affair is that Medicine Snake Woman, acting as an intermediary between whites and Indians, helped pave the way for the railroad and white settlers who would eventually displace her people.

The fur trade had made Culbertson a rich man. By 1858, when he left the employ of the American Fur Company, it was estimated that he had accumulated a fortune of $300,000. Culbertson, along with his wife and children, retired to his large estate named Locust Grove outside Peoria, Illinois, where he took up farming. He built a spacious, nine-room, beautifully furnished mansion for his family, staffed it with servants, and hired an English gardener to landscape the estate's three hundred acres, complete with a corral stocked with antelope, elk, and buffalo. The couple loved to ride, so the estate contained some of the finest horses in the area, which took blue ribbons in the horse shows at Cincinnati.

Soon after settling at Locust Grove, Culbertson decided to formalize his relationship with Medicine Snake Woman in a Christian marriage since he wanted to legally protect her property rights and those of the children in his estate. The marriage, which took place at the estate on September 9, 1859, was reported in the Peoria *Daily Transcript*. Fr. Scanlon, a Catholic priest from St. Joseph, Missouri, an old friend of Culbertson, performed the service. Many invited guests came to celebrate the wedding, including some former associates in the fur trade. The report noted that "Mrs. Culbertson is a lady of fine native talent."

Medicine Snake Woman enjoyed her years at Locust Grove. The last of her five children, Joseph, was born there in 1859. She loved her finely furnished home with its servants and her dresses with fine jewelry, especially stones with color, like rubies and emeralds. But every year she would set up a Blackfoot tipi on the lawn, dress in Indian clothing, and spend time in her tipi. It was her simple way of keeping in touch with the Indian world she had left behind in the mountains.

Often, Alexander and Medicine Snake Woman would break away from Locust Grove and take the riverboat up the Missouri River to visit friends and relatives. One Dr. E. J. Marsh, who met the couple on the steamboat traveling up the Missouri River in 1859, said that Mrs. Culbertson "dressed like a white lady and is said to be a very fine woman."

The noted Indian anthropologist Lewis Henry Morgan met Culbertson and Medicine Snake Woman, traveling with their two children to Fort Benton, on the same riverboat in May 1862. Like any proud mother, she showed Morgan a photograph of her eighteen-year-old daughter—most likely Julia—then at Locust Grove. Morgan commented that "It is a very beautiful face without a particle of Indian in it." Morgan met another daughter on the boat—most likely Fannie—then about twelve years old. He said that she was a "very handsome child, with bright eyes, brunette complexion, and hair slightly dark. She will make, when educated, a woman to command attention anywhere. She talks English only, having never learned Blackfoot." Morgan predicted that the two daughters would "of course both marry white husbands." Morgan's time with Mrs. Culbertson was well spent since he was engaged in a research project on American Indian kinship systems and Medicine Snake Woman provided him information pertaining to the Blood/Blackfoot.

By 1868 Alexander Culbertson's fortune was nearly gone. Years of lavish living and bad investments brought an end to life in Peoria. By the time creditors filed claims against the estate at Locust Grove, Culbertson and Medicine Snake Woman had already left for Fort Benton. But the golden age of the fur trade was over. Culbertson, a man who once ruled like a feudal lord over Fort Union and Fort Benton, was forced to make his living by engaging in small-time trade with the Indians and by serving as an interpreter at some of the agencies.

Medicine Snake Woman remained with Culbertson at Fort Benton until 1870; her name is on the fort's census for that year. Then she left her husband, going her own way. No one knows why. Within a short time, she returned to her people in Canada. Ms. Schemm, an earlier biographer, offered a simple explanation: "She had been away a long time and she chose to go back to her own people." She was relatively on her own by this time: Her two well-educated daughters remained back east, and in time both married white men; her two boys, familiar with both worlds—white and Indian—found work at the frontier forts and Indian agencies.

Major Culbertson spent his last days with his daughter Julia in Nebraska, where he died on August 27, 1879. By this time Medicine Snake Woman was living in the log house of her nephew on the Blood Reserve in Canada, drawing her rations from the Canadian government—a long way from the years she presided over two fur-trading forts on the Upper Missouri and at Locust Grove mansion in Peoria. One of the fur traders from Fort Benton saw her there in 1881. Despite the passage of time, she was still known as "Madam Culbertson." Medicine Snake Woman died in 1893, nearly seventy years old, and was buried among her people in the Indian mission cemetery near Standoff, Alberta.

CHAPTER 8

Eagle Woman: Peace Emissary

Eagle Woman, born in 1820, grew up in a well-connected family, her father, Two Lance, being a distinguished chief of the Two Kettles Lakota and her mother, Rosy Light of Dawn, a member of the powerful Hunkpapa Lakota.[1] When Eagle Woman was only five, she began to accompany her father to Old Fort Pierre, where he traded furs for European goods. Over time she became fascinated with the fort, its exotic goods, and the white men who ran it, especially the French-Canadian fur trader Honore Picotte.

At seventeen Eagle Woman became an orphan, losing first her father, then her mother. A year later the beautiful young woman "married" the much older Honore Picotte, who, at forty-two, was legally married to a French woman living in St. Louis. The marriage proved mutually beneficial—for Eagle Woman marriage to an important fur trader enhanced her position and that of her family; for Picotte it cemented ties with the Lakotas who traded at the fort.

Living at the fort close to her own people, Eagle Woman served as the fort's hostess, learning the ways of whites without losing ties to her own people. During the years she lived with Picotte, Eagle Woman gave birth to two daughters, Mary Louise and Zoe Lulu. Ten years after their marriage, Honore Picotte retired to live in St. Louis with his French wife and children. Despite his separation from Eagle Woman, Picotte did not neglect his parental obligation to provide for the education of his two daughters.

Moreover, when Picotte left for St. Louis in 1848, he entrusted Eagle Woman to his protégé, Charles E. Galpin, who managed the fur trade at Fort Pierre. Galpin, multilingual and multicultural in his outlook, was

---

1   In the last decade of her life, Eagle Woman shared stories about her life with Frances Chamberlain Holley, a local historian living in Bismarck, North Dakota. Holley published Eagle Woman's fascinating stories in *Once Their Home: or, Our Legacy from the Dakotahs* (1892). For a scholarly study of Eagle Woman's life, see John S. Gray's two-part essay, "The Story of Mrs. Picotte-Galpin, a Sioux Heroine: Eagle Woman Learns about White Ways and Racial Conflict, 1820–1868," *Montana, the Magazine of Western History*, 36 (Spring 1986), 2–21, and "The Story of Mrs. Picotte-Galpin, a Sioux Heroine: Eagle Woman Becomes a Trader and Counsels for Peace, 1868–1888," *Montana, The Magazine of Western History*, 36 (Summer 1986), 2–21.

roughly the same age as Eagle Woman. The two fell in love and married two years later. The union was lifelong, warm, and intimate, each learning the best of their respective cultures from the other. Eagle Woman gave birth to five children with Galpin: Samuel, Robert (who died young), Alma Jane, Richard, and Anne. Galpin proved a good husband and devoted father to his children and to Picotte's daughters as well.

Eagle Woman continued as hostess at Fort Pierre, and although she did not speak English, she made a good impression on the fort's many visitors. Army surgeon Dr. George L. Miller, who visited the fort in the 1850s, wrote favorably of the Galpins: "Agent Galpin of the fur company is remembered for his intelligence and kindness to me, especially on account of his bright-minded Sioux wife, whose hospitality we enjoyed in his wigwam, furnished with the richest furs and decorated with several children of the half-breed brand of their mixed parentage." The ethnologist Dr. Ferdinand V. Hayden, who stayed with the Galpins in June 1859, said of Eagle Woman: "She is a woman of much intelligence and fine natural capabilities and may be regarded as the highest type of her sex among the Indian tribes of the Northwest."

Throughout her life Eagle Woman served as a peace intermediary between her people and whites. In 1862 the Galpins played a role in saving several white captives held by the Santee Sioux. Eagle Woman explained to Frances Holley, an early biographer, how the rescue came about. In the spring of that year, Charles Galpin undertook a long journey up the Missouri River to Fort Benton to establish a new base for trading with the Blackfeet and Crows. Eagle Woman accompanied her husband with their four-year-old son, Richard, but tragedy struck at the fort, where the little boy died suddenly. Reluctant to bury the boy so far from home, the Galpins prepared the body for the long journey downriver to Fort Pierre.

During their return hostile Santee Sioux, who had fled Minnesota after a failed uprising, stopped their boat and threatened to kill them all. Eagle Woman, who knew some of these Indians, talked her way out of danger. While at the Santee Sioux village, the Galpins had recognized some white captives and quietly promised to rescue them. After burying their child near Fort Pierre, the Galpins arranged for friendly Indians (including two of Eagle Woman's brothers) to rescue the captives—two women and seven children. When the captives reached safety, Eagle Woman provided for their needs.

Eagle Woman frequently spoke out against cruelty of any kind, whether committed by whites or by Indians. When soldiers from Fort Randall, the

Eagle Woman (Matilda Galpin), circa 1880 REPRINTED FROM *ONCE THEIR HOME: OR, OUR LEGACY FROM THE DAKOTAHS*, BY FRANCES C. HOLLEY, 1892

Galpins' new home, killed seven Lakotas in 1863, Eagle Woman protested and declared that one of the men shot by the soldiers was a friendly chief of Two Kettles' band who had "never even looked cross at a white man; he was always kind and good."

Two years later Charles Galpin took his family to Fort Rice, where he served as the post's sutler. While there, Eagle Woman again courageously protested an act of cruelty, only this time she spoke out against her own people. On May 26, 1865, hostile Indians ambushed Lieutenant Benjamin Wilson, the post quartermaster, shooting him with three arrows. Eagle Woman rushed to the fallen officer and cradled him in her lap. As the Indians rushed Wilson for the kill, she shouted in defiance: "This man belongs to me now! You cannot mutilate him nor touch him! Begone, every one of you!" Meanwhile, she waved her shawl and signaled for help. The lieutenant's orderly, revolver drawn, rushed to help. The mortally wounded officer was taken to the post's hospital, where he lingered for seven days. At the dying officer's request, Eagle Woman visited him. While her brave intervention earned praise from soldiers, some Indians did not appreciate her actions. Later, Circling Bear, one of those who shot the deadly arrows, told Eagle Woman if he had known she was the one protecting the officer, he would have killed her, too.

In 1865 General Alfred Sully was anxious to end the hostilities that had broken out between Indians and soldiers on the Northern Plains. A large, hostile village was camped on the Little Missouri River. Sully wondered if the Indians there would meet with peace commissioners from Washington, and he approached the Galpins for help. Deciding to make the journey for peace despite personal risks, the pair left Fort Rice on September 1, 1865. After reaching the hostile village, they met in council with the chiefs and persuaded them to meet the peace commissioners. When the chiefs arrived at Fort Rice, they were greeted warmly by the Galpins, and true to their word, the chiefs met the commissioners and signed a peace treaty.

Given the diplomatic role Eagle Woman played in the peace process, Captain Adams, an officer at Fort Rice, heaped praise on her: "Mrs. Galpin . . . is one of the finest women in the world. . . . She speaks no English, only her native Sioux. She is a friend of her own race and also of the whites. Her friendship is not proved by words but by deeds."

Sadly, peace was short-lived. Starting in 1866 Red Cloud, the Oglala war leader, led his followers in a bloody conflict against the soldiers building a series of forts in the buffalo-rich Powder River country designed to protect the emigrants crossing the Bozeman Trail headed for mining camps in Montana.

After two long years of conflict, Congress decided to seek a comprehensive peace agreement with the Lakotas and other tribes. After arduous negotiations most Lakota chiefs, including Red Cloud, signed the 1868 Treaty of Fort Laramie. Some Lakotas refused to sign the treaty or come onto the reservation. Sitting Bull, the powerful Hunkpapa leader, was one of the most prominent dissenters. The peace commissioners looked for sympathetic supporters who could persuade the hostile Sitting Bull to come to Fort Rice and sign the treaty.

For this dangerous mission the peace commissioners enlisted the support of Father Pierre De Smet. The Jesuit priest, in turn, enlisted the support of his friends Charles Galpin and Eagle Woman. Galpin would serve as his interpreter. As for Eagle Woman, Father De Smet explained his reasoning to N. G. Taylor, who led the peace commission: "Mrs. Galpin, being of Sioux birth and a near relation to several war chiefs . . . exercises great influence among her people." Father De Smet, with Eagle Woman's help, put together a large party, which included seventy men, including prominent Lakota and Yanktonai chiefs, and ten women. They left Fort Rice on June 3, 1868, and traveled 350 miles on horseback to the hostile camp.

There are two different versions of this long, difficult journey to the Hunkpapa village. At Father De Smet's request, Charles Galpin kept a daily account of the mission, and the Jesuit priest based his official report on this journal. Many years later Eagle Woman told this same story to Mrs. Holley. Alongside the Galpin/De Smet account, Mrs. Holley's version appears overly dramatic and tends to exaggerate the dangers faced by the expedition.

Several days into the journey, Father De Smet sent four messengers to locate the village on the Powder River, carrying tobacco as a peace offering. The messengers returned a week later with eighteen warriors from the Hunkpapa village, who assured the peace delegation that the chiefs welcomed them "with open arms." Some days later as they approached the village, they were greeted by a large demonstration of warriors dressed in colorful war regalia. Contrary to Mrs. Holley's story, the delegation was in no danger: Four Horns and Black Moon, leaders of the village, shook hands with Father De Smet, Charles Galpin, and Eagle Woman.

Safely escorted into the village, the delegation was greeted by Sitting Bull, who provided them shelter in his lodge and an armed guard, fearful that some young, hotheaded warrior would take revenge for some previous loss at the hands of whites. Eagle Woman enjoyed the freedom of the camp and Galpin reported that she was invited to feast in many lodges, everyone treating her with great respect and kindness.

After some days a great council took place. Father De Smet urged the chiefs and war leaders to meet with the commissioners and make peace with whites. Black Moon spoke first, listing the many abuses his people suffered at the hands of whites, who, he insisted, should leave Lakota lands. Sitting Bull, leader of the warriors, spoke next. Although his speech was more conciliatory, he said that whites should stop spoiling Lakota lands. After the speech Sitting Bull, in a gesture of friendship, shook hands with Father De Smet, Charles Galpin, and Eagle Woman, a distinct mark of respect for this brave Lakota woman.

Despite their grievances against whites who invaded their lands, the chiefs agreed, out of respect for Father De Smet, to send a delegation to speak with the commissioners at Fort Rice. But Sitting Bull would not personally make the journey, telling Eagle Woman that he feared whites would take him prisoner if he went. Gall, one of his lieutenants, went in his place.

The Lakota delegation met with the peace commissioners on July 2, 1868. The commissioners explained the complex terms of the recently negotiated Fort Laramie Treaty. Gall, who spoke first, showed little interest in the provisions of the treaty, especially the article that established the Great Sioux Reservation. Instead, he told the commissioners that if whites wanted peace they should leave the Upper Missouri River area. Nonetheless, Gall signed the treaty, took his presents, and returned to his people. Sitting Bull had assured Father De Smet that he would abide by the agreement his delegates reached with the commissioners, but as Robert Utley pointed out in his biography of Sitting Bull, the great war leader gave the treaty terms even less consideration than Gall.

The peace commissioners, satisfied with the illusion of success, praised Father De Smet for bringing the hostile Lakotas to sign the treaty, and they appointed Galpin special interpreter for the Northern Lakotas. Eagle Woman received no public recognition from the commissioners, but Major General David S. Stanley recognized her role in the peace negotiations in a letter to Archbishop John Purcell, dated July 16, 1868: "This lady is a good Catholic and an excellent person, a striking example of what the influence of religion and civilization can accomplish for the welfare of the Indians." It appears that several days before this letter was written, Father De Smet had baptized Eagle Woman and blessed her marriage with Charles Galpin.

The Treaty of Fort Laramie established the Great Sioux Reservation, including most of the Dakotas west of the Missouri River. Agencies were established on the reservation to serve the needs of the different Lakota groups. The agency serving the Hunkpapas was first located at Grand River, and while Sitting Bull never came to the reservation, many Hunkpapa bands settled at the site. In recognition of his public service, Galpin was appointed agency interpreter, for which he received $150 monthly. The Galpins relocated to Grand River, where they set up their trading post. Eagle Woman accepted the move to help her people make the transition to a more settled way of life—not an easy task.

The Hunkpapas found the reservation a strange and unsettling place in the early days. They resisted the agent's efforts to start farming the land, and when government rations ran out (as they did in the first year), the Indians simply killed the agency beef they needed for their families. In these difficult times, Eagle Woman persuaded her husband to share store provisions with hungry families.

Tensions between agency whites and the Hunkpapas ran high, and on one occasion nearly erupted in bloodshed. Eagle Woman related the following story to Mrs. Holley. Some five thousand Indians (clearly an inflated number) surrounded and threatened agency whites. Eagle Woman became so disturbed at their violent behavior that she marched into the angry crowd shouting: "Cowards! To come here, five thousand of you, to slaughter a half-dozen white men! You have been killing their cattle right along, day after day, and not one of them said anything to you about the loss. . . . If you do kill one of their white men, war will be declared."

The hostile crowd quieted. Eagle Woman promised them a feast if they ceased threatening the whites. With provisions from the agent and from her own store, she prepared huge pots of coffee, generously sweetened with sugar. While food was being cooked, she distributed bolts of calico to the women and horses to some of the leading chiefs. She succeeded in preserving the peace. One of the agency whites, whose life Eagle Woman saved that day, later told Mrs. Holley: "As Mrs. Galpin stood in the midst of that immense crowd of blood-thirsty Indians, and argued and pled for the lives of the white men, regardless of her own perilous position, it was the grandest spectacle I ever saw."

The next few years were filled with both tragedy and happiness for Eagle Woman. Galpin, a devoted husband, good father, and friend to the Hunkpapas, took ill and died suddenly on November 30, 1869, at age forty-eight, leaving Eagle Woman a widow with two young girls to educate (Anne eight years old and Alma Jane thirteen). She took over her husband's post, becoming the first woman merchant among the Lakotas. Sammy, who had worked in his father's store, assisted his mother at the trading post, but in 1872 he suffered an untimely death from tuberculosis. Sammy, only twenty-two, was Eagle Woman's last surviving male child.

In the midst of all this sadness, there was some good news: Lieutenant William Harmon, who served as the commissary officer at Grand River, fell in love with the beautiful and talented Lulu Picotte. They were married in 1870 in a Catholic church in Sioux City, where Father De Smet gave away his goddaughter Lulu. After a splendid reception, the couple returned to Grand River, where Lieutenant Harmon resigned his commission in the army and served as agent for Durfee and Peck's trading post at the agency. Within a year Lulu gave birth to her first child.

Eagle Woman reentered public service in 1872. A special commission persuaded some of the nonreservation Lakota chiefs to go to Washington, D.C., to meet with the "Great Father." It was Washington's way to impress Indians with the power of white society. The Indian agent at Grand River consulted with Eagle Woman to select a delegation of "friendly" chiefs from the reservation to accompany their northern kin. A seasoned traveler, Eagle Woman guided the chiefs on their journey eastward.

The delegation stopped in Chicago, where they were greeted by the mayor. Eagle Woman sat with the chiefs. A Chicago reporter described her as a "pleasant appearing Indian woman . . . neatly dressed in modern style [with] two daughters at school in the east, whom she has supported by moccasin-making and beadwork among the Sioux."

Arriving in Washington, the delegation stayed for two weeks, visiting designated sites and meeting with various dignitaries, including President Grant. They also spent a few days in New York City before making the long journey back to Grand River.

In 1873 the flood-threatened Grand River Agency was relocated upriver to Standing Rock, the Hunkpapas' new home. Eagle Woman established her trading post at the new agency, but she ran into opposition from a group of Washington insiders who wanted to exercise a monopoly over all trading posts in the West. Eagle Woman boldly resisted all efforts to close down her trading post, arguing that as a full-blood Indian she had the right to trade with her own people.

It was during this difficult period that Eagle Woman again proved her value as a mediator between Hunkpapas and whites. When soldiers came in December 1874 to arrest Rain-in-the-Face for the alleged killing of some whites, Eagle Woman persuaded the Hunkpapas to avoid conflict with the soldiers by allowing the arrest, and she secretly warned their commanding officer that his troops would be attacked if he left the fort by a certain route.

Emboldened by her standing at the agency and the support of her own people (whom she helped in hard times with goods from her store), Eagle Woman refused to obey the call by John Burke, the Indian agent at Standing Rock, to close her trading post. Burke then asked Captain John S. Poland, who commanded Fort Yates, to close the store, but the officer, who disliked Burke and likely recognized Eagle Woman's importance, refused. Finally, Burke appealed to a federal marshal to confiscate Eagle Woman's goods, but he also declined. Defeated, Burke gave up the struggle in August 1875. The last word in the fight came from Lieutenant Colonel Pinckney Lugenbeel, who had been sent to investigate the Burke-Poland controversy. Recognizing Mrs. Galpin's right to maintain a trading post among her people, Lugenbeel concluded on a personal note: "I consider her a very meritorious person and trust that she will remain unmolested in her laudable efforts to educate her children. Mrs. Galpin is the bright particular star of the Sioux Nation, and I honor her for her former deeds and for her present unexceptionable conduct."

Eagle Woman's personal struggles gave way in the following years to larger issues affecting the Lakota Nation. In 1874, after Lieutenant Colonel George Armstrong Custer's expedition reported finding gold in the Black Hills, thousands of miners poured into the region. Reluctant to drive out the miners, Congress created a commission to buy or lease the Black Hills. Leading Lakota chiefs and thousands of warriors gathered on the White River in South Dakota to discuss Washington's offer. Eagle Woman accompanied a delegation of Hunkpapa chiefs from Standing Rock to the meeting. A reporter from the *New York Herald*, who noted her presence among the chiefs, reported that she was "carrying a sunshade over her bare head." He commented favorably about her appearance and pointed out that "her long and luxuriant black hair [was] tinged with gray"—a recognition that this active woman was getting older.

The proceedings went nowhere. Assembled chiefs and young warriors were bitterly divided over selling the Black Hills. Into the midst of these proceedings rode Little Big Man, a Powder River Lakota and one of Crazy Horse's lieutenants, armed and dangerous, threatening to shoot any chief who signed away the Black Hills. Little Big Man excited the warriors, who crowded dangerously against the one hundred soldiers assigned to protect the commissioners. The timely intervention of Young Man Afraid of His Horses and his Oglala warriors protected the soldiers from violence, while a mounted force of Standing Rock Hunkpapas, organized by Eagle Woman's supporters, shielded the commissioners from harm. Years later the Rev. Samuel D. Hinman, a member of the commission, said that Mrs. Galpin "had saved their [the commissioners] lives."

Eagle Woman played no part in the many troubles that followed the failed proceedings—the Great Sioux War of 1876 that led to Lieutenant George Armstrong Custer's defeat at the Little Bighorn and the constant warfare between the army and Powder River Lakotas, which finally led to the "surrender" of Crazy Horse, the flight of Sitting Bull's people to Canada, and the loss of the Black Hills and the Powder River country.

During the conflict the army took over the Lakota agencies. Congress created another Sioux commission and threatened to cut off supplies to the Lakotas if they did not cede the Black Hills and the Powder River country. With soldiers everywhere and food supplies low, the commissioners pressured Lakota chiefs at various agencies to sign away the lands in question.

When the commissioners reached Standing Rock Agency in October 1876, Eagle Woman graciously offered some commissioners the comforts of her home. Forty-nine Hunkpapa chiefs signed the forced treaty. Although she attended the meeting, Eagle Woman did not sign the document.

After the controversy over the treaty subsided, Eagle Woman gave her attention to the plight of her people and the welfare of her surviving children. She worked with Indian agent John Burke to establish a school for Indian children. Burke hired Louise Picotte De Grey, Eagle Woman's eldest daughter, to teach the first Indian day school at Standing Rock in January 1876. Well educated and fluent in Lakota and English, Louise ran a successful school program for thirty young Indians and twenty mixed-race students. Later, Louise established a day school just for girls. Josephine McCarthy, a mixed-blood who grew up at Standing Rock, was one of Louise's earliest students. Josephine said that Louise was a devout Catholic who taught the girls some English songs and how to recite in English the "Lord's Prayer" and the "Holy Mary Mother of God." Louise rewarded the girls with candy when they performed well in classroom exercises.

William Allen Rogers, an artist for *Harper's Weekly* who visited Standing Rock in September 1878, left an interesting description of Eagle Woman and her daughters: "This woman was a really fine character. She was the widow of an old French trader, and had on more than one occasion prevented attacks on the whites by her own people. She had several daughters who were educated and refined women." Rogers commented that Eagle Woman, dressed in Indian costume, greeted her guests in a pleasant manner. He noted that she was "reputed to be a rich woman [who] still carried on the trading business established by her French husband." The artist/reporter happily purchased from his host's trading post a "Sioux bead belt of great beauty and some handsome moccasins."

One by one Eagle Woman's daughters left her household. In 1879 Louise (whose first husband had died) married George L. Van Solen and had two children, but she still continued to teach classes for young Indian girls at Standing Rock. That same year Alma Jane married Henry S. Parkin, who purchased the famous Cannonball Ranch north of the agency. Anne married John F. Kennedy, a clerk at the agency, in 1882. Tragically, both Anne and John died within two years of their marriage. Eagle Woman's daughter Lulu Picotte-Harmon lived nearby in Bismark, North Dakota.

Politics entered Eagle Woman's life for the last time when in July 1881, after some years of living in exile in Canada, Sitting Bull "surrendered" and returned to the United States. Sitting Bull spent August at Fort Yates (which guarded Standing Rock Agency), where Eagle Woman renewed her old ties with the great chief before the army sent him to Fort Randall as a prisoner of war. Eagle Woman sent a letter to her stepson Charles Picotte at the Yankton Agency to look after Sitting Bull's needs.

Eagle Woman spent the remaining years of her life living at Standing Rock surrounded by old Indian friends, with whom she continued to trade, and her three surviving daughters, Louise, Lulu, and Alma Jane, and her grandchildren. Eagle Woman died at Alma Jane's Cannonball Ranch on December 18, 1888. Later, the family buried Eagle Woman alongside her beloved husband Charles Galpin in the cemetery at Fort Yates. Mrs. Holley, who sometimes exaggerated Eagle Woman's exploits, did not exaggerate when she called Eagle Woman "one of the most illustrious women of her time." She was truly a remarkable woman who tried to peacefully mediate between two worlds: the Lakota world of her ancestors and the emerging world of the whites.

CHAPTER 9

Cynthia Ann Parker: White Comanche

Cynthia Ann Parker was part of an extended, religion-driven, enterprising family, ever in search of the "promised land." Her grandfather, the "elder" John Parker, was the titular head of the family; a restless man ever in search of a place where he could perfect his primitive Baptist faith and secure the family's economic well-being. Wherever the elder John Parker went so did his growing family, which included eight sons and four daughters. His search for the "promised land" took the family from Virginia to Georgia to Tennessee, and then central Illinois, where Cynthia Ann was born in 1826 or 1827 to Silas and Lucy Parker. The promise of extensive tracts of free land finally drew the Parkers to Texas in 1833, where the Mexican government (which controlled Texas at that time) granted each Parker head of family some 4,600 acres of land. The move would dramatically change young Cynthia Ann's life.

When they reached Texas, the family located in various places. Daniel Parker, the eldest and most religious son, chose land closer to the settlements in southeast Texas, a place where his family and religious followers found safety and a sense of community. More daring and ambitious, James and Silas, two of the younger Parker boys, decided to take their extensive land grants farther north near the headwaters of the Navasota River, which flowed into the Brazos River. In the fall of 1833, this branch of the Parkers—James and Silas, along with their brother Benjamin and their father—settled with their families on their chosen land. Several other relatives joined them.

By all accounts the land was rich for farming, with deep black alluvial soil near the river. Rolling meadowlands with rich grasses would feed their livestock; timbered forest provided wood for their daily needs; and the nearby springs, creeks, and river provided life-giving water. The settlers got to work, building cabins, clearing land for farming, and, most important, building a fort for protection from Indians, which they completed in 1835.

Parker's Fort included six cabins inside the compound to house its residents. The whole area was enclosed by a high fence of sharpened, split cedar timbers, with a solid, heavy front gate. For added protection they built two-story blockhouses at each corner of the fort for observation and sharpshooters. As S. C. Gwynne pointed out in his fascinating book *Empire of the Summer Moon*, Parker's Fort was "a small—and prodigiously fortified—pastoral utopia." "Under normal circumstances," Gwynne argued, "a small group of defenders at Parker's Fort could have held off a direct assault from a large body of Indians."

But on the Texas frontier in 1836, the situation was far from ideal, much less normal. Parker's Fort (as the settlement was called) "was situated on the absolute outermost edge of the Indian frontier." Beyond it lay country long claimed by the Comanches, where hardly any settlements could provide refuge in case of attack. Fort Houston, the nearest fort, was many miles away. Parker's Fort was located in an extremely dangerous place: a place long subjected to raids by Comanches who resented white intrusion into their territory. The Parkers, who built such an impressive fort, clearly understood the dangerous place they were in—which makes it so difficult to understand why they acted as they did on that fateful day, May 19, 1836.

Ten men left the fort that day to work in the fields, carrying their old-fashioned, single-shot rifles. James Parker and Luther Plummer, his son-in-law, were in the fields. Luther was married to the beautiful, red-haired Rachel Parker Plummer, who, four months pregnant with their second child, was in the fort caring for their fourteen-month-old son, James Pratt. Eight women remained in the fort doing chores and looking after nine children at play. One of the children was the pretty, blonde-haired, blue-eyed, nine-year-old Cynthia Ann Parker. There were six men in the fort, including the family patriarch, John Parker. For some strange reason the men were unarmed and left *open* the great, protective gate to the fort, designed for protection against Indian attack.

Around ten in the morning, someone shouted that they spotted a large group of Indians carrying a white flag some two hundred yards from the fort. No one sounded an alarm for the men in the distant fields and no one bothered to shut the main gate. Benjamin Parker went out, unarmed, to speak with the Indians, who turned out to be mostly Comanches, perhaps one hundred warriors, with some women riding along. The Indians professed peace, but asked for a cow to kill and directions to a water hole. Benjamin offered to bring them food and went back to the fort and shared his doubts about the Indians' intentions with his younger brother, Silas

(Cynthia Ann's father). Silas warned Benjamin not to go back, but Benjamin gathered some foodstuff and bravely went back to the Indians, perhaps with a desire to placate them. Silas ran to his cabin for ammunition, asking his niece, Rachel, who was holding her firstborn child, to watch the Indian's movement.

Meanwhile, most of the remaining residents, mainly women and children, ran for their lives out the back gate in a desperate effort to reach the men in the cornfields roughly one mile away. Sarah Parker Nixon, Rachel's married sister, left immediately. Martha Parker, James's wife, followed with her four children. The elderly John Parker and his aged wife, Sally, assisted by Elizabeth Kellogg, Rachel's widowed aunt, ran as best they could, and so did Lucy Parker, Cynthia Ann's mother, with her four children.

When Benjamin reached the Indians, the worst happened. The Indians surrounded him. After brutally killing Benjamin, they charged the fort. According to Rachel, who ran with her child for the back exit, her uncle Silas got off one shot before being killed. Then an attacker killed Samuel Frost and his teenage son, Robert. All three were scalped.

Rachel did not get far. An Indian on horse gave chase, striking her on the head with a farm hoe. She fell to the ground, bleeding profusely. He then dragged her by the hair back to the main body of Indians, where he placed her on a horse. Desperately looking for her son, Rachel spotted him mounted on the back of an Indian's horse, crying for his mother.

Warriors then ran down the fleeing survivors, easily catching up with the elder John Parker, his wife, Sally, and daughter Elizabeth. After surrounding the trio and stripping their clothing, they killed and scalped John Parker in front of his wife who, in turn, they brutally assaulted, though she lived. Elizabeth was taken captive.

Next the warriors caught Lucy Parker, forcing her to surrender two children, Cynthia Ann and seven-year-old John Richard. Lucy and her two remaining children were brought back to the fort, where three men with rifles, who finally arrived from the fields, rescued them.

The battle was over in barely half an hour, resulting in five men dead, two women wounded, and five taken captive: Cynthia Ann, her brother John Richard, Rachel Parker Plummer and her child, James Pratt, and Elizabeth Kellogg. Before leaving, the Indians looted the fort and killed livestock. The survivors, led by James Parker, fled for their lives in a harrowing journey to Fort Houston, some sixty-five miles away.

As was their custom, the Comanches rode north to their home country, pushing their horses hard, creating distance between themselves and any pursuers. In her narrative written after captivity, Rachel Parker Plummer described what happened on that northward journey.[1] The Comanches stopped after midnight, secured their horses, lit a fire, and celebrated with a victory dance. Rachel was tied up, thrown on the ground, and struck repeatedly with warriors' bows. As the warriors yelled and danced "around the scalps," they continued to beat Rachel, her aunt Elizabeth Kellogg, and even the crying children. Rachel said that she would never forget the "dreadful, savage yelling!" "Enough," she added," to terrify the bravest hearts."

Rachel and Elizabeth may have been stripped of their clothing and raped that night as suggested in some recent studies of the Comanche raid on Parker's Fort.[2] But Rachel Parker Plummer in her narrative does not provide any detail of the sexual abuse she may have suffered at the hands of her captors—a natural reluctance for a woman of her day—but she does hint at the terrible ordeal she suffered. "To undertake to narrate their barbarous treatment would only add to my present distress, for it is with feelings of the deepest mortification that I think of it, much less to speak or write of it; I can almost fell [feel] the same heart-rending pains of body and mind that I then endured, my very soul becomes sick at the dreadful thought."

The war party traveled hard for five days. During this period Rachel said that she "never ate one mouthful of food, and had but a very scanty allowance of water." On the sixth day the Comanches divided their captives. Elizabeth Kellogg was given to a band of Kichai Indians who had participated in the raid. Cynthia Ann and her brother John went to a band of Comanches, probably the Nokonis. Rachel went with her son, James Pratt, to a different Comanche band. They allowed her to embrace and nurse the child, but when it became apparent that the child was weaned, they tore the child away. "He reached out his hands towards me," Rachel later wrote, "which were covered with blood, and cried, 'Mother, Mother, oh, Mother!' I looked after him as he was borne away from me, and I sobbed aloud. This was the last I ever heard of my little Pratt."

---

1   Rachel Plummer, *Narrative of the Capture and Subsequent Sufferings of Mrs. Rachel Plummer During a Captivity of Twenty-one Months Among the Comanche Indians*, Houston: 1839. This is a reprint of the 1838 edition with a slightly different title.

2   The rape of white women captives by Indians is a subject full of controversy. Certainly it occurred, but to what extent? For a revealing look at the historical literature, consult Glenn Frankel, *The Searchers: The Making of an American Legend*, New York: Bloomsbury, 2013, pp. 41–44.

The five captives disappeared into the vastness of the Southern Plains, their fate among the Comanches differing in time and treatment. But they were not forgotten. Shortly after the attack on Parker's Fort, James Parker, perhaps bearing some guilt for the disaster, took up the search for the captives, including his daughter and grandson. For nearly a decade, James undertook some nine difficult and dangerous trips into Indian land to rescue his family. He became famous throughout Texas (and perhaps the West) as "the man who searched for the Parker captives."[3]

James's first trip was successful. He found his sister-in-law, Elizabeth Kellogg, in Nacogdoches, East Texas. She had spent only three months with the Kichai Indians before a group of Delaware Indians purchased her freedom on August 20, 1836. They wanted $150 to compensate them for their efforts. Having lost everything in the attack on Parker's Fort, James was without money, but fortunately, his old friend Sam Houston put up the money. Elizabeth returned home to her family in Texas and likely lived a quiet life, never telling her story of captivity among the Indians.

But Rachel Parker Plummer, who survived a yearlong ordeal among the Comanches, did tell her story, giving a rare and valuable insight into the life of a white woman captive among the Comanches. Rachel spent her time with the Comanches in constant movement on the high plains. She had been given to an old man, his wife, and daughter as their servant. Lightly clothed, often cold, she was mistreated by the women. Although pregnant with her second child, they worked her hard, day and night. Her main job was to tend the horses every day and to dress a certain number of buffalo robes each month.

Rachel gave birth to her second child in October 1836. She feared for her child's life since she could not nurse the child and perform her daily workload. Rachel pleaded in vain with her "mistress" to protect the child. After several weeks warriors came and brutally killed the child. She assumed they came at the request of her "master," who "thought it [the child] too much trouble."

Desperate, despondent, and even suicidal, Rachel saw little hope in her future. Prepared to die rather than tolerate any more abuse, she physically fought with her "mistresses," mother and daughter, and both times won. Surprisingly, the Comanches did not punish her.

---

3   James Parker's story became the basis for John Ford's film *The Searchers*. For a critical study of the historical drama that began with the Comanche attack on Parker's Fort and the making of the film, see Glenn Frankel, *The Searchers*.

Rachel's horrific ordeal ended in August 1837 when a group of Mexican traders came to her village and offered her master a sufficient price for her freedom. He agreed, and Rachel began her long, difficult homeward journey. The Mexican traders took her on a seventeen-day journey to Santa Fe, New Mexico, where she was warmly welcomed by William and Mary Donoho, who had arranged for her purchase. Rachel suffered from exposure and malnutrition. Civil unrest in Santa Fe forced the Donohos to flee to their home in Independence, Missouri. It was a long, grueling journey of some eight hundred miles. Rachel went with them. It was in Independence that Lorenzo Nixon (Rachel's brother-in-law) found her. James Parker had sent him. Rachel was so anxious for home that she pressed Lorenzo to head out in the dead of winter. She arrived at her father's house in Texas on February 19, 1838—some twenty-one months after the attack on Parker's Fort. Months later Rachel reunited with her husband and soon became pregnant.

Rachel was ill from her time in captivity, the long journey back home, and the fact that while eight months pregnant with her third child she was forced to flee from her father's home in the dead of winter to escape from some vigilantes who threatened him. James and his family sought refuge in the home of his brother Joseph Parker, a wealthy landowner in Houston. It was in Houston that Rachel wrote a twenty-seven-page account of her captivity. The first edition of her *Narrative* was dated September 23, 1838. Rachel was seemingly aware of her precarious health, for she ended the preface to her captivity narrative with these prophetic words: "With these remarks, I submit the following pages to the perusal of a generous public, feeling assured that before they are published, the hand that penned them will be cold in death." Indeed, Rachel did not have long to live.

Rachel gave birth to her third child on January 4, 1839, but she had little time to enjoy the baby she brought into the world. Rachel died on March 19, 1839. She was only twenty years old. Two days later the child died as well.

Had Rachel lived a few years longer, she would have been reunited with her first (and only surviving) child. James Parker located his grandson James Pratt Plummer and his nephew John Richard Parker at Fort Gibson in May 1842. James was now eight years old; his cousin John thirteen. Both boys spoke no English. After some persuasion the boys returned with their uncle to Texas. James returned to live with his father, who had remarried after

Rachel's death; John returned to live with his mother, who had remarried after the death of her husband Silas at Parker's Fort.

James Parker made one last attempt to find Cynthia Ann (the last of the captives) in 1844, and then gave up the search. After searching for eight long years for the Parker's Fort captives, James was exhausted and needed to spend time with his family and landed interests. Besides, after reports came in from the field from various persons who had sighted Cynthia Ann, it became clear to James that Cynthia Ann was now a young woman who had been away for so long and with ties so close to the Comanches that she had no desire to be rescued. Seemingly lost, Cynthia Ann remained with her captives for twenty-four years, becoming a Comanche woman married to a Comanche warrior and lovingly raising three children.

What had happened to Cynthia Ann Parker? According to Comanche oral tradition, Cynthia Ann was adopted by a childless couple who raised her as their own. Peta Nocona, one of the young warriors who had raided Parker's Fort and may have placed the child on his horse, stayed close, later marrying Cynthia Ann when she came of age.

As a young girl, Cynthia Ann was treated differently by the Comanches than grown women like Rachel Plummer and Elizabeth Kellogg who were enslaved. She was a "loved captive" who was embraced and cherished and treated as a full family member. What did this mean? Unfortunately, Cynthia Ann never left any account of her early years among the Comanches, but another young captive girl did. Her name was Bianca "Banc" Babb. She was captured at age ten (one year older than Cynthia Ann) in September 1866. But unlike Cynthia Ann, Bianca was rescued after seven months with the Comanches. Bianca's story is the only first-person narrative describing a young girl's captivity.[4] The Comanches raided Bianca Babb's homestead in Texas on September 14, 1866. They killed her mother and captured Bianca along with her fourteen-year-old brother, Dot. Bianca and Dot were soon separated. When Bianca's band reached its home village on the Canadian River, the warrior who captured the girl turned her over to his sister Tekwashana, a widow without children.

---

4   Daniel J. Gelo and Scott Zesch edited and wrote an introduction to Bianca Babb's "A True Story Of My Capture By, And Life with the Comanche Indians," in "'Every Day Seemed to Be a Holiday': The Captivity of Bianca Babb," *Southwestern Historical Quarterly*, CVII (July 2003), 35–67; for a good account of Bianca's time among the Comanches, see Scott Zesch, *Captured: A True Story of Abduction by Indians on the Texas Frontier*, New York: St. Martin's Press, 2004.

Tekwashana did her best to look after the child. Her adoptive mother made her a new calico dress and when "mother" and "daughter" washed their dresses in the river on warm days, Tekwashana taught the young girl how to swim. Bianca slept comfortably in Tekwashana's tipi; on cold nights her adoptive mother would warm her by the fire and then wrap her in a buffalo robe for warmth. When food was plentiful, Bianca ate as any family member; when food was scarce she went hungry, though one little boy in the family shared his meat and corn with her. Bianca said that her Comanche "mother" was "always thoughtful of me and seemed to care as much for me as if I was her very own child."

Tekwashana looked to Bianca's appearance: She provided Bianca with brass bracelets, silver earrings with long silver chains that hung down over her shoulders, and an elaborate headdress. Tekwashana gave Bianca a horse, which she loved to ride as fast as she could, taking pleasure as her "long blond hair and pretty head dress float[ed] in the breeze."

Of course, like all Comanche children, Bianca had her domestic chores. She had to carry water for cooking, gather wood for the fire, and when the camp moved she had to pack the horses and, on the trail, look after the horses and even the puppies.

Bianca was made to understand by her adoptive mother (and perhaps other family members) that her "life was to be a regular Indian life" and even the children who came to play made her feel welcomed. "Every day," Bianca wrote in her narrative, "seemed to be a holiday." Despite such favorable treatment, Bianca longed to return to her Texas home and family. Such sentiments saddened her adoptive mother.

One day as Bianca returned to the village after collecting firewood, she found Tekwashana crying. It appeared that Bianca's father had finally arranged for her freedom. His representative offered the band $333 for Bianca's release, which was accepted. Tekwashana was so unhappy to lose her "adopted" daughter that she took the child and fled, but she was caught on the second day. After seven months with the Comanches, Bianca was joyfully reunited with her father in April 1867. Two months later her brother Dot was also rescued.

Bianca's story is instructive and gives some idea how Cynthia Ann was similarly treated by her adoptive parents. The difference, of course, was that Bianca's stay with the Comanches lasted only seven months; Cynthia Ann spent twenty-four years with the Comanches—enough time for her to forget her past and to forge a new identity with the Comanches. The Comanches called her Nautdah. Historians disagree about its meaning. Jo Ella Powell Exley, a biographer of the Parker family, gives the name a flowery description, "She Carries Herself With Dignity and Grace." But the journalist S. C. Gwynne, who has written on Quanah Parker and the Comanches, said that the name was given to Cynthia Ann by Peta Nocona and it meant "Some One Found," which seemed more telling.

Presumably, her adoptive parents loved and accepted the nine-year-old white child and made her understand that she was to be raised as a Comanche woman. Childhood did not last long among the Indians. Like all Comanche women, Cynthia Ann did all the hard domestic tasks: looking after the tipis, raising the children, making clothes, collecting water and gathering firewood for cooking, packing the horses when camp moved, butchering buffalo, drying meat, tanning hides, and making buffalo robes.

Sometime before 1845 Cynthia Ann (now a young woman in her late teens) married Peta Nocona, the young warrior who had taken part in the raid on Parker's Fort and probably made a claim to her person from the moment of capture. Already married to a full-blood Comanche woman, Peta was an enormous, muscular, dark-skinned man who by this time had become a prominent war chief, a good hunter, and a great raider who brought in many horses.

In time Cynthia Ann gave birth to three children. Her first, probably born in 1848/1849, was named Kwihnai (meaning "Eagle"), but is best known by his nickname Quanah, which most likely meant "fragrance" because he was said to be born in a bed of flowers. Within two years she had a second child with the unusual name of Peanuts, said to be so named because of his mother's fond memory of eating peanuts as a child back in Parker's Fort. Her last child was a girl named Topsannah, "Prairie Flower."

By this time Cynthia Ann had become, for all purposes, a Comanche woman. She enjoyed all the pleasures of a Comanche woman with a lodge to keep and a husband and children to look after. She also suffered the hardships Comanche women suffered: hard work, the danger of constant warfare, diseases like smallpox and cholera that decimated her band, and the constant struggle to find food from declining buffalo herds. Cynthia Ann spoke Comanche and some Spanish, dressed like a Comanche woman, with her blonde hair cut short and darkened and her skin tan. From a distance she blended in and looked like any Comanche woman, but up close

Cynthia Ann Parker nursing her daughter, Prairie Flower, circa 1861
THE TEXAS HISTORY COLLECTION, BAYLOR UNIVERSITY, WACO, TEXAS

her blue eyes reflected a white woman, although in all things Cynthia Ann considered herself a proud Comanche, as various whites who met her in the late 1840s and 1850s came to realize.

The first sighting of Cynthia Ann Parker by a white person came in April 1846 when she was nineteen. Indian agent Leonard H. Williams spotted her in a Comanche camp on the Washita River, but had difficulty communicating with her. He made a generous offer to buy her freedom, but to his surprise the Comanches refused to negotiate. Williams's superiors—Indian Commissioners P. M. Butler and M. G. Lewis—offered the best explanation of why the Comanches refused the offer: "The young woman is claimed by one of the Comanches as his wife. From the influence of her alleged husband or from her own inclination, she is unwilling to leave the people with whom she associates." The commissioners' report established the fact that by 1846 the nineteen-year-old Cynthia Ann Parker was already married to Peta Nocona.

Sometime in the early 1850s, Lucy Parker (Cynthia Ann's mother) sent her son John Richard (who had been captured with Cynthia Ann and freed) to find his sister and bring her home. Somehow, John found his sister, but she refused to listen to his pleadings. John told this story to Captain Randolph B. Marcy, the intrepid explorer of the Red River, who reported John's visit to the Comanches and noted why she refused her brother's request: "This woman has adopted all the habits and peculiarities of the Comanches; has an Indian husband and children, and cannot be persuaded to leave them."

This was the last time any member of the Parker family looked for their long-lost relative. Married, with children, Cynthia Ann now completely identified with the Comanche people. However hard to admit, John Richard confessed to Captain Marcy what his sister held dear—her husband, children, and the Comanche people—and "there she should remain."

The next white encounter with Cynthia Ann was not by design and not friendly. In November 1860 some fifty Comanche and Kiowa warriors, perhaps led by Peta Nocona, raided settlements in northwest Texas, stealing horses and killing settlers. Texans were outraged by these brutal attacks and demanded action. A full-scale operation was mounted in December against the raiders. Laurence Sullivan Ross led forty Texas Rangers, Sergeant John W. Spangler commanded twenty federal cavalry from Camp Cooper, and J. J. "Jack" Cureton captained some seventy local militia.

In the early hours of December 19, 1860, the Texas Rangers and cavalry soldiers located an Indian camp on Mule Creek, which flowed into the Pease River.[5] It clearly was not the main camp, but a small village of nine tipis with some fifteen people, mostly women, children, and older men, its warriors likely out hunting. It appeared from a distance that the camp's residents were getting ready to leave, perhaps having sighted the Texans' approach. Captain Ross ordered the Rangers to directly attack the camp, while Sergeant Spangler's cavalry maneuvered a flanking movement to prevent the

---

5   The most careful study of the Pease River fight that tries to make sense of the conflicting source material is Paul H. Carlson and Tom Crum's *Myth, Memory and Massacre: The Pease River Capture of Cynthia Ann Parker*, Lubbock: Texas Tech University Press, 2010.

Indians from escaping. The few older men were killed in the first strike and some women who tried to flee with their loaded horses were cut down by the soldiers. The fight ended quickly, with the Comanches losing everything in the village. Seven people were killed—four women and three men—the village destroyed. The Texans took numerous horses and pack mules loaded with buffalo meat.

Some Indians tried to flee, pursued by Ross and Texas Ranger Lieutenant Tom Kelliher. They caught up with a Comanche riding a splendid horse. Sensing danger from the pursuers, the rider reigned in the horse and cried "Americano!" Ross and Kelliher were surprised to find out that the rider was a woman carrying a small child in her buffalo robe. Kelliher guarded the captive while Ross pursued two riders on a second horse.

Ross caught up with the fleeing Comanches and fired his colt, which struck the rear rider who, falling, dragged the main rider from the horse. The second rider, a large man, landed on his feet and fired some arrows at his attacker; one of the arrows hit Ross's horse. Ross fired a shot that broke the Comanche's right arm; then he fired two more shots that hit the man, who staggered away singing his death song. Many years later Ross claimed that the dead warrior was Peta Nocona, the feared Comanche warrior. Peta Nocona's death at the Pease River fight is extremely controversial. Many years later Quanah Parker denied that his father was ever at the Pease River, and Horace P. Jones, an army interpreter, claimed that in the early 1860s he met Peta Nocona at Fort Cobb. Peta Nocona's death still remains a mystery; but in any case he never saw his wife Nautdah again. Paul H.Carlson and Tom Crum, in *Myth, Memory and Massacre*, provide a critical analysis of the primary documents relating to Peta Nocona's death.

Ross rode back to where Kelliher held the Comanche woman and child. She was filthy, covered with dirt and grease from butchering buffalo, but when Ross noticed her blue eyes and light hair, he realized that she was a white woman. The captive woman cried as she witnessed the destroyed village and its dead inhabitants, but she cried as much for her two boys whom she presumed dead.

Once in the soldiers' field camp, she shared her fears with Ross's interpreter, Antonio Martinez, who had been a child captive of the Comanches and knew their language. But Ross assured her the two boys were not dead and had escaped. After further questioning, Ross began to suspect that this captive white woman might be the long-lost Cynthia Ann Parker. Ross brought the woman and child to Camp Cooper. The women of the fort cleaned her and put white clothes on her. But Cynthia Ann ran back to her tent with her child, stripped off her new clothes, and put on a Comanche dress.

Ross and army officials sent word to her uncle Isaac Parker. (By now, James Parker, who had spent so many years searching for his relatives, was old, in ill health, and living some three hundred miles away.) Isaac arrived at the fort and, with the help of an interpreter, questioned the captive woman who displayed a good knowledge of what happened many years ago at Parker's Fort. At one point Isaac spoke her name to the interpreter. Without waiting for an interpretation, she "rose from her chair, and patting herself said: 'Me Cynthia Ann,'" convincing Isaac that she was his long-lost niece. His plan to take her and the child home to their Texas family, however, met with opposition. She did not want to go, crying for her lost Comanche world, her husband whom she presumed was dead, and her two lost boys.

So began Cynthia Ann Parker's second period of captivity. Uncle Isaac took Cynthia Ann and Prairie Flower back to his home in Birdville, north of Fort Worth. It was not a joyous homecoming. Her parents were dead: her father in the raid on Parker's Fort in 1836, her mother in 1852. Her younger brother Silas Jr. and sister Orlena were still alive and living in Texas, but she had not seem them in twenty-four years, and her brother John Richard (with whom she suffered captivity) had disappeared.

Uncle Isaac meant well, but Cynthia Ann did not adapt to her new surroundings. Frightened by the Texans who came to stare at the Comanche "squaw," she was unhappy, often despondent with her new life. She made no effort to learn English, sat for hours on the porch nursing Prairie Flower and staring into the distance, and tried repeatedly to escape with her daughter. She showed no appreciation for her rescue and continued to live in the Comanche way. The Parkers treated her as if she were "crazy"—a white woman who wanted to return to the Comanches.

Cynthia Ann proved too difficult for her aging uncle, so he sent her to live with his son William (Cynthia Ann's first cousin) and wife Mattie. The change of scenery did not lift her heavy-hearted spirits. On the first night Mattie prepared a bed for Cynthia Ann and Prairie Flower to sleep on, but in the morning she found them asleep on a buffalo robe on the floor. But when William invited to his house Coho Smith, a Texan pioneer who spoke Comanche, Cynthia Ann came alive. She engaged Smith in a spirited conversation, begging him to take her back to the Comanches and her two boys whom she missed dearly. She promised him horses, guns, and women if he would do so. But Smith thought the task too dangerous and declined.

Early in 1862 Cynthia Ann moved again, this time to the home of her brother Silas Jr. and his wife. Life was no better there. Cynthia Ann did not get along with her sister-in-law and kept trying to escape. She walked off down the road with Prairie Flower and when questioned she simply said that she was "going home, just going home." Sometimes she cut her hair short or slashed her arms and breasts with a knife, drawing blood in the Comanche way. Was this an act of mourning for her lost loved ones or simply an expression of her own misery? It was during her stay with Silas that he took her to Fort Worth, where a photographer took the famous picture of Cynthia Ann nursing Prairie Flower.

When Silas joined the Confederate army in April 1862, his wife sent Cynthia Ann and her daughter to live with Orlena (Cynthia Ann's sister) and her husband, Ruff O'Quinn, who owned a farm and sawmill. She would spend the remaining years of her life at her sister's home. Tom Champion, a distant relative, described her appearance at the time: "She was a very pretty woman, about five feet, seven inches tall, weighing 135 pounds, well built, beautiful blue eyes, light hair, and a very fair and sunny disposition." While not everyone would agree that Cynthia Ann had a "sunny disposition"—she had experienced too much suffering for that—T. J. Cates, one of her neighbors, added in support, "She was an open-hearted, good woman, and always ready to help somebody."

As Cynthia Ann moved farther away in time and space from her life with the Comanches, she slowly began to adjust to her new surroundings, relearning some English; learning how to spin, weave, and sew; excelling at tanning hides and plaiting or knitting ropes and whips (skills she learned as a Comanche). Lively and pretty Prairie Flower assimilated more easily; she quickly learned English and even attended school.

Although Cynthia Ann learned to slowly accept her family and new surroundings, she never entirely forgot the Comanche ways. Whenever some relative died, she cut her body and sang Comanche songs of mourning. And she never forgot or stopped crying for her two lost boys. Still, Cynthia Ann may have found some measure of belated happiness in her last years as a "captive" in Texas—until tragedy struck again. In 1864 Prairie Flower died from influenza and pneumonia at the age of nine. Cynthia Ann was devastated: Prairie Flower, her last visible tie to her old life with the Comanches, was gone.

Cynthia Ann lived for six more years. Quanah Parker's descendants believe that they were unhappy years as Cynthia Ann mourned for the losses she had suffered since the Pease River fight: her husband, her two boys, and her daughter's death. They believe that she slowly lost the will to live and was so weakened by self-starvation that she succumbed more easily to influenza. When Cynthia Ann died in 1870, she was buried next to her beloved daughter.

Isaac Parker, looking back with some regret at the role he played in Cynthia Ann's forced second captivity, said that she was "the most unhappy person [I] ever saw. She pined for her children and husband continuously. . . . She was as much an Indian as if she had been born one." Tom Champion added what has become a widely accepted truth: "I am convinced that the white people did more harm by keeping her away from them [the Comanches] than the Indians did by taking her at first."

Meanwhile, young Quanah (twelve when his mother and sister were captured) came of age among the fierce Quahadis Comanche, in time becoming a respected warrior who fought against the buffalo hunters at Adobe Walls (June 27, 1864) and Colonel Ranald Mackenzie's relentless blue-coat soldiers in the Red River War (1874–1875). But after Mackenzie destroyed their village in the Palo Duro canyon, the Quahadis were forced to surrender—the last of the Comanche bands to do so and to take up life on the reservation.

Quanah never forgot his lost mother and baby sister, and as soon as he settled on the reservation in April 1875, he began to make inquiries, assisted in his search by Colonel Mackenzie. It was Mackenzie who gave the young man the sad news that his mother and sister had passed away. Mackenzie even wrote to Isaac Parker (then eighty-two) on Quanah's behalf, but got no response. Quanah also advertised in Texas newspapers for a picture of his mother. Laurence Sullivan Ross, who had captured Cynthia Ann during the Pease River fight, responded by sending a copy to Quanah of an old picture of Cynthia Ann nursing Prairie Flower. Quanah framed the picture and placed it in his bedroom. Sometime, he posed for a photograph sitting next to the picture.

As he got older, Quanah longed for the return of his mother's remains to be buried near his home in Oklahoma. In the late fall of 1910, Quanah sent Aubrey Birdsong, his son-in-law, to Texas to find his mother's gravesite. After some searching and with the help of local Texans, Birdsong found Cynthia Ann's gravesite in the lonely Fosterville cemetery. When he dug up the gravesite, he found a small skeleton, presumably Prairie Flower, lying beside Cynthia Ann. He placed the child's bones in the same casket as Cynthia Ann "with the girl's remains placed as if she were in the arms of her mother."

Birdsong hurried the casket back to Oklahoma, where it was displayed (December 10, 1910) at the Post Oak Mission in Cache, Oklahoma, a few miles from Quanah's home. Quanah gave a simple, but moving speech: "Forty years ago my mother died. She was captured by Comanches, nine years old. Love Indians and wild life so well, no want to go back to white folks. All the same people anyway. God say. I love my mother."

As it turned out, Quanah did not have long to live and died on February 23, 1911. The family buried him next to his mother. Cynthia Ann was finally reunited with one of her lost boys.

CHAPTER 10

Monahsetah: Custer's Captive "Wife"

On a cold, wintry morning in late November of 1868, Lieutenant Colonel George Armstrong Custer's Seventh Cavalry stormed into Black Kettle's peaceful and unsuspecting Cheyenne village camped on the Washita River. Despite some resistance, the village was overwhelmed in a short time. Indian casualties were high: Black Kettle, who had survived the massacre at Sand Creek four years earlier, was killed along with some fifteen warriors, sixteen women, and nine children. Fifty-three Cheyennes were captured, mostly women and children. Custer ordered the village and all its supplies burned and some 650 horses destroyed.

Prior to departing the bloody battlefield, Custer assembled the captives. Speaking through his interpreter, Rafael Romero, Custer assured the troubled women that they would be kindly treated on their journey to Camp Supply. In the midst of this gathering, a strange incident took place, which Custer later recorded in his colorful book *My Life on the Plains*. An older woman boldly stepped forward and selected a young woman from the crowd. She then placed the young girl's hand in Custer's and spoke some words in her language that Custer said sounded like some sort of "benediction." Not desiring to give offense, Custer remained a passive participant. Then the old woman uttered what seemed to Custer like a prayer to the "Great Spirit," and at the same time she was moving her hands over the faces of the young woman and Custer. Finally, the curious Custer broke his silence and asked Romero, "What is this woman doing?" Romero smiled and said, "Why, she's marryin' you to that young squaw!" Custer immediately broke off contact, thanking the older woman and her young friend for their kind offer, which he firmly but respectfully declined.

Later, Custer asked Romero why the elderly woman performed the "marriage" ceremony. Romero replied, "That's easy enough to understand; she knows they are in your power and her object is to make friends with you as far as possible." Romero went on to explain that once "married," Custer

Women and children captured at the Washita fight. Monahsetah, Mahwissa, and Sioux Woman are not in the photograph, as they had left a few days earlier to accompany General Custer, circa 1869.

COURTESY OF THE NATIONAL PARK SERVICE, LITTLE BIGHORN BATTLEFIELD NATIONAL MONUMENT, LIBI_00019_00392, W. S. SOULE, "PRISONERS CAPTURED IN THE BATTLE OF THE WASHITA – SCOUT WITH THEM."

would become a relative with all the familial obligations to provide and care for his Cheyenne "kinfolk."

Peter Harrison, Monahsetah's foremost biographer, calls Custer's account "something of a whimsical tale." He does not think it happened as Custer described, and even if it did, he did not think that Monahsetah was the young woman "married" to Custer. But why would Custer make it up? It does not seem overly strange that in the midst of some carnage, an older Cheyenne woman, fearful for the safety of the young captive women and children, would reach out to the soldier-chief for protection by "marrying" her to a beautiful young woman. The "marriage" ceremony goes a long way to explain the role that the two women—but especially the younger woman—would play in the unfolding drama with Custer.

The older woman (she was thirty-four) was Mahwissa, literally translated as Red Hair, later as Red Dress. She was married to Chief Wolf Looking Back, a member of Black Kettle's ruling entourage. Mahwissa was an important figure in her own right. Younger Cheyenne women of the village held her in high regard. She had survived the attack on Black Kettle's village at Sand Creek in 1864, and during the fight she courageously assisted a young woman who had gone into labor.

The younger woman was Monahsetah, who had just turned nineteen. She was the daughter of Chief Little Rock, who was killed at the Washita, and Skunk Woman, who survived. She called herself Meyouzah (Morning Walker), though some Cheyennes (like her cousin Kate Bighead) called her Meotzi (Goes at Sunrise). Custer called her Monahsetah (The Young Grass that Shoots in the Spring), by which she is best known in the historical literature.

For the next several months, Monahsetah's life would be caught up with Custer's. Barely twenty when he met her, Custer, who had an eye for the "ladies," was taken by the young woman's beauty. He describes her beauty in some detail in *My Life on the Plains*:

> *Little Rock's daughter was an exceedingly comely squaw, possessing a bright, cheery face, a countenance beaming with intelligence, and a disposition more inclined to be merry than one usually finds among the Indians. . . . Added to bright, laughing eyes, a set of pearly teeth, and a rich complexion, her well-shaped head was crowned with a luxuriant growth of the most beautiful silken tresses, rivalling in color the blackness of the raven and extending, when allowed to fall loosely over her shoulders, to below her waist.*

Louise Barnett, a Custer biographer, speculated that next to the "feminine and sweet-faced Libby [Custer's wife], [with her] little curls framing a lovely oval face with rounded cheeks," Monahsetah had, for Custer, "sex appeal."

The beautiful Indian woman was young, but not innocent or virginal. As a fifteen-year-old young woman, she lived through the horror of Colonel John M. Chivington's attack on Black Kettle's village at Sand Creek in November 1864. Fleeing from the battlefield, a soldier's bullet struck in the back of her leg, breaking a bone below the knee. Unable to run or walk, she found shelter in the pits dug by other refugees from the attack. Custer did not know that she had already been scarred by warfare.

In the time they were together, Custer learned that Monahsetah had been married to a warrior named Little Eagle. At the time of the marriage, Monahsetah was just eighteen; her new husband was twenty-eight. The marriage was short-lived. Evidently, Little Eagle did not completely win his young wife's heart, but he did satisfy Little Rock with eleven horses, making him a good son-in-law. The marriage was troubled from the start, since Monahsetah did not play the role of a dutiful Cheyenne wife. Nor did time soften her heart. Her husband tried to win her over with kindness, but failing that, he began to assert his husbandly authority. Monahsetah reminded her husband that she was the daughter of a chief and would not suffer any indignities. The young wife forced the breakup of their marriage when she used a small pistol concealed beneath her blanket to shoot Little Eagle in the knee. Sometime in the late summer or early fall of 1868, Monahsetah returned to her father's lodge and Little Rock gave back the eleven ponies. Monahsetah came away from the failed marriage pregnant. She gave birth to a girl she named Bird Girl.

Late November 1868 found Little Rock camped with his family at Black Kettle's village on the Washita. When Custer's soldiers attacked the village, Monahsetah with her little baby sought safety in her father's tipi hiding under buffalo robes. Monahsetah survived the fight, but her father, Little Rock, and her fourteen-year-old brother, Hawk, did not.

When Custer first met Monahsetah, she was a divorced woman with a child. Custer shared the first part of Monahsetah's story with the readers of *My Life on the Plains*—that she was a beautiful, strong-willed woman who resisted her husband's control by shooting him in the knee—but he did not acknowledge that she was a young mother. Likewise, he shared Monahsetah's story with his wife, Elizabeth Bacon Custer, but he never shared with anyone (perhaps, with the exception of his brother Tom, who was with him at the Washita) that he was attracted from the beginning to this captive woman, though Elizabeth and any careful reader of *My Life on the Plains* should have guessed from his glowing description of Monahsetah that Custer was charmed by this young, beautiful Indian woman. And it would appear that, over time, Monahsetah became attracted to "Long Hair," as the Cheyennes called Custer.

White and Cheyenne sources testify to the intimate relationship between Custer and Monahsetah. Captain Frederick Benteen, who served with Custer at the Washita (though he was no friend of his superior officer), told a fellow soldier that Custer invited his fellow officers "to avail themselves of the services of a captured squaw" and that "Custer took first choice, and lived with her [Monahsetah] during the winter and spring of '68–'69."

Benteen later elaborated that "Custer slept with her all the time, although she was pregnant and gave birth to a male child." Benteen was wrong. Monahsetah was not pregnant at the Washita. She already had given birth to her first child from her failed marriage to Little Eagle. Why did Benteen say this? Benteen had an intense dislike of his glory-hunting superior and took delight in damaging Custer's reputation. It was bad enough that Custer forced himself on a young, captive woman; worse still, Benteen may have reasoned, if she were pregnant.

Ben Clark, the trusted and fair-minded scout for the Seventh Cavalry at the Washita, told Walter M. Camp in 1910 that "many of the squaws captured at the Washita were used by the officers." Clark noted that "Custer picked out a fine looking one and had her in his tent every night." John Ryan, a sergeant in the Seventh Cavalry, remembered that a captive woman assisted Mrs. Courtenay, Custer's cook, in her duties. The young woman learned some English and became a favorite with the troops.

The Southern Cheyennes have long believed that Custer and Monahsetah shared an intimate relationship. Kate Bighead, an elderly Cheyenne woman who was Monahsetah's cousin, told Thomas B. Marquis that she had been at the Washita and in the camp of the fleeing Cheyennes. Kate Bighead saw Custer and Monahsetah (who Kate called Meotzi) often together, and was convinced that they enjoyed a sexual relationship.

In the 1930s Charles Brill, a historian who wrote a critical study of Black Kettle, Custer, and the fight at the Washita, interviewed Magpie and Little Beaver, two elderly Cheyennes who had been at the Washita. Although they were younger than Monahsetah at the time of the fight (Little Beaver was twelve, Magpie in his early teens), they knew the young woman's story with Custer. Little Beaver's mother, Red Dress (another name for Mahwissa), told her son that the officers mistreated the women prisoners from the first day. She went on to say that Custer chose Monahsetah on the first night and that a "*mutual* [italics mine] friendship seemed to spring up between them immediately." While Kate Bighead bore no animosity toward her cousin for taking up with Custer, Magpie told Brill that the Southern Cheyenenes were displeased with Monahsetah because "she had displayed a preference for her captor so long as he would keep her with him."

But, what choice did Monahsetah have? She was a captive dependent on the affection of the soldier-chief. Monahsetah had survived in turn Sand Creek, a bad marriage, the Washita, and the loss of her father and brother.

Although still a young woman, these experiences had toughened her for the present ordeal of "sleeping" with Long Hair.

Still, by becoming closer to the soldier-chief (as Mahwissa planned with the "marriage" ceremony), Monahsetah hoped that Long Hair would better protect and care for the captives, which included her child. And for Monahsetah there was the "marriage" ceremony, which she may have taken seriously even if Custer did not; so in going with Custer, she was, in effect, going with her "husband."

Brave Bear, a Southern Cheyenne warrior, thought it deplorable that Custer took Monahsetah as his sexual partner, despite the fact that she was in deep mourning for her father and younger brother. As a commanding officer, Custer clearly abused the power of his office to force a sexual union with a young, captive woman. He was guilty of the same charge of rape that was leveled against Indian men who forced themselves on captive white women. The same would be true of his fellow officers who took advantage of these young captive women.

After the Washita the surviving Cheyennes fled the area. Custer returned to Camp Supply with his captives, where he was warmly received by General Philip Sheridan. The captive Cheyenne women and children were sent north to Fort Hays—but three remained behind. General Sherman wanted to visit the site of the Washita fight. Custer, who led the expedition, selected three Cheyenne women to serve as his guides: Mahwissa, her companion Sioux Woman, and the young Monahsetah. Peter Harrison, Monahsetah's biographer, maintains that Monahsetah left behind her child, Bird Girl, with her paternal grandmother, Tovish.[1]

Sheridan and Custer left Camp Supply on December 7, 1868, and reached the Washita in a few days. Sheridan canvassed the site and then the military party headed south to Fort Cobb. Sheridan desired to bring in the fleeing Cheyennes peacefully. An Apache scout was sent out to locate the Cheyenne camp and, as a gesture of goodwill, Mahwissa went with him. Before she left, Custer "loaned" Mahwissa his hunting knife. The Indian scout returned some days later without Mahwissa, who claimed that she wanted to come back but the chiefs in Stone Forehead's village would not let her. The message may have been true, but it's just as likely that Mahwissa invented an excuse to stay with her people. Later in the campaign, Custer would meet Mahwissa

---

1   Harrison is insistent on this point. Monahsetah had given birth to a baby before the Washita. Neither Sheridan nor Custer would have allowed a seven-months-pregnant woman to accompany them on such an expedition.

in Stone Forehead's village. "She recognized me at once," Custer wrote in *My Life on the Plains*, "and laughed when I . . . referr[ed] to the hunting knife I had loaned her."

Custer decided, with Sheridan's permission, to take a highly select group of soldiers in the field to track down the Cheyennes. Monahsetah and Sioux Woman accompanied him on this dangerous journey. Custer hoped that these women would serve as peace envoys and help him establish "friendly" contact with their people. Custer wanted to bring in the Cheyennes peacefully and rescue the two white captive women held in Stone Forehead's camp.

Custer left Fort Cobb on January 21, 1869, for what amounted to a fruitless search for the elusive Cheyennes who had fled to the vastness of east Texas. After traveling 180 miles with supplies running low and no sign of the main Cheyenne camp, Custer decided to return to the newly established base at Medicine Bluff Creek. Custer spent three long weeks at his new base, plenty of downtime to carry on his sexual relationship with Monahsetah.

The ever-relentless Custer organized a larger force that set out in search of Stone Forehead's Cheyenne village on March 2, 1869. Monahsetah and Sioux Woman rode again with the soldier-chief. Somewhere along the way as Custer traveled toward Texas, Sioux Woman managed to escape, but Monahsetah remained with Custer until the end of the expedition.

During Custer's sortie west, Monahsetah road freely without guards. She made herself useful to Custer in many ways. She established a close relationship with Mrs. Dennis Courtenay, Custer's Irish cook. (Mrs. Courtenay's husband was a soldier in Custer's command.) Monahsetah may have helped Mrs. Courtenay with her cooking chores.

Monahsetah served Custer as a scout. One time on the journey, Custer came across a deserted campsite. He called Monahsetah to investigate the site. After some time Monahsetah told Custer in sign language that some twelve lodges had been camped there and that they left two weeks earlier.

Custer pushed on and tracked the fleeing Cheyennes to their main village on the Sweetwater River in Texas, but they were ready for him. Sioux Woman had arrived there before the troops and warned them that the soldiers were coming. Stone Forehead, the Keeper of the Sacred Arrows, decided to talk instead of fight. He invited Custer to his lodge to smoke the peace pipe. It was during this "smoke" that Stone Forehead tipped the ashes from his pipe on Custer's boots and placed a curse on him: that if he ever attacked a Cheyenne village he would suffer a disaster. Custer recorded the incident in *My Life on the Plains*, but it's unlikely he understood the full meaning of Stone Forehead's utterance. (Stone Forehead's curse came true some years later when Custer struck a Lakota/Cheyenne camp at the Little Bighorn.)

Custer searched but did not locate the captives in the village. According to Custer, he consulted Monahsetah and she told him that the captives were in the village. Whether she had some prior knowledge of the white women's presence in the camp or just guessed, Custer could not order an attack for fear that the captives would be killed. Custer decided on a desperate measure. He took captive four chiefs and threatened to kill one if the white women were not released. A delegation came from the village but paused outside the sentry lines, fearful for their safety. Custer appealed to Monahsetah. She agreed to serve as a mediator but wisely feared that as she passed through the soldiers' picket line at night they might mistake her for an enemy and shoot her. Custer escorted her safely through the picket line and waited for her return: "Starting at once in the darkness," Custer wrote in *My Life on the Plains*, "she clung to my hand with the natural timidity of a child." Custer paints an endearing scene, but Monahsetah was no timid child.

Even though she could have easily stayed in the Cheyenne village, a strong and self-confident Monahsetah freely returned with some Cheyennes to the soldier camp. Custer evidently sensed that the readers of *My Life on the Plains* would express some surprise at this turn of events, so he explained that Monahsetah knew one day the soldiers would return her to her people and that until then "she would receive kind treatment at our hands and be exposed to less personal danger and suffering during hostilities than if with her village." Perhaps. But it's just as likely that she returned because she understood that her well-being and that of the captives depended on her good relations with Custer and the soldiers. And one has to admit the possibility (hard as it may be) that this young woman had become fond of Long Hair and that was not something Custer could say to his readers.

Custer left Texas in late March of 1869, his mission only partially completed. He had rescued two white captives and received promises from the Cheyennes that they would return to their reservation when their ponies were strong enough for the journey. Custer headed for Camp Supply, and after his men and horses rested, they pushed on to Fort Hays in the Smoky Hill region of Kansas, which they reached on April 7, 1869. Peter Harrison,

Monahsetah's most recent biographer, suggests that by this time in the journey Monahsetah realized that she was pregnant with Long Hair's child.

As in the past, Monahsetah rode freely without guard. When they reached Fort Hays, Monahsetah visited the captive Cheyennes in the stockade to bring them news of their people. She visited with her grandmother Tovish, who had cared for her child, Bird Girl, while she was in the field with Custer. Then she returned to the freedom of the soldier camp—but Long Hair was not there for long.

Custer left Fort Hays for Leavenworth, Kansas, to spend time with his wife, Elizabeth Bacon Custer. She returned with her husband to Fort Hays late in April, but sometime before her arrival, Monahsetah had been conveniently sent back to live with the captives at Fort Hays.

For reasons not entirely clear, Custer took Elizabeth to meet Monahsetah and her baby. By now Custer had already shared Monahsetah's story with his wife. Many years later Elizabeth Custer shared the story of her meeting with Monahsetah in her third book about life in the field with General Custer, *Following the Guidon*. Elizabeth admitted that she was at first fearful of meeting the young woman. "When [her] soft eyes smiled on me," Elizabeth confessed, "I instantly remembered how they must have flashed in anger" when she shot her husband. "How," Elizabeth exclaimed rather dramatically, "could I help feeling that with a swift movement she would produce a hidden weapon, and by stabbing the wife, hurt the chief who had captured her." In fact, Monahsetah had had plenty of opportunity to kill Custer, the "big chief" who led the attack on Black Kettle's village in which her father died. If Monahsetah had attacked Elizabeth, the motive would be jealousy, not revenge against the husband. Did Elizabeth, at some level, think that?

As if to temper her husband's glowing description of Monahsetah that he penned in *My Life on the Plains*, Elizabeth said that she was not overwhelmed at first with the young woman's appearance: "Her face was not pretty in repose, except with the beauty of youth, whose dimple and curves and rounded outlines are always charming. The features of the Indian woman are rarely delicate, high cheek bones and square jaw the prevailing type." But when Monahsetah "let the blanket fall from her glossy hair, [and] her white, even teeth gleamed as she smiled," Elizabeth had to admit that "the expression transfigured her, and made us forget her features."

Monahsetah was asked to bring the baby, which she did gladly. Elizabeth's response was less than flattering: "It was a cunning little bundle of brown velvet, with the same bright, bead-like eyes of the rest." According to Elizabeth, Monahsetah then made a strange request to the childless couple: Would they care for the child until she should "return to her people?" Elizabeth was at a loss how to respond, but George politely declined the generous offer.

In mid-June the captives were finally released at Fort Hays. Custer said that although Monahsetah was "gladdened" to once again see her people, she "exhibited marked feelings of regret when the time for her departure arrived." Why would that be so? Custer explained rather smugly to his readers that "she had grown quite accustomed to the easy, idle life she had led among the troops as compared with that mere existence of toil and drudgery to which all tribes of Indians consign their squaws." Elizabeth Custer gave a more personal, slightly condescending, account of the leaving. "Monahsetah walked out of the gate, carrying her 'pappoose' on her back, smiling and shy, and showing some regret at departure for she had thriven in the idle life." The soldiers and bystanders called "Goodbye, Sallie Ann" (which, Elizabeth explained, was the name given to her fondly by Tom Custer). "'Sallie Ann' came over to where we waited to say a special good bye to us and . . . she raised her liquid eyes coyly to smile and bid adieu."

Monahsetah may have shown some regret in leaving (though it's not likely for the reasons alleged by George and Elizabeth Custer), but it's just possible that she regretted leaving the man she had been intimate with for some months—the man she considered her "husband" and father of the child growing inside her. Besides, like most Cheyennes, she may have felt uncertain about the future as her people headed for the newly established reservation at Darlington in Indian Territory.

Although Custer never returned to her life, Monahsetah had a namesake from Long Hair to keep her company: a little boy, according to Southern Cheyenne oral history, first reported in Charles Brill's *Conquest of the Southern Plains*. Little Beaver, Mahwissa's son, told Brill that according to his mother, Monahsetah became Custer's lover and the young woman gave birth to a son, "yellow-haired and fair-skinned," whom she called "Yellow Swallow." But if there was a "second" child, this "yellow-haired and fair-skinned" boy was most likely born late that year at the Darlington Agency in the south, and not in the summer of 1869 at Fort Hays as Mahwissa (called Red Dress by Brill) suggests.

Peter Harrison has made the most careful study of Yellow Swallow, though even he can't resolve all the questions pertaining to the boy's controversial birth and life. Harrison professes no doubt that Custer fathered the child. He suggested that the most likely time for conception occurred during the three-week period the troops spent quietly at Medicine Bluff Creek in February 1869. If that was the case, then the baby was most likely born in November 1869 when Monahsetah was at Darlington. The birth of Yellow Swallow may have brought some comfort to Monahsetah because a few months earlier she had lost her first child, Bird Girl.

Harrison had to admit that there was "no family tradition or oral history among the *direct* [italics mine] descendants of Monahsetah's relations to the paternity of Yellow Swallow." But he did locate one descendant of Mahwissa who confirmed (what Little Beaver, Mahwissa's son, already told historian Charles Brill) that Monahsetah did have a child with Custer.

While many Cheyennes (and white historians) accept the birth story of Yellow Swallow, not all do. Kate Bighead, our main source for the affair between Custer and Monahsetah, does not mention the birth of Yellow Swallow. John Stands in Timber, a prominent North Cheyenne tribal historian, goes further; he does not accept the idea of a relationship, much less a child, between Custer and Monahsetah.

There is no consensus among Custer scholars. Jay Monaghan, for instance, does not admit the relationship or a child; Robert M. Utley, on the other hand, accepts the relationship and the possibility that the "second" child may have been Custer's. Jeffrey D. Wert devoted some careful attention to the controversy. He tends to be skeptical but not dismissive of the possible relationship between Monahsetah and Custer—but he does not believe Custer could have "fathered" a child in any case because Custer had gonorrhea while at West Point and was most likely sterile from the infection. West Point doctors treated gonorrhea with various metallic solutions, which at best were palliative in nature but did not destroy the bacterium that could render its victims sterile.[2] This may possibly explain why George and Elizabeth Custer were never able to conceive a child. Wert suggested that if anyone fathered a child with Monahsetah, it was more likely Tom Custer,

---

2 Mary Ampola, M.D., shared with the author medical literature that supported Wert's assertion that untreated gonorrhea likely let to Custer's sterility.

who, according to Captain Benteen, also slept with the young woman. Elizabeth Custer may have inadvertently suggested as much when she noted in *Following the Guidon* that Tom Custer was friendly with Monahsetah, who delighted in the name "Sallie Ann" that he gave to her. Unlike his brother, Tom Custer did father a child with a young woman back home in Monroe, Michigan.

If, however, one accepts the birth story of Yellow Swallow, which has some reference in Cheyenne oral tradition, the question of what happened to this child became the stuff of legend. There are many possibilities, but Charles J. Brill in his study of Custer, Monahsetah, and the Washita fight offered the most sensible account. In a letter to Mari Sandoz (January 2, 1950), Brill reported that after the birth of Yellow Swallow, Monahsetah brought her two children south (Bird Girl was still alive) with her to the Darlington Agency, the base for the Southern Cheyenne in Indian Territory. Yellow Swallow was raised in the south, where he attended school with other Indian children and suffered an early death at the age of twenty.

Peter Harrison's *Monahsetah* charts roughly the same course as Brill but with some surprising variations on the story. According to Harrison, Monahsetah followed the Cheyennes to the Darlington Agency, where Yellow Swallow was born a short time after the tragic death of her firstborn, Bird Girl. Sometime after the birth of Yellow Swallow, Skunk Woman, Monahsetah's mother, adopted the boy and raised him as her own. Such adoptions were not unusual among the Cheyennes, but why this particular adoption? Perhaps Skunk Woman may have wanted to spare her young daughter the embarrassment of raising a child born from the forced union with Long Hair, the destroyer of the Cheyenne village on the Washita. Yellow Swallow was a reminder of that relationship. Perhaps Monahsetah had second thoughts and less maternal feelings for Long Hair's child. And Monahsetah had one more consideration to consider: At Darlington, she reunited with her first husband, Little Eagle. The death of their first child, Bird Girl, may have brought them together. It's possible that Little Eagle did not relish raising the child of the white officer.

Yellow Swallow lived at Darlington in Skunk Woman's house. He attended school at Darlington, where he took on the Anglicized name Guy Little. Yellow Swallow lived a tragically short life. He died in 1889, at the young age of twenty. Monahsetah provided the brief details about Yellow

Swallow in a testimony she gave at an heirship hearing to dispose of Skunk Woman's lands to her descendants. Harrison cited the documents and noted that it's the only record of Monahsetah's own words. In her testimony Monahsetah (now known in the civil records as Morning Alfrey) referred to Yellow Swallow as Skunk Woman's son. She said that Yellow Swallow died at the age of twenty (in 1889) and then added rather sharply that he "never married, nor had any children."

Despite the emphatic statement by Monahsetah that Yellow Swallow "never married, nor had any children," the fascinating story of Monahsetah, Custer, and Yellow Swallow has not died. Periodically, young people emerge who call themselves Custer's descendants—all of them flowing from the "birth" of Yellow Swallow. In January 1973 AIM militants took over the famous Wounded Knee battle site in South Dakota as a protest against United States Indian policy. Mary Crow Dog, a young Brulé Lakota woman from the Rosebud Reservation (in south-central South Dakota), was part of this historic takeover. In *Lakota Woman*, her compelling story of this dramatic period, Mary Crow Dog reported that during the takeover and siege at Wounded Knee, two brothers, Charles and Robert, joined the protesters. These two young men claimed to be great-grandsons of Custer and Monahsetah. Mary Crow Dog said that these two boys were part Lakota—that Yellow Swallow had moved north and "married a Sioux woman, moving in with his wife's tribe into which he was adopted."

At the 2004 meeting of the Western History Association, a young woman named Gail Kelly-Custer delivered a paper to a skeptical audience entitled "General Custer's Secret Indian Family, or How I Discovered My Heritage," in which she claimed that she was a descendant of Monahsetah and George Armstrong Custer. Three years later Gail Kelly-Custer published a book dealing with her ancestors, *Princess Monahsetah, the Concealed Wife of General Custer*. Simply told, this is her story.

Gail Kelly-Custer starts, of course, at the beginning with the "love affair" between Custer and Monahsetah, which led to the love child whom Kelly-Custer calls "Yellow Hair." So far, Gail Kelly-Custer has not strayed too far from the historical record. But then the story gets really interesting. According to Gail Kelly-Custer, General Custer recognized his child, and concerned about the boy's future, he asked his half brother, Brice Custer, to raise the child in case of his death, which Brice agreed to do. Upon General Custer's death, Brice took Yellow Hair back to Ohio, presumably with

Monahsetah's consent. Brice named the boy Josiah Custer. Young Josiah attended school in Ohio, but after graduation he returned to live with his mother at the Darlington Agency in Oklahoma. Josiah spent his years in Oklahoma, married, raised a family, and became a farmer, living a quiet life. While growing up, Gail Kelly-Custer knew little of this history, but, in time, she discovered that Josiah Custer was her great-grandfather.[3]

What happened to Monahsetah after she left Custer at Fort Hays? Kate Bighead related that when Monahsetah returned to live among her people, several Cheyenne men wanted to marry her, but she would have none of them. "She said that Long Hair was her husband, that he had promised to come back to her, and that she would wait for him. She waited seven years. Then he was killed." Monahsetah mourned for him; like a good Cheyenne wife, she "cut off her hair and gashed her arms and legs."

Kate Bighead finished the story. A year after Custer's death, Monahsetah married a white man named [John] Isaac, settling in Oklahoma. The couple had several children. Monahsetah lived to old age and died in Oklahoma, sometime in January 1921. One of her daughters relocated to the Northern Cheyenne Reservation in Montana. Thomas B. Marquis, who recorded Kate Bighead's life, included a beautiful picture of Monahsetah's daughter carrying her own little child in typical Cheyenne fashion. The picture is dated 1927, with the daughter's married named inscribed as "Mrs. Ben Shoulderblade."

Kate Bighead was generally a reliable "reporter" of military events, but her account of Monahsetah's life after she left Long Hair is part romance, part fiction, and part history. Peter Harrison's *Monahsetah* fleshed out the full story.

After the Cheyenne captives were released from Fort Hays, Monahsetah followed her people to Indian Territory, where she lived out her life on the Cheyenne Reservation. Within a year she experienced the death of Bird Girl and the birth of Yellow Swallow (which Kate Bighead never mentioned). She did not spend seven years pining for Custer's return. Back on the reservation, she reunited with her first husband, Little Eagle. They lived together long enough for Monahsetah to give birth (sometime in 1871) to a baby boy

---

3   In his fascinating book *Custerology*, Michael A. Elliott claimed that Gail Kelly-Custer's *Princess Monahsetah* is a novel (and not a work of history as Gail Kelly-Custer asserts), and given its highly imagined scenes and dialogue, I'm inclined to agree with Elliott's verdict. It's unfortunate that given the highly controversial nature of the Yellow Swallow/ Josiah Custer story, Gail Kelly-Custer provided not one shred of historical documentation to back up her claims that she is a descendant.

they named Wolf Belly, later known by his Anglicized name, Sampson Kelly. Shortly thereafter, Little Eagle disappeared from Monahsetah's life.

With one brief exception, Monahsetah lived a quiet life on the reservation. There was one brief moment of excitement. In September 1874 Cheyennes attacked the family of John and Lydia German as they crossed the Kansas plains. They killed the parents and three children, taking four captives. In time two of the German children were recovered, but two remained in captivity in Stone Calf's village. A rescue effort was set in motion at Fort Sill, led by scouts Rafael Romero and Isaac Alfrey. Monahsetah was asked to join the rescue team. As a former captive herself who had assisted Custer in rescuing two captive women from Stone Forehead's camp on the Sweetwater in Texas, Monahsetah was a natural choice. Monahsetah knew Rafael Romero. He had served as Custer's scout at the Washita. Romero was the intermediary between the captive women and Custer's officers. Romero took advantage of the captives as well. He forced a sexual union with Standing In Sand Hills, a young captive woman who later gave birth to his child. Romero married the young Cheyenne woman and went to live with her people. Isaac Alfrey was a twenty-five-year-old scout who had lived his life with the Cheyennes. Some years later Monahsetah would marry him.

It was not a dangerous mission. Stone Calf had already agreed with the authorities at Fort Sill to surrender his band and to release the German girls. On February 27, 1875, the trio took custody of the young girls and brought them safely back to the Darlington Agency. That was it: a brief moment of excitement from the everyday life on the reservation.

A year after the rescue of the German girls, Monahsetah had started a relationship with Joe Jarvis, who worked as a scout, interpreter, and teamster at Fort Sill. Monahsetah soon became pregnant and gave birth to Glenna Eunice Jarvis on April 6, 1877. The union was short-lived. For reasons not known, the couple decided to separate, each going their own way.

Monahsetah did not stay single for long. Sometime in 1879 she formed a relationship with a Hispanic man named Flacco, who had lived among the Cheyennes as a hunter/warrior. At the time she lived with Flacco, he worked as a hunter providing meat for the garrison at Fort Reno. They did not remain together for long. Flacco left Monahsetah for another woman.

Still a young woman in her early thirties, Monahsetah had two children to care for, Wolf Belly and Glenna. Monahsetah needed a male companion to help support her two children, though it's hard to understand why she

Monahsetah (Morning Alfrey) with last her husband, Ike Alfrey (center), son Sampson Kelly (far left), and son-in-law John Block (kneeling), circa 1914 COURTESY OF THE CHISHOLM TRAIL MUSEUM, KINGFISHER, TEXAS

chose David Trempe, who was thirty years older. Despite their age difference, Monahsetah became pregnant and gave birth to a boy they named
Joseph Trempe. Once again Monahsetah was abandoned. Her husband left
her for an older woman.

Monahsetah's last relationship came in 1885. She married Isaac "Ike"
Alfrey—the same man she rode alongside ten years earlier to rescue the
German girls. This was most likely the [John] Isaac Kate Bighead referenced
in her memoir. On November 10, 1885, Monahsetah and Alfrey came
together in a traditional Indian ceremony, but several months later the
couple married in a Christian ceremony. From this moment Monahsetah
was referred to as Mrs. Morning Alfrey in the agency records. On April 14,
1886, Monahsetah gave birth to her last child, Mary Alfrey. In addition to
Monahsetah's four children—Wolf Belly, Glenna, Joseph, and Mary—Ike
brought two girls, Jennie and Sadie, into the household.

In 1891 the Alfreys settled down on their allotted land. Ike and Monahsetah built a frame house to live in. The marriage did not always go smoothly.
After the death of his daughter Sadie, Ike began to drink. Monahsetah left
him, but Ike eventually returned to live out his life with Monahsetah.

Time passed. Monahsetah lived through good times and bad. Monahsetah's children married and in time they presented her with grandchildren.
Mary, her youngest child, married Ben Shoulderblade. They went to live on
the Northern Cheyenne Reservation in Montana. Kate Bighead knew her.
And Dr. Thomas Marquis photographed Mary with her child in 1927. He
wrote across the picture, "Meotzi's daughter."

There were, of course, deaths as well. Yellow Swallow, her tie to Custer,
died in 1889. Her elderly mother, Skunk Woman, passed away in 1901.
And her son Joseph Trempe, who spent years away from the family as a student at a Mennonite school in Kansas and at Carlisle in Pennsylvania, died
in 1903. Joseph was barely twenty-one.

Monahsetah was not spared from further harm. In 1910 she went blind,
most likely from the infectious disease trachoma. Still, she carried on. In
1914 she posed next to her son Sampson and her husband Ike in a group
portrait. At sixty-five she was still an attractive woman. The years passed.
Monahsetah lived long enough to become a great-grandmother. But time
took its toll. Monahsetah died on January 25, 1922. The undertaker said
that she died from "old age."

She was buried on her family farm with a simple stone marker that read:

Morning Alfrey
1849–1922
age 73

The beautiful young woman captured at the Washita lives on in legend, in Cheyenne oral history, and in the historical literature. Monahsetah's name will forever be linked in the minds of the Cheyennes with the fight at the Washita, Long Hair, and Yellow Swallow. Kate Bighead shared with Dr. Marquis a telling anecdote: one of her granddaughters was called Meotzi. At times, Kate Bighead said, the young people make fun of her and say: "You are Custer's Indian wife."

CHAPTER 11

Pretty Shield: Remembering the Old Days

In March 1931 Pretty Shield, an elderly Crow woman who lived in poverty in a one-room cabin on the Crow Reservation, told her story to Frank B. Linderman, a Montana pioneer. Pretty Shield was one of the few Crow women who felt comfortable sharing her life story with a Euro-American. An admirer of Pretty Shield, Linderman wrote to his daughters, "Pretty-shield is a wonderful old soul. I like her very much. She did the best she could, and never once hesitated for a name or a date, or a location. I never saw such a memory—and above all, she loves fun—is funny herself. . . . The old agency records show that she is 74, and yet her mind is as bright as a new dollar."

The feelings were mutual. Pretty Shield admired Linderman, calling him Sign Talker, because he was fluent in sign language. Alma Hogan Snell, Pretty Shield's youngest granddaughter, recalled in her insightful book *Grandmother's Grandchild*, how much Pretty Shield liked talking to Linderman and how pleased she was when he came to the reservation. "Oh, my friend is coming," she would say. "My friend is coming. Sign talker. Sign Talker is coming. I have to be ready." Ever mindful that Pretty Shield was caring for her many grandchildren, Linderman brought her tanned deer and elk skins that she could use to make dresses for her granddaughters, and he gave her silver dollars to buy food at the general store.

Alma recalled the moment when someone presented Pretty Shield with the first copy of Linderman's book on her grandmother's life story, *Red Mother*. "She took it," Alma remembered, "and held it to her breast, close to her, close to her like it was important." Anna Sloan, the wife of the agency clerk, who was likely present at the moment when Pretty Shield received her first copy of the book, noted: "When Pretty Shield understood what it was she was getting, she held the book tight to her and tears came into her eyes, she said, 'tanks, tanks, tell him tanks.'" Later, Linderman came by with a personal copy for Pretty Shield. He said that she could have as many copies

Pretty Shield PRETTY SHIELD-CROW, BOX 22, RICHARD THROSSEL PAPERS, ACCESSION
NUMBER 2394, AMERICAN HERITAGE CENTER, UNIVERSITY OF WYOMING. PHOTOGRAPHED BY
RICHARD THROSSEL

as she wanted for her grandchildren, but Pretty Shield said, "I want just one. When each one reads it they can tell me over again."[1]

Based on what she told Linderman, Pretty Shield was born in March of 1857 somewhere near the Missouri River. Her mother and father were both Mountain Crows and belonged to the Sore-Lip band. Pretty Shield was the fourth child in a family of eleven children. Her paternal grandfather, who possessed a powerful war shield, handsomely painted half red and half blue, bestowed on her the name Pretty Shield.

---

1   John Day published the book in 1932 with the title *Red Mother*. The University of Nebraska reprinted it in 1972 under the title *Pretty Shield: Medicine Woman of the Crows*. All quotes in this chapter come from the reprint edition. For a more complete understanding of Pretty Shield's life, especially the long years on the Crow Reservation, Alma Hogan Snell's *Grandmother's Grandchild* serves as an invaluable companion to Linderman's *Pretty Shield*.

Pretty Shield always remembered with fondness her early years on the Great Plains. "We were a happy people when I came onto this world," Pretty Shield told Linderman. "There was plenty to eat, and we could laugh." When she was three years old, she was sent to live with her mother's sister, Strikes With An Axe, who had suffered great loss: The Lakotas had killed her husband and two little girls. Mourning for a long time, Strikes With An Ax grew thinner and weaker. Pretty Shield's mother sent her to the sister "to heal her heart." Although technically an "aunt," in Crow culture a mother's sister is like a second "mother."

Pretty Shield did not see this move as a hardship and was happy with her second mother since Strikes With An Axe raised her with love, like her own daughter. Besides, the Crow bands frequently intermingled and Pretty Shield was often reunited with her biological mother, her father, and her many siblings. (The relationship was so close that when Pretty Shield married Goes Ahead, Strikes With An Axe came to live with them.)

Enjoying a happy childhood, Pretty Shield played with her girlfriends, swimming in the summer and sliding down hills in the winter on sleds made from buffalo ribs. But so much of Crow girls' playtime was designed to bring them slowly into womanhood. Pretty Shield carried her doll on her back just like Crow mothers, and she had a child's tipi that she pitched alongside her second mother's lodge. All her girlfriends did the same, creating a play village. They rigged small travois to some dogs, pretending they were moving camp, just as boys pretended they were real scouts riding on the ridges. Pretty Shield told Linderman: "That was a happy time on a happy world. There was always fat meat, and glad singing." She could not help but compare those "happy times" to the hard, impoverished life she experienced on the reservation.

Playing with dolls was fun, but as the girls got slightly older they wanted to "play" with real babies, failing to understand the challenges. Pretty Shield describes one incident that turned from joy to fright. As the camp moved, Pretty Shield and her girlfriends hung back, racing their horses and stopping to swim in a creek. A lone woman rider leading a packhorse with a two-year-old girl strapped on top stopped to water her horses, though she was anxious to catch up to the main party. Pretty Shield suggested the woman ride on while they took care of the baby on the slower packhorse. The woman foolishly agreed.

The girls played for some time with the baby, named Turtle, but soon realized the sun was going down and the village had moved farther away.

Pretty Shield led the second horse with the baby "strapped" in as the girls started to race their horses. Suddenly, Pretty Shield realized that the baby was not on the pack horse. She shouted to her friends: "Stop! Stop! We have lost the baby!" The girls quickly turned back to look for the baby, fearful for the child's safety as they noticed a buffalo herd moving in their direction. They soon encountered a group of young men hunting buffalo and pleaded for help. After chiding the young girls for their carelessness, the young men rode away, looking for the baby. The girls followed. A short time later, Pretty Shield saw the young men sitting on their horses in a circle. None got down, so Pretty Shield feared the worst. She rushed to the spot and found the young men laughing. "And there, face upward, and sound asleep, lay the baby, unharmed."

Pretty Shield took the child in her arms. When the party of young girls reached the village in the dark and returned the child, its worried mother scolded all of them, but especially Pretty Shield, for their foolishness. Pretty Shield never "borrowed" a baby after that. When she told Linderman this story many years later, she noted with sadness that of the ten girls that rode with her that day, only three were still alive.

Pretty Shield shared with Sign Talker other misadventures growing up—like the time her horse was surrounded by a buffalo herd and her father rescued her, or the time she rode her father's favorite buckskin horse as the animal ran into the midst of a buffalo herd, or the time she and her friends were stranded up a tree to escape a bear that turned out to be old and harmless. These adventures frightened her at the time, but looking back from old age, she laughed at her youthful indiscretions.

Pretty Shield fondly recalled the "play" of her youth, but, surprisingly, she had little to say about the domestic chores all young Crow girls were expected to perform, part of the necessary education that prepared them for life as wife, mother, and keeper of the lodge. Surely Pretty Shield's mother(s) did not neglect the age-old task of preparing her for womanhood—or was she as the only child of her aunt/mother so indulged that she was spared domestic chores? Pretty Shield does say in her autobiography that she was aware of the responsibilities that would fall on her as she became a woman, married, and had children. Even as a young girl, she was captivated by a woman who lived in her village. The woman's name was Kills-Good and she was married to Long-Horse, a Crow chief. Kills-Good was a "tall handsome woman with a soft voice." She was beautiful in appearance and demeanor;

she kept the most handsome lodge in the village; she provided the best for her daughter; and she made her husband so happy that he lovingly combed his wife's hair. Pretty Shield confessed that she "tried hard to be like her, even after I grew up and had children of my own."

When she was thirteen years old, Pretty Shield's father promised her in marriage to Goes Ahead, a good warrior and hunter, but the marriage would not take place until she was sixteen. Pretty Shield described to her granddaughter Alma one of her first meetings with Goes Ahead. "When I was thirteen years old, I still went out to play. Goes Ahead would stop by and say to me, 'How are you?' I would tell him, 'All right.' I wouldn't stay and talk with him too much because I wanted to go out with my girlfriends and play. But I knew that this was the man I was going to marry. Goes Ahead just stood there and he'd smile—kindly man. He'd smile at me and he'd say, 'Go, go. They're [her friends] getting away from you.'" Pretty Shield left but she thought: "So this was my man. He was *eechik,* good-looking. He always kept himself neat, his hair done up, always wore abalone."

The marriage took place as planned when she turned sixteen. Pretty Shield said, "It was a happy affair but it was frightening to me [too]." Goes Ahead's family prepared a tipi for Pretty Shield furnished with household items and clothing she would need for married life; Pretty Shield's father and brothers presented Goes Ahead with clothing, weapons, and horses. When the time for the ceremony arrived, a crier went through the camp inviting all to come and celebrate the wedding and enjoy good food. Pretty Shield shared her memories of Goes Ahead and the wedding with her granddaughter Alma.

Linderman asked Pretty Shield if she married for love. "No. No." She smiled. "Young woman did not then fall in love, and get married to please themselves, as they now do. They listened to their fathers, married the men selected for them, and this, I believe, is the best way." It was natural that her father promised Pretty Shield to Goes Ahead, since he was already married to Standing Medicine Rock, Pretty Shield's older sister. In time, when Pretty Shield's younger sister, Two Scalps, turned sixteen, Goes Ahead claimed her as his third wife, the marriage of sisters to one man being a common practice among the Crows.

Pretty Shield confessed to Linderman that Standing Medicine Rock was not a good woman since she flirted with other men. Pretty Shield talked to her older sister about her conduct, but it did no good, although Pretty

Shield had to admit that her older sister had good qualities. She was attractive, kept a neat lodge, and was a hard worker who excelled at dressing robes. Two Scalps, the third sister, behaved as a proper wife and Pretty Shield had a good relationship with her. It is not clear that Goes Ahead knew of his first wife's flirtations, and if he did, he made no effort to divorce her. Pretty Shield's granddaughter Alma suggests that Goes Ahead did not want to separate the sisters: "This was a *strong family unit*, Pretty Shield and her sisters and Goes Ahead."

Perhaps because she was the only one who gave him children, Pretty Shield was Goes Ahead's favorite wife. "It was *my* face," she proudly told Linderman, "that he painted when he gained that right by saving a Crow warrior's life in battle. And it was I who rode his warhorse and carried his shield."

Sometime after the marriage, Pretty Shield gave birth to her first girl child, Pine Fire. When the time came for the delivery, Pretty Shield went to a special birth-lodge where her mother and a midwife would assist in the delivery. (As was customary, her father gave a horse and robes as a gift to the midwife.) Pretty Shield described to Linderman the Crow way of giving birth. Two stakes had been driven into the ground, surrounded by a thick pile of robes. Pretty Shield knelt on the robes and took hold of the two stakes and in this way gave birth to her first child. The midwife cleaned the baby, wrapped her in soft buckskin, and handed the child to Pretty Shield, who then took charge. Pretty Shield would carry the little girl wrapped in soft buckskin for the next six months until the time came to place her in a cradleboard, which made handling the baby easier.

Over time Pretty Shield gave birth to five children, experiencing the best of all worlds. "The happiest days of my life were spent following the buffalo herds over our beautiful country. My mother and father and Goes Ahead my man, were all kind, and we were so happy. Then, when my children came I believed I had everything that was good on this world."

But such happiness was not to last. Two of her children, a boy and girl, died young. When her daughter died, Pretty Shield mourned the loss for more than two months. She slept little, "sometimes lying down alone in the hills at night, always on hard places." She ate only enough to keep herself alive, always "hoping for a medicine-dream, a vision that would help me to live and to help others." One morning, after a night spent in the hills, she spotted a woman walking in the distance. Pretty Shield thought she recognized the woman as one who died four years ago. The woman stopped to stare at the ground. The woman beckoned a frightened Pretty Shield onward. As Pretty Shield drew near, she realized that the woman "was not a real woman, but that she was a Person [apparition], and that she was standing beside an ant hill."

The Person said, "Come here, daughter." As Pretty Shield drew closer, the Person told her, "rake up the edges of this ant hill and ask for the things that you wish, daughter," and then the Person disappeared. Pretty Shield raked up the edges of the ant hill and made her wish: "Give me good luck, and a good life." From that moment the ants became Pretty Shield's lifelong friends. "And even now," she told Linderman, "the ants help me. I listen to them always. They are my medicine, these busy, powerful little people, the ants." Pretty Shield also believed the ant-people gave her name-bestowing power, helping her to name all her children and grandchildren.

Pretty Shield also shared her medicine-dream with her granddaughter Alma. In addition to telling Pretty Shield they were her friends, the ants offered encouraging words to her: "No obstacle is too great. Keep working, keep doing what you are doing, and you will have what you need." Pretty Shield took their message to heart and always told her grandchildren to work hard like the ants and never "step on them." Once, Pretty Shield and Alma were in the hills digging turnips when Pretty Shield spotted an ant pile. She removed some colorful beads from her pouch and "sprinkled" them on the pile, telling the ants, "I brought you some little beads. I thought you would like them because they're so pretty. I brought them for you as a *gift*, and I want you to have them." Alma saw the ants take the beads into their hold.

Pretty Shield worked hard at being a good mother and wife, and for years she enjoyed a good life. Her three children—Pine Fire, Little Woman, and her son Good—lived to adulthood, making Pretty Shield a grandmother many times over. All the while, Goes Ahead remained her constant companion.

But the ants could not protect Pretty Shield from all life's pain, such as the suffering that comes with the natural death of one's mother or father. For some reason Pretty Shield did not say much in her memoir about her birth mother, who died suddenly in her early fifties. Pretty Shield, who was thirty-two at the time, never forgot that moment. She and her father were away from the village. Her mother, who appeared "well and strong," went out to water her husband's favorite horse and on the trail "met" two of her sons who had been killed in war. After watering the horse, she went to her lodge. When Pretty Shield and her father returned, her mother told them what happened: "I am going to The-beyond-country now. My sons have come to take me there." Then, Pretty Shield said, "She laid down on her robe, and went away, sleeping."

Pretty Shield spoke in more detail of her father's story, remembering him as a "kind man," "never cross," with a big heart, yet with one fault: "He liked other women besides my mother pretty well."

Although a small man, her father was a fierce warrior who hated his people's enemies. One time, Lakota and Cheyenne warriors attacked their Crow village while camped on Pryor Creek. Her father rode though the camp on a gray horse, having stripped and painted his face and body yellow, with shivery lines zigzagging through the yellow paint. He gave the Crow war cry and charged the enemy "armed with only his medicine, the stuffed skin of the long-legged owl, tied on his head, and his coup stick." So strong was his power, the Lakota and Cheyenne warriors scattered before his charge. Crow warriors followed and drove the enemy away from their village.

Her father lived to be an old man, dying not at the hands of his enemies, but from smallpox, which claimed a hundred Crow lives in one month's time. (Pretty Shield herself had contracted smallpox at seventeen, surviving with the help of Sharp Skin, a medicine man.) She exclaimed with some sorrow that "until the bad-sickness came to our world my people were scarcely ever sick."

Even as Pretty Shield provided for the needs of Goes Ahead and her children, she was a keen observer and critic of the political/military conflicts of her day. How could it be otherwise? Having been surrounded by warriors and warfare her whole life, she explained to Linderman, "There was always war. When our enemies were not bothering *us*, our warriors were bothering *them*, so there was always fighting going on somewhere. We women sometimes tried to keep our men from going to war, but this was like talking to winter-winds."

There were, of course, warriors in her family: Her father had been a fierce defender of his people, her two brothers had been killed in warfare, and Goes Ahead was a member of the warlike Fox Society, which Pretty Shield supported only out of loyalty to her husband. "We women did not like war," she exclaimed, "and yet we could not help it, because our men loved war. Always there was some man missing, and always some woman

[had] to go and live with her relatives, because they [women] were not hunt-ers. And then there were the orphans that war made. . . . You see that when we women lost our men we lost our own, and our children's, living. I am glad that war has gone forever. It was no good—*no good!*"

Despite her condemnation of warfare, Pretty Shield expressed an admi-ration for the heroic role women played in defending the people—a role, she complained to Linderman, that the men did not like to talk about.

Once when Pretty Shield was only eight years old, the Lakotas attacked her small village. The Crows quickly formed a defensive circle with their tipis, breastworks were quickly thrown up, and the horses brought inside the circle. There was a large gap between two tipis that little Pretty Shield tried, in her childlike innocence, to close by setting up her play-tipi in the open space to keep out the enemy. One elderly woman picked up the brave little girl and took her back to the safety of her mother's tipi. In the midst of the fighting, with arrows and bullets flying everywhere, Strikes-Two, a sixty-year-old woman, rode around the camp on her gray horse. Carrying only her root-digger and singing her medicine song, she shouted to the villagers to sing, "They are whipped. They are running away, and keep singing these words until I come back." Strikes-Two then charged the Lakotas "waving her root-digger and singing that song." The enemy, overwhelmed by her medicine power, turned and fled the scene. "I *saw* her, I *heard* her," Pretty Shield told Linderman, "and my heart swelled, because she was a woman."

Pretty Shield felt the same pride about two Crow women who fought with the blue-coat soldiers against their mutual enemy, the Lakotas, at the Battle of the Rosebud, June 17, 1876. She told Linderman a rich story—which none of the Crow men who fought there had revealed—about the heroic deeds of The Other Magpie, a young woman who sought revenge for her brother's death at the hands of Lakotas, and Osh Tisch/Finds Them and Kills Them, a Crow batée, who for one day fought like a warrior.

Pretty Shield was most proud of Goes Ahead, who scouted for Lieu-tenant Colonel George Armstrong Custer at the Little Bighorn. After the fight Goes Ahead shared with Pretty Shield what happened that fateful day—and many years later she shared this colorful and highly questionable account with Sign Talker.

Goes Ahead stayed close to Harry Moccasin and White Man Runs Him that fateful day. As they explored the trail, the three scouts spotted many signs that indicated the Lakota/Cheyenne village was large, with many warriors. They tried to warn Custer, but he urged them forward. The scouts went on to Hawk's Nest in the early morning hours of June 25, and it was Goes Ahead who first sighted the great Lakota horse herd on the west side of the Little Bighorn. Again they warned Custer that it was a large village, but he would not turn away from the impending conflict. Pretty Shield thought the conflict inevitable. "But Son of the Morning Star [which she called Custer] was going to his death, and did not know it. He was like a feather blown by the wind, and *had* to go."

Of course, it may have not been fate but foolishness and drinking that caused his death and that of his soldiers. Goes Ahead had told his wife that Custer "drank too often from the straw-covered bottle that was on his saddle." Pretty Shield told Sign Talker that "too much drinking may have made that great soldier-chief foolish on that day when he died." Some soldiers may have drunk whiskey that day, as many Crow scouts claimed, but it's highly unlikely that Custer was one of them. Most Custer scholars reject the Crow assertion that Custer drank whiskey that fateful day, since he had given up drinking years before.

Goes Ahead claimed that he rode down to the Little Bighorn River with Custer, where the Son of Morning Star was shot. Some years later Goes Ahead showed Pretty Shield the very spot where it happened. She so believed her husband that she told Linderman, "The monument that white men have set up to mark the spot where Son of the Morning Star fell down [Last Stand Hill], is a lie. He fell in the water." Goes Ahead's claim is highly questionable, according to most scholars.

Goes Ahead survived the fight and returned to his village. The war was over for Goes Ahead; he never fought again.

Pretty Shield lived more years of her life on Crow Agency than she did in the nomadic days, yet she had little to say to Linderman about those long years on the reservation. "There is nothing to tell," she said, "because we did nothing. There were no more buffalo. We stayed in one place, and grew lazy." Linderman asked Pretty Shield what happened when the buffalo went away. "Ahh," Pretty Shield exclaimed, "my heart fell down when I began to see dead buffalo scattered all over our beautiful country, killed and skinned, and left to rot by white men, many, many hundreds of buffalo." At first, the people could not believe, even then, that "the white men could kill *all* the buffalo." Although the Crows believed the buffalo would return, they did not. Hunters went in all directions looking for buffalo, but found "nothing."

"After this," said Pretty Shield, "their hearts were no good anymore." The Crows had suffered a great ecological disaster.

Forced by treaty onto a reservation, the Crows stayed in one place, growing sicker and passive. It was hard for Pretty Shield since she had loved the nomadic life, the excitement of moving camp from one beautiful place to another. Now white men began to fence the land, even Crow land that they leased. Pretty Shield hated fences, telling her granddaughter Alma: "Why is it that they put up fences? If you keep something in a fence too long, it will die. Let it go its way."

Although the Crows suffered a loss of land, population, and spirit in the early days of the reservation, they lived in the most beautiful country in Montana. New leaders emerged and slowly they rebuilt their horse herds and acquired cattle from the BIA for ranching. Pretty Shield thought the Crows "might have managed to get along if the White Chief in Washington had not leased our lands to white stockman," some of whom shot down Indian horses "because they wanted all the grass for themselves." The Crows suffered, what one historian said of the Lakota, their second "ecological disaster," which, more than anything, impoverished them.

Although Pretty Shield did not reveal to Linderman much about her everyday life on the reservation, her granddaughter Alma left a rich and detailed record of her grandmother during these long years at Crow Agency. In some ways the reservation was harder on men than women. Goes Ahead was no longer the hunter and warrior of the family, but Pretty Shield continued her domestic life, keeping Goes Ahead's lodge, looking after her three surviving children—Pine Fire, Little Woman, and Good—and watching her many grandchildren grow. During the early 1900s, Goes Ahead and Pretty Shield lived near Hardin in a two-room log house, with a shed where Pretty Shield kept her dried food like jerky, roots, and berries. Their children lived nearby.

In the 1890s Goes Ahead made a life-changing decision. He became a convert to Christianity, a follower of Jesus, "The One Pierced in the Hand," who gave up his life (like a good warrior) to save his people from sin. In the old days, Goes Ahead had been a medicine man who healed the sick through herbal medicines. But once converted, he threw all his medicine bundles in the Little Bighorn River. Some traditionalist begged him not to, but Goes Ahead was committed to his new faith and baptized in the Baptist church, where he served as a deacon.

Pretty Shield was baptized at the same time. Goes Ahead asked his wife to forgo her role as a medicine woman, but she took longer to give up her healing powers. Alma remembered her grandmother using her medicine to cure people afflicted with various bodily pains. As long as there were interpreters to translate the service into Crow, Pretty Shield went to church services. When the church stopped having interpreters, Pretty Shield stopped going: "I don't understand the words," she explained, "so I get sleepy."

When Goes Ahead became ill and knew the end of his life was near, he had a vision in which Jesus fought the "evil one" for his soul—and Jesus won. "Now," Goes Ahead said, "it won't be long until he'll be coming after me." Goes Ahead built his tipi on the banks of the Little Bighorn, a river that he loved, with Pretty Shield at his side. Goes Ahead died in 1919 and was buried in the National Cemetery at the Little Bighorn.

Pretty Shield remained a widow for twenty-five years. Some older men wanted to marry her, but she refused. "No," she said to one man. "It's not that I don't like you. I appreciate your concern and everything, but I belong to *Basaakoosh* [Goes Ahead]. I want him to see me as he left me." After her husband died, Pretty Shield received a monthly pension check, thirty to thirty-five dollars, from the U.S. government for Goes Ahead's service as a scout for the army. Pretty Shield never forgot Goes Ahead, telling Linderman, "Since my man, Goes Ahead, went away twelve snows ago my heart has been fallen down. I am old now, and alone, with so many grandchildren to watch."

In 1924 more tragedy followed with the unexpected death of her daughter Little Woman. She had "stepped into a horse's track that was deep in the dried clay, and hurt her ankle." The doctor said she had a form of bone disease that could not be cured. "I did not believe it," exclaimed Pretty Shield, "and yet she died, leaving six little children." Alma, the youngest, was not yet two. Shortly after, Pine Fire died, leaving behind her children. Pretty Shield lamented that these deaths would not have happened in the old days. Her son Good was the only surviving child.

By the time Linderman arrived on the scene in 1931, Pretty Shield was raising two families of grandchildren on very little money, relying on Goes Ahead's monthly pension and money she received from leasing her allotted land. From the moment her daughters died, Pretty Shield worried about her grandchildren's future. "I wonder how my grandchildren will turn out," she said to Linderman. "They have only me, an old woman, to guide them, and plenty of others to lead them into bad ways." She prayed every morning for their well-being and for the strength to help them grow up in a world she did not understand.

Prior to 1931 Pretty Shield had lived in the rural area of Benteen, where she had a hard time transporting the grandchildren to school. She had to make two trips a day with her horse-drawn wagon across the Little Bighorn River to reach the highway where the bus picked up the children—a difficult trip for an elderly woman. But when Alma started school, Pretty Shield moved to town at Crow Agency, within walking distance to the school Alma attended.

The family lived in a "frame house covered with tar paper." Alma said, "It was nice, a warm place, but it was just the one big room." The house was simply furnished with only basic necessities: a homemade cupboard made of orange crates, a large table for eating with benches that slid under the table, a large bed for the granddaughters who lived with her, a corner stacked with boxes for clothes, a washbasin and dipper (Alma's task was to carry water from a pump at her uncle's house nearby), and a Monarch stove in the middle of the room. Pretty Shield slept in a corner of the room on a pallet bed with a mattress and a buffalo robe for a cover. There was no running water or electricity, only oil lamps and candles.

Pretty Shield had little, but she always provided for her grandchildren's basic needs. Always working and instructing the grandchildren to do the same, she told them, "Don't sit around!" or "Don't waste the day, because it's not a long day." She worked hard preparing meats (domestic cattle and wild game that her grandson hunted), dressing hides, collecting wood and wild foods, and sewing clothes, which she washed in the river. While cleaning clothes in the river, Pretty Shield took time to swim, which she loved to do.

Clearly, Pretty Shield preferred the old ways. Looking the part of an old Crow woman, she wore long dresses, with a blanket and shawl wrapped around her. Yet slowly, she adopted some modern touches, small and large. She still walked in moccasins, but in wet times used waterproof overshoes for protection. She discovered that manufactured combs with big teeth worked better than porcupine tails. She used metal needles and thread, and only used sinew for her moccasins. She discovered that store-bought Fels Naphtha soap cleaned clothes better than pounding. She preferred traditional foods, but enjoyed eating canned tomatoes mixed with macaroni.

As time passed, Pretty Shield accepted technological changes that seemed incongruous with her earlier background. She used her lease money to buy a gasoline-operated washing machine with a hand-wringer, letting her granddaughters Pearl and Mayme operate it, for she would not touch it.

In 1935 Pretty Shield, Pearl, and Mayme pooled their lease money to buy a car, a blue-gray Ford. The girls would take Pretty Shield into the town of Hardin to shop for groceries, but one day Pearl and Mayme argued over who should drive the car. Perhaps annoyed at their bickering, Pretty Shield grabbed the key, started the car, put it into gear, and drove forward, thrashing the washtub, running over the wood pile, and crashing into the shed door. Pretty Shield got out and rather mysteriously said, "There it is. That's what I'll do."

As a traditional Crow woman, Pretty Shield did not feel that a book education was essential for a young girl destined for motherhood, but under pressure from the Indian Agency, she sent the girls to school, though like many Crow mothers she preferred the day school on the reservation to distant boarding schools. When Cerise, the oldest granddaughter, was sent to an Indian boarding school in Oregon, Pretty Shield was "very distrusting." She feared that the Indian Agency was taking her granddaughter away and she would never see her again. Alma remembered that "when Cerise left, Grandma ran down the railroad tracks, following the train and crying." Fortunately, Cerise returned home after one year in school.

Alma attended the day school at Crow Agency. Pretty Shield was fine with that, but one day Alma came home early, the palms of her hands swollen. Alma told her grandmother that the principal struck the palms of her hands with a rubber hose because she had misbehaved in class. Pretty Shield was furious, and grabbing her hatchet, she headed for the principal's office, where she confronted him. "You bad," she said in her broken English. "You bad." Pretty Shield chased him around the room, and fortunately for the principal, some teachers intervened and calmed the situation. Alma said that the principal didn't use the hose very much after that.

After Alma finished the sixth grade at the Crow Agency day school, the same principal recommended that she attend an Indian vocational school in Pierre, South Dakota. Alma thought that he wanted to get rid of her, and Pretty Shield did not want Alma to leave. However, Mayme persuaded her grandmother that it would be best for her younger sister to receive a good education. Pretty Shield, who reluctantly agreed to let Alma go, finally began to understand what was happening. Alma remembered her grandmother's insightful words: "I understand. Now, I'm beginning to understand what it's all about. They want *all* our children to be educated in their way—the white man way. I know there's no stopping it. That makes me sad because I am going to have to let the old ways go and push my children to this new way. It breaks my heart to do this."

Pretty Shield felt increasingly at odds with this modern world. Sadly, she told Mayme, "I'm too much a part of the past. I'll continue to live that way. I have no reason to change, but looking to the future, they [the grandchildren] must go. They must go. When one of my grandchildren leaves me and goes somewhere like Cerise did, it tears my heart out. It hurts. It hurts, and I feel so helpless. It's just as if I'm nothing. I'm nothing no more; where I was capable, where I prided myself in keeping my lodge, here I am at the brink of no more."

Pretty Shield loved her grandchildren. They were her responsibility and it was her duty to protect them from harm in the modern world, but she wondered whether she any longer had knowledge or authority to control their actions. She shared her fears with Linderman. "I hope I can save my grandchildren. But times have changed so fast that they have left me behind. I do not understand these times. I am walking in the dark. Ours was a different world before the buffalo went away, and I belong to that other world." She told Linderman that in the old days, a parent never had to strike a child. Children listened to their parents and did what they were told. But that was no longer true in the reservation era where dangers abounded, especially for young women, who were increasingly exposed to drinking, smoking, immodest dress, white dances, and young men who would compromise their virtue.

In order to protect her granddaughters from harm, Pretty Shield did the unthinkable; she struck her grandchildren. "There seemed to be nothing else to do," she confessed to Linderman. "Times and children have changed so. One of my granddaughters [Frances] ran off to a dance with a bad young man after I had told her that she must not go. I went after her. . . . I brought her home to my place, and used a saddle-strap on her. I struck hard, Signtalker. I hoped it helped her, and yet I felt ashamed of striking my grandchild. I am trying to live a life that I do not understand."

Pretty Shield did not tell Linderman that she also struck Alma, her youngest grandchild. Alma, who was seventeen at the time, told what happened. She and her girlfriend were in town talking to a young man. It was all quite innocent. Pretty Shield saw them and misread the situation. Pretty

Shield was mad. She threw a stone at the young boy, who ran away. Alma tried to hide but her grandmother caught her and "slapped" her across the head. Alma told Pretty Shield, "You hurt me." "It's better to hurt you," Pretty Shield replied, "than to let you chase wild. You have no ears for me, for my words, so I have to let you know that what I tell you, I mean."

Pretty Shield lived long enough to see her grandchildren grow up and take their place in the world. She had raised with love the many grandchildren left in her care since the death of her two daughters in the 1920s. By the early 1940s, most of the grandchildren were married and working in the outside world. Some had children of their own, making Pretty Shield a great-grandmother. She was now in her late eighties, and the years had taken their toll.

Until she got very old, Pretty Shield relied on her own medicine for sickness, but now that no longer worked. In the final days of her life as she lay dying, the doctor said, "It's just old age and a broken heart. There's nothing physically wrong with her." Alma said that her sisters believed that she wanted to be with Goes Ahead.

The family gathered around her—George, Frances, Cerise, Pearl, Mayme, and Alma. George read the Twenty-third Psalm and placed a crucifix in her hand. Pretty Shield spoke in turn to each of the grandchildren. Even on her deathbed, she thought of the grandchildren. She told Mayme that the pension check was due. "Go get it," she said, "and get some food." She told the other grandchildren, "You're going to be all right." But she was concerned about Frances, who had so many children to look after. Finally, she took Alma's hand and said, "You will go and make it. Whatever you put your efforts in will be so."

Then Pretty Shield pointed and said, "Four people are coming. I must go." Pretty Shield died that day, April 30, 1944, at age eighty-eight. Alma said she died happily since she was going to meet Goes Ahead. After a religious service at the Baptist church, Pretty Shield was buried in the same grave with Goes Ahead in the National Cemetery at the Little Bighorn.

CHAPTER 12

Buffalo Bird Woman:
Keeping the Traditions Alive

Gilbert L. Wilson, a Presbyterian minister and aspiring ethnologist, came to the Fort Berthold Reservation in North Dakota in July 1906 to study the old-time crafts and customs of the village people—the Hidatsa, Mandan, and Arikara—who called Fort Berthold their home. Reverend Charles Hall, the Congregational minister at Fort Berthold, suggested that Wilson take up his studies at Independence, a distant settlement overlooking the Missouri River. It was a fortuitous decision.

At Independence, Wilson met Henry Wolf Chief, a prominent member of the Hidatsa community, his nephew Edward Goodbird, who was educated and bilingual, and, most important, Buffalo Bird Woman, who was Goodbird's mother and Wolf Chief's older sister. The trio shared their life story with Wilson that summer—and for the next twelve summers.

Wolf Chief, Goodbird, and Buffalo Bird Woman were close-knit members of one family and clan. While each shared their knowledge of the old Hidatsa way with Wilson, they were at different places in their lives when Wilson first met them in 1906.

Wolf Chief, in his late fifties, had lived the traditional life of a Hidatsa man. He was a handsome man who dressed in fashionable clothes and pursued women, a brave man who hunted buffalo and fought the people's enemies, and a spiritual man who fasted and prayed and suffered in search of a vision. But by 1906 Wolf Chief no longer looked back with nostalgia on the old days as did his older sister. During the reservation era, he adapted in many ways to the white-man's world, learning to read and write, opening a general store, becoming a commercial farmer and rancher, serving as an Indian Judge on the Court of Indian Offenses, and becoming a Christian.

Goodbird, in his mid-thirties when he met Wilson, was born too late to live the old lifestyle. He never counted coup against the enemy, or went on a communal buffalo hunt, or achieved a spiritual vision. Goodbird's parents,

Son of a Star, Goodbird, and Buffalo Bird Woman, circa 1906 COURTESY OF MINNESOTA HISTORICAL SOCIETY, GILBERT WILSON PHOTOGRAPH COLLECTION, I.63.NO.135. PHOTOGRAPHED BY GILBERT WILSON

Son of a Star and Buffalo Bird Woman, were traditional; but as a young man who came of age on the reservation, Goodbird transitioned more easily from the old to the new, attending the white-man's school at an early age, becoming an accomplished farmer, rancher, and landowner, and converting to Protestant Christianity. He eventually became a leading preacher and minister of the Congregational church at Independence. Goodbird faced the future with hope and confidence. In 1914 Wilson published Edward Goodbird's life story in *Goodbird the Indian: His Story.*

Buffalo Bird Woman was an elderly woman at sixty-seven when Wilson met her. The best and happiest years of her life were behind her, and she did not seek to follow the path of her younger brother and son. Having long gloried in the traditional life of a Hidatsa woman, she mastered the domestic crafts, excelled in her role as keeper of the garden, enjoyed a long, loving relationship with her husband, Son of a Star, and took pride and joy in her only child, Goodbird. She lived all her life according to the ideal of the Hidatsa woman—and much of that was now challenged or lost in the reservation era.

So, she welcomed into her life this proper and curious white man who wanted to record the skills and customs of the old days. Buffalo Bird Woman saw in Wilson a way to pass on her knowledge to future generations.

Impressed with Buffalo Bird Woman, Wilson found her a "wonderful old lady, a born storyteller with a genius for detail." As he got to know Buffalo Bird Woman over the years, he came to realize that though "conservative, and sighing for the good old times [and] ignorant of English," she had a "quick intelligence and a memory that is marvelous." He noted that Buffalo Bird Woman's "lore seemed endless and her delight at telling it was almost embarrassing." Despite her age, Wilson expressed some amazement that "in the sweltering heat of an August day she has continued dictation for nine hours, lying down but never flagging in her account, when too weary to sit longer in a chair." Throughout it all, the faithful Goodbird served as his mother's interpreter and Wilson's guide to the world of the Hidatsa.[1]

In 1921 Wilson published Buffalo Bird Woman's autobiography, *Waheenee, An Indian Girl's Story Told By Herself.* What follows is the story Buffalo Bird Woman told to Wilson.

Buffalo Bird Woman's birthplace was a Hidatsa/Mandan village at the mouth of the Knife River where it flowed into the Missouri River. Known as village people, the Hidatsas and Mandans lived in earth lodges and farmed corn, beans, and squashes in the rich bottomland alongside the Knife and Missouri Rivers. In 1837 a smallpox outbreak struck the Knife River villages, devastating the Hidatsas and the Mandans. It's estimated that the Hidatsa lost half their population; the Mandan losses were even higher. About three years after the smallpox outbreak, Buffalo Bird Woman was born, sometime in 1839–1840.

Her father was Small Ankle; her birth mother was Weahtee. But Small Ankle had also married three of Weahtee's sisters: Red Blossom, Strikes Many Women, and Stalk of Corn. The Hidatsa practiced "sororal polygyny." According to Hidatsa custom, Weahtee's daughter called her mother's sisters "ika," which meant mother; the young child was surrounded with four loving mothers, instead of one.

When she was ten days old, Buffalo Bird Woman's birth mother gave a feast and invited an old man, Nothing But Water, to give her a name. He called her Good Way, and he prayed that the child would go through life "by

---

1   Carolyn Gilman and Mary Jane Schneider's *The Way to Independence* captures the special relationship Wilson had with Wolf Chief, Goodbird, and Buffalo Bird Woman.

a good way; that she may grow up a good woman . . . and that she may have good luck all her days." But Good Way was not lucky: she was a sickly child. Since the Hidatsa thought that sickness was a sign from the gods, her father decided to give her a new name, one that would move the gods to help her. He renamed her Waheenee-wea, which meant Buffalo Bird Woman. She was named after the brown cowbird, or buffalo-bird, as it was called in Hidatsa country. She assumed that her father chose this name because birds were his spiritual protectors. "Perhaps," she thought, "the buffalo-birds had spoken to him in a dream." Carrying the name her father gave her all her life, Buffalo Bird Woman lived to be an old woman who believed that "it [her name] has brought me good luck from the gods."

When she was around six years old, the Hidatsa and Mandan decided to relocate their villages farther north along the Upper Missouri River. Looking for a place rich in good soil and timber, they hoped to find greater safety from increasing raids by the Sioux. Their journey ended at a hooklike bend in the Missouri River and here they established their new village, which they called Like a Fishhook. Buffalo Bird Woman came of age in this village. The Arikaras joined Like a Fishhook in 1862.

When her people arrived at their destination in the spring, Buffalo Bird Woman described the scene. Since they lacked enough time to erect an earth lodge before planting, Buffalo Bird Woman's mothers put up their tipis instead. Then her mothers and her grandmother, Turtle, cleared land near the river, planting seed corn, squash, beans, and sunflowers. In the fall they harvested their crops and then, as was their custom, sought a sheltered place in the protected woods along the river to build their small winter lodges.

But not all members of Buffalo Bird Woman's family returned from winter camp; smallpox had followed her people north. She lost her mother, her mother's sister Stalk of Corn, and her brother. Buffalo Bird Woman was lonesome in the winter lodge and often wept for her birth mother. Fortunately, she had her mother's surviving sisters, Red Blossom and Strikes Many Women, who loved her as their own child, and Turtle, who would raise her with grandmotherly love.

In the following spring her family returned to Like a Fishhook to plant their fields. Red Blossom and Strikes Many Women used iron tools, axes, and heavy hoes (gotten from European traders) to clear the land, but Turtle was old-fashioned. "I am an Indian," she said, "I use the ways my fathers used." Turtle dug weeds and bushes with a wooden digging stick, the point sharpened by fire, and then dug the ground with an old-fashioned bone-bladed hoe, "made of the shoulder blade of a buffalo set in a light-wooden handle, the blade firmly bound in place with thongs." When the fields were ready, they planted seed corn, squash, beans, and sunflowers.

After planting, Red Blossom and Strikes Many Women built their earth lodge, which Buffalo Bird Woman called their "real home." Since women owned the lodge, which they passed on to their daughters, they had the right to initiate construction. The women of the household staked out the dimensions of the earth lodge, marked where the holes for the four central posts should be dug, and supervised the men erecting the heavy frames. The four tall posts that supported the roof were the center of the earth lodge. As a Hidatsa, Buffalo Bird Woman believed that "the four posts were alive and we prayed always and made offerings. We thought the house to be sacred and the posts upheld it." When completed, the earth lodge measured some forty feet across, large enough to house all the related women, their husbands, and children, with room for the dogs and special horses.

Buffalo Bird Woman and Goodbird said that Like a Fishhook numbered some seventy Hidatsa and Mandan lodges, a noisy, busy, and crowded village. The earth lodges were clustered on a bluff overlooking the Missouri River, with an open space in the center for religious ceremony. Her family's earth lodge faced west in honor of the birds and thunder. Fortified for protection from its enemies, the village was surrounded by a four-foot ditch and earthen embankment encircled by a log palisade. The residents left and entered through two hinged gates. Each morning when the bells rang, the women left to tend their gardens in the rich bottomlands along the river while the men drove their horses out to graze on the grassy plain. Buffalo Bird Woman's family field measured about 180 by 90 yards. At night the bells rang again, and they all returned to the safety of their lodges.[2]

Throughout the spring, summer, and early fall, this was the ritual of the people who lived in Like a Fishhook. Then, as cold approached, the people left for their winter lodges in some sheltered location along the river bottom where they found wood for their fires. The village residents continued this pattern until around 1866 when they started to build cabins next to their

---

2   Based on Buffalo Bird Woman's description of her mothers' earth lodge, Frederick Wilson (who illustrated his brother's research) drew a detailed sketch of the interior of the earth lodge. He also drew a detailed map of Like a Fishhook village. See Gilman and Schneider, *The Way to Independence*, pp. 10–11, 18–19.

earth lodges, where they lived in the winter. Buffalo Bird Woman's family had a pair of dwellings: an earth lodge and a cabin.

Looking back at her "girlhood as the happiest time of [her] life," Buffalo Bird Woman had many girlfriends, although Cold Medicine, her younger sister, was her constant companion. The girls played the ball and stick game, in which two teams of girls tried to get the ball past the other team's goal. They also played a game with a soft ball that they bounced with their foot to see how long they could keep it in the air without letting it touch the ground. In winter they coasted down hills on small sleds made of buffalo ribs, and in the summer they slid down steep, grassy hills on buffalo skins.

Buffalo Bird Woman loved to play house with her girlfriends, all of whom had dolls and put up play tipis. Sometimes, little boys joined in their play and each girl selected a boy for her "husband." They sent the boy-husband to "hunt" for food and he returned with some meat from his mother, which the girls used to prepare a feast like their mothers did after a buffalo hunt.

In time boys and girls began to play separately, in preparation for their different roles in Hidatsa society. If Buffalo Bird Woman wandered outside that role, she was challenged. When she wore her father's hunting cap, Turtle would laugh and cry out, "Hey, hey, that is a warrior's cap. A little girl cannot be a warrior." In turn, when she became a mother, Buffalo Bird Woman warned Goodbird not to play with girls because, if he did, "he [would] grow up to be a woman."

As Buffalo Bird Woman grew older, she spent less time playing and more time with household tasks. Around age twelve, her mothers started to prepare her for womanhood and marriage. Fetching water from the Missouri River was an everyday chore that she enjoyed because it gave her the chance to "gossip" with her girlfriends. She learned how to sweep out the lodge, gather driftwood from the river, dress hides, cook, sew with awl and sinew, and decorate clothing with porcupine quills dyed in color.

One day stood out for Buffalo Bird Woman. Her family gave her a black puppy that she called "Blackie." Grandmother Turtle helped her raise and train the dog for the day when he could draw a travois loaded with wood or household goods. After two years Turtle thought Blackie was ready for work and she built a travois for the dog to draw. Turtle said to Buffalo Bird Woman: "Your dog Sheepeesha [Blackie] is now old enough to work and my little granddaughter, too, must learn to be useful." Buffalo Bird Woman accompanied her mothers to collect wood. She understood the significance of the moment. "Owning a dog, and invited to go with my mothers to get wood, I felt that in spite of my girlish years I was almost a woman now." She returned to the lodge and proudly told Turtle, "Grandmother, my dog has brought home a load of wood."

Next to building a lodge, perhaps no skill was more important to a young Hidatsa woman than planting and harvesting the family's garden. Buffalo Bird Woman spent many summer days with her grandmother in their three-acre field, fenced with sunflowers to separate it from their neighbors' fields. She watched how her mothers and grandmother cleared the area to be planted with seed corn, beans, and squash, then learned how to plant the seeds. While young, Buffalo Bird Woman's first task had been to chase the crows from eating the seed. As the plants grew, her mothers and grandmother built a watch-station in the fields—a simple platform from which Buffalo Bird Woman and her sister Cold Medicine could watch over and protect the ripening plants, especially corn, from rapacious crows and magpies, mischievous boys, and wandering horses.

"We cared for our corn in those days," Buffalo Bird Woman exclaimed, "as we would care for a child; for we Indian people loved our fields as mothers love their children. We thought that the corn plants had souls, as children have souls, and that growing corn like to hear us sing, as children like to hear their mothers sing to them." Buffalo Bird Woman called the songs young women sang to the corn "gardeners' songs," songs that were often "love-boy" songs—songs in which young girls teased their "sweethearts." But not always. Sometimes the songs simply teased boys or young men who thought too highly of themselves, and sometimes the songs simply celebrated the special friendship one girl had with another, her eekupa (her "chum"). Whatever the songs, the corn liked to hear the girls sing.

Corn was sacred to the people. When Buffalo Bird Woman once spilled a few kernels of corn on the floor, Turtle said to her grandchild, "Do not do that. Corn is sacred; if you waste it, the gods will be angry." To make her point, Turtle told her grandchild the following story about an Arikara woman who thought she picked all the corn in her fields, but as she was leaving with her harvest, she heard a small voice like a baby calling, "Please, please do not go. Do not leave me." The woman thought that a baby was hidden in the field, so she desperately searched but found no child. She again started to leave, but still the little voice cried out, so she searched again, finding no one. Once more she started to leave the field, but still the voice cried out. So, the woman searched every corn hill, lifting every leaf. "And, lo, in one corner of the field, hidden under a leaf, she found a tiny nubbin of yellow corn. It was the nubbin that had been calling to her." Turtle's message to her grandchild was clear: "For so the gods would teach us not to be wasteful of their gifts."

As a young girl approaching womanhood, Buffalo Bird Woman received moral instruction from her family. Her mothers said to her, "We are a family that has not a bad woman in it. You must try hard not to be naughty." Big Cloud, her grandfather, gave her good advice: "My granddaughter, try to be good, so that you will grow up to be a good woman. Do not quarrel nor steal. Do not answer anyone with bad words. Obey your parents, and remember all that I say." Buffalo Bird Woman listened carefully to her mothers and grandparents, and all her life, she strove to be the ideal Hidatsa daughter, wife, and mother.

When she turned fourteen years old, Buffalo Bird Woman began to think herself "almost a young woman." Like most, she dressed up and looked pretty, painting her face, "red all over the face, but deeper and heavier on the cheeks." She also made use of perfumes, so boys began to notice her. Some of the boys smiled at her as she came up from the watering place, but as a proper young woman from a good family, she did not smile back.

However, she did not discourage the attention of Sacred Red Eagle Wing, a good-looking fifteen-year-old young man who asked her mothers' permission to accompany Buffalo Bird Woman as she went picking berries in the woods, to protect her from enemies lurking there. "I felt quite grown-up," Buffalo Bird said, "to know that a young man wanted to go berry picking with me." As it turned out, there was no enemy in the woods, so the young man helped Buffalo Bird Woman collect Juneberries, although the shy, proper young woman did not talk with the young man or, she regretted to say, even thank him for his help.

But the young man was not discouraged and showed up at corn-harvest time, the "busiest and happiest time of all the year." Her mothers prepared a big feast for relatives and friends who helped the family husk corn, while Buffalo Bird Woman bathed in the river, putting on her best dress and painting her face. Men and women sat on opposite sides as they husked corn, with Sacred Red Eagle Wing sitting opposite Buffalo Bird Woman. Red

Hand, a handsome young warrior who sat next to Sacred Red Eagle Wing, also looked favorably at Buffalo Bird Woman. "I was glad," she said, "that I was wearing my elk-teeth dress." "He is a young man," she thought, "not a boy like Sacred Red Eagle Wing."

After the feast the women carried the husked corn back to the village. As Buffalo Bird Woman gathered some strings of corn, Red Hand approached. Without saying a word, he laid the strings of corn on his pony and started for the village so that Buffalo Bird Woman thought he admired her. "Red Hand is brave, and he owns a pony," she said to herself, and she forgot all about Sacred Red Eagle Wing.

Just then came the roar of guns. A party of Lakotas appeared on the hillside overlooking the cornfields. Her father, Small Ankle, sprang for his war pony, followed by Red Hand as a fight ensued. When a Lakota warrior charged the Hidatsa, Red Hand rode out to meet him. The Lakota warrior shot an arrow that caught Red Hand's pony in the throat. The horse fell, but Red Hand landed on his feet and fired his gun, wounding the Lakota warrior, who dropped his bow and arrows and fled back to his own line. More Hidatsa warriors came from the village, driving away the Lakotas. The Hidatsa returned with one scalp, and people celebrated their victory with a scalp dance praising Red Hand's bravery.

Buffalo Bird Woman's "relationship" with Red Hand quickly ended, as she later explained to Wilson. "The next day I was coming from the watering-place with my kettle. Just ahead of me walked Waving Corn, a handsome girl two years older than I. Red Hand passed by; shyly I looked up, thinking to see him smile at me. He was smiling at Waving Corn."

Buffalo Bird Woman got over her disappointment. "And so I grew up," she said, "a happy, contented Indian girl, obedient to my mothers." Continuing to work at domestic chores that would prepare her for marriage, her family started to recognize her industry and skill. Her aunt presented her with a beautifully decorated woman's belt for her skill in dressing skins. "To wear a woman's belt," Buffalo Bird Woman said, "was an honor. I was as proud of mine as a war leader of his first scalp." She was also given a brass ring for embroidering a robe for her father with porcupine quills and a bracelet for "embroidering a tent cover with gull quills dyed yellow and blue."

Evidently others in the village began to notice that this was a desirable young woman for marriage. One day Hanging Stone came to the lodge and offered Small Ankle four horses, expensive blankets and calico, and three flintlock guns for Buffalo Bird Woman to marry his stepson, Magpie. Small Ankle refused, saying his daughter was too young, and he returned the gifts. Hanging Stone was persistent, returning the next day with the three guns, some expensive cloth, and four horses—but this time two of the horses were prize hunting horses, fast enough to overtake a buffalo.

Small Ankle was impressed with Hanging Stone's sincerity. He asked his wives what they thought of the offer, but they said that he should do as he thought best. Small Ankle reconsidered the offer. Since he thought Magpie a kind young man and a good hunter, it would be a good match. He then spoke to Buffalo Bird Woman. "My daughter, I have tried to raise you right. I have hunted and worked hard to give you food to eat. Now I want you to take my advice. Take this man for your husband. Try always to love him." As a dutiful Hidatsa woman, his daughter agreed to the wisdom of his decision.

Buffalo Bird Woman's mothers prepared a feast for the wedding celebration, which Cold Medicine and Buffalo Bird Woman took to Hanging Stone's lodge. Small Ankle also sent three horses, plus a prized weasel-skin cap and an eagle-feathered war bonnet, each worth a good horse. After the girls left, Magpie's relatives came to feast on the foods brought by the girls. The relatives, in turn, brought gifts for the newlywed bride, which were taken to Small Ankle's lodge. After this mutual exchange of goods, Buffalo Bird Woman went back to Magpie's lodge and invited him to come and live in her lodge. Magpie followed a few minutes later, for "young men did not walk through the village with their sweethearts in the daytime. We should have thought that foolish. And so I was wed." (It's clear from Buffalo Bird Woman's account that her sister, Cold Medicine, was involved in the wedding ceremony. But, for whatever reason, she did not make clear that Cold Medicine was also to marry Magpie, though the marriage would not be consummated until her sister came of age.)

After the marriage Small Ankle gave further instruction to Buffalo Bird Woman. "My daughter," he said, "you are married, you must stay home and try to be a good worker; you will sometimes not want to do your work; you will think it is too hard but stand up, and see if you can not do it any way." Buffalo Bird Woman did not disappoint her father. In addition to excelling in the domestic chores, Buffalo Bird Woman also wanted to become a skilled craftswoman—to master the sacred crafts of basket making, tipi making, house construction, and pottery making. In Hidatsa society the right to such "sacred knowledge" had to be purchased from a teacher. Buffalo Bird Woman acquired the rights to the first three. She was most proud of her right to construct the earth lodge, especially to "trim" the four sacred posts, for which she gained great respect and many gifts from the people at Like a Fishhook.

Buffalo Bird Woman's marriage to Magpie, which was childless, lasted thirteen years until he died from tuberculosis. She mourned for a year until Son of a Star, a Mandan, took notice of the young widow. He smiled pleasantly at her whenever they met and, one day, he told her, "I am going to marry you! My people have put up four horses for me." Her mothers and father, who liked the kindly Son of a Star, were in favor of the union. "He is brave, daughter," Small Ankle said. "He wears two eagle feathers, for he has twice struck an enemy, and he has danced the death dance. Three times he has shot an arrow through a buffalo." So Buffalo Bird Woman married again, in what was a good and happy lifelong marriage.

About a year after she married, Buffalo Bird Woman, thirty at the time, gave birth to a baby boy, her first and only child. The Hidatsa were on a rare buffalo hunt, having camped for the night on a sandbar where the Yellowstone joined the Missouri River on a cold and windy November day. Her father had struck a warm fire in the tipi. Many years later Buffalo Bird Woman still remembered the moment.

"The wind died at evening," she said. "Twilight fell, and the coals in the fireplace cast a soft, red glow on the tent walls. I sat near the tent door. With the robe drawn over my shoulder to keep off the chill, I raised the skin door and looked out. The new moon, narrow and bent like an Indian bow, shone white over the river, and the waves of the swift mid-current sparkled silvery in the moonlight. . . . Over all rose the roar, roar, roar of the great river, seeping onward we Indians knew not where." She remembered that the sleeping dogs awoke around midnight and started to "howl" at the moon, while far out on the prairie rose the wailing of a coyote. "The dogs grew silent again, and curled up, nose-in-tail, to sleep." And, sometime that night, her son entered the world.

At first light Son of a Star came into the tent. "His eyes were smiling," Buffalo Bird Woman recalled, "as he stepped to the fireplace, for they saw a pretty sight. Red Blossom was giving [the baby] a bath." The baby "squalled loudly." Son of a Star laughed. "It is a lusty cry," he exclaimed. "I am sure my son will be a warrior." But given the year his first child was born—1869—

Son of a Star was engaged in wishful thinking. The age of the warrior and buffalo hunter was nearly over.

Ten days after the birth, Buffalo Bird Woman asked her father to name the child. Small Ankle called him Goodbird since Small Ankle's gods were birds. Buffalo Bird Woman explained that "the name was a kind of prayer that they [the gods] remember and help my little son."

By the time Goodbird was born, the white world had already intruded on their village. French traders had arrived and established trading posts, like Fort Berthold, where they exposed the village tribes to European goods. Blue-coat soldiers, who had appeared in 1864, were welcomed because they protected the village against raids by the Lakotas. These soldiers stayed three years, and then moved fourteen miles east to establish Fort Stevenson. Some years later an Indian agent arrived at the Fort Berthold Agency to serve as representative for the United States to the Hidatsa, Mandan, and Arikara (who had joined the village in 1862). He came to administer the annuities promised under the 1851 Treaty of Fort Laramie, but he also came to change the fabric of tribal society and assimilate the village tribes into white society. In 1876 the Reverend Charles L. Hall, a Congregational minister, arrived at Like a Fishhook to Christianize the village people and expose them to a Euro-American way of life. The presence of whites in their village, especially the Indian agent and the missionary, presented challenges and opportunities.

By 1877 there were two schools at Like a Fishook—one founded by the Indian agent, the other by Rev. Hall. "Many of the older Indians," Goodbird said, "would laugh at any who tried to learn to read. 'You want to forsake your Indian ways and be white men' they would say."

But there were many in the village who wanted their children to learn English.

Buffalo Bird Woman's elderly father encouraged his sons and grandsons to go to school and learn English. Goodbird, age eight, was the first in the family to attend the mission school, doing so with the approval of his father, Son of a Star. Goodbird noted that his grandfather was "deeply interested in [his] studies." Small Ankle said that "it is their books that make white men strong. The buffaloes will soon be killed; and we Indians must learn white ways, or starve." Goodbird called his grandfather a "progressive old man."

Wolf Chief (Buffalo Bird Woman's brother) took his father's advice and sought an education, but he did so differently than Goodbird. He first sought instruction from a friend (a white man who had married into the tribe) in the three essential disciplines: reading, writing, and arithmetic. Wolf Chief progressed in his studies, and the following year, at age thirty, he enrolled in the public school. Despite the hardship for someone his age to begin schooling, Wolf Chief persisted in his studies—he saw education as a way to advance in the white man's world.

A few years after Goodbird started school, the Indian agent established a boarding school at Fort Stevenson. School officials wanted Goodbird to attend the boarding school, but his parents refused to let him go away. "No," they said, "we have a school here. Let him attend the missionary school." His parents feared, as did most Hidatsa parents, prolonged separation from their children. Buffalo Bird Woman spoke for many when she said, "it is a very hard thing for us to have to let our children be taken from us and sent away to school where we cannot see them." Besides, Buffalo Bird Woman had reservations about the learning experience of the boarding schools, especially as it affected their young girls. "In old days," she said, "mothers watched their daughters very carefully; and girls did not give birth to babies before marriage. But after schools were started on this reservation, then our daughters began to have babies before marriage, for they now learned English ways."

Rev. Hall also established a church at Like a Fishhook. On Sundays young Goodbird, with his parent's permission, attended service and heard Rev. Hall's sermons about Jesus. Goodbird began to think and read about Jesus and Christianity, but he was a long way from becoming a convert. His father and uncle were sympathetic to Rev. Hall's message but were too wedded to the traditional Hidatsa religion. As Son of a Star told his son, "the old gods are best for me." Buffalo Bird Woman did not speak to the new religion, but it's unlikely that she ever considered becoming a Christian, for, like her husband, she was faithful to the old ways.

Life for the Hidatsa, Mandan, and Arikara residents of Like a Fishhook underwent a dramatic change in the mid-1880s. The Indian agent argued that the time had come for the Indians to take their allotment of land, each individual family member to receive roughly 150 acres. Buffalo Bird Woman's extended family (joined by several related family groups) left Like a Fishhook in June 1885 and journeyed forty miles up the Missouri River to where a tall hill stood above a sharp curve in the river. The Hidatsa called the place Awatahesh (the "hill by itself"); later, Rev. Hall called it Independence. Buffalo Bird Woman's family decided to take their allotments of land at this place. Although the allotment policy broke the ancient community way of life the Hidatsas had enjoyed at Knife River and Like a Fishhook, Buffalo Bird Woman's family allotments were clustered so that they still enjoyed a sense of community.

Son of a Star built a log cabin on the high benchland overlooking the Missouri River. In the old days Buffalo Bird Woman would have designed and built the earth lodge, but a cabin was not considered sacred space, so Son of a Star took over responsibility for building the house. The cabin looked like a typical white person's cabin, but with some crucial Hidatsa differences. The iron stove was placed in the center of the main room with the smoke hole in the roof, similar to where the fireplace in the earth lodge was located, and the front door stood open for guests to enter, with benches lining the walls for women and men to sit.

However much Buffalo Bird Woman sighed for the old days, change was inevitable. It's not clear that she was ever comfortable living in a log cabin or that she ever learned to cook, as did Goodbird's wife, on an iron stove. She did make some small concessions to white ways: Goodbird said that his parents learned to use milk from whites. "We were very fond of it," he said. "We had cream in our coffee, and make biscuits with it. Sometimes we made butter." Buffalo Bird Woman did not favor the new style of living. "Children were then [in the old days] in every lodge," she said, "and there were many old men in the tribe. Now that we live in cabins and eat white men's foods, the children and old men die; and our tribe dies."

By settling at Independence, Buffalo Bird Woman's family gained some measure of freedom from the reach of the Indian agent, missionary, and school teacher, but it was only a matter of time before they followed the people to the new site. The Indian agent challenged Hidatsa religious practices, marriage customs, ceremony, and dance. When the Indian agent forbade the self-torture ritual for those seeking a vision, Son of a Star reacted with anger. "The government does wrong," he said, "to forbid us to suffer for our gods." Buffalo Bird Woman also resented the Indian agent's intrusion, expressing dislike of white men's laws. "I do not understand them nor know how to make them rule my life."

Goodbird and Wolf Chief were far more comfortable in the white man's world. Adapting to new conditions, they took up farming in the white man's way, planting cash crops with mechanical equipment on the land located between the river and bluffs and raising cattle. But Buffalo Bird Woman was unmoved by this new development in agriculture, continuing to plant, with great success, her garden of corn, beans, and squashes using the old-fashioned garden hoe. Her corn, planted and cultivated in the old way, took first place in the reservation's first agriculture fair in 1911.

When Rev. Hall came to preach at Independence, the first meetings were held in Goodbird's cabin, with Goodbird translating for Rev. Hall. In time some residents of Independence formed a Christian congregation. After many years of study and thought, Goodbird at age thirty-five was baptized and joined the church. He understood that he had reached a turning point in his life. "I am travelling the new way, now," he said. "I can never go back to Indian ways again." When Rev. Hall established a preaching station at Independence, he asked the faithful Goodbird to serve as assistant missionary. Wolf Chief converted as well and became a leading member of the Congregational Church.

After suffering for many years from a crippling disease, Son of a Star died in 1906 at age seventy-six. Goodbird said that his father "always remained true to his beliefs and would not desert his gods." Buffalo Bird Woman mourned the death of her husband in the Hidatsa way by cutting her hair short and wearing it loose.

In the summer of the year that Son of a Star died, Gilbert Wilson came to Independence. It was an auspicious moment, for Buffalo Bird Woman had found someone who was truly interested in learning about the ancient lifestyle of the Hidatsa, a way of life that was slowly disappearing among her people. Buffalo Bird Woman's story can be found scattered in the vast trove of material collected by Wilson, but it's best captured in her nostalgic autobiography, *Waheenee*.

A look inside the book is instructive: In chapter after chapter Buffalo Bird Woman delighted in describing life in a Hidatsa village during the old days, but she spent less than two brief pages describing life on the Fort Berthold Reservation where she spent long years of her life. She did not look forward like Goodbird; she looked back with sadness on the loss of the old ways. She closed the book with a nostalgic comment on life in the old days. "I am an old woman now," she lamented. "The buffaloes and black-tail deer are gone, and our Indian ways are almost gone. Sometimes I find it hard to believe that I ever lived them."

She was proud, however, of Goodbird's accomplishments in the white man's world, since he read books, owned cattle and a farm, lived in a house, was a leader among the Hidatsa, and helped his people "follow the white man's road."

"But for me," she said, "I cannot forget our old ways." She confessed to Wilson, "Often in summer I rise at daybreak and steal out to the cornfields; and as I hoe the corn I sing to it, as we did when I was young. No one cares for our corn songs now." Buffalo Bird Woman closed her story with a sad remembrance of her earlier life at Like a Fishhook village:

Sometimes at evening I sit, looking out on the big Missouri. The sun sets, and dusk steals over the water. In the shadows I seem again to see our Indian village, with smoke curling upward from the earth lodges; and in the river's roar I hear the yells of the warriors, the laughter of little children as of old. It is but an old woman's dream. Again I see but shadows and hear only the roar of the river; and tears come into my eyes. Our Indian life, I know, is gone forever.

That old Hidatsa way of life may be gone, but thanks to Buffalo Bird Woman and Wilson, the Hidatsa world of the earth lodge villages will never be forgotten.

CHAPTER 13

Josephine Crowfeather: Catholic Nun

In November 1884 Father Francis Craft, a Catholic priest, arrived at Standing Rock for missionary duty among the Hunkpapa Lakota. There he met Josephine Crowfeather, a young Lakota woman. For the next decade, their religious lives would be bound together.

Francis M. Craft was born in New York City on September 23, 1852. His father was a distinguished surgeon at Bellevue Hospital in the city; his mother was a direct descendant of the revolutionary war hero Nathanael Green. There was some Indian "blood" in the family tree: Francis's paternal grandmother, Rebecca Basset, was the daughter of a full-blood Mohawk woman.

The Crafts were longtime members of the Episcopal Church; but, for reasons that are not entirely clear, Francis converted in 1874 to the Roman Catholic faith. "Called . . . by God," to the priesthood, he entered the Society of Jesus in 1876. While following a rigorous program of study in philosophy and religion, Francis found time to study the missionary activity of the Catholic Church, especially among Native Americans. He admired the work of the French Jesuits among the Iroquois and was fascinated with the story of Kateri Tekakwitha, a young Mohawk woman noted for her purity and her desire (never realized) to found a religious order of American Indian sisters.

Francis left the Jesuit seminary in 1880, finding it difficult to follow the ascetic and disciplinary ideals of the Jesuits. Francis decided on a new course of action: a life of missionary activity among the western Indians. In late 1879 Francis had met a Benedictine monk, Abbot Martin Marty, who had established a missionary outpost among the Hunkpapa Lakota at Standing Rock Agency in Dakota Territory and was looking for recruits. Francis, eager to join the movement, finished his religious studies out west, and in March 1883 Marty (by that time Bishop of the Dakota Territory) ordained him as a diocesan priest.

Bishop Marty sent Fr. Craft to work among the Brulé Lakota at the Rosebud Agency. Fr. Craft spent less than two years at Rosebud, where he was accepted as a "relative" by Spotted Tail's family and immersed himself in the culture and language. Unfortunately, he alienated the Episcopal minister and Indian agent, who ordered the priest to leave. Bishop Marty sent Fr. Craft to the friendlier Catholic enclave at Standing Rock in November 1884.

At Standing Rock, Fr. Craft performed the usual chores of a Catholic priest, serving eleven mission stations throughout the vast land. He also founded a day school for Indian students, but his greatest interest lay in recruiting young Lakota women for the Benedictine convents, even though this was opposed by the Benedictine Nuns and Father Stephan, director of the Bureau of Catholic Indian Missions. This is how Josephine Crowfeather entered Father Craft's life.

Josephine Crowfeather, the daughter of Joseph Crowfeather, a Hunkpapa chief, was born in 1868. Her Lakota name, "Ptesanwanyakapi," which translated as "They see a White Buffalo Woman," bore religious significance. White Buffalo Woman held a sacred place in Lakota history as the legendary woman who brought the sacred pipe and, along with the holy men, the seven sacred rites that guided the Lakotas along the right path of life, a path blessed by Wakan Tanka, the Great Mystery. Josephine represented a tangible link with the sacred past, and the Lakotas called her a "sacred virgin." Her status as a special child was only confirmed when her father carried her into battle against the soldiers because he believed she would protect him from harm, which she did. Both returned unharmed.

Josephine was baptized as a Roman Catholic at fourteen years of age on June 29, 1882, at St. Benedict's Mission at Standing Rock. She had expressed for some time a desire to follow the religious life, and Fr. Craft encouraged Josephine in this direction.

From his early days at Standing Rock, Fr. Craft became close to Josephine Crowfeather's family, referring to Josephine as his "sister" in the Lakota way. While Fr. Craft mentored several young Lakota women toward the religious life, Josephine was clearly his favorite. It's possible that from his early days at Standing Rock, Fr. Craft thought of establishing an order of Indian sisters and that he thought Josephine the ideal candidate to lead the order. Why Josephine Crowfeather? Thomas W. Foley, Craft's biographer, speculated on the priest's choice of Josephine: "Whether it was the sacred nature of her past that intrigued him, or her own religious calling, or that she stood by him in the Sitting Bull affair—or perhaps for all these

Josephine Crowfeather, Sacred White Buffalo Woman, and her spiritual mentor, Father Francis M. Craft

reasons—Josephine's successful vocation and eventual salvation became an obsession [with him]."

Trouble arose with Sitting Bull after Fr. Craft recruited Josephine and several young Lakota women for the Benedictine school, St. Scholastica, at Fort Yates. Like many Lakotas at Standing Rock, Sitting Bull may have resented the removal of these young women from Lakota society and made wild charges of moral impropriety against Fr. Craft. But young Josephine rushed to defend the priest. "When all others left me to fight alone against slander & calumny," Fr. Craft noted in his journal—later published under the title *At Standing Rock and Wounded Knee*—"she was the *only* one to give me sister's sympathy & affection."

On June 22, 1888, Josephine Crowfeather and Anne Gaudreau left the Benedictine school at Fort Yates to attend the Benedictine convent in Zell, South Dakota. Fr. Craft had arranged the journey and paid for their dowry to enter the novitiate. It was all part of Fr. Craft's grand religious plan for his "sister" Josephine, the leader of his future order of Indian sisters.

But everything did not go as planned. In early August visiting sisters from Zell summoned Fr. Craft to meet them at St. Scholastica's school at Standing Rock. Fr. Craft feared the worst and was right. Josephine was there. It appeared that she had written Bishop Marty and the Mother Superior of her desire to return home, informing them that she never wanted to go to the convent, but that Father Craft and Sister Gertrude at St. Scholastica had "coaxed" her to do so. Fr. Craft explained her action with some sympathy in his journal: "The poor child had the usual severe attack of homesickness, desolation, & temptation against vocation, and, not knowing what she said, wrote to Mother Gertrude & the Bishop, asking to return."

Fr. Craft had a long talk with Josephine. She appeared in a better frame of mine and asked him to write Bishop Marty and explain that she would like to try again with the sisters at St. Scholastica. Fr. Craft wrote a long, pleading letter, but Bishop Marty instructed the sisters to return Josephine to her father—a decision the priest refused to accept.

Journeying to Chicago, Fr. Craft met with Bishop Marty and Fr. Stephan, Director of the Bureau of Catholic Indian Missions. Bishop Marty wanted Fr. Craft to establish a new mission at Fort Berthold (the home of the Three Affiliated Tribes: Mandan, Hidatsa, and Arikara) under the direction of Fr. Stephan and the Bureau of Catholic Indian Missions. Clearly, Bishop Marty wanted Fr. Craft removed from Standing Rock and his jurisdiction, but the priest refused to leave Standing Rock until Josephine's religious vocation was secured. Doubtful that Indians could serve as priests or nuns, Fr. Stephan dismissed the idea. But Bishop Marty, who showed a little more faith in the idea of Indian sisters, agreed that Josephine could pursue her religious vocation. With this assurance from Bishop Marty, Fr. Craft agreed to relocate to Fort Berthold.

Fr. Craft hurried back to Standing Rock, where he was greeted by Josephine. Within days he was back on the road. In early September 1888 Fr. Craft took Josephine, her sister Claudia, and four other young Lakota women (Alice White Deer, Jane Moccasin, Mary Black Eyes, and Bessie Yellow Bear) to the St. Francis Xavier Academy, which had been established by Sisters of the Holy Childhood at Avoca, Minnesota. After staying a few days to make sure that Josephine and her companions were comfortable and safe in their new surroundings, Fr. Craft left for Fort Berthold.

Fr. Craft kept in close touch with Josephine, sending her a special rosary and religious literature, all designed to bolster her resolve to persevere in her vocation. Avoca was a good choice. She wrote Fr. Craft on December 21, 1888, telling him that she and Claudia were well and enjoying their experience at St. Francis Xavier Academy.

With Josephine safe at Avoca, Fr. Craft journeyed to the Fort Berthold Reservation, where he established the Sacred Heart Mission and began work on a school, St. Edward's, funded by Katharine Drexel, a wealthy Philadelphia heiress and philanthropist. Fr. Craft hoped that, in time, the mission and school would be staffed by Indian sisters under his leadership.

Josephine did not remain long at Avoca. With Fr. Craft's support she left Avoca about four months after arriving and entered the novitiate with the Benedictine Sisters at Zell, South Dakota, having put behind her any doubts about her religious vocation. Fr. Craft's grand plan that Josephine become a nun and lead an order of Indian sisters was coming to fruition. On Easter Sunday (April 21, 1889), Josephine began that journey by taking on the religious habit of the Benedictine Sisters.

One year later, again on Easter Sunday, Josephine took her final vows at the Benedictine Motherhouse in Yankton, North Dakota (it had moved from Zell). She wrote the good news to Fr. Craft, who was in New York raising funds for his mission at Fort Berthold. She had taken the name Sister Mary Catharine, the name of Kateri [Catharine] Tekakwitha. Fr. Craft

Mother Mary Catharine (Sacred White Buffalo), circa 1890 COURTESY OF THE DEPARTMENT OF SPECIAL
COLLECTIONS & UNIVERSITY ARCHIVES, MARQUETTE UNIVERSITY LIBRARIES, BUREAU OF CATHOLIC INDIAN MISSIONS, ID 00242

had realized his dream for Josephine Crowfeather, linking the "Lily of the Mohawk" with the "Lily of the Dakota."[1]

Sister Mary Catharine and the other novices still at Avoca sought, with Fr. Craft's help, to join the Sacred Heart Mission at Fort Berthold. It happened in stages. In June, at the end of the school year, James McLaughlin,

_____
1   Josephine Crowfeather was not the first Lakota to take her vows as a Benedictine sister. Ellen Clark, a half-blood, was the first Lakota to enter the Benedictine order at Zell in 1885. She took the name of Sister Gregory. Theodora Piiciyawi, a full-blood, took her final vows as a Benedictine sister on May 12, 1889. She took the name Sister Mary Gertrude. Fr. Craft had conducted the investiture ceremony. At the time of her induction, Sister Mary Gertrude was gravely ill from tuberculosis, and she died on June 14, 1889.

the Indian agent at Standing Rock, instructed the Mother Superior at Avoca to return all the Lakota students to their homes, but Fr. Craft's postulants objected. They feared that if they returned home, they would not be allowed to continue with their vocation. They wrote Bishop Marty, who permitted the young women—Claudia Crowfeather, Jane Moccasin, Alice White Deer, Nellie Dubray, and Louise Bordeaux—to continue their studies at the Benedictine convent at Yankton, South Dakota.

Fr. Craft arrived at Yankton in November, having received a letter from Sister Mary Catharine. Claudia, her sister, was very ill with tuberculosis. Bishop Marty and the doctor wanted Claudia returned to Standing Rock, but Josephine objected to the separation. Fr. Craft came armed with authorization from his new superior, John Shanley, Bishop of Jamestown, North Dakota, to withdraw Sister Mary Catharine and the five postulants to the Sacred Heart Mission at Fort Berthold. Sister Mary Bridget (Annie Pleets) refused to follow Fr. Craft, writing her superior, "I am more happy when I'm alone among the white Sisters than . . . with any of my [Indian] companions, especially Sister Catharine Crowfeather, who caused more trouble than anyone else." Nonetheless, Fr. Craft finally had in place the nucleus for the creation of the Indian sisters that he had long contemplated.

Fr. Craft arrived at St. Edward's School at Elbowoods, North Dakota, at the beginning of a cold winter. Without heat in the building and no supplies, he had six young Lakota women to care for—and, somehow, he found a way. He converted the building into both a convent (Sacred Heart) and boarding school (St. Edward's), the convent serving as the motherhouse of the Indian Benedictine Sisters. Life proved hard at the mission, but Sister Mary Catharine and the postulants carried on as best they could under Fr. Craft's direction.

Sister Mary Catharine was appointed Mother Superior of the Community by Fr. Craft. She wrote Sister Gertrude at Yankton on December 10, 1891, that the five postulants—Alice White Deer, Nellie Dubray, Jane Moccasin, Susan Bordeau, and Mary Black Eyes (a Standing Rock Lakota who had joined them later)—had received the holy habit of the Indian Congregation of the Order of St. Benedict in early December on the Feast of the Immaculate Conception.

Claudia Crowfeather, who was dying from tuberculosis, had taken her vows on December 6. Perhaps she should never have left the comforts of the Yankton motherhouse since the Belgian and Swiss sisters at Yankton did not think Claudia had long to live, and perhaps, reflecting a foreign bias, they did not think Fr. Craft would succeed in creating an order of Indian sisters. In all fairness to Fr. Craft, he had warned Claudia about the poverty and suffering that awaited her at the Sacred Heart Mission, "but she insisted on coming with us, preferring to die in labor for God and her people than to live without it." Sister Mary Theresa (as she called herself) died soon after, on December 13.

Immensely proud of Mother Mary Catharine and his Indian sisters, Fr. Craft wrote to a fellow priest that "These Indian Sisters have passed through trials that would have shaken most vocations." Their perseverance, he added, "proves that our Indian race is capable of all the good and the spiritual advantages that race prejudice has so long refused them." Fr. Craft railed against those in the church who held "the absurd theory that Indians cannot be priests or Sisters."

Fr. Craft was not alone in his suspicions. Mother Mary Catharine expressed similar reservations to Mother Gertrude at the Yankton mother-house on March 17, 1892. "We are doing well now," she wrote, "but I don't know if we will be allowed to go on. Everyone seems to want to stop us because we are Indians. I hope God will keep us; His Church seems to desert us."

The charge of bias against Indian sisters was not unfounded. The European-born sisters at Yankton and church leaders such as Fr. Stephan at the Bureau of Catholic Indian Missions shared the widespread belief that most Native Americans (especially full-bloods) could not perform at a high enough level in white institutions. But the doubt expressed was not directed only against the Indians. There were those, especially the Benedictine sisters, who doubted the ability of a diocesan priest (who belonged to no religious order and had no training in the Sisterhood) to establish a new Benedictine Order of Indian Sisters. And there were some church leaders and Bureau of Indian Affairs officials who did not like Fr. Craft, a person who challenged the authority of those who did not agree with his position.

Despite difficulties, Fr. Craft and Mother Mary Catharine moved forward with their plans. They guided the young Lakota women in Sacred Heart Convent and administered St. Edward's School. By spring 1892 ten students enrolled in the day school and ten enrolled in the boarding school. For the moment the commissioner of Indian Affairs still honored the contract with religious schools and paid St. Edwards for each pupil.

When Bishop Shanley visited Sacred Heart Mission in October 1892, he wrote his benefactor Katharine Drexel that he "found the Indian sisters happy, obedient, pious—but unspeakably poor; living on salt-pork and bread. It is Bethlehem." Bishop Shanley brought Fr. Craft and the sisters some money—$600 from Katharine Drexel and $400 from his own funds—so that, as he boasted to Miss Drexel, "one thousand dollars has started a convent and kept six Sisters and a priest one year and a half."

The bishop viewed Fr. Craft's work as an "experiment." Evidently, he too questioned the Indian sisters' ability to run a school. He told Miss Drexel: "I have some hopes of starting a good school at [Fort] Berthold next summer. The Indian community will come to Fargo and support itself by needlework. Some other teaching order will surely be found to take charge of the School." It would seem that there were few in the Catholic Church who shared the enthusiasm and faith that Fr. Craft, Mother Mary Catharine, and the Indian novices had in their ability to create an order of Indian sisters.

That faith would soon be tested further. In the spring of 1893, Mother Mary Catharine became gravely ill, suffering from tuberculosis, the same disease that struck her sister Claudia and many young Lakotas who grew up on the crowded and unhealthy reservations. She had experienced symptoms for some time. As early as August 1891 when she notified Fr. Craft that her sister Claudia was ill, she told the priest, "I think I catch cold or something that I commence cough too, and pain on my chest." In March 1892 when writing Mother Gertrude in Yankton of her sister's death, she mentioned that she also suffered all winter from a bad cold of the lungs.

Her condition deteriorated in the winter and spring of 1893. Fr. Craft wrote his artist friend, James E. Kelly, on February 6, 1893, that "Rev. Mother Catharine is still very weak. Her health has been badly shattered by hardship and anxiety." In March and April, as her consumptive condition worsened, Indian leaders came to express their respects and pray for her recovery. But there was no recovery from the dreaded disease.

On Sunday, May 2, 1893, Mother Catharine asked the sisters to dress her in full religious habit and take her to the chapel. Her habit was made from the "blood-stained and bullet torn cassock" that Fr. Craft wore at Wounded Knee, where he was stabbed in the tumult, and the crucifix she embraced was worn by Fr. Craft in the same fight. The sisters lay her on a pallet before the altar, singing Latin, English, and Lakota hymns in honor of Venerable Katari Tekakwitha. Fr. Craft said mass and distributed communion to Mother Mary Catharine and the sisters, and while he recited the prayer for the dying, Mother Mary Catharine, holding her crucifix, died.

She was twenty-six years old. At that moment of passing, Fr. Craft noted that "her Lord came for her, blessed her, and took her with him, [and] she was gone while the incense smoke still floated about the altar."

Mother Mary Catharine was buried next to her sister Claudia (Sister Mary Theresa) in the Catholic cemetery at Elbowoods, North Dakota. There they lay quietly until the 1950s, when the Corps of Engineers built the Garrison Dam and Lake Sakakawea flooded good parts of the Fort Berthold Reservation. The graves of Mother Mary Catharine and Sister Mary Theresa were relocated to Queen of Peace Cemetery near Raub, North Dakota, their gravestones incorrectly marked as "Sister Catharine, Grey Nun," and "Sister Theresa, Grey Nun."

Fr. Craft paid Mother Mary Catharine a fitting tribute:

When the story of Mother Catharine's life is told the Church will know how to appreciate her work and will understand how deeply both Church and Indians are indebted to her. By the successful establishment of her Indian congregation, under trials and difficulties more than usually cruel and severe, she has removed from her Church and her people a reproach of four centuries' standing, and triumphantly vindicated the Catholicity of her church and the spiritual and mental capacity of her race.

CHAPTER 14

Sanapia: Comanche Medicine Woman

Sanapia practiced her craft as a medicine woman and eagle doctor for many years in southwestern Oklahoma. A medicine woman cured the patient's physical ills whereas an eagle doctor cured the psychosomatic illnesses that ghosts inflicted on their victims. In 1967 David E. Jones, a young anthropologist, began an ethnographic study of her life and work. Sanapia was seventy-two years old. During their three years together, Sanapia and the young man became so close that she "adopted" him as her son.

In addition to telling her life story, Sanapia hoped to record the secrets of her profession so that her grandson could continue her work. Unsure that she would live long enough to instruct her grandson, she told her "adopted" son, "You got to write down all those medicines what I tell you . . . write it on a book and keep it until he [the grandson] gets old enough. If I'm still living two or three years, well, if I pass away then you could just tell him that . . . just to give him what you [are] taking down." Sanapia did not pass on her spiritual powers to her grandson. She died without a successor, the last Comanche eagle doctor. But the story of her remarkable life and medicine powers live on in David E. Jones's influential study, *Sanapia, Comanche Medicine Woman.*

Born at Fort Sill, Oklahoma, in the spring of 1895, Sanapia did not know the exact date of her birth, so she arbitrarily set it as May 20. Her birth name was Mary Poafpybitty, the sixth of eleven children, but the first girl in the family. (Sanapia is a pseudonym, bestowed on her by David E. Jones.)

Her father, David Poafpybitty, was a poor Comanche farmer who, as an adult, converted to Christianity and abandoned Comanche spiritual practices. He became a devoted member of the Presbyterian Church and chose to follow the customs of white society. A photograph of her father and his wife showed him with his hair cut short, posing in a dark jacket, white shirt, and tie. Sanapia had mixed feelings about her father, sometimes calling him "a good Christian man and a good father," and other times speaking of his white, Christian ways as a source of embarrassment to her mother and family.

Sanapia (Mary Poafpybitty) and family. Sanapia's father, David, is the second person standing on left and her mother, Chappy, is the third person standing on left. Sanapia is the adult woman seated.
COURTESY OF THE MUSEUM OF THE GREAT PLAINS, ARTHUR LAWRENCE COLLECTION, ID. 87-P5:663

Sanapia's mother, Chappy [Chapty] Poafpybitty, was totally different from her husband. A traditional Comanche woman who was well known for her skills as a medicine woman and an eagle doctor, she resisted her husband's attempts to introduce white customs into the home. In the same photograph described above, Chappy was attired in traditional Comanche dress, apron, sash, and buckskin moccasins. Although her mother knew and understood English, she never spoke it in a white man's presence, having Sanapia serve as her translator. Once, when Sanapia complained about the task and told her mother to speak English, her mother replied that when whites learned Comanche, she'd speak English. Somehow, despite their differences, her father and mother survived a long-term marriage.

As a young child, Sanapia was raised by her grandmother, whom she remembered fondly. Her grandmother—half Comanche, half Arapaho—encouraged her granddaughter to remember the old ways and old stories. From her early childhood days, Sanapia was urged to follow the spiritual calling of her mother, though at first she refused.

Her mother's brother, a leader in the Native American Church, whose central sacrament was the sacred use of peyote, also urged her to become

147

a medicine woman and an eagle doctor. When Sanapia suffered a serious illness, her uncle cured her, but he made the girl promise that when she came of age she would follow her mother's calling. He gave her a new name, "Memory Woman," so that she would not forget the promise she had made.

When she was seven, her parents sent Sanapia to the white boarding school at Cache Creek Mission in southern Oklahoma. She liked her teachers, all missionaries, who taught her how to read the Bible along with reading and writing English. At one point the Indian agent wanted to send some girls to Haskell, an Indian boarding school in Kansas, but Sanapia's parents, fearing for their daughter's safety, refused to let her go. During summer vacations she returned to her parents' home, where she worked hard on her father's farm.

Prior to Sanapia's last year at school, her mother offered to train her as a medicine woman during summer vacation. Although she was reluctant to begin the arduous training program, Sanapia gave in to the pressure from her mother and maternal grandmother and consented to begin the first stage of the program: that of identifying and preparing the various floral and herbal plants that a medicine doctor needed to treat illnesses.

Leaving school in 1908 at age fourteen, Sanapia returned home to begin a rigorous three-year training program designed by her mother and uncle to give her the knowledge, ethics, skills, and supernatural power (*puha*) to become a medicine woman (*puhakut*)—a course of study with which her Christian father apparently did not disagree.

Having completed the first stage of her training—the knowledge of medicinal plants—Sanapia was then instructed by her mother and uncle in diagnosing patient illness and applying the proper treatment. For the next three years, she assisted her mother and uncle in their doctoring activities, which allowed her to observe the actual treatment of patients and learn what the proper relationship should be between a doctor and patient.

Throughout this period Sanapia had "long, long talks" with her mother and uncle, who carefully instructed her about the proper behavior of a medicine woman and eagle doctor. Above all, she had to live an honorable life—the Medicine (the power/puha) demanded this. Sanapia understood that the Medicine and the puhakut are one: If she led a dishonorable life, she brought disgrace on her power. As a medicine woman and eagle doctor, she must not sing her own praises, for the healing power she possessed came through the supernatural power she received from her mother and uncle and not through her own person. She learned that a medicine doctor, out of respect for her power, must be paid for her services, but with the exception of some green cloth and tobacco, the amount must be left to the patient. And once she received payment, she must "give away" some of it to those around her as a way of honoring her medicine.

During her long training, Sanapia was closely observed by her mother, uncle, and grandparents. Each had to give their approval and blessing before the process was completed. Her maternal uncle had already given his blessing when he cured his niece from influenza in the early 1900s. Her maternal grandmother gave her blessing for her granddaughter to become a medicine woman and eagle doctor when Sanapia was fourteen years old. Next, her paternal grandfather, a "strong peyote man," gave his blessing. But the final and most important blessing came from her mother, and with her mother's blessing began the actual transfer of spiritual power.

The first stage in the transfer involved her mother installing power in Sanapia's hands and mouth, the two areas of the body where an eagle doctor's powers are best located. After her mother built a fire of pecan wood, dry leaves were placed on the hot coals and her mother sang her "Medicine" song while blessing her daughter with the rising smoke. Then her mother took a live coal from the fire with her bare hands and handed it to her daughter. At first Sanapia refused, but at her mother's insistence she took the hot coal and found it did not burn her. She felt a "chill" in her hands, which signified that the power was present.

The mother then began the transmission of supernatural power to Sanapia's mouth. She brushed two eagle feathers across her daughter's opened mouth four times, and in the course of the fourth movement, one feather disappeared. Her mother said that the feather had entered her mouth and would be a part of her. Sanapia later told Jones that she did not believe that the actual feather entered her mouth, "but rather [it was] the idea, the essence, or the Medicine which the eagle feather symbolized." The first phase ended with the mother applying red paint to Sanapia's face, forearms, and legs.

Along with the power came two powerful *tabus* or "rules." One, Sanapia could not eat any kind of fowl; if she did, the feather in her throat would kill her. Secondly, Sanapia could not allow people to pass behind her carrying food, especially meat, while she was eating. The mother explained that this was true of the eagle whose powers she carried.

The mother and uncle watched Sanapia closely for several months to make sure that she suffered no ill effects from the infusion of the eagle "power." During this period the uncle instructed his niece as to the many medicinal uses of peyote. When Sanapia showed no negative effects from the first transmission of power, her mother initiated the second stage: the magical insertion of an "eagle egg" into her daughter's stomach, which would increase her eagle power. Like the eagle feather, Sanapia believed it was the "essence" or "idea" of the eagle egg (and not the actual egg) that entered her stomach. Once again, with so much power came more tabus: Sanapia could not eat eggs or the visceral organs of animals. She found these rules so onerous that she later sought ways to circumvent the restriction.

In the third power transmission, Sanapia received from her mother and uncle her "Medicine" song. It is through her "Medicine" song that Sanapia communicates with the supernatural realm—the ultimate source of her power. When she sang her powerful "Medicine" song—which she did rarely and only in times of great need—she was actually summoning the spirits of her mother and uncle to come to her aid. She remembered the words of her mother: "When you come by yourself like that, when you don't have no place to go for help, when you got no one to lean on for help, sing this song. What you want, you going to get. I'll be listening to you. When you sing this song, I'm going to hear you singing and I'm going to help you."

One last test remained. Sanapia was instructed to spend four days and nights in seclusion and meditation in a remote place. During this time ghosts would likely struggle for control of her "medicine." Frightened, she refused to spend her nights alone in the darkness. So she went to the hill during the day and returned secretly to spend the night safely under her front porch, returning to the hill in the early morning hours. She never told her mother or uncle. (Sanapia later regretted her "cowardly" conduct.)

Sanapia returned home on the fifth morning. Her mother greeted her with the traditional blessing and for the first time addressed her daughter with the title "puhakut." Close friends of the family congratulated her with gifts; they received gifts in return for honoring Sanapia. The family sponsored a peyote meeting to announce to the community Sanapia's new status as a medicine woman and eagle doctor.

At the same time, Sanapia's elderly mother chose to end her career as a medicine woman and eagle doctor, perhaps tired of the demanding work. It was a strange move for her mother to make since Sanapia could not begin her career as a medicine woman and eagle doctor for many years until after menopause. Later, Sanapia questioned the wisdom of mother-daughter succession, especially if the mother withdrew from the profession (as her mother did), since it meant that the people would have no eagle doctor until the daughter in question became eligible. The problem, of course, would not arise if a mother installed her power in a son.

When Sanapia became a puhakut at seventeen, her mother and older brother decided she should marry. Her brother had a good friend, a hard worker, who spent one summer on their father's farm. Her mother liked the young man and encouraged her daughter to marry him. Admitting to Jones that she was young and didn't think much about marriage or love, she nonetheless followed her mother's suggestion. She bore one child but then, strangely, left her husband at the urging of her mother. Jones merely recorded the incident without any explanation for the sudden end of the marriage or why Sanapia's mother changed her mind about the young man. But Sanapia told a different story to Letha Barksdale, who interviewed her on July 13, 1967. She confessed to Ms. Barksdale that she divorced her first husband because he chased other women.[1]

A year later Sanapia married a second time to a man she was fond of and with whom she had a son and daughter. When he died in the early 1930s, she was emotionally devastated, reacting to her profound grief by drinking excessively, engaging in sexual promiscuity, compulsive gambling, and outbursts of temper. Sanapia called these years "the time I was roughing it out."

During this terrible time in her life, Sanapia's sister approached with a plea to cure her sick child. It was a fateful moment in her life. At first she refused her sister's request, perhaps feeling ashamed of her bad behavior and doubting her power to do good. But remembering her mother's instruction that a medicine doctor could not refuse to help someone in need, Sanapia went with her sister and cured the child. "I thought that was some kind of sign," she told Jones, "so I thought that I might try to make something out of this doctoring." The cure of her sister's child had reawakened her spiritual calling.

When Sanapia married for a third time in the early 1940s, she abruptly put an end to her wild ways. After menopause she earnestly began her long

---

1   Ms. Letha Barksdale's interview with Mary Poafpybitty Neido/Sanapia can be found in the Doris Duke Oral History Collection at the University of Oklahoma's Western History Collections, Vol. 28, ID # 103, Document # T-89.

career among the Comanches as a medicine woman and eagle doctor. She was still practicing when Jones met her in the late 1960s.

Sanapia's healing powers were unique. According to Jones's analysis, she blended the three great religious influences of her life: "the Christianity of her father, the peyotism of her uncle and paternal grandfather, and the more customary Plains pattern of vision quests and guardian spirits as embodied by her mother, the eagle doctor."

Although not formally a Christian like her father, Sanapia drew inspiration for her work from the New Testament where Jesus, and then later his disciples, had the power to heal those afflicted in mind and body. Like the disciples, Sanapia believed that she drew from Jesus the power in her hands to cure the sick. The same was true of peyote. She believed that peyote was good medicine given by God to Indians to help them cure sickness. Sanapia attended peyote meetings, but did not believe she had to be a formal member of the Native American Church to use peyote in her cures, arguing it belonged to anybody who needed it. And, like her traditionalist mother, Sanapia was infused with the power of the eagle. "The eagle," she said, "got more power than anything living. . . . It's got Medicine to help people get well . . . to cure them."

Jones estimated that each year Sanapia treated some twenty patients suffering from various illnesses and doctored six cases of ghost sickness. She kept her medicines in a leather "travel case." Because her "medicines" were sacred and powerful, she allowed no one to touch the box or its contents. With Sanapia's permission Jones has left a detailed description of the contents of her travel case, which he broke down into non-botanical and botanical medicines.

Sanapia's most revered non-botanical item was the tail feather from a golden eagle: the spiritual source of her medicine power. She wrapped the feather and all her medicines in black cloth, a symbol of her power as a medicine woman. Sanapia employed the feather to "fan" smoke from smoldering cedar coals over her patients and to "tap" or "fan" her patients four times (a sacred number) so that the power of the eagle would cure them.

In addition, she carried in her travel case four crow tail feathers to be tied on the door of the house as a protective amulet against ghosts. Slivers of glass were used to make very small incisions in the flesh of her patients while drawing blood, after which she sucked away the sickness (like a headache or vertigo) using a "sucking horn." For children she had a small piece of white otter fur or four porcupine quills placed on live coals, using the smoke as a cure. To strengthen bones and treat sprains, Sanapia had "bone medicine" ground into a powder and mixed with water. "Indian lard" was used as a "salve" to treat severe burns and liquefied as a remedy for constipation. After every treatment she applied "red paint," the color of the earth, calling upon mother earth to bless her patients. Finally, she carried a Bible, something her mother had not done, to pray to Jesus for power to cure her patients.

Sanapia collected her botanical medicines in the late fall when they were completely matured. Jones provided a long list of her medicinal plants, listing each plant by its Comanche name, followed by Sanapia's description, then the Latin designation, and finally its popular American name. (I have chosen to follow the American designation.) She believed that the sun and the earth powered the growth of the medicine plant, and accordingly, she collected mostly the root (surrounded by earth) or the top of the plant (fueled by the sun). The roots were cut, cleansed with water, and properly stored for use.

Peyote was Sanapia's most utilized medicine—the most powerful plant in her arsenal to cure sickness. She used it as a painkiller and sedative, giving the patient four peyote buttons to eat. For colds, pneumonia, and internal disorder, she gave the patient "peyote tea" (the buttons were dried, pulverized, and boiled in water). For localized pain—arthritis, severe headaches, and heart pains—Sanapia applied thin slices of peyote to the affected area. Like peyote, the "red berry cedar" had widespread use, and after every treatment she sprinkled dry cedar leaves on hot coals and fanned the cedar smoke over her patients in a blessing ceremony. For women suffering menstrual cramps, she used the dry pulverized root of the cedar mixed in water.

She gathered a wide assortment of plant materials that she used to treat a variety of illnesses. Sanapia collected "sneezeweed" in the early fall, drying and pulverizing the flowers. Patients suffering from sinus congestion or head colds could breathe the dust through an inhaler that she invented for this purpose. "Mescal beans" were ground, pulverized, and boiled; Sanapia used the liquid as eardrops for earaches and sores deep in the ear. She used the powdered root of the "prickly ash" to treat toothaches and burns. The root of the "iris" plant, which Sanapia's mother transplanted from eastern Oklahoma at an earlier time, was mixed in water to treat colds, upset stomach, and sore throat. Sanapia treated insect and spider bites by applying moist pulp—she chewed leaves from the "gray sage" plant—over the affected areas of her patient. For external signs of eczema and rashes, Sanapia gathered the flowers of the "broomweed" plant, which she boiled into a jelly and then applied over the affected areas.

The traditional Comanche of the twentieth-century reservation era still believed in ghosts. When afflicted, the victims could call upon the special services of Sanapia, one of the last eagle doctors among the Comanches who knew how to cure "ghost sickness."

Since Sanapia had never seen a ghost (she believed that ghosts were afraid of her powers), she was not absolutely sure of their essence. Sometimes she thought ghosts were the spirits of evil men that lingered after their deaths; sometimes she thought that ghosts were "malevolent" forces that roamed the earth, not necessarily the spirits of deceased evil men. In either case these dark forces caused harm to old-time Comanches who believed in such spirits. Ghosts (perhaps assuming some "humanlike" shape) usually afflicted their victims in the dark of night when a person was most susceptible and frightened. In the daylight ghosts showed themselves in the "whirlwinds" or "dust devils" that blew in semi-arid southern Oklahoma.

When a ghost struck, it had the power to "deform his victims, usually by causing contortions of the facial muscles and in some instances paralysis of hands and arms." Sanapia called this distortion of the body "ghost sickness" or "twisted face." She said that this facial paralysis was not the result of a stroke, as some white persons alleged. She could tell the crucial difference: The victims who suffered from "ghost sickness" gave off "an offensive odor" and possessed "an aura of evil," neither of which were present in a stroke victim.

Sanapia shared with Jones the elaborate treatment for curing "ghost sickness." It began when the person afflicted with "ghost sickness" sent an intermediary—preferably an older woman—to arrange the preliminaries for the first interview between the patient and the puhakut. At the time of the first interview, the afflicted person humbly requested her help, which, as an eagle doctor, she could not refuse. The patient offered the standard ritual items of payment: a piece of dark green cloth, a small bag of Bull Durham tobacco, and four corn-husk cigarette papers. The patient rolled a cigarette, took four puffs, and then handed it to Sanapia who, in turn, took four puffs to seal the contract between them.[2] After smoking, Sanapia said to the patient, "Tell me your troubles." It was during this conversation that she made her diagnosis and decided on her treatment.

After this interview Sanapia instructed the patient to bathe in the stream near her house, for given the nature of the treatment, it was essential that the patient be clean. She treated her patient three times daily—at sunrise, midday, and sunset—for two days. At sunrise, on the day she began treatment, Sanapia (accompanied by the patient) prayed to the earth and the sun, which the eagle was associated with, and which are considered the two greatest sources of power in the nomadic Comanche culture.

After prayer Sanapia placed cedar on live coals, empowering her eagle feather by waving it four times through the smoke, then cleansing herself with the smoke. Finally, she fanned the patient with her eagle feather. After that she took the Bible and prayed to "God and Jesus and especially the Holy Ghost" to help her cure the patient. Next she handled "Chief Peyote," drawing its power into her hands. When it was over, she had appealed for spiritual assistance from three power sources: the eagle, Christianity, and peyote.

After these preliminary moves, Sanapia began the treatment proper, placing the root of the bekwinatsu plant (milkweed), one of her major medicines, in her mouth and masticating it to a moist pulp. (She said that the bekwinatsu plant, along with peyote and cedar, possessed supernatural power.) She spewed some of it over the patient's face, head, and arms, and then rubbed some of the moist pulp over the afflicted bodily areas. Finally, she asked the patient to swallow the remainder of this pulp. Sanapia then chewed another piece of the bekwinatsu root together with a few leaves of sweet sage and then applied her mouth to the "contorted areas of the patient's face to suck out the sickness."

After this first session, Sanapia placed cedar on live coals and fanned the patient with the smoke, then "smoked" the eagle feather and herself. After this she washed her hands and rinsed her mouth to destroy any "poison" that remained. The first treatment was over.

At midday, for the second treatment, Sanapia followed the same ritual as at sunrise. After this session she determined if progress had been made. If

---

2   Ernest Wallace and E. Adamson Hoebel, *The Comanches: Lords of the Southern Plains*, p. 180, stated that "when smoking ceremonially, it was [for the Comanches] an oath, a signature to an agreement, a pledge on the part of the smoker."

so, she continued the same treatment at sunset, but, if not, then she intensified her effort by organizing a special peyote meeting. She repeated the same ritual used in the earlier sessions, but with the patient chewing four peyote buttons and drinking a special peyote "tea." Sanapia spewed the same peyote tea over the patient's afflicted face, head, and hands.

If peyote failed to cure the patient, Sanapia invoked her ultimate source of power, the calling of her Medicine Eagle through the intercession of her mother and uncle. She did this only at the sunset ceremony on the second day. After the usual ritual treatment, she sang her medicine song, at first with the patient and then by herself, singing the song over and over late into the night until the spirits of her mother and uncle appear to help her as they promised long ago. On two rare occurrences in her life, the Medicine Eagle appeared before her, and with this power—the medicine feather and medicine smoke—she could cure her patient. On the morning of the third day, she prayed with the cured patient, painted his body red, and gave him the traditional blessing. The "doctoring" was over.

Over a long career as an eagle doctor, Sanapia cured many patients of the "ghost sickness," but not all. If by the morning of the third day the patient had not recovered, she began the treatment again for two more days. If the patient had not recovered by the end of the fourth day, Sanapia had to admit that her powers were not sufficient to cure the person, and she suggested that he visit the white doctor to find what comfort the doctor could offer. But she really knew that the patient was going to die, though she could not bring herself to tell him that sad news. She made this judgment based on long years of diagnosing patients' physical conditions and an inner "voice" that tells her, "He's dead right now, he's dead right now."

Sanapia served as a medicine woman and eagle doctor for some thirty years among the Comanches, proud that she possessed the spiritual power necessary to cure people of their ills, physical or psychosomatic. Jones reported that Sanapia doctored people from other tribes in the area as well: Wind River Shoshones, Southern Cheyennes, Northern Arapaho, Kiowa, and Kiowa-Apache. But she knew that among the Comanches she was a controversial figure.

Comanches who held to the old ways of life respected the wisdom and spiritual gifts of Sanapia. A Kiowa woman whose niece was treated by Sanapia offered a favorable opinion: "She sure is a good old woman . . . pretty for an old woman too. . . . I took my niece to her once and she cared for her and got her well in a few days. I tell other people about how she took care of my little girl and they might go to see her if they get sick bad or if their family might get sick."

However, younger and more assimilated Comanches thought that Sanapia was an "eccentric old woman." Some thought that she was "ridiculous"; others doubted her medicine powers, and still others feared her power as evil. One informant captured for Jones all the negative opinions about Sanapia: "I don't know much about it. I've heard some of my people talking about an old woman who lives south from here. They say she can curse you if she wants to and make you sick. . . . She supposed to be a bad one, but I never seen her. I don't believe that s[t]uff about curses myself but a lot of people . . . Indian people . . . do. You better watch out. They say she can do it." The Comanche make no basic distinction between a medicine man and a sorcerer. Medicine was a two-edged sword that could be used for good or evil. There is no record that Sanapia ever used her power to harm anyone.

Sanapia feared that as the Comanches moved into the modern white world, they would have less need of her services, yet she desperately sought a successor to carry on the family tradition. A medicine woman should transmit her powers to her favorite daughter, but Sanapia's daughter had no interest in acquiring her mother's power. Sanapia told Jones that her daughter was "too much like a white man." Sanapia's younger son tried to follow his mother's path, but she ruled him out because he lacked sincerity. Her next choice was her grandson, but she feared that her daughter would not allow it.

During Jones's stay with Sanapia, her eldest son seemed like a possible successor. She had not considered him because he had moved away from Comanche society. However, in his late forties the son changed, taking a renewed interest in the Comanche language and peyote. Besides, he was a person of good character, so essential for a Comanche eagle doctor. Sanapia spoke to him about becoming a medicine man and eagle doctor and he agreed to think about it, but did not take up his mother's calling. Because Sanapia's request presented a hard choice for her children, none followed her path.

Sanapia understood that as her people moved increasingly into the white world, they would have less need for the puhakut's services. She confessed to Jones that she had outlived her times. Jones said that when he and Sanapia spent time in Oklahoma City and Wichita, watching cars on the highway, the tall skyscrapers, and the crowds of white people, she "would speak of the incongruity of herself and the twentieth-century world in which she live[d]."

Speaking of her grandmother who predicted all this change, Sanapia said, "Maybe I should be with her now because my way is getting no good up to today. Maybe I should be dead too. Even my own kids growing up like white peoples, and they think I'm just a funny old woman. I know they do! But I ain't got too many more years to go yet. And here, you, a white person asking me all those old ways and my kids go around here and there and don't even talk to me about those things. It is sure is funny, ain't it?"

Sanapia died in January 1979 (some accounts date her death in 1984), the last of the Comanche eagle doctors, the last practitioner of an ancient Comanche tradition. But the spirit of her life and work lives on for future generations in David E. Jones's splendid ethnographic biography, *Sanapia: Comanche Medicine Woman*.

CHAPTER 15

The La Flesche Sisters: Walking in Two Worlds

The La Flesche sisters—Susette, Rosalie, Susan, and Marguerite—are recognized as among the most important biracial Indian women in nineteenth-century America, having left their mark on their Omaha tribe and the larger Euro-American world. As they moved between the two worlds, they were profoundly influenced by their parents, especially their father, Joseph La Flesche Jr.

Joseph La Flesche Jr. was biracial: His father, Joseph La Flesche Sr., was a French-Canadian fur trader; his mother, Watunna, was most likely a member of the Ponca tribe. When young Joseph was around five, his mother left her husband and married a member of the Omaha tribe. The young boy lived with his mother and, for some time, with his aunts. In his early teens Joseph went to live with his father, hunting and trading among the Missouri River tribes and living for a time in St. Louis, where he learned French. So Joseph's worldview expanded beyond the boundaries of the Ponca/Omaha tribes to the larger Euro-American world.

In the late 1830s Joseph and his father worked at Peter Sarpy's trading post in Bellevue, Nebraska, the heart of Omaha country. Here young Joseph spent less time with his father hunting and trapping and more time with the Omahas, especially the chiefs and older men, who instructed him in tribal ways. Joseph had decided to live his life with the Omahas, but, given his contact with the outside world, he believed early on that if the Omahas were to prevail as a people, they would have to adapt to the ways of the advancing white world.

It was at the trading post that young Joseph met Mary Gale, Sarpy's stepdaughter, who was biracial. Her father, Dr. John Gale, was an American army doctor stationed at Fort Atkinson; her mother, Nicomi, was of mixed Omaha/Oto/Iowa heritage. When Dr. Gale was ordered back to St. Louis, Nicomi remained behind, keeping the child under her care. After Gale's death his friend Peter Sarpy married Nicomi and raised Mary as his own. Despite attending school in St. Louis, where she learned French and perhaps some English, the young woman was proudly Indian and, like her mother, spoke only the Omaha language.

Joseph La Flesche Jr. and Mary Gale married sometime in 1845–1846. In 1848 Mary gave birth to her first child, Louis, who did not live to adulthood. Four girls followed. The daughters—Susette, Rosalie, Susan, and Marguerite—all thrived and, drawing from their parents' guidance, brought prestige to the La Flesche name.

At some point Joseph caught the attention of Chief Big Elk, who shared the young man's concern for the future of the Omahas in an ever-expanding white world and accepted Joseph into the family's clan. In the tribal census for 1848, Joseph La Flesche took the name Estahmaza, "Iron Eye." Some five years later, when Young Elk (Big Elk's son) died, Iron Eye became one of the principal chiefs of the Omahas.[1]

In his capacity as chief, Joseph went to Washington, D.C., in 1854 and negotiated a treaty with the United States by which the Omaha ceded their hunting grounds north of the Platte River and west of the Missouri River, receiving in exchange a permanent reservation of roughly 300,000 acres of land bordering the Missouri River (some seventy miles north of present-day Omaha City) and the promise of $40,000 in goods and cash annually for forty years.

The tribe selected a spot located on Blackbird Creek near the Missouri and moved to their new location. In the summer of 1855, Joseph at first built an earth lodge, but within two years he erected a two-story frame house that served as a residence for his family and a place for his trading operation. Norma Kidd Green, in her comprehensive study titled *Iron Eye's Family: The Children of Joseph La Flesche*, claimed that Joseph was the first Plains Indian to build his own frame house. He cleared the rich bottomland near the river and planted corn, wheat, potatoes, fruit, and vegetables, and he encouraged his followers—the "young men's party"—to likewise build frame houses in their new village and farm the rich land. Some nineteen of his followers did so. Traditionalists who lived in earth lodges called it, with some suspicion, "the village of 'make-believe' white men."

Joseph persuaded the Presbyterian missionaries to follow the Omaha tribe from Bellevue to the new reservation, where they built a mission and school.

---

1   Some scholars maintain that Joseph succeeded Big Elk, but John M. O'Shea has made a compelling case in "Omaha Chieftainship in the Nineteenth Century," *Ethnohistory,* 39 (Summer 1992), 329–30, 338–39, 347, fn. 5, that Joseph succeeded Big Elk's son.

Encouraging young Omahas to study in the white man's school and listen to the teachings of the missionaries, he argued that they would all have to live in the white man's world. His own children all attended the mission school, and over time Joseph and his family became close to the Presbyterian Church.

By the 1860s Joseph recognized dramatic changes in the Omaha's world; so, when the time came for Joseph to pierce his son's ears and tattoo his daughters with a red dot on the forehead and a blue four-pointed star on the throat, he refused to do so. When asked why he failed to follow the ancient ceremonies, Joseph replied: "I was always sure that my sons and daughters would live to see the time when they would have to mingle with the white people, and I determined that they should not have any mark put upon them that might be detrimental in their future surroundings."

While Joseph urged his people to adopt some aspects of the dominant society, he never advocated complete assimilation into the white world, nor did he ever deride those members of his tribe who maintained the traditional ways of life. He continued to maintain the Omaha language in everyday life and went on the annual buffalo hunt well into the 1870s. Like many Omaha men, Joseph engaged in polygamy. In the mid-1850s he married an Omaha woman named Tainne (Elizabeth Esau) and had three children with her: Francis, Lucy, and Carey. His relationship with his wives is controversial. As he drew closer to the Presbyterian Church, Joseph separated from Tainne in the mid-1870s. Perhaps after converting to Christianity, Joseph did not feel it proper to have two wives. In any case he continued to provide for Tainne and their children.

Joseph found value in the Euro-American ideas of white education, Christianity, commercial farming, allotment of land, and citizenship. But he insisted that such ideas be accepted within the context of Omaha society— at best a difficult task, a delicate balancing between two cultures; at worst a threat to Omaha culture and traditions. By following his lead, Joseph's daughters chose a tough path.

Susette La Flesche Tibbles was born in an earth lodge in 1854, probably in the Omaha's principle village of Bellevue near the Missouri River in what whites called Nebraska Territory. A year later the child accompanied her parents as they relocated to the new reservation. When she was around three years of age, she underwent the traditional "Turning of the Child Ceremony," which recognized the child as a formal member of the Omaha tribe. It was at this ceremony that she received her tribal name, Inshta Theamba, "Bright Eyes."[2] None present at the ceremony could have imagined that one day this little girl's tribal name would be known throughout the United States.

As a young girl, Bright Eyes experienced some aspects of traditional Omaha society, living briefly in her parents' earth lodge and later, when her father built a frame house, often staying in her "oldest" grandmother's earth lodge, where she listened to traditional stories and ate delicious cakes made of parched ground corn, honey, and buffalo marrow. She spoke the Omaha language, accompanied her father on the annual buffalo hunt, and observed traditional Omaha rites. But the Omaha world was changing, and Joseph La Flesche knew that his daughter would have to embark on a new journey that allowed her to live in the coming white world.

When Susette was six, her father sent her to study at the reservation's Presbyterian mission school. Unlike other students, Susette had received her English name from her father, not the school teachers. Living at the school six days a week, she dressed like a white girl, in a wide calico skirt and loose blouse with long sleeves and high neck, buttoned up the back. She spoke only English and learned to read and write in English. Excelling in her studies, Susette developed a love of books and learned domestic skills. All the students were exposed to the Christian faith, especially on Sundays. While Susette liked school and her teachers, who influenced her life, she took pleasure in Saturdays when she returned home as Bright Eyes, surrounded by her loving Omaha family.

The Presbyterian mission school closed in 1869 after losing federal funding. Susette was fourteen, too old to attend the daytime agency school. Then, in 1872, Miss Read, a former teacher at the mission school who was now headmistress at the Elizabeth Institute for Young Ladies in Elizabeth, New Jersey, offered Susette a scholarship. At the age of eighteen, Susette left the reservation to attend the new school, becoming the first Omaha woman to travel so far away for an education. She spent three years at the Elizabeth Institute, excelling in her studies and graduating with honors in 1875.

Susette returned to the Omaha Reservation with the intent of teaching in the agency day school, but the Indian agent rejected her application.

---

2   Dorothy Clarke Wilson's *Bright Eyes: The Story of Susette La Flesche, an Omaha Indian* is one of the few full-length biographical studies on Susette's life. It is well researched but contains invented dialogue and scenes that are more literary in nature than historical.

Susette "Bright Eyes" La Flesche Tibbles COURTESY OF NEBRASKA STATE HISTORICAL SOCIETY, RG2026.PHO.000005

Susette refused to back down. She wrote a letter to the commissioner of Indian Affairs and reminded him that by law, a qualified Indian deserved preference over a white person. She called it a "farce" to educate and "civilize" Indians and then deny them the opportunity to use their knowledge. She closed by threatening to go to the press and expose the injustice.

The commissioner insisted that Susette had to pass a state examination and send in a certificate from the Nebraska school committee. The Omaha agent refused permission for her to leave the agency to take the test, but

Susette slipped away, and then took and passed the exam. Her persistence paid off in 1877 when she was finally offered a teaching position in the agency school at twenty dollars per month, half of what a white teacher received. But it was a start. Assigned to an old schoolhouse two miles from her home, Susette moved into the house and started teaching. In time, with the help of the Presbyterian minister, she started a Sunday school and, with her own money, bought a small organ to expose her students to music.

Susette spent two years absorbed in teaching but remained fully aware of what was happening in the larger white/Indian world around her. Fluent in English and Omaha, many of her Omaha neighbors came to her for help, far from the agent's eyes, to write letters to various Indian Bureau officials in Washington on their behalf.

Meanwhile Susette followed the plight of the neighboring Poncas, who had been forced to leave their homes and fields along the Niobrara River in northeastern Nebraska and sent south to Indian Territory in 1878. She and her father were especially concerned because one of the Ponca leaders was White Swan, Joseph's half brother. The Poncas were the victims of Washington's ignorance: In 1868 congressional peace commissioners had negotiated a treaty with the Lakotas that inadvertently included Ponca territory. Despite their innocence, the Poncas were forced south.[3]

Suffering in Indian Territory from extreme heat, lack of food, and disease, many Poncas died. On January 2, 1879, Chief Standing Bear and some thirty Poncas, mostly women and children, left Indian Territory and headed north to their homeland on the Niobrara River. Chief Standing Bear had promised his dying son that the boy's bones would be buried with his ancestors in their native land. In early March the weary and hungry travelers reached the Omaha Reservation, where Joseph La Flesche gave them food and shelter as well as a plot of land, tools, and seeds to grow food.

Despite the Omaha embrace, soldiers arrived in March and arrested the Poncas for leaving Indian Territory without permission. They were taken to Fort Omaha and imprisoned until their return south. The plight of Chief Standing Bear aroused a number of Nebraskans, lay and religious, who spoke out against the imprisonment and organized the Omaha Ponca Relief Committee, which filed suit in federal court charging that the Poncas had been deprived of their civil rights under the Fourteenth Amendment.

---

3   Joe Starita's "I Am a Man": Chief Standing Bear's Journey for Justice is one of the best accounts that documents the trials of Chief Standing Bear and the Poncas.

Thomas H. Tibbles, a crusading reporter for the *Omaha Herald*, became a leading advocate for Chief Standing Bear and the Poncas.

Tibbles needed an Omaha to write on behalf of the Poncas, so Omaha elders entrusted Susette with the task. She wrote an eloquent account of the plight of the Poncas and their betrayal by the United States government. On April 30, 1879, Susette met Tibbles at the trial in Omaha—the beginning of a relationship that would change her life. She and her father were thrilled with Judge Elmer Dundy's decision that the Poncas were "persons" under the law and could not be imprisoned without cause. Standing Bear was free but still without a home, since the federal government planned to appeal the decision.

The Omaha Ponca Relief Committee then planned a larger campaign on behalf of the Poncas: an eastern lecture tour with Tibbles and Chief Standing Bear designed to heighten public awareness of the issues. Another purpose of the tour was to raise cash to finance their long-range plans: first, to push the issue of Indian citizenship all the way to the Supreme Court, if necessary; and, second, to restore the Poncas to their rightful land along the Niobrara River.

Needing information about the plight of the Poncas in Indian Territory, the committee suggested that Joseph and Susette visit their relatives in the south. Father and daughter were shocked at the desperate condition of the Poncas. When the La Flesches returned, Episcopal Bishop Robert Clarkson, a member of the committee, asked Susette to present her findings before a largely white audience in an Omaha church. Shy by nature, she accepted the invitation with some trepidation. Tibbles attended, doubtful that this small Indian woman could command a large, white crowd. He observed that she stood nervously at the podium for some time. Then she began to speak "in a rich voice which carried clearly to the crowded church steps." Tibbles took notes. Susette spoke with passion and simple eloquence about the plight of the Poncas and closed her speech on a personal, even bitter note:

> *The soldiers drive Standing Bear and his wife and children from the land that belonged to him and his fathers before him—at the point of a bayonet; and on the way [south to Indian Territory] his daughter [Prairie Flower] dies from the hardship of the journey. The Christian ladies of Milford, Nebraska, come to the Indian camp, pray for the dying girl, and give her Christian burial. Oh, the perplexities of this thing they*

*call civilization! Part of the white people murder my girl companion
and another part tenderly bury her, while her old father stands over her
grave and says: "My heart breaks."*

Overwhelmed with emotion, Susette suddenly stopped speaking. But
the silence was broken by the audience, which went wild in their enthusiasm, with some women weeping openly and men loudly shouting their
support for the Poncas.

The Omaha Ponca Relief Committee was so impressed they decided
that Susette should accompany the lecture tour to interpret for Chief Standing Bear and speak in her own voice about the plight of the Indians. Shy
and reserved, uncomfortable with large crowds and public speaking, Susette
was reluctant to go. At first Joseph refused to send his unmarried daughter
so far from home to strange cities surrounded by white men not members of
her family. But when word came that Congress entertained a bill to remove
the Omahas to Indian Territory, Joseph relented. He allowed Susette to go
on the condition that his twenty-two-year-old son, Francis, a child from his
second wife, accompany the tour and serve as her guardian.

The group left in October of 1879 and traveled by train to Chicago,
where they were well received. After a brief stop in Pittsburgh, they moved on
to Boston, which many considered the country's literary and reform capital.

Sadly, tragic news followed on their way to Boston: Tibbles's wife,
Amelia, had died, leaving behind two children cared for by family and
friends, and Chief Standing Bear's brother had been shot by a soldier. The
tour nearly ended, but Standing Bear, despite his sorrow, urged a depressed
Tibbles to continue with the lecture tour.

Warmly welcomed in Boston, they spoke in churches, meeting halls,
and private homes, and at receptions and dinners. Throughout the demanding trip, Susette often suffered from exhaustion. But when Tibbles tried to
shield Susette from the endless speeches, receptions, and handshaking, she
always replied, "The lives of my father, brothers, and sisters, and of thousands of other Indians depend upon the success of this agitation. Everything
else has failed for a hundred years. It is better for me to die than all the
Indians should be exterminated."

On stage the tall, dignified Chief Standing Bear stood dressed in full
Indian regalia. Francis dressed handsomely in eastern clothes and eventually
took up the task of interpreting for Chief Standing Bear. While Susette did

some interpreting, she delivered prepared speeches. Dressed in a simple black dress, with a white collar and a bonnet framing her face, she made a fine impression on her audience as she spoke in eloquent English about the plight of the Indians. Reporters who covered the lectures referred to Susette by her Omaha name, Bright Eyes, sometimes Inshta Theamba.

They made their first presentation at the Horticultural Hall in October. Chief Standing Bear told the tragic story of his people as Susette interpreted. Then she spoke with simple eloquence. She thanked the people of Boston for their sympathy and help. She shared the tragic story of the Poncas: the loss of their ancestral homeland, the forced march south, Chief Standing Bear's desperate flight home, and his fight for the right to return to his land. She ended on a strong note: "Your government has no right to say to us, Go here, or Go there, and if we show any reluctance, to force us to do its will at the point of a bayonet." She asked, "Do you wonder that the Indian feels outraged by such treatment. . . . Oh, I wish I could tell you the story as it should be told!" The room erupted in applause and someone presented her with a bouquet of flowers.

The trio also spoke before five hundred Boston businessmen at the Merchant Exchange. Susette followed Chief Standing Bear and Tibbles. After a long speech, she closed with a simple but profound question that became central to her thinking. What did her people want? "It is a little thing," she said, "a simple thing, which my people ask of a nation whose watchword is liberty; but it is endless in its consequences. They ask for liberty, and law is liberty." Bright Eyes understood her American audience, which prided itself on its founding principles as a nation.

Tibbles was taken aback by the profundity of Susette's declaration that "law is liberty." He suggested in his autobiography, *Buckskin and Blanket Days*, that Susette's declaration was spontaneous—that she realized the power of liberty when she observed that Bostonians moved about freely (they were citizens under the law) whereas her people (wards of the government) could not freely leave the reservation. But it's more likely that Susette had been thinking of this question for some time because she penned the very same words—that "law is liberty"—in the introduction she wrote for Tibbles's book *The Ponca Chiefs*, which came out while they were on tour.

While in Boston Bright Eyes met many famous figures, but the three most memorable were Henry Wadsworth Longfellow, Helen Hunt Jackson, and Alice C. Fletcher. She met Longfellow, one of her favorite poets, at a private reception. He gave her a copy of his poem *Hiawatha* as they held a long, private conversation. At the end Longfellow told Tibbles: "I've been a student of the English language all my life, and I would give all I possess if I could speak it with the simplicity, fluency, and force used by that Indian girl."

The writer Helen Hunt Jackson attended one of the lectures. She was so impressed with Chief Standing Bear and Bright Eyes that she became an ardent champion of the Ponca cause and Bright Eyes's friend. A few years later Helen Hunt Jackson published *A Century of Dishonor*, a passionate account of Washington's betrayal of the American Indian.

Alice C. Fletcher, a noted anthropologist at the Peabody Museum in Boston, became a lifelong friend of Susette and the Omahas. But she connected best with Francis La Flesche, who shared his wide knowledge of his people. Friends and collaborators, they worked together for years studying Omaha culture and in 1911 published their findings in a classic work, *The Omaha Tribe*.

On December 2, 1879, they gave their last lecture in Boston at the famous Faneuil Hall, the cradle of American liberty. Susette was the first women to speak at Faneuil Hall. They left Boston, having raised considerable money for the cause and made important friends.

The quartet continued its exhausting journey to New York City, where they were warmly received, the reporters fascinated with Bright Eyes's dress and appearance. Next they went to New Jersey, where Susette had the pleasure of seeing her sisters Marguerite and Susan, who were studying at the Elizabeth Institute for Young Ladies. The next stop was Quaker Philadelphia, where Susette declared that "the solution of the Indian problem, so called, is citizenship." By February they arrived in the nation's capital.

Chief Standing Bear and Bright Eyes testified before a Senate subcommittee investigating the Ponca removal. Bright Eyes was invited to the White House for an informal meeting with President Rutherford B. Hayes and his wife, during which the president shared his concern with the plight of the Poncas. This quiet, eloquent, and passionate young Omaha woman had come a long way. Only a few years before, she had struggled to find a teaching position in an agency day school; now she was meeting with the president of the United States.

Having been gone a long time, the four returned home in the summer. Despite an exhausting trip, they had raised money for the cause, aroused the public conscience, and even stirred politicians in Washington to address the question of the Poncas' removal. Although the Poncas had suffered such an injustice that they could never be made whole, in time they received a small measure of justice. Washington provided land and financial compensation for the Ponca tribe in Indian Territory and Nebraska to rebuild. Chief Standing Bear's refugees, who had endured so much, finally received a parcel of land in their ancestral homeland on the Niobrara River.

Susette was happy to be home but, after the drama of the past seven months, struggled to find herself. Encouraged by Helen Hunt Jackson, she started to write, completing a children's story, "Newadi," about her great-grandmother and Omaha life, published by *St. Nicholas* magazine. Susette also worked with Tibbles on a novel, *Ploughed Under, the Story of an Indian Chief.* She wrote the introduction, in which she stated that the answer to the vexed "Indian question" was citizenship, protection under the law, and freedom from the Indian Bureau. She added a bitter note: "The huge plow of the 'Indian System' has run for a hundred years, beam down, turning down into the darkness of the earth every hope and aspiration which we have cherished."

Susette did not generally attack white people as such. After all, she had become friends with white missionaries, school teachers, and eastern reformers. Still, she had her moments of doubt about the loss her people suffered with the coming of whites. In June 1883 *Wide Awake*, a children's magazine, published her story "Omaha Legends and Tent Stories." "When thinking of those old days," she wrote, "so happy and free, when we slept night after night in a tent on the wide trackless prairie, with nothing but the skies above us and the earth beneath; with nothing to make us afraid; not even knowing that we were not civilized, or were ordered to be by the government; not even knowing that there were such beings as white men; happy in our freedom and our love for each other—I often wonder if there is anything in your civilization which will make good to us what we have lost. I sometimes think not, unless it be the wider, fuller knowledge of God and his Word."

Her life took an unexpected turn in 1881 when Thomas Tibbles proposed marriage. He was fifteen years older with two daughters, but she accepted his offer. Married on July 23, 1881, in the mission chapel, Susette wore a wedding dress provided by her eastern friends. Her father and mother and sisters approved the marriage, but Francis disliked Tibbles from the beginning and did not attend the wedding.

The couple spent their first year in Omaha with the two children, during which time Susette found the transition difficult, especially relating to Tibbles's daughters. But the family moved to a house near the Omaha Agency within the year, where the girls attended the mission school. Surrounded by her loving family, Susette's relationship with the girls improved. At the same time, new tension arose within the La Flesche family. Politics and land were the issues.

The Omahas were preoccupied with the question of land in the early 1880s. Congress passed an allotment act in 1882 that granted land to individual members of the Omaha tribe. The division of land challenged tribal unity, but it seemed the safest way to protect their land. Alice Fletcher and Francis (who worked for the BIA in Washington) were charged with the task of apportioning the land. Miss Fletcher persuaded the Omahas to select their farmland in the rich Logan Valley. Joseph and his extended family (including Susette) relocated near the town of Bancroft to begin farming their allotted land. Tibbles built a sod house on Susette's land.

The Omahas, secure in their allotments, looked ahead: They developed plans for self-government and land management. After allotment, thousands of acres of tribal land remained for development. The Omaha created a rich pastureland, which white cattlemen could lease for a fee, the income shared with all the people. Rosalie La Flesche and her husband, Ed Farley, played a major role in managing this pastureland.

However, the highly opinionated Tibbles disagreed. He and Susette thought the programs were ill-advised and premature. They advised the Omahas to press for citizenship first and only then take up with self-government and the common pastureland. Their position created conflict within the La Flesche family, especially with Ed and Rosalie.

Fortunately for the family, Tibbles tired of farming, preferring the life of an itinerant lecturer. When the two Tibbles girls went away to school in Lincoln, Nebraska, Susette joined her husband on an eastern lecture tour. After the tour she wanted to return home, but Tibbles accepted an offer to lecture on Indian culture in Great Britain. They left the United States in May 1887 and spent one year traveling widely throughout the British Isles. Bright Eyes shared stories about her people, but everywhere she went the English treated her like a stereotypical Indian "princess," which she did not appreciate.

When they returned home, Tibbles gave little thought to farming. He leased the farm and joined the editorial staff at the *Omaha World-Herald*.

The Tibbles moved to Omaha, where townspeople referred to her as Mrs. Thomas Tibbles. It would be a long time before Bright Eyes returned home to live with her family on familiar land.

Joseph La Flesche, the family patriarch, died on September 24, 1888. (Grandma Nicomi had died the year earlier.) With Joseph's death the old Omaha world began to vanish.

However, in the Dakotas, the Lakotas were trying to restore the world of the past through the Ghost Dance. They hoped to dance back the buffalo and their ancestors. Tibbles was sent to cover the Ghost Dance, and Bright Eyes went with him. After celebrating Christmas in the Episcopal church on Pine Ridge, Tibbles was in the field on December 29, 1890, when the blue-coat soldiers rounded up Big Foot's band of ghost dancers and brought them to Wounded Knee. On his way back to Pine Ridge to report the story, fighting broke out. Bright Eyes was at the Episcopal church when soldiers brought in wounded Indian women and children. She spent the night nursing the wounded. The contrast between the Christmas message and the slaughter of innocent Indian women and children was not one she was likely to forget.

Wounded Knee was Tibbles's last involvement with the plight of Plains Indians. He spent the next decade fighting on behalf of oppressed western farmers, with Bright Eyes by his side, largely cut off from the everyday life of the Omahas. During this period the Tibbles lived in Omaha, Washington, D.C., and again in Omaha. Susette found time to enjoy the cultural and artistic life of the city.

Her writing in this decade focused mainly on the politics of Free Silver and Populism, but she found time to sketch and paint, pursuing a love for drawing that she had shown years earlier as a student in the mission school. In 1898 she collaborated with Fannie Reed Griffin on a book titled *Oo-mah-ha Tawathe* (Omaha City). Susette provided illustrations of Indian life for the book, which claimed that her drawings were "the first artistic work by an American Indian ever published."

It was most likely her last piece of work. Never robust, Susette suffered physically and emotionally in her last years. Tibbles thought she was simply "homesick," but the problem ran deeper. They moved back to the reservation in 1902. In times of trouble, it seemed best that she be surrounded by the familiarity of the land and family that she loved.

This must have been a time of great reflection for Susette as she returned to the reservation. She had labored in her speeches and writings to protect the Ponca refugees and her Omaha people in their ancestral land. That was good. She had worked for allotment and citizenship as a way to protect the people and the land, but that did not always work out well. Many Omaha farmers had leased or sold their land for quick money, impoverishing themselves in the long run. Drinking was more widespread on the reservation than in the old days when Joseph La Flesche was alive. Still, there were good things happening. Francis was working in Washington on the history of the Omahas; Marguerite was a school teacher; Susan was a doctor serving her people; Susette's nieces and nephews were going to school and entering the professions. She had done the best she could for her people.

Susette enjoyed the warmth of her family, her elderly mother, her younger sisters Marguerite and Susan, and her nieces and nephews, but only for a short time. She died on May 26, 1903, at the age of forty-nine. They laid her to rest in the cemetery near Bancroft beside the loved ones from her past: her father, her grandmother Nicomi, the oldest grandmother Memetage, and her sister Rosalie. The epitaph on the tombstone read fittingly, "She Did All That She Could To Make The World Happier And Better." Engraved on the tombstone was an arrow poised for flight inside an unstrung bow, which her biographer Dorothy Clarke Wilson said symbolized a "life fulfilled and ended."

—◦—

Rosalie La Flesche Farley, born in 1861, took a different life path than her older sister, Susette. Susette went east to school and used her learning and knowledge of white society to storm the country in defense of the victimized Poncas, becoming a national figure known as "Bright Eyes." Rosalie, on the other hand, spent most of her life on the reservation, a pioneer farm woman who raised a large family and quietly worked for the good of her people.

Rosalie's education was confined to the mission school and the Quaker day school at the Omaha Agency. She did not venture far away to study as her older sister had, but continued her education by wide reading and far-flung correspondence. She noted with pleasure that her husband, on one of his trips, bought her a needed dictionary and a complete set of the novels of Charles Dickens. She became, in time, the principal letter writer of the La Flesche family.

Rosalie, at nineteen, married Edward Farley, a thirty-year-old Irish immigrant, in a religious ceremony at the Presbyterian mission in 1880. The

Rosalie La Flesche Farley COURTESY OF NEBRASKA STATE HISTORICAL SOCIETY, RG2026.
PHO.000003

couple worked at the mission school, Ed as an industrial teacher who trained boys as farmers and Rosalie as a teacher of English language and religion for boys and girls. In time they left the mission and took up farming and raising stock on their allotted land.

Ed built a home on their allotted land that, when completed in 1884, remained as the center for the Farley–La Flesche families for more than eighty years. Rosalie spent her married life here, caring for her growing family of ten children. Childbearing took its toll on Rosalie.

Although Ed had hired help for the house and farm operations, Rosalie worked constantly around the house. Her diaries list the many chores of an Omaha farmwoman: killing animals for food, bottling preserves, preparing and cooking food, baking bread and donuts, washing and ironing clothes, cleaning house, putting up curtains and rolling wallpaper, sewing dresses for the girls, planting flowers in the garden, and nursing sick children. This work went on day in and day out—and all in the midst of bearing ten children and raising the eight who survived.

However, Rosalie's busy life extended far beyond the daily chores of maintaining a home and raising children. Of all the sisters, she made her home the center of La Flesche family life. Visitors, white and Indian, always ended up at Rosalie's place.

Alice Fletcher, the noted anthropologist, first stayed with Rosalie in the fall of 1881 when she and Francis La Flesche began their study of the Omaha tribe. Rosalie and Alice became dear friends. Alice Fletcher was always welcomed at Rosalie's home. Rosalie assisted Alice and Frank in their work, obtaining tribal artifacts and information. In a separate study of the Omaha earth lodge, Alice formally recognized the assistance rendered in the project by Rosalie and Mary Gale (Joseph's wife).

Rosalie corresponded regularly with Mrs. Sara T. Kinney, who presided over the Connecticut Women's Indian Association, which provided financial assistance for Indians building homes. Phillip and Minnie Stabler (an Omaha couple who had studied at the Hampton Normal and Agriculture Institute, a coeducational school for black and Indian students that offered vocational and academic programs) moved into the first house on the Omaha Reservation financed by the Connecticut women. Serving as a mediator, Rosalie informed Mrs. Kinney of the costs involved and what household items she should send to the new homeowners, while at the same time explaining the financing issues to Phillip and instructing Minnie how to write thank-you letters to the Connecticut women.

When Mrs. Kinney and her husband visited the Omaha Agency in 1891, they stayed with Rosalie and were charmed by their reception. Before they dined outside on a delicious meal of prairie chicken, one of the children said prayers. In the evening the adults gathered inside for a discussion, and Mrs. Kinney observed that "at one end of the room in a prettily draped bay window was a table with magazines, *Harpers*, *Century*, *Youth's Companion* and the *Agriculturist*." She added a favorable impression of Rosalie: "She is sweet, gentle, modest, wise, far-sighted, quick-witted, refined Christian woman, yet an Indian, has never been in any school but a reservation school and (seldom) more than fifty miles from home."

There were others who came to Rosalie's home and became friends: Mrs. Amelia S. Quinton, president of the Women's Indian Association and an ardent Presbyterian; a Miss Heritage from Philadelphia (one of Susan's friends), who became close to Rosalie and her children; and John C. Fill-more (a noted musician who worked with Miss Fletcher on a book dealing with Omaha music and song) sent his son to Rosalie's to recuperate after an illness. He evidently recovered his health and became strong enough to spend six weeks on the range cooking for Ed's hired cowboys.

At the same time the Farley home was always open to their Indian relatives, a familiar tipi pitched in the yard. The Ponca chief White Swan (Joseph's half brother) came to visit, and so did his daughter. On one trip that coincided with the Fourth of July, Ed killed several "beeves" to celebrate the occasion. Some of Mary Gale's Otoe relatives also came to visit.

Financially astute and a good correspondent, Rosalie was deeply involved in the daily life of her Omaha neighbors. Norma Kidd Green, the biographer of Joseph La Flesche's family, said that Rosalie "became the banker, the go-between, the chief financial officer for the tribe." Her Omaha neighbors bought on credit from nearby merchants in Bancroft, often borrowing money for various activities. Rosalie kept the separate accounts owed by different tribal members. Merchants and creditors showed up at agency headquarters when the Omahas received their annuity payments from Washington. So did Rosalie, making sure that exchanges between the Omaha and their creditors were honestly handled.

Various eastern organizations and individuals also loaned tribal members money for various needs. All depended on Rosalie to keep the accounts, handle the correspondence, and ensure payment, placing great demands on her time and patience. On one occasion she wrote to Alice Fletcher, who had arranged many loans: "I collected only $45.00 on the notes you left with me; $25.00 from Schyler Wells . . . $10.00 still due, which must come from his crops . . . $10.00 from Albert Pappan on his $37.00. Little Heel $10.00, the balance on his $20.00, Migazhega had to pay on a horse so could do nothing but would chop wood this winter to earn money."

Sometimes tribal members who did not promptly pay their debts frustrated her. In another letter, presumably to Alice Fletcher, she shared her concerns. "[I] have sent word to Sindahaha that he must bring some money and make a payment as I have written so many times to Mrs. Kinney that he would pay and that I could not write another letter. . . . I could not go on forever making excuses for them. . . . I have to go over and see Tae-on-haha and poke him up. Dear me if they don't do any better what are we going to do with them."

But, more than an accountant, Rosalie had a larger vision for Omaha economic development. She agreed with Ed and many tribal leaders that the Omahas should manage tribal land for a profit. After individual allotment began in 1882, thousands of acres of unallotted land were set aside for future generations and owned by the tribe. Whites were allowed to graze their cattle on this land for a fee, but their cows wandered onto Omaha farmland, destroying crops. Alice Fletcher suggested that the Omahas fence their pastureland and create a cooperative grazing program where tribal members could graze their cattle free but whites had to pay a fee. Tribal leaders selected Rosalie's husband, Ed Farley, to manage the pastureland—to put up the fence, lease the land to whites, manage the herd, and collect the fees. After deducting his expenses and fees, Ed would share the profits with the tribe.

Ed was a farmer/cattleman. He took out a twenty-year lease on 18,000 acres of tribal land at four cents an acre, which came to $720 yearly. By 1888 Ed ran some 5,000 head of cattle on the tribe's pastureland. He sold his cows to the slaughterhouses in Omaha and Sioux City at a good profit.

While Ed managed the pastureland, Rosalie handled the business transactions, negotiating the leases, managing the accounts, and writing the correspondence. Since she was bilingual, Rosalie served as mediator between Ed and tribal leaders, becoming a trusted interpreter. The tribe's representatives valued Rosalie's expertise and linguistic skills. In 1887, after the Dawes Act declared that holders of allotted land were "citizens," the Omaha sent a delegation to Washington to discuss how "citizenship" would affect their right to self-government. Rosalie took her father's place as a delegate.

Other than the trip to Washington, D.C., Rosalie did not often travel far from her place on the reservation. She did accompany Ed, with two young children, to the Chicago Columbian Exposition. Like many Nebraskans who lived through the drought and bank failures in the early 1890s, the Farleys were financially pressed, but her half brother Frank sent her eighteen dollars for the trip. She was, at first, overcome by the crowds and noise, but with Ed's company and Miss Fletcher's guidance, she thoroughly enjoyed the experience. Rosalie made one last trip away from home in July 1898, going by train to Omaha to visit the Trans-Mississippi Exposition. There she attended the lecture on Omaha music presented by Francis, Miss Fletcher, and the musicologist John C. Fillmore. The talk was illustrated by professional musicians and six Omaha who sang traditional songs.

It was likely her last trip. By the late 1890s, Ed was handling most of the business transactions Rosalie had conducted for years. She was ill, and had been for some time. Her diary and letters are replete with signs of physical illness. Years of bearing children (she had her last child in 1897 at age thirty-six), maintaining a home for Ed and her surviving eight children, managing a farm, welcoming visitors to her home, serving as a correspondent, accountant, and adviser for many of her Omaha neighbors—all had taken a toll on her physical well-being. By the spring of 1900, Rosalie was so weak that she spent most of her time in bed, looking out the window at the spring flowers and up the hill where Ed was planning a new house. She did not live to see that house. On May 9, 1900, her eighteen-year-old son, Jack, wired his uncle Francis, "Mama died this morning. Come at once."

The community, Indian and white, mourned her passing. A eulogy for Rosalie appeared in the *Omaha Bee*:

> *Mrs. Farley never severed her relations to the tribe . . . was one of its most influential personages. Old Iron Eye [her father] was a keen, strong man and although he left . . . other children, his mantle fell on his daughter. She was a woman of rare business qualifications. . . . But her influence among the Omaha was not due [only] to her sagacity, she was an earnest Christian woman who . . . persistently and unselfishly sought to induce the tribe to accept the benefits of education and Christianity. She was the resource of the poor, the sick and the improvident, her life was a benediction, truly she was one of the most remarkable women of the state.*

Rosalie was buried in the cemetery near the town of Bancroft alongside her father and her maternal grandmother, Nicomi. The epitaph on the stone marker said simply: "The nobility and strength of two races were blended in her life of Christian love and duty."

~

Susan La Flesche Picotte was the youngest of the La Flesche sisters born to Joseph La Flesche and Mary Gale. Unlike Omaha girls of old, Susan did not undergo the traditional "Turning of the Child Ceremony," so she had no traditional Omaha name, nor did her father tattoo her body with the "mark of honor." Like her older sisters—Susette, Rosalie, and Marguerite—Susan was raised to live in two worlds: the traditional world of her mother and grandmother Nicomi and the more progressive world of her father.

As a young child, Susan learned to do simple, traditional domestic chores: foraging for wood, carrying water, helping around the lodge. As an adolescent, she learned to erect a tipi, dress skins, dry buffalo meat, and plant and harvest crops. Dressed in calico with her hair in braids, she learned proper social etiquette and good manners from her mother and grandmother. On cold winter nights, she warmed herself in her grandmother's lodge, listening to ancient stories.

But her father believed that more was needed for his children than a traditional upbringing since they would have to function in a white world. So, like her sisters, Susan received an education in "white man's" schools. She spent a brief time in the mission school before it closed and then attended the agency day school run by the Quakers, studying reading, writing, spelling, arithmetic, history, and geography, with a little emphasis on vocational training. While the Quakers exposed their students to Christianity, they did not directly proselytize like the Presbyterian missionary teachers.

Proficient in English, Susan and her sister Marguerite followed Susette's educational path by attending the Elizabeth Institute for Young Ladies in 1879. They spent nearly three years away from home studying more advanced courses in English, literature, foreign language, philosophy, physiology, drawing, and music, returning to the reservation in 1882. Susan and Marguerite found positions as assistant teachers at the mission school, which had reopened.

After two years at home, Susan and Marguerite continued their education at the Hampton Normal and Agriculture Institute. Well prepared, Susan completed the three-year academic program in two, graduating on May 20, 1886, with distinction. Chosen by the faculty as salutatorian, Susan delivered the opening address, "My Childhood and Womanhood." Alice Fletcher, who had become a close friend of the La Flesche family, noted that Susan "looked well, spoke clearly and everyone was delighted with her."

Hampton had not been all study. Susan lived in Winona Lodge, where she formed friendships with Indian women from many tribes, as well as a warm relationship with Thomas Ikinicapi, a young full-blood Sioux from the Dakotas. She described T.I. (as she called him) "*without exception* the handsomest Indian I ever saw." There were mutual feelings of friendship, perhaps love, but Susan had already decided to pursue a career in medicine.

Hampton expected that educated Indians would return to their reservations as teachers of "civilization" and "Christianity" for their people. Like all Hampton students, Susan did some teaching in the summertime, but she believed she could do more good by working as a physician for her people, especially women and children. Challenging gender and racial stereotypes in the dominant society, it was not unusual for a Plains Indian woman to pursue the life of a healer.

Dr. Martha M. Waldron, Hampton's resident physician, probably influenced Susan's choice to attend the Women's Medical College of Pennsylvania, founded by Quakers. Alice Fletcher secured funds for Susan's medical education from the women's branch of the Connecticut Indian Association, while the BIA provided a yearly stipend. General Samuel Armstrong, Hampton's principal, writing a letter of support for Susan, said that she was "the finest, strongest Indian character we have had at the school. She is a level-headed, earnest, capable Christian woman."

A young Indian woman in the big city, Susan found a room at the Philadelphia YWCA. Welcomed by the college faculty, she plunged into her studies, attending daily lectures and taking exams in basic courses. Fond of anatomy, she easily took to dissecting cadavers and took some delight in sharing with her sister Rosalie the gory details. She found time to observe clinical practices and surgery at the Women's Hospital in Philadelphia.

The first semester was difficult. Alone in the city, Susan was homesick for her family and missed her sister Marguerite and Indian friends at Hampton. Thomas Ikinicapi wrote her loving letters, urging her to come for Christmas to Hampton. She did. They spent considerable time together, but in the end Thomas wanted a deeper commitment than Susan was prepared to give, so they parted sadly. Devoted to her medical studies, Susan had promised her patrons in Connecticut that she would remain single for a few years after her studies to devote her time to medical work among her people. She wrote Rosalie and tried to make light of her predicament: "Friendship [with Thomas Ikinicapi] is all it can be. . . . I shall be the dear little old maid and come and see you all and doctor and dose you all. Won't that be fine?"

Susan's second and third years were even more intense. She attended lectures every day in the major disciplines, but with special emphasis on obstetrics and gynecology, since the school assumed their female students would mainly serve women. Despite a busy schedule, she did clinical work at the Women's Hospital and other health facilities in Philadelphia.

Although her studies were rigorous, Susan did take time from her studies to enjoy Philadelphia. In company with some of her white college friends, she traveled freely throughout Philadelphia, visiting its historical sites. She heard Frances Willard give a lecture on temperance; she visited the Academy of Fine Arts and enjoyed the paintings of Benjamin West; she attended the theater, where she saw Lily Langtry perform in *Wife's Peril;* she took in recitals and opera at the Philadelphia Academy of Music, where she enjoyed Gilbert and Sullivan's *The Mikado* and Handel's *Messiah.* She also made friends outside the college. The W. W. Heritage family took special interest in Susan, often inviting her to their lovely home for tea or dinner, while their daughter Marian became a constant companion. Susan enjoyed an experience few Omaha women could ever hope to realize.

While she mingled freely in white society, Susan did not forget her Indian roots. Concerned about her family, she wrote constantly to her sisters and spent the second summer at home looking after her aging parents and working on her father's farm. She kept in touch with faculty and Indian friends at Hampton, teaching there one summer. Shy at first, she took to speaking before missionary societies about the plight of Indian people. She also spent time with destitute Indian boys and orphans cared for in charitable and educational institutions in Philadelphia.

Susan did not disappoint her supporters, receiving her medical diploma on March 14, 1889, the leading student in a class of thirty-six and the first Native American woman to become a physician. After commencement she completed an internship, serving four months as assistant to the resident physician at Women's Hospital and gaining valuable medical experience.

True to her promise, she returned home to the Omaha Agency in August 1889 to begin work as a family doctor looking after the health of her people. Dr. Susan La Flesche was twenty-four years old. At first the BIA appointed her as a physician for the students at the agency boarding school at an annual salary of $500. On her own time, Susan extended her medical services to students attending the mission school and then to the larger Omaha population that came to her for help. By December the BIA designated her as physician to all the Omaha people. She now had 1,244 patients, and the bureau eventually gave her a $200 raise for her good service.

Despite her busy schedule, Susan took on the role of medical missionary for the Women's National Indian Association. Paid $250 yearly, Susan looked after the spiritual needs of her patients, conducting school and morning services on Sundays as well as prayer meetings on Wednesdays. She encouraged Christian ceremonies for marriage and burial.

Susan maintained an office in the agency school, where she examined patients, dispensed medications, inoculated the young, and offered general advice on how to prevent sickness by following guidelines on cleanliness, hygiene, and good housekeeping. As predicted, she served more women and children than men, since Omaha women felt more comfortable with a woman doctor who spoke their language than with a white male doctor.

Dr. Susan also made house calls, covering more than 1,350 square miles of difficult roads. When possible, she walked. For patients farther away, she rode a horse. When that proved difficult, she rented and then bought a team of horses with a carriage. After returning home after a long day, she kept a lantern in her window so that anyone who needed help could find her.

During the four years Susan served as the agency physician, she treated acute and chronic illness: influenza, dysentery, cholera, tuberculosis, and eye-related disorders such as conjunctivitis and trachoma. She enjoyed her work as a doctor and was well respected for her devotion and medical skill.

But the demanding work took its toll. Susan was never robust. She suffered her first breakdown in December 1892 and was bedridden for several weeks with severe pain in her ears, head, and back of the neck, an illness that plagued her for the rest of her life. She resumed her medical work after she recovered, but in the fall of 1893, she suffered another bout, recuperating at her mother's house for fifty days. Shortly after, Susan resigned her position as agency doctor to conserve her strength and look after her ailing mother.

On June 30, 1894, Susan's life took a surprising turn when she married Henry Picotte, a Yankton Sioux, in the local Presbyterian church. Henry, a thirty-five-year-old divorced father of three, was the brother of Charles Picotte, Marguerite's first husband, who had died from tuberculosis. The marriage surprised her family and eastern friends, with her Connecticut patrons assuming they had lost Dr. Susan once she became a married woman. Susan's Philadelphia friends, such as Marian Heritage, thought that she had not made a good choice for a husband, but Susan defied all their expectations.

Susan was thirty years old and had always wanted children. Life was fleeting; she had experienced the deaths of her brother-in-law, Charles Picotte, and her first love, Thomas Ikinicapi, who also died from tuberculosis. Susan expressed her love for Henry, whom one friend said was a "handsome man with polite ingratiating manners, and a happy sense of humor."

The couple settled on Susan's allotment. Henry cared for the farm, proving to be a supportive husband and good father to their two children, Caryl, born in 1895, and Pierre, in 1898. Dr. Susan, in defiance of Victorian ideals, went back to work as a private physician with Indian and white patients in the town of Bancroft, where they settled. At first she operated mostly out of her home, but in time she conducted house calls. Sometimes she took one of the children with her, but on most occasions Henry or family members looked after the two boys. Dr. Susan continued to provide medical care for the Omahas throughout the late 1890s despite the fact that she was never entirely free from pain.

The new century opened on a troubling note for Susan. Her sister Rosalie died in 1900, Susette died in 1903, and her husband, Henry, died in 1905 at age forty-five. Henry's death from tuberculosis, complicated by heavy drinking, brought a personal dimension to her campaign against drinking, a campaign that Susan had fostered throughout her years as a doctor.

It was a campaign begun by her father many years earlier. As a doctor, Susan witnessed firsthand the destructive impact of alcoholism on her patients: fights, spousal abuse, illness, poverty. Alcoholism cut close to home. There were members of her family, like her brother-in-law Noah (married to her stepsister Lucy), who drank too much, her bother-in-law Ed Farley (who indulged until Rosalie laid down the law), and most tragically her husband, Henry, who drank heavily. Susan lectured on temperance and advocated legislation against the sale of alcohol on the reservation and in the nearby towns.

When the Omahas began to take up with the "peyote cult" in the early years of the 1900s, Susan at first branded it an "evil" like alcohol and supported federal efforts to suppress it. But the Omaha followers of peyote blended Christian principles with traditional beliefs, and as Dr. Susan studied the peyote movement among the Omahas, she began to realize that its adherents led sober and industrious lives. Before she died Dr. Susan wrote to her half brother Francis, arguing that peyote religion had beneficial qualities.[4]

---

4 I am indebted to Benson Tong's excellent biography, *Susan La Flesche Pictotte, M.D.*, Norman: University of Oklahoma Press, 1999, pp. 129–31, for this insight into Dr. Susan La Flesche's changing position about the use of peyote among the Omahas. Tong included in his picture-portfolio a photograph of Susan observing a peyote religious meeting.

Dr. Susan La Flesche Picotte COURTESY OF NEBRASKA STATE HISTORICAL
SOCIETY, RG2026.PHO.00071

Henry's death left Susan a widow with two young children to care for in addition to her elderly mother, who lived with her. In 1906 she received a timely offer from the Presbyterians. Recognizing Susan's devotion to the Christian faith, the Presbyterian Board of Home Missions appointed her as missionary to the Omahas, the first American Indian appointed by the board. They provided Susan a temporary house near the agency headquarters and a salary.

So, in addition to her medical work, Susan began serving the Blackbird Hills Presbyterian Church, which was without a pastor, preaching the gospel in Omaha to the small congregation, instructing the young, holding Christian services for the dead, and encouraging young couples to marry in the church. Susan's zeal and devotion to the faith and the church revived the congregation. Even after a new pastor arrived in 1908, Susan continued to teach Sunday school.

By then Susan lived in Walthill, a new railroad town carved from reservation land, which became a "dry" town largely because of her efforts. She built a modern two-story house with a fireplace, furnace, kitchen, living room and dining room with large windows, and an indoor bathroom with a bathtub. Marguerite and her second husband, Walter Diddock, lived across the street. The two families—Marguerite with four children, Susan with two children and her elderly mother—lived close, like an old Omaha extended family. Susan and Marguerite became pillars of the community, with Susan becoming a leading figure in the new, largely white Presbyterian church in Walthill and serving as president of the church's missionary society.

Along with her involvement in the life of Walthill, Dr. Susan continued her demanding schedule as a practicing physician in the town and surrounding reservation area. She took time from her busy schedule in late 1909 to become involved in tribal politics.

The land question came to a head in 1910. Members of the Omaha tribe had received their individual allotted land in 1885, with the major proviso that the land would be held in trust for twenty-five years. Until then tribal members who held allotted land could not lease or rent their land without the approval of the Indian agent. Then Washington decided to extend the trust period for an additional ten years, implying that the Omahas were not intelligent enough to wisely manage their own allotments. Tribal leaders, along with Dr. Susan, protested. Having come to resent the stifling bureaucracy in Washington that impeded self-development among her people, Susan accepted the challenge to fight despite having been ill for a good part of 1909. She suffered from a nervous disorder that brought on profound physical and mental exhaustion and experienced, once again, profound pain in her head and ears, which led, over time, to her becoming deaf.

Susan wrote and agitated on behalf of the Omahas, whom she argued were as "independent and self-reliant . . . [and] as competent as the same number of white people." The tribe sent a delegation to Washington in January 1910 to argue their case and insisted that Dr. Susan lead the delegation. Despite her recent illness, she felt she had to go. Susan wrote to a friend, "The Omahas depend on me so, and I just have to take care of myself until the fight is over." Susan spoke with passion and logic before the secretary of the Interior on February 7, 1910, arguing that most Omahas were competent to manage their own affairs and that the remaining few would become capable of managing their land and lives once freed from the stifling bureaucratic hand of the BIA.

The appeal was successful. The BIA loosened the restrictions and a few hundred tribal members gained full legal title to their lands. One reporter for the *Fremont Tribune* praised Dr. Susan for helping the tribe draw up a "second declaration of independence." But the victory proved a mixed blessing. Many of the Omahas who received full title were not ready to manage their lands, as Susan should have realized. In a matter of years, many sold or leased their lands for quick and easy money, which soon vanished from their hands.

After Susan returned from Washington, she resumed her demanding practice, traveling now by car to visit her distant patients. She turned more and more to larger questions of public health, coming to believe that the early detection and prevention of disease and hygienic care were more important than prescribing medicine. Susan became an accepted member of the Thurston County Medical Society and the Nebraska State Medical Society, but she accomplished her greatest good as the Chair of the State Health Committee of the Nebraska Federation of Women's Club, which pressured the state legislature for remedial measures.

Dr. Susan spent considerable time investigating tuberculosis, which ravaged the Native American community, recommending some commonsense measures to stay healthy and avoid sickness, such as cleanliness, fresh air, good food, and exercise. She urged broader measures to prevent the disease, including monthly checkups for boarding-school students and measures to avoid contagion once it appeared. She understood how germs spread and spoke against the common drinking cups, winning legislation for disposable cups and utensils and drinking fountains in the schools and public places. She campaigned to raise awareness of dangers posed by the fly, using graphic posters revealing how flies spread disease, and urging Nebraskans to eliminate breeding places and use window and door screens.

Susan had long wanted a local hospital for the Omahas, so that they would not have to travel far to Sioux City or Omaha for treatment, and worked hard to make that dream a reality. In 1911 the Presbyterian Home Mission Board contributed more than $8,000 for a hospital. Susan appealed to eastern friends and religious organizations for additional money. Walter and Marguerite Diddock donated a one-acre site overlooking the town of Walthill. Opening on January 8, 1913, the hospital, intended for the Omahas, soon treated whites as well. The new facility boasted ten beds in the general ward, five private rooms, a small children's ward, an operating room, two bathrooms, a laundry, a kitchen, and a reception room. It was a clean, modern facility with access to steam heat, electricity, and city water.

The hospital was Dr. Susan's last great accomplishment. Because her health began to fail, she served the hospital as chief physician in a limited capacity, as she suffered increasing pain in her head, neck, and ears. At long last doctors realized that she suffered from bone cancer. In February and then again in March 1915, surgeons operated to remove diseased bone, but it was too late. Nursed at home by her sons, Caryl and Pierre, and by a niece (Marguerite's daughter), Dr. Susan died on September 18, 1915, at age fifty.

A simple funeral ceremony was held in her home, where she was surrounded for the last time by family and friends. Three Presbyterian ministers presided, and after the ceremony an elderly Omaha said prayers in the Omaha language. Susan was buried in the Bancroft cemetery alongside her husband, where her cemetery stone read, "Until the day dawns."

Tribute poured in from the many people who recognized her unselfish devotion to her people. The Reverend D. E. Jenkins wrote a fitting eulogy: "Dr. Picotte gave herself unselfishly, passionately and often with what amounted to reckless disregard of herself to the task of relieving, helping and uplifting the Omaha Indians. By day and night she dreamed dreams and saw visions of larger and better things yet to come for her beloved people." Jenkins understood that though educated in the Euro-American way, Susan came home to live and work among her own people, the Omaha.

Some months after her death, the hospital was named "Dr. Picotte Indian Medical Mission." It was later renamed the "Dr. Susan La Flesche Picotte Memorial Hospital," serving whites and Indians until 1947. One of the last Omaha to die in the hospital was her beloved sister Marguerite.

Marguerite La Flesche Diddock, like all her siblings, was exposed at birth to two different ways of life. Born in 1862 she spent her first years in her father's two-story frame house while nearby lived Nicomi, her maternal grandmother, in a traditional Omaha earth lodge.

Joseph La Flesche wanted all his children exposed to Euro-American education and culture. So Marguerite, like her sisters Susette and Rosalie, attended the Presbyterian mission school and, when the mission school closed, studied at the Quaker agency day school.

Despite years of indoctrination, Marguerite was not completely won over to the white way. At fifteen she wrote an interesting letter to the *St. Nicholas* magazine, one of the best "juvenile" periodicals of the late nineteenth century. After a simple introduction, Marguerite expressed a great regret: "Sometimes I am sorry that the white people ever came to America. What nice times we used to have before we were old enough to go to school for then father used to take us on the buffalo hunt. How glad we used to be when the men were bringing in the buffaloes they had killed! Whatever the white men take away from us, they cannot take away the love of roaming."

But the old days were gone. In 1879, when Marguerite was seventeen years old, she followed in Susette's path by attending the Elizabeth Institute for Young Ladies in Elizabeth, New Jersey. (Susan, her younger sister, went with her.) Marguerite spent three years at the Elizabeth Institute, studying reading, writing, and arithmetic, along with higher-level courses in philosophy, physiology, and literature.

Marguerite and Susan returned to the Omaha Reservation in 1882. Then, in late summer of 1884, Marguerite and Susan decided to continue their education at Hampton Normal and Agriculture School in Hampton, Virginia, which had opened after the Civil War as a school for freed slaves but now welcomed Indian students as well.

The sisters lived in Winona Hall, a dormitory for Indian girls. (Lucy, their half sister from Joseph's second marriage, was already at the school, living with her husband, Noah, in one of the separate cottages for married couples.) The sisters excelled in their academic and vocational programs and enjoyed the coeducational social life at the school.

By all accounts Marguerite had blossomed into a very pretty woman and within a few months was courted by Charles Felix Picotte, a handsome mixed-blood from the Yankton Agency in North Dakota. They fell in love. Susan wrote: "Mag [a family nickname for Maguerite] and her Felix [Picotte] have a mutual admiration society. He says 'Daisy [Marguerite] is so good to me; life could not be without her.' She says, 'Charles is so good to me. I don't think it would be possible to quarrel.'" Susan added that Charles "is one of the gentlest men I have ever seen." Before leaving Hampton, Marguerite and Charles were engaged.

Marguerite was influenced by Hampton's mission of "self-sufficiency through assimilation"—that its students would take up the task of promoting "Americanization" among their own people. Marguerite considered becoming a missionary after graduation and, in the words of her Indian school friends, "lighting up of our people . . . in the new good way." It was a less critical comment on the "coming of white people" than she expressed in her teenage letter to *St. Nicholas* magazine.

Marguerite graduated in 1887 along with Charles Picotte. Her senior composition, "Customs of the Omahas," won special honors, and Hampton officials asked her to read the essay as part of the commencement exercise.

Marguerite and Charles returned to their respective reservations, but the separation was difficult and within a year they married. Marguerite spent her married years teaching at the Presbyterian mission school while Charles managed much of the La Flesche family land. Tragically, the marriage was short-lived; Charles died from tuberculosis within four years.

After Charles's death Marguerite continued to teach school. But she did more than impart the rudiments of learning. Like a missionary, she exposed the Omaha youngsters to the larger white Christian world and was especially interested in getting the Omaha to marry legally and in the Christian church, forsaking old customs.

At this time she met Walter Diddock, a longtime Nebraskan with some understanding of the Omahas. Walter worked for the Omaha Agency as an industrial teacher and farmer, helping Omaha men learn modern farming. The two fell in love and married on June 29, 1895, at the Blackbird Hills Presbyterian Church, beginning a lifelong, happy marriage.

In 1896 the BIA appointed Marguerite as a field matron to the Omahas at an annual salary of $720. The BIA officials founded the field matron program in 1890 because "they had concluded that the persistent traditionalism of most native women impeded general Indian advancement." Designed to help Indian women break from the past, field matrons exposed them to the "higher" principles of Victorian domesticity.

In the first decade of the program, field matrons were mostly single, middle-class white women driven by Victorian missionary or Indian reform

Marguerite La Flesche Diddock COURTESY OF NEBRASKA STATE HISTORICAL SOCIETY, RG2026.PHO.000004-B

sentiment. But lacking linguistic and cultural ties, they often found it diffi-cult to establish working relationships with native women.

Marguerite was the first field matron to work with Omaha women and only one of two Indian women in the program. With her knowledge of Omaha and Euro-American values, she could function as a bridge for her people between two worlds. She would serve for four years.

Marguerite's task was not as difficult as that of some field matrons work-ing with the more nomadic tribes. The Omahas were a village people with long and friendly ties to the white world. Half of the Omaha women lived in frame houses and had some understanding of Victorian domesticity; but the other half lived in poor, overly crowded log cabins and needed more assistance in the transition to white ways. Marguerite offered her clients an introduction to more modern ways of engaging in household tasks. With the help of her physician-sister, Marguerite advised her clients how to better care for their family's health.

As part of her mission, Marguerite took on the difficult task of counseling Omaha couples to follow legal Christian marriages. In light of her constant complaints, the Omaha Indian Agent suspended entitlement payments to those who refused to follow the Euro-American marriage contract. Some traditional Omahas, who long resented the La Flesches' insistent emphasis on biculturalism, accused Marguerite of being overzealous and partisan in her desire to challenge traditional customs.

At the same time Marguerite's work did not always endear her to BIA officials. Fluent in Omaha and English, Marguerite spent considerable time serving as scribe and interpreter for her people. BIA officials were suspicious of her use of the Omaha language and her close personal relations with Omaha women. They were equally concerned that so much of Marguerite's scribal work concerned tribal landholding and property law, which had little to do with the policy goals of the field matron program—particularly the Americanization of Indian women.

Marguerite resigned her position as field matron in 1900. No reasons were stated for her resignation, but Lisa E. Emmerich, who studied Marguerite's work as a field matron, suggested that Marguerite "may have proven herself to be too much a Euro-American for the Omahas and too much an Omaha for the OIA [Office of Indian Affairs]."

In 1906 Marguerite and Walter bought a lot across from her sister Susan in the new town of Walthill. The Diddocks built a large, frame, two-story, well-furnished house with all modern amenities, including a bathroom—a far cry from the simple frame house Joseph had built a long time ago. Marguerite raised her four children in this house while, across the street, her sister Susan lived with her two boys and the sisters' mother, Mary Gale. The two families were close, like the extended Omaha family of old.

An active member of the new community, Marguerite was a founding member of the new Presbyterian church and active in the Missionary Society, hosting many church activities in her home. For other Omahas living in the town who lacked proficiency in English, Marguerite interpreted at their church weddings and funerals. She also supported many community projects, including lecture series, concerts, volunteer clubs, and the town library. Anne P. Diffendal, a teacher and archivist, noted that Marguerite "typified the Victorian penchant for improvement."

Marguerite outlived all her siblings, the last of the remarkable La Flesche sisters. She spent her final days in the Dr. Susan La Flesche Picotte Memorial Hospital, named for her beloved sister. She died in 1945 at the age of eighty-three.

CHAPTER 16

Josephine Waggoner: Lakota Historian

Two years before Josephine McCarthy Waggoner died, George F. Will, her friend and editor, suggested that as part of her historical manuscript on the Lakotas, she write her own life story. Josephine replied in the most self-effacing way. "My story is so dull and prosaic it wouldn't be worth reading. You know . . . I didn't do much for my race. . . . I got married and lived on isolated ranches living only for myself and my family. I am hardly worthy of writing a biography of myself. I never did anything very uplifting that would be considered great."

How wrong she was! Josephine Waggoner lived through an exciting period of history as the Lakota people moved from the nomadic, buffalo-hunting days to the late-nineteenth- and twentieth-century world of the reservation. She had an incredible memory of all that she experienced and the innate historical sense to collect and record, from a Lakota perspective, the life story of her people. When she died in 1943, she left behind a rich and wide-ranging manuscript of her people's history and culture. Sadly, it lay largely ignored for some seventy years, consulted only by a handful of historians. Much later, Emily Levine resurrected the unpublished manuscript in all its glorious parts. Brilliantly edited and illustrated, with a splendid introduction, copious notes, and a strong bibliography, the handsome book from the University of Nebraska Press bears a title Josephine Waggoner would have loved: *Witness: A Húnkpapha Historian's Strong-Heart Song of the Lakotas*. *Witness* is the work of a remarkable Hunkpapa Lakota woman who made a "great," "uplifting" contribution for her people.[1]

Josephine Waggoner was born on October 28, 1871, in her grandmother's tipi on the Grand River Agency. Her mother, Wind Woman, was raised as a traditional Hunkpapa Lakota woman and had been married twice before, first to a Hunkpapa warrior who died fighting the Crows and

---

1 Josephine Waggoner, *Witness: A Húnkpapha Historian's Strong-Heart Song of the Lakotas*, edited and introduced by Emily Levine, Lincoln: University of Nebraska Press, 2013.

Josephine Waggoner, circa 1912 WAGGONER FAMILY COLLECTION, COURTESY
OF LYNNE ALLEN

then to a white frontiersman, Ben Arnold, with whom she had one child, Marcella.

Charles H. McCarthy, Wind Woman's third husband, named their new-born child Josephine in memory of his sister. McCarthy was an Irish immi-grant who operated a trading post on the east side of the Missouri River, across from the Grand River Agency. Wind Woman's family traded at the post; McCarthy noticed the young woman and, following Lakota customs, approached the young woman's brothers, who approved the marriage and received gifts of guns and ammunition. Dressed in her finest clothes, Wind Woman married McCarthy in a Catholic ceremony officiated by a priest. Josephine said that her father always treated her mother with respect.

The family took up residence at Apple Creek, near present-day Bismarck, North Dakota, where McCarthy operated a farm, owned town lots, and ran a prosperous livery and feed business. Wind Woman excelled at tanning hides and making gloves, buckskin suits, and moccasins, which she sold to the officers at Fort Lincoln, pleasing the likes of General Custer, Captain Tom Custer, and Captain Myles Keogh. Josephine bragged that her mother's "beadwork was beautiful, her color combinations were perfect—she was an artist in that line."

A founding member of Bismarck, McCarthy was elected the first sheriff of the newly formed Burleigh County. In January 1875 he and his deputy were in pursuit of a murderer when their sleigh broke through the ice on the Missouri River and both men drowned, their bodies never found. Josephine noted that her mother was "prostrate with grief. She knew that she was alone and without a protector."

The executor of McCarthy's estate allotted nothing to Wind Woman from the sale of her husband's property. So in June 1875 Wind Woman, with $300 of her own money, loaded her belongings—a large tent, three trunks of goods, dishes, bedding, groceries, cooking utensils, and a stove with pipes—onto a sixteen-foot prairie schooner and headed back with her two daughters to the newly formed Standing Rock Agency.

The family was assigned to Goose's band and received rations distributed by the chief: flour, sugar, coffee, beans, rice, salt pork, soap, baking soda, and other sundries. Within a month Wind Woman moved into a one-room log cabin and continued her trade by selling buffalo caps and mittens, leather moccasins, and buckskin suits to the soldiers and civilians at Fort Yates. Eventually she accepted a job as "matron" for the men working at the agency. Josephine said that her mother made beds, swept the floor, and washed the men's clothing.

Some Hunkpapa who were dissatisfied with life at the agency left in the summer of 1875 to join the nonagency Lakotas on the Powder River. Wind Woman, along with her mother, brothers, and two girls, joined the exodus using a big black mare to carry her possessions on a travois. At the time Josephine was only four, but she possessed a remarkable memory of the journey. When she spotted the camp on the Powder River, she remembered that "it was a beautiful sight to see the countless white tents that were pitched in a circle on the green grass. The winding river was lovely with its border of dark green trees." Getting a brief taste of how the Lakotas had lived freely on the high plains, she concluded that the Powder River Lakotas "were living a great deal better than the agency Indians."

Wind Woman spent the summer tanning deer hides, returning with the children to the agency in November 1875 with three horses loaded with her summer's work. (Josephine's grandmother and uncles remained in the Powder River country.) Again Wind Woman made needed money by selling her wares to soldiers and civilians at the fort while setting up home in a log cabin.

Happy to be back at Fort Yates living in their log cabin, Josephine remembered the winter of 1875–1876 as bitterly cold. Lakota families came regularly to the agency headquarters for their annuities: clothing, blankets, quilts, shoes, cooking utensils, knives, thread, awls, and other household goods. At the same time they sought shelter from the cold in every public building at the agency and in the log-cabin homes of friends and relatives. Wind Woman's home was always filled with guests as she served hot coffee with hard bread.

Josephine was too young to personally experience the events that led to the Great Sioux War and the Lakota/Cheyenne victory over General Custer and the Seventh Cavalry at the Little Bighorn on June 25, 1876. But she guessed that something ominous had happened. Three relatives came to her home, presumably from the Powder River country, with some important news, so Wind Woman sent the girls out of the house. The next day Josephine overheard her mother tell a neighbor: "Don't repeat it, but my cousins just came in. . . . They don't want it known here among the white people. Every soldier of the Custer command from Fort Lincoln that went out west has been killed—even the Ree scouts and the Crow scouts are all killed."

After the disaster at the Little Bighorn, the Lakota agencies were taken over by the army, which began a campaign to dismount and disarm the agency Indians, lest they assist the "hostile" Indians. Josephine, with her mother and sister, watched from a high hill outside Fort Yates as soldiers brought in thousands of horses from outlying areas. The scene was so dramatic that Josephine remembered it vividly many years later and wrote with great sympathy and insight of that traumatic moment in the life of the Hunkpapas: "So the horses were all gone. The life, the hope, the pride of the Indian was gone with them." Josephine explained that in the "machine age," no one could fully understand the love an Indian had for a "spirited, courageous horse," comparing it to the love one had for a "beloved child."

Later, Josephine, her sister Marcella, and the other children would climb the hill behind Fort Yates but could not see a horse. She wrote poetically that "every tent seemed to be silent except where the children were crying for food. Silence, because there was no enjoyment in talking, no enjoyment in singing, only a wailing song came at times with the wind, a song of grief and regret."

Louise Picotte, Eagle Woman's daughter, established the first school on the reservation in January 1876, holding classes at first in the front room of Eagle Woman's trading post. Later, a two-room log school was built containing a classroom and kitchen where the girls could eat. Marcella, five years older than Josephine, went every day; Josephine went sporadically. "I went," she said, "more to play than learn." Louise taught the girls to sing a few English songs. The officers and their wives from Fort Yates visited the school and brought candy. A devout Catholic, Louise taught the girls the "Our Father" and the "Hail Mary," which they sang out loud in their broken English and were rewarded for singing with pieces of candy.

In spring 1878 the Benedictine Sisters opened a boarding school at Standing Rock. Josephine and Marcella transferred to the new school and lived in a dormitory with bunk beds. The building was enclosed by a stockade. Josephine said that she talked to her mother through cracks between the walls. The Sisters were good teachers and Josephine's command of English improved.

Late that year the government built a new boarding school sixteen miles south of Fort Yates, also run by the Benedictines, officially called St. Benedict's Agriculture Boarding School, although everyone called it simply the "Farm School." Josephine and Marcella joined the Farm School in November 1878 and remained there throughout 1879, 1880, and part of 1881. In the spring of 1881, they were allowed to return home for the first time.

Sometime during this period, Wind Woman had married a man by the name of Silk, but he died a year or two after the marriage. Josephine noted that her mother "was always unlucky with her husbands." In another tragedy a child named Mary, born from this union, drowned in the Missouri River.

When Josephine arrived home from the Farm School, the Hunkpapas were returning from their exile in Canada, where many fled after the Little Bighorn fight. Wind Woman, Josephine, and Marcella went to the dock to welcome home their grandmother and relatives. Sadly, her grandmother, who Josephine loved dearly for her traditional cooking and stories of the old days, was sickly from the long, hard time in Canada.

Sitting Bull and his close followers arrived last at Fort Yates, where the army took him as a prisoner to Fort Randall. Josephine described the dramatic scene, which has seldom been reported. When the day arrived that Sitting Bull and his followers had to board the steamboat that would take them into exile, the old chief faced a critical moment—resist and die or go to prison. Some feared that Sitting Bull would invite death, but his beautiful daughter, dressed in her finest clothes, urged her father to live. Sitting Bull hesitated, then strode before the soldiers "like a caged lion," and broke out in song—a "song of regret, sorrow, and grief." The crowd grew silent. His daughter led the chief safely down the gangplank, accompanied by his close followers. As the boat pulled away, the "Indians in the boat were singing a brave song, while voices on the shore were wailing a farewell."

In October 1881 Josephine, nearly ten, went east with some two dozen Hunkpapa boys and girls to study at Hampton Normal and Agriculture Institute in Virginia, a bold experiment in biracial, co-ed education. The Indian Bureau paid the expenses for Indian students to attend the school. Josephine was part of a large contingent of Lakota students who attended Hampton over the years for its academic and vocational programs. When she arrived, Josephine noted the lush Virginia surroundings of Hampton, which overlooked the beautiful Chesapeake Bay, a sharp contrast to the high, dusty plains of the Dakotas.

Spending three years at Hampton, Josephine admired her teachers, mostly from New England, for their patience and skill. She admitted that many Indian students, including herself, had no great desire to learn. "None of our parents," she said, "encouraged us to study." But she admired the black students, since many of the older students worked during the day and attended night classes and the younger students worked long and hard over their books. "The colored students were an inspiration to us," Josephine admitted. While not a great student, she progressed from the fourth to the eighth grade in two years.

After her third year at Hampton, Josephine returned home in 1884. By this time Wind Woman had married her fifth husband, Charles Papin, a mixed-blood Ponca. Once again the union was short-lived, for Papin died in 1888.

While home, Josephine spent time at her aunt's place, a short distance from the cabin of Sitting Bull, who had returned from Fort Randall in 1883. Getting to know Sitting Bull, his mother, wife, and sister, Josephine spoke with him on many subjects. Bilingual in Lakota and English, Josephine read and wrote letters for Sitting Bull.

A year after leaving, Josephine returned to Hampton for another three-year term, living in the new Winona lodge, a dormitory for Indian girls. She moved up the academic ladder, but Hampton was not all work. Saturday was a day of leisure and games and Sunday a day for church, with a song service in the evening by the Hampton Minstrels, a well-respected group of black women who sang gospel and folk songs.

As part of Hampton's "outing system," Josephine spent a happy summer with a New England family who lived in North Egremont, Massachusetts. She went to the home of Dr. Louisa Millard Clark, a well-respected homeo-pathic doctor. Working in the kitchen alongside Mrs. Dean, the cook, Jose-phine gathered herbs for Dr. Clark. At times she went with the doctor to meet patients. When it came time to leave, the family packed a trunk with delicious food. "We cried in each other's arms when I left," Josephine said. "I grew so fond of these people. I knew I would never see them again. They were good people."

Josephine returned to Standing Rock in May of 1888, claiming she left Hampton to accompany home a seriously ill friend, Rosa Bear Face. In fact, Josephine had been expelled from the school for dating a black student. Despite her expulsion, Josephine expressed fond thoughts of the school and its teachers. "When I think of Hampton," she said, "I think of everything that is pure, good, and holy."

Educated and bilingual, Josephine found various places to work at Standing Rock. She briefly assisted her former teacher Louise Picotte (who had married and become Louise Van Solen) at an agency day school, and then she worked as an interpreter and nurse (having evidently acquired some skill in this profession at Hampton) for the Congregational church and mission hospital near Fort Yates. While at the hospital, she met her future husband, Private Joseph Franklin Waggoner.

In late August Josephine began work as an interpreter and housekeeper for Rev. F. M. Weddell at St. Elizabeth's, the Episcopalian mission at Wakpala on Oak Creek, earning five dollars a month. Wind Woman and Marcella were members of this community. The church's most prominent member was Gall, a onetime warrior now turned devout Christian. Josephine credited Gall with a profound insight to the Christian concept of the Trinity—the Father, the Son, and the Holy Spirit—when in a speech Gall referred to the Trinity as "ice, snow, and water," saying "it was all the same thing only in different forms." At Episcopalian conventions she met such leading Native American priests as the Reverend Philip Joseph Deloria, who served for many years at Standing Rock, and the Reverend Charles Smith Cook, who served at Pine Ridge.

All the while Josephine continued to read and translate letters for Sitting Bull that came from Pine Ridge and from Walker Lake, Nevada, the home of Wovoka, the Ghost Dance prophet. The last time she met Sitting Bull was in January 1889 at Thunder Hawk's place. She read a letter from Kicking Bear (who had been to Nevada to meet Wovoka) telling his people "to stand firm, to keep praying and dancing [the Ghost Dance], for the Messiah would soon be here." According to Wovoka (as related by Kicking Bear), the coming of the Messiah would usher in a new world: The Indian dead would reappear on earth, the buffalo would return, and whites would vanish from the earth. Wovoka prophesied that this cataclysmic event that foretold the end of the white world would take place through supernatural and not military force, but whites misunderstood the peaceful nature of Wovoka's message and feared the ghost dancers would stage an uprising.

Understanding the New Testament, Josephine connected the Christian message of the second coming of the Messiah and the Kingdom of God to the beliefs of Ghost Dance followers. "Jack Wilson's [Wovoka] new religion," Josephine said, "coincided with the teachings from the Bible." She voiced no objection to Wovoka's metaphysics, but was troubled that the ghost dancers misunderstood the message, telling Thunder Hawk that the "Great Spirit never planned for all the white people to be extinguished." She convinced some of her listeners, but not all.

Sitting Bull relocated to the Grand River, where his followers passionately embraced the Ghost Dance. Sitting Bull's leadership of the Ghost Dance movement alarmed James McLaughlin, the Indian agent at the Standing Rock Agency and a fierce opponent of the old chief who refused to bow to McLaughlin's authority. On December 15, 1890, McLaughlin made a fateful decision. He decided to disarm the movement by ordering the Indian Police to arrest its leader, Sitting Bull. Expecting trouble, the army sent a contingent of soldiers to back up the Indian Police. Private John

Franklin Waggoner, Josephine's husband (they had married a year earlier), was part of the expedition. In the ensuing conflict, Sitting Bull was killed along with some of his followers and Indian Police. After Sitting Bull's body was brought back to Fort Yates, Josephine, with great sadness, helped prepare it for burial. Her husband, a skilled carpenter, built a simple "rough pine box" and Josephine witnessed the burial.

Some of Sitting Bull's followers fled from Grand River and joined Big Foot's Miniconjou ghost dancers, but they were captured by soldiers from the Seventh Cavalry and brought to Wounded Knee Creek at Pine Ridge. On December 29, 1890, soldiers attacked, and during a desperate fight, many Indian men, women, and children were killed. Josephine talked to survivors, Indian and white, who fought at Wounded Knee. Even though she did not approve of the Ghost Dance, she knew that the killings were morally wrong. "It was an easy matter," she said, "to conquer this friendly band of disarmed Indians. . . . What if they were in the wrong and suffering under a false illusion because they had a wrong idea about the Messiah? Should such a massacre take place?"

A year before the massacre, on Thanksgiving Day 1889, Josephine and Private John Franklin Waggoner had crossed the Missouri River to attend a dance in Winona. While there, the temperature dropped severely and the river began to freeze, making it too dangerous to return. The couple spontaneously decided to be married by a justice of the peace in Winona.

Josephine said at one time that she "did not know that getting married would change my life to an entirely different aspect." For the next twenty-five years (as she stated in a letter to her editor George Will), "I . . . lived on isolated ranches living only for myself and my family." It's interesting that in her wide-ranging manuscript, there's only one brief chapter on her married life. She believed that her life as a farmer/rancher raising many children was not deserving of historical attention.

The newly married couple lived in a log cabin at Fort Yates, where their first child, Ramona, was born in 1890. Two years later Daphne was born. Waggoner received his discharge from the army in 1892 and a monthly pension of fifty dollars.

The family moved to Four-mile Creek a few miles south of Fort Yates, living in a comfortable one-room cabin, with a steady supply of fresh water from the creek. Frank later added two rooms and built most of the family's furniture. While her husband did the heavy labor around the farm—building a sod barn for the animals and digging a rock-lined well, an ice cave, and a root cellar—Josephine busily tended house and garden. She grew potatoes, beans, melons, and other vegetables in her garden, preserving most but selling some to nearby residents for extra money. She milked cows, stored the milk and butter in a well to keep it cool, collected eggs from chickens, preserved meat in her root cellar, and dried and preserved wild fruit.

Josephine worked hard on the farm while raising Ramona and Daphne and giving birth to three more children. But all did not go well. Maude, her third child, at age three, fell off her high chair and damaged her spine so severely that she never recovered to lead a normal life. David, her fourth child and first boy, died of influenza, and finally, in 1899, she gave birth to a healthy boy, John.

Life was hard, sometimes tragic at Four-mile Creek. Fortunately Josephine was close to her family, which offered some comfort. Wind Woman, who lived nearby, was a weekly visitor, much to her grandchildren's delight. In 1893 Marcella and her two children moved in with Josephine, and they lived as an extended Lakota family, speaking the language of their people.

Close to the Congregational church, which she attended with her children, Josephine was friendly with Mrs. Reed, the minister's wife, who had tragically buried two children during the influenza outbreak. As a favor to Mrs. Reed, Josephine joined a sewing society that made clothing for the missions.

Sometime around 1900 Frank and Josephine relocated to a new farm/ranch on Goose Flats, sixteen miles west of the agency, where the land was especially rich. During this time Josephine gave birth to three more children: Luzetta, Ernest, and Lester.

Sometime after 1906 the allotment program began in earnest at Standing Rock. Josephine took her allotted land in the far western boundary of the reservation, implying at one time that she took her allotted land so far from the agency and her neighbors in part because her "impulsive," "rash," and "quick-tempered" husband did not get on easily with Indians. She would spend the rest of her life on this ranch.

In her mid-to-late thirties, she gave birth to two more children: Aurelia and, finally, Wayne. As her children grew older, Josephine sent them to boarding schools off the reservation: Carlisle, Haskell, and Flandreau. In time most returned and took their allotments near Josephine's place, so in her later years Josephine was surrounded by her grandchildren.

As her children grew and left the house, Josephine found some time in the 1920s to paint and write poetry and stories about her people. Billy Irons, Josephine's grandson, visited his grandmother during this time, often finding her sitting at her sewing machine, which, when the top was down, served as her writing desk. She would tell Billy there was fry bread on the stove, which he understood to mean that he should not disturb her writing. Sometimes Josephine was so busy with her grandchildren or chores, she could only work at night—in the kitchen so the light would not disturb her sleeping husband.

In the early 1920s Josephine wrote her recollections of Wind Woman's second husband, frontiersman Benjamin Monroe Connor (better known as Ben Arnold). Her account filled fourteen notebooks. Lewis F. Crawford from the South Dakota Historical Society made use of her material in his book *Rekindling Camp Fires: The Exploits of Ben Arnold* (1926). Despite his heavy reliance on her work, Crawford only made passing reference to Josephine's writings.

By the end of the 1920s, despite her age, illness (diabetes), and daily struggles with hard economic times, Josephine gave considerable time and attention to recording and writing Lakota history. Given her place at Standing Rock, she gathered her oral history mostly from the Northern Lakota and their Yankton relatives. She told Walter Stanley Campbell (one of her correspondents, who wrote under the pen name of Stanley Vestal) in a letter dated October 30, 1929, of her intentions: "I am also writing but maybe that is as far as it will be. *My work is for the Indians* [italics mine]. They don't study history much, are not interested, but I believe they would be from someone they knew."

Josephine maintained a lively correspondence with white historians seeking personal information from her. She complained to George Will, "I receive many letters from strangers wanting information. I would have to hire a typist to answer them." While writing his biography of Sitting Bull, Stanley Vestal was a frequent correspondent, sometimes making heavy demands on her time. Despite hard times and illness, Josephine did her best to provide information for Vestal's biography with the hope, she reminded him, "of a substantial payment when your book is published as you promised me." Vestal recognized her contribution in his book (published in 1932), but it's unlikely that he provided her with very much financial assistance.

Josephine Waggoner (on the right) with Susan Bordeaux Bettelyoun (on the left) at the memorial to honor Crazy Horse at Fort Robinson, Nebraska, circa 1930s WAGGONER FAMILY COLLECTION, COURTESY OF LYNNE ALLEN

Frank I. Herriott, a professor at Drake University in Des Moines, Iowa, approached Josephine in 1931 for information about Inkpaduta (Scarlet Point), a prominent war leader of the Wahpekhute Santee Sioux. Inkpaduta had been involved in the fight at Spirit Lake in northern Iowa in 1857 that killed some forty settlers, fought in the Santee Sioux uprising in Minnesota in 1862, and then crossed the Missouri to join Sitting Bull's Hunkpapa Lakotas. Years later Inkpaduta fought against Custer at the Little Bighorn, after which he followed Sitting Bull to Canada. Josephine had long been interested in Inkpaduta's military career, considering him a patriot and hero in defense of his people. She obtained firsthand material on Inkpaduta's war exploits as early as 1918 from one Mrs. Bull Ghost, who was a close relative. Josephine was always eager to provide an Indian point of view to set the record straight. She sent Herriott a long chapter she had written on Inkpaduta. Herriot was gracious; he respected Josephine's historical work and publicly recognized her contribution to his writing on Inkpaduta.

The 1930s brought hard times to Dakota ranchers: drought, dust storms, loss of grasslands, and falling agriculture prices. Frank and Josephine did not escape the Great Depression, losing their home and land because they could not pay their taxes or meet the obligations on their heavily mortgaged land. Frank was too proud to stay with his children so, in February 1932, they moved into the Old Soldiers' Home in Hot Springs, South Dakota. The Old Soldiers' Home had been founded in 1889 for veterans of the Civil and Indian wars. In the late 1930s Frank and Josephine were able to repurchase their ranch, where they lived simply off the land, spending the warm months at their ranch and wintering at the Old Soldiers' Home.

Surprisingly, Josephine found new opportunities for her research and writing at the Old Soldiers' Home. From Hot Springs she visited the Oglalas at Pine Ridge and the Brulés at Rosebud to gather additional stories from tribal elders and old warriors, complementing the oral accounts she had already gathered from the Northern Lakotas. At the Old Soldiers' Home, she met old-timers who enriched her knowledge of the Lakota past: John Bruguier Jr., who served as a scout during the Ghost Dance troubles; Philip Wells, a frontiersman and army interpreter who survived the fight at Wounded Knee; and, most important, Susan Bordeaux Bettelyoun.

The two elderly women had much in common. Susan, born in 1857 at Fort Laramie, Wyoming, was some fourteen years older than her newfound companion. Her father, James Bordeaux, was French-American; her mother, Red Cormorant Woman, was Brulé Lakota. Susan spent her early years at her father's trading post some eight miles downriver from Fort Laramie on the North Platte River, surrounded by French fur traders, their Indian wives and mixed-blood children, blue-coat soldiers and civilian workers from Fort Laramie, and emigrants (many Mormons) headed west on the Overland Trail, which passed the trading post.

When she was around eight years old, Susan's father sent her to a French community in Hamburg, Iowa, where she joined some of her siblings at a Catholic school, spending four years away from home. In 1870, at age thirteen, she returned to her parents' home, located near the first agency for Spotted Tail's Brulés. Major Poole, the Indian agent, had established a school for Indian children. His two daughters taught at the school but they did not speak Lakota, so they hired Susan, who was bilingual, to help them in the classroom.

In 1874, at age seventeen, Susan married Charles Tackett, an educated mixed-blood. Two years later Susan gave birth to her first child, Marie. For a time Charles served as a scout and interpreter at Fort Robinson, Nebraska.

While stationed there, Susan met Chief Red Cloud and the fabled warrior Crazy Horse. Unfortunately, her marriage was short-lived; Charles Tackett left Susan in 1878 and married Spotted Tail's daughter.

Susan carried on as best she could without parents to depend on, since both had died. In 1884 she moved to Anoka, Minnesota, where her daughter, Marie, attended St. Ann's School. Susan found work as a matron in the girl's building. After four years she returned to the Rosebud Agency while Marie stayed behind to finish her education.

In 1891, an important year for Susan, Marie returned but died soon after at age fifteen. That same year Susan married Isaac P. Bettelyoun, a college-educated mixed-blood who worked for a long time as a clerk and farmer at Rosebud, also serving for a brief time as a scout and interpreter for the army. Susan was employed as a field matron for the Indian Office, entrusted with educating Indian women at Rosebud in the ways of Victorian domesticity.

Susan and Isaac left government service around 1906 to begin life as farmers and ranchers. But by 1933 age and ill health forced them to move to the Old Soldiers' Home in Hot Springs. Isaac died shortly after and Susan stayed on.

Susan Bordeaux Bettelyoun had an interesting story to tell about life among the French fur traders and the Brulé Lakotas in the last half of the nineteenth century. But Susan was old and so severely rheumatic by this time that writing proved difficult. Josephine Waggoner was a natural collaborator with a keen interest in Lakota history, and a good writer.

They started to work together in 1933, and within a year Josephine shared their plans with Addison E. Sheldon, the director of the Nebraska State Historical Society. Sheldon encouraged the two women in their historical project and promised assistance, even publication. Susan and Josephine followed a plan of action: Susan dictated her stories and Josephine wrote them down in longhand. After each section was complete, they sent it on to Sheldon, who made corrections, had it typed, and sent it back to the authors. The first handwritten section was sent to Sheldon early in 1935, and by 1937 a first draft of the Bordeaux/Waggoner manuscript was completed. But they were no closer to publication. In time Susan and Josephine became impatient, then frustrated and angry with Sheldon's failure to find a publisher. Finally, sometime in 1940, Susan requested that Sheldon return the manuscript, but it's not clear she ever received it. As feared, Susan

Bordeaux never saw her manuscript published. She died on December 17, 1945, and for many years the manuscript lay on the shelf at the Nebraska State Historical Society, where it was consulted by many western historians. Finally, Emily Levine discovered the Bordeaux/Waggoner manuscript. After long years of research, she published the document with the title *With My Own Eyes*. It is the indispensable book for understanding the life and work of Susan Bordeaux.[2]

While Josephine Waggoner collaborated with Susan Bordeaux, she continued her own writings on the Lakotas. Throughout the 1930s she shared her emerging manuscript with Professor Herriott of Drake University, who admired her work but was unable to find a publisher. George F. Will, vice president of the State Historical Society of North Dakota, obtained a copy of Josephine's manuscript in 1939. Impressed with her work, he requested that Josephine (then age sixty-nine) prepare a final draft of the manuscript. She sent the chapters to Will as she completed them, the last in June 1941.

Throughout 1941 and into the summer of 1942, Will worked on arranging Josephine's manuscript into an acceptable narrative. But Josephine suffered from diabetes and loss of eyesight and ended up in a Bismarck hospital in the summer of 1942. When Will visited and brought flowers, Josephine reminded him that "time is short," fearing that after ten years of working on her manuscript she would not live to see it published. She was right. Josephine Waggoner died at her daughter Daphne's house on February 14, 1943. Seventy long years later, Emily Levine published *Witness: A Húnkpapha Historian's Strong-Heart Song of the Lakotas*—Josephine Waggoner's great work.

Despite not being professionally trained and having a limited academic education, Josephine Waggoner was a historian. Indeed, she thought of herself as a historian writing a far-reaching history of the Lakota people, although there are elements of her life in the story. The individuals she interviewed, Indian and white, and the white historians she corresponded with understood the extent of her historical ambitions.

Somehow, perhaps by sheer will, she developed the necessary skills to write a grand history of the Lakotas. She possessed a keen memory that allowed her to recall events from an earlier time, and she personally knew many of the participants who left their mark on the history of the Lakotas.

---

2   Susan Bordeaux Bettelyoun and Josephine Waggoner, *With My Own Eyes: A Lakota Woman Tells Her People's History*, edited and introduced by Emily Levine, Lincoln: University of Nebraska Press/Bison Books, 1998.

For the people or events she did not personally experience, she sought out individuals, Indian and white, who had firsthand experience, traveling the Lakota reservations and interviewing tribal elders, historians, and chiefs. She read widely, cited these sources in her text, and attached a rudimentary bibliography at the end of her manuscript—an impressive methodology for one self-taught.

With the exception of a few white historians, Josephine Waggoner was far ahead of her time in collecting and using winter counts in her study of Lakota history. The Lakota name for these picture calendars is *waniyetu wówapi. Waniyetu* means "winter," a time of the year when most winter counts were kept, and *wówapi* refers to a document that can be marked and read or counted. The Indian artists who maintained the winter counts created a pictographic image that best represented the most significant event—such as a tribal fight, horse raid, buffalo hunt, severe weather, or disease—affecting the tribe/band/familial unit in that year. The winter counts were not complete histories in any sense of the term, but yearly markers that served the tribe and individuals as a calendar. The four winter counts Josephine collected are presented in *Witness*.

As already noted, Josephine had emphatically stated that her work was intended for Indians. Josephine wanted to write a book celebrating Lakota history and culture, a book that her people would read and appreciate, but it's also clear that Josephine intended her book to educate white historians, who sometimes distorted or disparaged Lakota history and society.

She was particularly troubled by the remarks of Doane Robinson, a popular South Dakota historian, who said in his book *A History of the Dakota or Sioux Indians* (1904) that "These people [the Sioux] have no reliable traditions of their origins. Most of their so-called traditions are mere invention, varying from the prosaic to the fantastically poetic." Robinson's remarks seemingly applied to the controversial question of Sioux origins, but Josephine rightly saw it as a challenge to the larger question of legends as a source of Lakota history, asserting that "most of the stories told [by the elders] are not mere inventions of fanciful minds." She believed that somewhere behind the legends, stories, and myths there is a history of something that actually happened in the far past. "We should," Josephine said, "study the legends and stories of places and happenings told in living languages, before they are extinct, to help us preserve [Lakota] history." It was a remarkable declaration.

Based on the legends and stories she heard from Lakota elders, Josephine ventured to tell the story of Lakota beginnings in a section of her book that her editor, Emily Levine, entitled "Dakota/Lakota Ethnography, Culture and Society." It was a bold undertaking with limited success since history, lived and recorded, was her strong point, not the study of the past shrouded in legend and myth.

As related by Left Heron, the well-respected Oglala historian that she met at Pine Ridge in 1934, and other tribal elders, Josephine told the story of how the Great Spirit created the first human beings to inhabit the earth, how fire came to the people, and how the people sought contact with the spirit world through the Vision Quest (one of the seven rites brought to the people by White Buffalo Calf Woman). From the more reliable winter counts, she described how the Sioux found the first horse, the "holy dog."

Josephine's most speculative section deals with Sioux origins. She disagreed with Robinson's conclusion that the Sioux originated in the Great Lakes region and then migrated onto the Great Plains. Based on her interpretation of the oral sources she had collected and her readings of some questionable historical and linguistic literature, Josephine postulated that the ancient ancestors of the Sioux originated in Central America. According to Josephine, those ancestors then migrated to the Atlantic Seaboard. Sometime around the end of the tenth century, White Buffalo Calf Woman appeared to the people, bringing them the Sacred Pipe, a symbol of peace between nations, and urging the people to move far west to buffalo country. So these people, who became the Sioux, started on their long journey across the country to the region of the Great Lakes and on to the Great Plains. Josephine's story, however vivid, is at variance with most Lakota accounts. In his "generational" winter count, Battiste Good, a Brulé Lakota, dated the coming of White Buffalo Calf Woman to his people in the year 901, which is, strangely enough, not far off from Josephine's own reckoning—but Battiste Good has the sacred woman appearing to the people in the Black Hills region of South Dakota, the heart of Sioux country, and not somewhere along the Eastern Seaboard.

Josephine is on more solid ground in the next major section of her book, which Levine designated as "Tribal History/Her life." The two sections are sometimes separate and sometimes they come together because Josephine Waggoner was never so interested in telling her own story except as it was part of the larger story of her people. Levine calls Josephine Waggoner's approach "bio-history." Again her task was twofold: to share with her people the greater story of their history and to educate white people about the true story of the Lakota Nation.

Josephine was angry at the work of one nineteenth-century writer, J. W. Foster, a Massachusetts geologist who explored the West and wrote an influential book, *Mississippi Valley*, in 1869. Wandering far from his expertise, Foster expressed harsh views of Indians, believing in a crude form of "manifest destiny"—the right of the superior white race to expand across the continent even if it meant that they had to "subdue" and "exterminate" the Indian.

Steeped in ignorance and prejudice, Foster held the American Indians in low regard, believing they had little knowledge of the arts, no agriculture apart from cultivating a patch of corn, and no sophisticated form of architecture. "They live," he said, "a listless and degraded life" roaming the land in search of game and "gorging themselves like beasts of prey."

Nor did Foster respect the Indian art of warfare. Even possessed of white weapons, he did not think that the Indian warrior "exhibit[ed] the steady valor and efficient discipline of the American soldier," being good at guerrilla warfare but lacking the ability to devise tactics and strategy like whites. Foster questioned the Indians' right to govern the land. Thinking the Indians were "feebleminded" and "incompetent," Foster recommended that the United States care for the Indians in "asylums" or "reservations." If, in time, the Indians were to die out, that was just the law of nature at work, the weak giving way to the strong.

Josephine rightly feared that many Americans shared to some extent Foster's harsh views. She sought to deal with Foster's negative portrait by presenting a far more favorable view of the ordered world of Lakota society.

Lakota society, Josephine explained, was tribal in nature. Within each tribe—for instance, the Hunkpapas—there were a number of prominent bands, each ruled by one or more traditional chiefs. The tribe was governed by band chiefs sitting in council, along with four selected magistrates. The council's decisions—for war, peace, the buffalo hunt—became law, providing an ordered way of living.

The Lakotas lived by the hunt, though women collected and preserved wild foods. When scouts sighted a buffalo herd, they reported the good news. Prior to the hunt, the people prayed to the Great Spirit for success. The tribal hunt was governed by the council, which proscribed the rules of the hunt and appointed one of the war societies to keep order and punish anyone endangering the hunt. The band chiefs divided the meat and skins so that "every man or head of family, sick, poor, or aged, received their share to an equal amount."

As a child, Josephine had spent a summer with the Lakotas living the old lifestyle in the Powder River country. Years later in her writings, she remembered the beautiful setting, the tipis pitched in a circle on green grass along the Powder River. The people were healthy in that pure, uncontaminated environment, with plenty to eat and clear water to drink. It was a good way of life.

In the old days parents controlled their children, teaching them their duty to society. Mothers paid special attention to their daughters, training them in domestic arts from an early age. When girls reached puberty and were old enough to marry, a special ceremony was held by the parents, who gave away presents in honor of their daughters coming of age. Friends and relatives spoke to the young girls, instructing them "how to lead a good, pure life, clean and virtuous." There was no premarital sex or children out of wedlock.

Admiring Lakota women as wives, mothers, and grandmothers, Josephine believed most women were "patient and content. They accept cheerfully their share of the labor of keeping the family fed and comfortable." Women worked hard, but so did men, contrary to the "lazy" Indian stereotype. "Indian husbands," Josephine said, "felt just as responsible for keeping their families fed as any American father."

Josephine was proud of Indian men, seeing them as brave, honest, and intelligent. While at Hampton, Josephine heard many fine white orators, but she also heard orators among the Indians—including Gall, John Grass, Running Antelope, and Sitting Bull—who "could not be excelled for their expression, impression, and language." "Men," Josephine exclaimed, "that could speak and think like they did are not savages; they are intelligent and as natural as nature made them."

Josephine affirmed that most Lakota men "love[d] their country, their nation, and their homes." Warriors, she said "were protectors of their tribes, their homes, and their rights. They were willing to die for this cause. Some of them who gave up their lives to this cause were the bravest men that ever lived." They were not bloodthirsty savages, as Foster would have Americans believe, but patriots and heroes.

Although Josephine was too young to have personally witnessed the long period of warfare between the Lakotas and invading soldiers, her account of the Great Sioux War and its aftermath is straightforward history, written largely from conversations with those Indians who fought in the struggle (she interviewed many) and from white sources such as Stanley Vestal's biography *Sitting Bull* or George Bird Grinnell's *The Fighting Cheyennes*, which she cited in her bibliography. But it lacks the vibrancy and immediacy she brought to the writing of Lakota history that she personally experienced.

As a Hunkpapa, Josephine dates the end of the Great Sioux War not in April 1877, when Crazy Horse came in to Fort Robinson, but in 1881, when Sitting Bull's Hunkpapas surrendered at Fort Yates. Ten at the time, Josephine personally witnessed this dramatic moment and never forgot the scene. Still, Josephine followed Sitting Bull's fortunes. She was close to the events that ended his life on December 15, 1890, and to the "massacre" (those are her words) of Big Foot's ghost dancers at Wounded Knee on December 29, 1890, which Josephine understood marked the end of their old world.

With the exception of a brief summer spent among the Hunkpapas in the Powder River country when she was four, Josephine Waggoner spent most of her life on Standing Rock Reservation. Not always happy with reservation life, she wrote a poem, reprinted in *Witness,* called "Reservation Blues." The first four lines read, "I have no use for civilization / I just cannot think of living that way / It only means hard times and starvation / Back to the hunting days I want to stray." Josephine did not suffer the same culture shock as many nomadic Plains Indian women, such as Pretty Shield, Iron Teeth, and Kate Bighead, who were forced onto the reservation.

Suddenly, a Hunkpapa warrior who had been free to wander the plains could no longer leave the reservation without the agent's permission. When the agent allowed the Hunkpapas in the 1880s to hunt deer or buffalo off the reservation, a scout or Indian Police had to accompany them. Josephine personally experienced the loss of freedom to do as she pleased when she married Private Waggoner and the agent denied her rations for one year because she left the reservation without permission.

Josephine was one of the few Indian women to write about life on the reservation, the good and the bad. With buffalo disappearing, the Indians were dependent on government rations, issued every two weeks: beef on Fridays and flour, sugar, and coffee on Saturdays. Families came to agency headquarters from surrounding areas, staying for a few days. But unfortunately, while they were away, their homesteads suffered as range cattle destroyed their gardens and rustlers stole their cows and horses. Despite this, the Hunkpapas saw ration days (especially when the weather was good) as a time to socialize with friends and relatives. But it was not always a good time. Rations were not always sufficient. Then, Josephine said, "the rest of the time it was starvation." She recalled the winter of 1881 as especially hard, given the bitter cold. Provisions were just wheat and corn for months, and Indians died from cold and hunger.

Over time many Hunkpapas slowly adapted to reservation life, replacing their tipis with log houses, taking up farming and raising livestock, sending their children to schools, and embracing one of the Christian churches springing up at Standing Rock: Congregational, Episcopalian, and especially Catholic, the latter of which many older people found more congenial to their love of ceremony and ritual. The transition to the new faith was not easy. Josephine described how the men came to church in their finest regalia; they sat on the floor and smoked the pipe and whenever the priest said something profound they "would all exclaim a loud *Hau!* to show their agreement—almost the same as saying 'amen.'"

Certainly, all did not go well on the reservation. Josephine complained (like Pretty Shield before her) that the younger, more educated generation "did not believe in the customs of their forefathers . . . [and] it is sad to say that the more educated they are, the more liquor they consume. One is not safe in town where there are Indians on a payday night." Like the La Flesche sisters, Josephine warned against the dangers of alcohol, especially for the young. In the old days parents controlled their children, she noted, and it was rare for a daughter to give birth to an illegitimate child. Now, Josephine lamented, young girls drink and get pregnant out of wedlock. But there was no going back.

In her great work, *Witness*, Josephine Waggoner included a section called "The Lives of the Chiefs," an ambitious project. In it she covered the entire Sioux Nation, which included the Santee Dakota, the Yankton and Yanktonai Nakota, and the Teton Lakota (composed of Hunkpapa, Oglala, Brulé, Miniconjou, Sans Arcs, Two Kettles, and Blackfeet Sioux). These biographical sketches constitute a remarkable portrait of the Sioux Nation.

There are, in all, sixty portraits. It's not surprising that the Hunkpapas (Josephine's tribe), with thirteen portraits, constitute the largest number of sketches, and that her portraits of her Hunkpapa kinsmen are the most interesting. Some of Josephine's figures were prominent leaders of their respective tribes who were well known, such as Sitting Bull, Inkpaduta, Spotted Elk/Big Foot, Gall, Red Cloud, and Spotted Tail, but some were minor players in the drama who would have been lost to history without her effort. The essays vary in length and quality. Some constitute full-length portraits, while others, however brief, remain valuable because they are the only written material we have on these lesser-known Sioux. Some are mere fragments that add little to the historical literature.

Josephine was at her best when she wrote from personal knowledge or when she could locate family members or close friends for more information on the subject. It's amazing how many people she personally knew or interviewed. Her biographies on the Hunkpapas, the Miniconjous, and their Santee/Yankton allies (with whom she had more contact) are rich and illustrative; but her biographies of the Oglalas and the Brulés (with whom she had less personal contact) generally suffer in comparison, with the exception of the piece she did on Spotted Tail. It's surprising, for example, that she wrote only two paragraphs on Crazy Horse, who fought so bravely against the soldiers, considering that she and Bordeaux included a chapter on this famous warrior in their manuscript.

Josephine's subjects were men, with a focus on the lives of the chiefs. Occasionally she makes reference to women. She included a simple page on the Hunkpapa Eagle Woman, who played a leading diplomatic role in the 1860s trying to bridge the divide between the whites and her people. Josephine also mentions in passing Josephine Crow Feather, who became one of the first Indian women to head a religious order, Louise Picotte (Eagle Woman's daughter), one of the earliest teachers at Standing Rock, and Good White Buffalo Cow Woman, who was present at the Battle of the Little Bighorn. It would have been fascinating to read more about the accomplishments of these notable women from a Native American woman's perspective.

Billy Irons, Josephine's grandson, once commented that it was too bad that his grandmother did not start sooner with her historical writings. But it was truly remarkable that despite all the odds against her—as an Indian woman with a limited education, spending her early years on a remote Indian reservation and then living as a pioneer ranch woman in isolated places in the Dakotas raising her family, despite age and illness—that this

Indian woman willed herself to become an accomplished historian, working for years in unrewarded labor on a manuscript celebrating the history and culture of her people.

The tragedy is well known: She never lived to see her monumental work published. But many long years later, Josephine Waggoner found the perfect editor and collaborator in Emily Levine (the editor she so desperately needed in 1940), and now, after seventy years have passed since her death, *Witness* bears testimony to Josephine McCarthy Waggoner, a remarkable Hunkpapa/Lakota historian.

CHAPTER 17

Zitkala-Ša: Woman of the World

As a child on the Yankton Reservation in South Dakota, she went by the name of Gertrude Simmons, though her true last name is a mystery. Her mother, a full-blood Yankton Sioux, Reaches for the Wind (Tate Iyohin Win), was listed on the tribal census rolls as Ellen Simmons. Married to three white men in succession, Ellen had a number of children besides Gertrude. The marriages were apparently not happy and, in at least one instance, involved violence and abuse.

After Ellen's first husband died, leaving her with a son, Peter St. Pierre, she married an Anglo man, John Haysting Simmons, with whom she had a second son, David. Ellen's relationship with John Simmons was not happy, so she left him and married a French-Canadian named Felker, who was most likely Gertrude's biological father. But he played a small role in the family. Years later Gertrude wrote that her mother left her father because he "scolded" young David, which Doreen Rappaport, in *The Flight of Red Bird: The Life of Zitkala-Ša*, interpreted as a "beating," an unacceptable act in Plains Indian family life. Ellen even refused to give Gertrude her father's last name, but instead gave her the name of her second husband, Simmons. Ellen Simmons banished Felker and any memory of him from her daughter's mind. Gertrude never acknowledged her biological father and always presented herself as a full-blood Sioux, later taking the Lakota name Zitkala-Ša, "Red Bird."[1]

Gertrude grew up without a father, living solely under the loving care of her mother, a woman she described many years later in an autobiographical essay, "Impressions of an Indian Childhood," published in *Atlantic Monthly* in January 1900, as "sad and silent," a woman pained by family loss and living in poverty. (At this point Gertrude took the name Zitkala-Ša for her literary works.) Ellen Simmons, who hated all white men and blamed them

---

1   Nancy M. Peterson, who wrote an essay on Zitkala-Ša in *Walking in Two Worlds: Mixed-Blood Indian Women Seeking Their Path*, affirmed that the French-Canadian Felker abandoned his wife before their child was born.

for the poverty of her life on the reservation and the deaths of her brother and elder daughter who died from white man's disease, taught her children to fear and hate the "bad paleface[s]."

Looking back at her early years at Yankton with fondness, Zitkala-Ša remembered best a "wild little girl of seven," clad in a brown buckskin dress and soft moccasins, "free as the wind that blew my hair, and no less spirited than a bounding deer." She said, "These were my mother's pride, my wild freedom and overflowing spirits." Poetics aside, Gertrude's childhood was not entirely free of discipline. She spent two years at an agency day school.

But little Gertrude's quiet life with her mother at Yankton was soon interrupted. Quaker missionaries visited the reservation to recruit young children for their school, White's Manual Labor Institute in Wabash, Indiana, where they would be "civilized" and "Christianized." (Her older half brother David had attended the school for three years.) After the Quakers tempted the young, eight-year-old girl with the promise that she could eat all the "red apples" she desired and ride on a train, Gertrude begged her mother to let her go. Ellen Simmons was torn: She did not want her young daughter to leave and attend a white boarding school, but she understood that Gertrude needed an education to survive in the encroaching white world. Painfully, she relented and let her go. It would prove a momentous decision in both their lives.

It's not clear that mother or daughter understood that young Gertrude would stay away for three long years. Gertrude had mixed feelings about her first years at White's Institute. She was a bright student who took easily to learning English, with a youthful appreciation for literature and music. But there was much she disliked about the place, which she shared in the second of her autobiographical essays, "The School Days of an Indian Girl," which *Atlantic Monthly* published in February 1900. Zitkala-Ša (as she was known professionally) complained most bitterly when the matrons cut her long hair. "Among our people," she declared, "short hair was worn by mourners, and shingled hair by cowards!" She also resented the daily routine, the wearing of white clothing, the strange foods. While there she suffered the death of a "dear classmate," who died reading about Jesus. Zitkala-Ša lashed out at the matron for the "cruel neglect of [the student's] physical ills." She wrote, "I blamed the hard-working, well-meaning, ignorant woman, who was inculcating in our hearts her superstitious ideas."

When the three-year term ended, the eleven-year-old Gertrude returned home, where she remained for four unhappy years. Unlike her older half brother David, who spent three years at boarding school and then settled down at Yankton to farm, Gertrude no longer felt comfortable in her old surroundings. Though she disliked the Quaker teachers, she missed her studies and briefly attended the bilingual Santee Normal Training School in Nebraska, but found it unsatisfying.

"During this time," she said rather dramatically, "I seemed to hang in the heart of chaos, beyond the touch or voice of human aid." Her older brother did not understand her feelings and her mother, saddened and troubled by the girl's unhappiness, could not reach her. Even nature had no place for her. "I was neither a wee girl nor a tall one," she lamented, "neither a wild Indian nor a tame one." Gertrude broke the impasse in her life by returning in 1892 to White's Institute to complete her studies, defying her mother's wishes that she remain at home.

Gertrude spent three more years developing her skills in writing, oratory, and music. She became so proficient in violin and piano that she taught music to the younger students. In time Gertrude became more accepting of the school. When White's Institute could not meet its quota of Indian students (paid for by the BIA), school officials sent Gertrude and Louise Goulette west to recruit young people for the school. The two young women recruited twenty-nine Indian students from Pine Ridge Reservation.

At graduation in 1895, Gertrude gave an oration entitled the "Progress of Women." She railed against the inequality of women and declared that "half of humanity cannot rise while the other half is in subjugation." A reporter for the *Wabash Plains Dealer* exclaimed (perhaps with some hyperbole) that Gertrude's speech was a "masterpiece [that] has never been surpassed in eloquence or literary perfection by any girl in this country." A Quaker woman in the audience was so impressed with Gertrude's speech that she offered to pay the young woman's tuition at Earlham, a Quaker college in Indiana.

The beautiful and talented nineteen-year-old Gertrude once again sought her mother's permission to attend college. But Ellen Simmons wanted her daughter to give up her white studies and return to live among her own people. Once again her daughter disobeyed her. Gertrude did not return home that summer. She stayed in Wabash and taught music to young students who lived in the neighborhood.

Zitkala-Ša holding an Indian basket, 1898 GERTRUDE KASEBIER PHOTOGRAPHY COLLECTION, DIVISION OF CULTURE & THE ARTS, NATIONAL MUSEUM OF AMERICAN HISTORY, SMITHSONIAN INSTITUTION. PHOTOGRAPHED BY GERTRUDE KASEBIER

Gertrude's decision to continue her education caused a break with her half brother David Simmons and his wife, Victoria, who lived and worked at the Yankton Agency. Victoria was angry with Gertrude's decision. She declared that since Gertrude had deserted her home she should give up the family name. When Gertrude published her first autobiographical essay in *Atlantic Monthly* in 1900, she decided that the time had come, and she chose Zitkala-Ša as her Lakota name.

Gertrude would blossom at Earlham, but it would take some time to get over the sting of her mother's disapproval. She spent a quiet first semester keeping her distance from other students, although that all changed when she won a college-wide oratorical contest to the cheers, best wishes, and a bouquet of roses from her classmates. "This friendly token," she admitted, "was a rebuke to me for the hard feelings I had borne them." Several weeks later Gertrude represented Earlham in a statewide oratorical contest in Indianapolis, giving a learned speech entitled "Side by Side," which celebrated the virtues of Native American and Anglo societies.

Warmly applauded by her classmates, Gertrude was "embittered" when a group of opposing students unfurled a white banner with the picture of an Indian girl and the hurtful word "squaw" underneath the figure. Gertrude took her sweet revenge when the jurors awarded her second prize and the "white flag dropped out of sight, and the hands which hurled it hung limp in defeat."

In the short and happy time that she remained at Earlham, Gertrude refined her gift for writing, oratory, and music and became an accomplished violinist. She did not graduate from Earlham because of recurring bouts of illness, both physical and psychosomatic in nature. Deborah Welch, Zitkala-Ša's biographer, speculates that her illness resulted from the tension and guilt she experienced from her conflicted desires: the love for her mother and Sioux identity versus her strong ambition to succeed as an American Indian in the larger Anglo world.

Gertrude chose not to return to the limited world of the reservation. Her pride prevented her from returning since she could not bear her mother's reproach that she had sacrificed her family and culture for so little accomplishment in the white world. She decided that she would continue the journey she had begun years ago—she would use her literary and musical talents on behalf of the American Indian. She simply told her mother that she had accepted a teaching position at Carlisle Indian Industrial School in Carlisle, Pennsylvania, the first and most famous off-reservation boarding school for Native American students.

Captain Richard Henry Pratt, who founded Carlisle in 1879, believed that an English-speaking education was key to assimilating Indians into white society. He once boasted: "In Indian Affairs I am a Baptist, because I believe in immersing the Indians in our civilization and when we get them under, holding them until they are thoroughly soaked." In cruder terms, to save the man, you would have to kill the "Indian" in him.

Pratt thought he made a good choice in hiring Gertude Simmons, a well-educated and talented young Sioux woman who could serve as a role model for his younger students. But Pratt's observation was superficial; he did not understand her deep feelings for native society. In her third essay, "An Indian Teacher among Indians," published by *Atlantic Monthly* in March 1890, and in her later writings, Zitkala-Ša would expose and challenge Pratt's biased worldview and educational philosophy.

Gertrude spent eighteen months at Carlisle, which she saw as a steppingstone for her larger literary and musical ambitions in the Anglo world. Teaching was not her first desire, and during her first year at Carlisle, Gertrude gave a solo violin concert for a literary society in Washington, D.C., attended by President William McKinley. She toured with the Carlisle Band as a violin soloist and orator, earning rave reviews for her recitation of the famine scene from *Hiawatha*.

In the summer Pratt sent Gertrude west to recruit students. She went with some reluctance, but it gave her the chance to visit Yankton. She found her mother older, poorer (her brother David had lost his clerk's position to a white man), and angrier still at whites encroaching on Yankton land.

Gertrude returned to Carlisle, to her "small white-walled prison" room, ever more suspicious of Pratt's assimilationist policy and the arrogance of white teachers towards their Indian students. She ended her essay on "An Indian Teacher among Indians" with a question: She wondered how many visitors who passed through Carlisle "paused to question whether real life or long-lasting death lies beneath this semblance of civilization."

Once again Gertrude questioned her life's choices. "Like a slender tree," she wrote, "I had been uprooted from my mother, nature, and God." But once again she decided to continue her journey. She left Carlisle at the end of her third semester and headed for Boston to pursue her musical career at the prestigious Boston Conservatory of Music.

Gertrude enjoyed the social and literary scene in Boston, and, in turn, the city's literary society welcomed this lovely and talented young Sioux woman. Literary critics soon experienced the richness of her writings. For the first three months of 1900, the *Atlantic Monthly* published Zitkala-Ša's three autobiographical short stories, moving from childhood on the Yankton Reservation, to her student days at White's and Earlham, and her teaching days at Carlisle. She now came to be known by her Lakota name, Zitkala-Ša. She had made such an impression that *Harper's Bazaar* in its April issue for 1900 included her in a column entitled "Persons Who Interest Us." The piece said:

> *A young Indian girl, who is attracting much attention in Eastern cities on account of her beauty and many talents, is Zitkala-Ša. . . . [She] is of the Sioux tribe of Dakota and until her ninth year was a veritable little savage, running wild over the prairie and speaking no language but her own. . . . She has also published lately a series of articles in a leading magazine . . . which display a rare command of English and much artistic feeling.*

While literary critics praised Zitkala-Ša's writings, some of her former Quaker friends and teachers grumbled that she failed to recognize and appreciate the people and institutions that educated her along the way. Worse still, it seemed that in her last essay about teaching at Carlisle, she had begun to question the value of white education, confirming their worst fears in a short story she wrote for the *Atlantic Monthly* in March 1901, titled "The Soft Hearted Sioux."

The story concerns a young Sioux boy of sixteen who left the dreams of his parents that he become a warrior and a hunter and instead attended a missionary school. Ten years later he returns to his people as a Christian missionary, a stranger to his family and tribe. The young man's father is starving to death, but the son's Christian message of a loving Jesus will not save him. His mother urges her son to hunt for meat, but he has lost the skill. Finally, in desperation, he kills a cow and the rancher who tries to stop him. The young man returns with the meat to the tipi, but the father has died. Arrested and sentenced to die, he wonders who will greet him, a forgiving Jesus or his father welcoming him back as a son. He is not afraid.

Zitkala-Ša's former mentors denounced the short story as an attack on white, Christian education. A negative review in Carlisle's *The Red Man* said the piece was "morally bad." Pratt called the story "trash" and Zitkala-Ša herself "worse than a pagan." She did not back down and responded by calling Pratt "woefully small and bigoted" while defiantly insisting that she would continue to speak her own mind.

While Zitkala-Ša pursued her musical and literary career in Boston, she had to deal with more intimate questions of love and marriage. Sometime around 1900 she met Carlos Montezuma, a college-educated Yavapai (Mohave-Apache) Indian who had a private medical practice in Chicago. When and how they met is something of a mystery. Ruth Spack, who has made a careful study of their early correspondence, suggests that they first met when the two traveled together with the Carlisle Indian School Band in March/April 1900. She was twenty-four; he was thirty-six. Unfortunately, the couple said little of their relationship, but by February 1901 they were secretly engaged, talking of love and marriage. Carlos Montezuma was not Zitkala-Ša's first love interest. While at White's Manual Labor Institute, she met Thomas Marshall, a Lakota from Pine Ridge. They reunited at Carlisle in 1897. Unfortunately, Marshall died an untimely death from measles in 1899 while attending Carlisle's Dickinson College. During their courtship Zitkala-Ša teased Montezuma by listing the many admirers who pursued her, but in the end she confessed that she found something special with him: "I require food for the intellect and spirit quite as much as my meals each day. It pleases me to know you too are made that way."

But difficulty with the relationship first emerged in Zitkala-Ša's early letters to Montezuma in which she talked about love and a future marriage. She told Montezuma she did not intend to give up her literary work and that she planned to return to Yankton for at least a year, to look after her elderly mother, teach in the reservation school, and spend time with the "old people" to gather material for her stories. (Ginn and Company Publishers had offered her a contract for a book of old Indians legends.) She wanted Montezuma to come to Yankton with her and take on the position of agency physician. Montezuma had worked as agency physician before and had no desire to leave his practice in Chicago and return to an impoverished reservation. He wanted her to come and live with him in Chicago after they married. But she had no desire to live as a physician's wife in the big city and lose her identity, as many Anglo women did when they married. In these letters she began to question whether she was suited for domesticity and even marriage itself.

There were also political differences between the couple that, if left unresolved, would wear on the relationship. Montezuma believed in full assimilation, endorsing Pratt's educational philosophy, the abolition of the BIA, and an end of the impoverished reservation system, with American Indians taking their full place in Anglo-American society. While Zitkala-Ša wanted the American Indians to adopt some aspects of Euro-American education, technology, and health care, she did not want to see the loss of the Indian identity, best preserved on the reservations, which remained, for many, their homeland.

Zitkala-Ša rejected the Euro-American notion of civilization and argued for the natural superiority of native society. "I will never speak," she exclaimed, "of the whites as elevating the Indian!" She reminded Montezuma that if "the character [of greatness] was not in you—savage or otherwise—Education *could not* make you the man you are today." She saw native people as possessing intellectual, spiritual, and artistic qualities that made them capable of higher goals than those promoted by the domestic and manual training of boarding schools like Carlisle.

Roughly a year after they met, the couple reunited in Chicago in May 1901 as Zitkala-Ša worked her way west to the Dakotas. Despite being unable to reconcile their personal or political differences, they did not end the relationship. She continued her conversation with Montezuma from the Dakotas.

Zitkala-Ša spent some time at the Fort Totten Agency in North Dakota to interview elderly Sioux for her book on Indian legends. "It was a good time," she told Montzeuma, "talking Sioux with the old ones & gathering fine old legends." She still harbored hopes for reconciliation with Montezuma, telling him she hoped to write the book "when I am in our own house."

All did not work out as she planned when she reached Yankton. She did not find a teaching position, and her aging mother proved extremely difficult. Still, she managed to finish a draft of her book on Indian legends by late summer and even correct the proofs. *Old Indian Legends* appeared in 1901, illustrated by Angel De Cora, a well-known Native American artist. In the preface Zitkala-Ša hoped, perhaps naïvely, that these stories, which she had heard since childhood from many Dakota elders, would reveal to all Americans, including the "black-haired aborigine" and the "blue-eyed little patriot," their common humanity.

Zitkala-Ša continued to send her short stories to eastern magazines. In 1902 *Everybody's Magazine* published "A Warrior's Daughter." On the surface it's a simple story about Tusee, a young Dakota woman who goes on a war party and saves her captive lover by killing one of the enemies. But on a deeper level, it reflects Zitkala-Ša's deep-seated belief that Native American women of her time must find, like Tusee, the "warrior's strong heart" to engage in the struggle to save their people.

In December 1902 *Atlantic Monthly* published Zitkala-Ša's "Why I Am a Pagan" (which she later retitled as "The Great Spirit"): a direct challenge to Pratt, who had earlier called her "worse than a pagan." The narrator of the story, Zitkala-Ša herself, listened with respect to the native Christian preacher though he spoke "most strangely the jangling phrases of a bigoted creed" that damned to hell "the folly of our old beliefs." The narrator preferred to such dogma a belief in "the voice of the Great Spirit" heard everywhere in nature and the universe.

As her literary career blossomed, Zitkala-Ša's relationship with Montezuma began to slip away. As early as October 1901, she wrote him, "I have a friend out here who claims all I can give by the laws of natural affinity." She made clear that "another holds my regard." Montezuma demanded the engagement ring back, but Zitkala-Ša claimed she lost it. The Zitkala-Ša/Montezuma affair ended on a bad note, and the two would not correspond again for years.

The other man in question was Raymond T. Bonnin, a Yankton Sioux. Raymond's mother was Yankton; his father was of French descent. Zitkala-Ša may have met Raymond at the Standing Rock Agency, where she clerked for a time. He was younger than her by a few years. Although not as well-educated as she was, he was ambitious and, as a Sioux, he desired to work among native peoples. Doreen Rappaport reasoned that Raymond "reconnected [Zitkala-Ša] to her people, language, and traditional ways." They married on August 10, 1902.

The marriage is hard to fully understand given Zitkala-Ša's earlier confession to Montezuma that she was ill-suited for domesticity and marriage. Her biographer, Deborah Welch, does not think it was a love affair, but a way out of Yankton and her failed relationship with Montezuma. In any case, seven months after their marriage, she gave birth to her only child, Raymond Ohiya Bonnin.

Zitkala-Ša found more than a husband at Standing Rock; she found religion, too. She was so impressed with the goodness of the Benedictine missionaries that she converted to Roman Catholicism—a religion so rich in ritual and ceremony that it appealed to many Sioux. Still, it was a surprising move for a woman who had in an earlier essay questioned the Christian dogma of the missionaries, celebrating, instead, the "voice of the Great Spirit" as found in nature.

In 1903 Raymond accepted an offer from the BIA to serve as property clerk at the Uintah/Ouray Agency at Fort Duchesne, Utah, far from Sioux country. For many years the rising literary star disappeared in the Utah desert. Zitkala-Ša tried to provide a home for her husband and child, but domestic life never appealed to her.

Not content to stay home, Zitkala-Ša tried to find a teaching position at the agency, but the BIA declined her request. Finding other ways to become involved with the Ute community, she began to teach music to the school children and by 1904 formed a band that gave concerts for the community. Zitkala-Ša also organized a basket-weaving class for the Ute women. The baskets were sold and the money used to help alleviate poverty on the reservation. She used the class as a way of sharing with the women new ideas about hygiene, medicine, and education for their children. Although her desire to help was sincere, she never felt truly comfortable among the Utes. Perhaps it was her background as a Sioux, which she always thought of as the ideal tribal group, or her educated status that made her describe the Utes as "victims" of their "ignorance, superstition, and degradation."

In the spring of 1905, the BIA offered Zitkala-Ša a teaching position with an annual salary of $600, but the next year she resigned her position and returned to Yankton to care for her dying mother. Sadly, her mother never reconciled with her disobedient daughter. She returned three months later to Fort Duchesne, but in her absence the BIA had filled her teaching position.

Zitkala- Ša was set adrift. Depressed by her mother's death and personal rejection, surrounded by an impoverished people, lonely and isolated in a faraway place, she appeared lost. In this environment she found it extremely difficult to resume her promising literary career.

Sometime in 1908 Zitkala-Ša met William F. Hanson, a young Mormon who had studied music at Brigham Young University. They decided to collaborate on an opera that revolved around the Sun Dance, despite the fact that it had been banned by the BIA and denounced by Christian missionaries. Zitkala-Ša insisted that the Sun Dance opera should represent the sacred ritual of the Lakota, even though it was not clear that she had a deep understanding of the Lakota Sun Dance.

The Lakota Sun Dance was an ancient and venerable religious ceremony. The Lakotas refer to it as *Wi wanyang wacipi*, the "sun gazing dance." They believe that it was brought to the people by the legendary White Buffalo Calf Woman, a spiritual messenger sent by Wakan Tanka, the Great Mystery. The Lakotas celebrated the Sun Dance in the summer when the tribe gathered. During the ceremony the pledgers vowed to undergo a self-torture ritual by piercing their flesh and staking themselves to the sacred tree. The pledgers thanked Wakan Tanka for some personal blessing they had received, but on a far deeper level, they offered up their physical suffering to Wakan Tanka for the good of the people. The Sun Dance restored tribal harmony, renewed the world in all its bounty, and revived the mysterious powers that ensured the well-being of the tribe. The people left the Sun Dance reassured about their future; the pledgers left the Sun Dance honored by their people, and proudly carried their scars with honor the rest of their lives.

Zitkala-Ša played traditional Sioux songs on the violin and flute (Raymond had given his wife a native flute as a wedding present), which Hanson converted into a European musical score. Together they wrote a libretto. (There's a copy of the Sun Dance libretto in Zitkala-Ša's *Dreams and Thunder: Stories, Poems, and the Sun Dance Opera*.) Actually, *The Sun Dance Opera* is concerned less with the display of sacred ritual than with a melodramatic love triangle.

In this opera Ohiya, a young Sioux warrior, pledges to undergo the torture rite of the Sun Dance to prove himself worthy of his love for Winona, a beautiful Sioux maiden, so that she would not fall for the charms of the evil Shoshone, Sweet Singer, who also desires her. Some native scholars later dismissed Zitkala-Ša's Sun Dance opera "as a ridiculous expression of tribal tradition." Certainly, the musical score and especially the libretto do not measure up to the sacred nature of the ritual involved in the Sun Dance. The Sioux Sun Dance was a spiritual experience: A person who pledged the rite of self-torture did so for deeper reasons than winning the love of an Indian maiden.

Throughout 1913 *The Sun Dance Opera* played in various Utah locations and was well received. The opera ended Zitkala-Ša's quiet period in the Utah desert, demonstrating once again to the larger world her literary and musical creativity.

But *The Sun Dance Opera* created tensions in her home life. Zitkala-Ša spent time away from the agency working on the opera, and even when

Zitkala-Ša, dressed in Indian regalia, circa 1913 COURTESY OF THE PHOTOGRAPHIC ARCHIVES, HAROLD B. LEE LIBRARY, BRIGHAM YOUNG UNIVERSITY, PROVO, UTAH, MSS 299, H27, 1659. PHOTOGRAPHED BY WILLIAM WILLARD

home, she was engaged in literary and musical activity. Raymond felt neglected. Unhappy with his life at the agency, Raymond's frustration spilled over into angry words. He accused his wife of not loving him, of paying more attention to Asa Chapman, a clerk at the agency, than to him. Somehow the internal quarrel spread beyond the confines of their home, and Zitkala-Ša felt compelled to write a long letter to Father William H. Ketcham, director of the Bureau of Catholic Indian Missions, professing her innocence. Zitkala-Ša was distressed at Raymond's jealous accusations. She admitted that she was friends with Asa Chapman, with whom she enjoyed literary conversations, but that was all. She professed her love for Raymond. In time tensions eased between them, but never entirely.[2]

In the spring of 1913, Zitkala-Ša made a trip east, stopping in Chicago to meet Carlos Montezuma. The meeting was friendly, with no sign of animosity despite the painful separation that had taken place eleven years earlier. Montezuma must have shared some news about the Pan-Indian Society of American Indians (SAI), which had formed two years earlier, because Zitkala-Ša referred to it in a letter she wrote to Montezuma the day after their meeting.

In the letter Zitkala-Ša began by expressing her pleasure at the restoration of their friendship. She apologized for not attending the planned SAI meeting in Denver. "It is not that I lack interest or even public spirit," she explained, "but my *duties* seemed to limit me to the home." And, tellingly, she added, "I am returning to Utah . . . because Mr. Bonnin insists on it." Zitkala-Ša felt compelled to express some regret for the long-ago separation. "In all sincerity I want to say you had a narrow escape—but you escaped. I was not worthy because I did not recognize true worth at the time. . . . I humbly beg your forgiveness for my gross stupidity of former years—which was not relieved by my misfortune to lose what I could not replace." (Deborah Welch said that this last line was ambiguous. Was Zitkala-Ša referring to the engagement ring or Montezuma?) She shared her inner tension with Montezuma. "My duty as mother and wife of course keep me in the west; but now I can hardly stand the inner spiritual clamor to study, to write—to do more with my music—Yet duty first!"

---

2   In a long, emotional letter to Fr. Ketcham, dated October 4, 1913, Gertrude Bonnin revealed the tensions in her marriage but professed in bold letters "I AM INNOCENT OF ANY IMMORAL ACT." A copy of this letter can be found in the Marquette University Raynor Memorial Libraries, Bureau of Catholic Indian Missions Records (Series 1-1, General Correspondence, Box 87, Folder 13).

The Bonnins, husband and wife, were at a crossroad. Zitkala-Ša's letter revealed the tension between them. Clearly Raymond wanted to stay in Utah where he had a good position, and perhaps he feared he would lose his wife if she returned east and joined Montezuma and the SAI. Clearly Zitkala-Ša felt that Utah had become like a prison, entrapping her talent and ambition.

Her duty as mother eased in 1913 when Raymond and Zitkala-Ša placed Ohiya, their ten-year-old son, in a Benedictine boarding school in Illinois. Although the Bonnins were members of the Catholic Church, it was a surprising move for a woman who had spent her early years denouncing the pernicious impact Christian boarding schools had on Native American youth.

The Bonnins reached a temporary compromise in 1914, when Zitkala-Ša accepted a position on the SAI advisory board (Montezuma may have recommended her), but, at least for a time, she agreed to operate from her home base in Utah. The SAI was not a perfect fit for Zitkala-Ša, but it provided a way back into the mainstream of the movement for Indian rights. Most members of the SAI were well-educated, acculturated Indians who looked to the future, not the Indian past. They wanted self-determination and protection for Indian rights, but stressed education, assimilation, and citizenship as the best way to achieve those goals. Like most members, Zitkala-Ša wanted to extend the benefits of Anglo-American knowledge and technology to Indian people, but she respected Indian civilization and resented the assault on Indian land and culture made by advocates of acculturation. Prepared to fight for the "Indian right to survive as Indian" put her at odds with some members in the SAI.

In keeping with SAI goals, Zitkala-Ša established at Uintah the first SAI community center, where Ute women would take on Anglo practices of hygiene, health care, education, and homemaking. The community center was the first and last womanly task that she would take on for the SAI.

Zitkala-Ša's life took a turn in 1916 when the SAI appointed her as national secretary, a position that meant the Bonnins would have to move to SAI headquarters in Washington, D.C. They arrived in the nation's capital as the country was preparing to enter World War I. Raymond began his study of law, but left to enlist in the United States Army, rising to the rank of captain. Zitkala-Ša plunged into her work as national secretary for the SAI, a life far more desirable than anything she had experienced in Utah. She would never look back.

Prior to Zitkala-Ša's arrival, men dominated the SAI in numbers and voice. Most of the SAI's female members were young and single and taught in Indian schools or worked for the BIA. Although well-educated, they were inclined to accept the subordinate role of women in American society, working behind the scenes to keep the organization going. Zitkala-Ša challenged the gendered order of the SAI, standing alone in seeking power and leadership positions. As national secretary, she was the only woman to serve on the SAI Executive Council. By 1918 Zitkala-Ša had taken over the position as treasurer and editor of the society's journal, *American Indian Magazine*. In her leadership positions, she did not limit herself to women's issue like education and health care, but argued for larger issues such as land ownership and water rights, so essential for tribal survival.

As a Pan-Indian movement, SAI proposed to speak with one voice for all Indians, but that proved elusive. The leaders largely agreed that they wanted to bring the American Indian into the mainstream of Anglo-American society, but they differed, sometimes strongly, as to how to achieve that goal. The SAI needed a strong, unifying leader to mediate the differences, but that was not a role a strongly opinionated Zitkala-Ša could play.

Carlos Montezuma held the most extreme views. He argued that the BIA and the reservation system kept Indians in poverty; thus it would be better to immediately end both and allow native peoples to thrive in American society. Others, such as Marie Baldwin, who worked for the BIA, called for the gradual end of the bureau as native peoples became more self-sufficient. Zitkala-Ša offered a third option, which set her apart from most "progressive" members of the SAI, who stressed full assimilation into American society. She saw the reservation not as an impoverished prison, but as a homeland, a place where Indian culture was preserved and where all Indians (even those who lived outside) could go to replenish their Indian identity.

The SAI professed to transcend tribal boundaries and speak for all Indians, but in reality some members held tribal loyalties that aggravated tribal division within the SAI. Zitkala-Ša's Sioux heritage, for example, was "the core of her identity." She constantly challenged the more acculturated members of the SAI with a constant "harkenening to her Sioux past." As editor of *American Indian Magazine*, she devoted a special issue to the Sioux. At the annual meeting of the SAI in Pierre, South Dakota, in 1918, she strongly supported the election of Charles Eastman, a Santee Sioux, as president of the society. With Eastman as president of the society, and Zitkala-Ša serving as national secretary/treasurer and editor of the magazine, the Sioux dominated the national office, much to the displeasure of some.

Peyote further divided the SAI. Zitkala-Ša had witnessed the use of peyote among the Utes at Uintah around 1913–1914. She came out strongly against peyote, which she condemned as a hallucinatory drug no different from alcohol—which damaged the physical, moral, and spiritual state of native people—and she refused to accept the religious significance of peyote in the emerging Native American Church as part of Indian tradition like the Sun Dance or the Ghost Dance. Zitkala-Ša had joined Mormon and Episcopal missionaries in opposing the spread of peyote at Uintah, and in 1917 she supported legislation in Utah and Colorado outlawing the use of peyote.

Zitkala-Ša continued her campaign against peyote within the SAI, where many members joined her crusade. Congress proposed legislation to outlaw the use of peyote and the Senate sub-committee on Indian Affairs asked her to testify. A piece in the *Washington Times* dated February 17, 1918, which announced that Zitkala-Ša would testify before the committee, included a picture of her dressed in Indian regalia.

A few days later James Mooney, a noted ethnologist from the Smithsonian who had personally studied the Ghost Dance religion and peyote religious practices, appeared before the committee to oppose the law outlawing peyote. In his testimony Mooney questioned Zitkala-Ša's knowledge of the peyote religion (she had never attended a peyote meeting as he did), and he ridiculed her mismatched Sioux outfit. Zitkala-Ša appeared before the committee the next day. Though shaken by Mooney's criticism, she refuted Mooney's assault on her character and listed intelligently her arguments against the use of peyote. In the end she employed a racial argument and asked the committee members who they should trust more: an Indian woman who had lived for a long time among the Ute people and knew the truth about peyote from firsthand experience or a white man who was an occasional visitor among Indian peoples. Interestingly, Francis La Flesche, an Omaha Indian who worked for the BIA, testified as to the beneficial aspects of the Native American Church, whose followers' use of peyote made them sober and productive members of their society. Francis relied on firsthand testimony of his noted sister, Dr. Susan La Flesche, who worked among the Omaha Indians.

The internal divisions among SAI members took its toll on the SAI. Fewer than thirty members attended the SAI meeting in Pierre, South Dakota, in 1918. The pro-peyote supporters stayed away, as did those who were tired of SAI factionalism and failures. For the moment Zitkala-Ša seemed in charge. But when she supported Carlos Montezuma's resolution to abolish the BIA, it alienated many bureau members, who saw it as a radical measure endangering reservation Indians, especially the elderly. A year later, at the annual conference in Minneapolis, the pro-peyote supporters returned in numbers and elected one of their own, Thomas Sloan, as president. Zitkala-Ša refused to accept the new leadership and resigned from all her offices in the SAI.

Raymond Bonnin wanted to return to South Dakota, but Zitkala-Ša did not. She took some time away from politics to assemble the short stories she published years ago into a collection entitled *American Indian Stories*, which came out in 1921. Once again Zitkala-Ša had established her literary credentials. But politics, not literature, had become her true cause, and she devoted the rest of her life to the task of securing the land base and cultural survival of the American Indian.

Needing a new base for her political work, Zitkala-Ša found it in the Greater Federation of Women's Clubs, which in 1921 appointed her an investigator for the newly established Indian Welfare Committee. In this capacity she joined Matthew K. Sniffen from the Indian Rights Association (IRA) and Charles H. Fabens from the American Indian Defense Association (AIDA) to investigate the theft of oil-rich Indian lands in Oklahoma. The trio spent two months in Oklahoma and found cases of wholesale abuse of the Indian populations by unscrupulous probate judges and lawyers who were charged to administer the land holdings of Indians deemed "incompetent" to manage their own lands. In 1924 the trio published their findings in a short pamphlet that said it all in its title: *Oklahoma's Poor Rich Indians: An Orgy of Graft and Exploitation of the Five Civilized Tribes, Legalized Robbery*.

While Sniffen and Fabens explored the legality of the corrupt probate/lawyer system, Zitkala-Ša used her literary gifts to expose the cruel exploitation of elderly women and children by corrupt lawyers who had been their "guardians." Their pamphlet prompted a congressional investigation but powerful interests blocked any action and, in the end, the congressional committee exonerated the probate courts. But the Oklahoma state legislature passed a law that placed some modest restrictions on lawyer/guardian fees. The system frustrated Zitkala-Ša.

After the setback in Oklahoma, Zitkala-Ša found shelter in John Collier's newly formed American Indian Defense Association. Collier, a kindred soul who rejected the further loss of Indian land and viewed the reservation and Indian culture as a refuge from the perils of modern society, gave her a voice in the early 1920s. But Zitkala-Ša had alienated too many former members of the SAI and too many officials in the BIA. In 1923, for example, when the secretary of the Interior formed the Committee of One Hundred to advise him on Indian policy, she was not invited.

Although she was sympathetic to Collier and the AIDA, Zitkala-Ša still longed for a Pan-Indian organization that would fight to protect Native American rights. In 1926 she and her husband cofounded the National Council of American Indians (NCAI), prompted in great part by the passage in Congress of the Indian Citizen Act (1924), which established citizenship for all American Indians. Zitkala-Ša had long advocated for the right of citizenship. With the NCAI the idea was to create a bloc of Indian voters, especially at the local and state levels, engaged in politics to protect the land and culture of American Indians within the American political system.

Zitkala-Ša served, unpaid, as president; Raymond served, with modest pay, as secretary-treasurer. Basically, they were the face and workforce of the organization. Each summer they traveled throughout reservation country gathering information and hearing complaints. Then they returned to Washington to argue before the BIA and Congress in support of Indian claims to land, better schools, and housing. Working alone, without staff and without money, she carried on the struggle for the rest of her life.

In one last major fight in the 1930s, Zitkala-Ša engaged with her old friend John Collier, who had become commissioner of Indian Affairs in Franklin D. Roosevelt's first administration. She remained sympathetic to Collier's goal of stopping the further loss of tribal/individual lands and preserving Indian culture, but she later opposed a major part of the Indian Reorganization Act (IRA) of 1934, which called for creation of written constitutions—a new form of elective government that would replace the traditional tribal council. Ever determined that Indians would decide their own destiny, Zitkala-Ša parted with her friend when he presumed to know what was best for Indian people. Both she and her husband considered the IRA as one more scheme by the BIA to control tribal life. They returned to Yankton and succeeded in persuading many of their kinsmen to reject the IRA. Zitkala-Ša and her allies proposed an alternate constitution that would place more power in an enlarged tribal council that would extend voting rights to all Yanktons living off the reservation and allow tribal membership for their children. Zitkala-Ša had strong personal reasons for advocating the last clause. Collier rejected the compromise and the conflict raged on.

Her last years were difficult as she and Raymond struggled financially. They had to look after their grown son, Ohiya, who suffered from severe diabetes and, in time, came with his wife and four children to live with them. Zitkala-Ša's health began to deteriorate, and she started to question her life's work.

During this period, Elaine Goodale Eastman, an old friend from the SAI, wrote to Zitkala-Ša to praise her work on behalf of American Indians. Responding with doubt of her accomplishments, she wrote, "I appreciate your genuine desire to give me credit for having tried to render service to the Red Race. But though it took a life time, the achievements are scarcely visible!!! It is even a most strenuous effort to stand still and hold fast the small grounds that have been gained."

Her biographer, Deborah Welch, believed that Zitkala-Ša "died a sad and profoundly disillusioned woman." Facing death, she believed that the American Indian was still "a veritable prisoner of war," subject to the whims of the BIA. Perhaps. But Zitkala-Ša was too hard on herself. The damages inflicted on the American Indians by whites had been long in coming and could not be reversed in a year, a decade, or even a generation. The New Deal years heralded the beginning of change: the defense of the land base, the preservation of culture, and a greater voice for Indians in their own affairs. Zitkala-Ša had waged the good fight in that long struggle to achieve self-determination for Indian peoples.

On January 25, 1938, Zitkala-Ša fell into a coma and was taken to Georgetown Hospital, where she died the next day at age sixty-one. With irony the hospital's postmortem report simply listed her as "Gertrude Bonnin from South Dakota—Housewife." Though Zitkala-Ša was nominally a Catholic, a memorial service for her was held at the Church of the Latter Day Saints in Washington. William Hanson came from New York City, where he was staging a revival on Broadway of *The Sun Dance Opera* that

Zitkala-Ša had worked on some twenty-five years earlier. John Collier was also present to pay respects to Zitkala-Ša, one of "the most sincere and persuasive advocates" for Indian rights. She was buried at Arlington National Cemetery (Raymond was a veteran). The epitaph on her marker read more fittingly: "Gertrude Simmons Bonnin—'Zitkala-Ša' of the Sioux Indians."

CHAPTER 18

Lost Bird: Sacred Child of the
Wounded Knee Battlefield

On a cold, wintry New Year's Day in 1891, three days after soldiers from the Seventh Cavalry massacred hundreds of ghost dancers at Wounded Knee, Dr. Charles Eastman, the Santee Sioux Agency physician on the Pine Ridge Reservation, led a search party to find survivors. George E. Bartlett, one of the searchers, thought he heard the cry of a child. Locating the source of the cry, Bartlett found seven dead women lying close together covered with blankets. As he turned over the frozen bodies, he was startled to find a baby girl, still alive, wrapped in the arms of a dead woman. Somehow the cold, hungry, frightened baby had survived under her mother's frozen corpse in a blinding blizzard with temperatures under forty below zero. Ironically, the child, wrapped in a shawl, wore on her head a buckskin cap with an American flag embroidered in bright beadwork.

Bartlett carried the child safely back to Pine Ridge, where he placed the little girl with John Yellow Bird and his wife, Anne, who ran a trading post. Anne, who lovingly nursed the child back to health, called her "Okicize Wanji Cinca," the Child of the Battlefield. This lost child was tormented her whole life by the mystery of the events that had led her mother to the killing fields of Wounded Knee.

By the late 1880s the Lakota people had suffered years of hard times living on the Great Sioux Reservation in the Dakotas. They were virtual prisoners, their past life as a free, nomadic people only a bitter memory, especially for the older generation who remembered a happier life on the Great Plains.

The sacred Black Hills and the buffalo-rich Powder River country were "stolen" by the whites, the buffalo killed off, their beloved war-leader Crazy Horse dead, and Sitting Bull confined to the Standing Rock Agency. Subjected to constant pressure by the BIA to abandon their "savage" way of life for the "civilized" lifestyle of whites, they chafed under Indian agents who challenged the traditional power of the chiefs and replaced the military societies with appointed Indian Police. At the same time Christian missionaries opposed their cultural and religious practices, even outlawing the Sun Dance. White teachers in the schools turned children away from tribal traditions, and Indians were encouraged to farm and live in log cabins like whites.

The 1880s were a bad decade for the Lakotas. Years of drought destroyed their meager crops and diseases struck down their much-needed livestock. Epidemics of measles, whooping cough, and influenza hit young and old alike, and many died.

In the midst of these disasters, Congress pressured the weakened Lakotas in 1889 to negotiate a new agreement by which they lost half their land and the Great Sioux Reservation was broken up into six smaller reservations: Pine Ridge, Rosebud, Lower Brulé, Crow Creek, Cheyenne River, and Standing Rock. Many of the older, more traditional leaders opposed the "sale" of land. Speaking for many, one elderly Lakota bitterly told the Reverend William J. Cleveland, "They [the whites] made us many promises, more than I can remember, but they never kept but one; they promised to take our land and they took it." Congress aggravated the problem in 1890 when they cut some $100,000 destined for the Lakota. The beef rations fell dramatically and many Lakotas went hungry.

All this pressure to change their old way of life had a devastating impact on the Lakotas. Historian Robert Utley, in *The Last Days of the Sioux Nation*, one of the classic studies on the Ghost Dance and Wounded Knee, noted that after many years of forced assimilation "a pervasive feeling of bitterness, helplessness, and futility gripped the Sioux."

In the midst of these deep troubles, the Lakotas began to hear vague but wondrous news: A messiah, who had appeared beyond the Rockies, promised Indians that the day was near for their deliverance from the oppressive world of white dominance. George Sword, captain of the Indian Police at Pine Ridge, captured the feelings of his people at this time. "In 1889," he reported, "the Oglalas heard that the Son of God had come upon the earth in the west. They said the Messiah was there, but he had come to help the Indian and not the whites, and it made the Indians happy to hear this."

In the fall of 1889, chiefs from Pine Ridge, Rosebud, and Cheyenne River sent delegates west to meet the messiah, who they found on the Paiute Reservation in Nevada. His name was Wovoka, the Cutter, though some called him Jack Wilson. When a young man in his twenties, Wovoka went to live and work for David Wilson, a rancher in Mason Valley, where he got his adoptive name. As a Christian, the rancher read the Bible aloud nightly for family and workers, and Wovoka came to know about Jesus, the "messiah," and the messiah's anticipated second coming from the gospel texts.

Wovoka was a well-known shaman among the Paiutes in the late 1880s, but his fame as a holy man reached far beyond his tribe after he experienced the great vision of his life. Wovoka later shared his vision with James Mooney, the famed Smithsonian ethnologist who wrote *The Ghost Dance Religion and the Sioux Outbreak of 1890*, the first major account of those events. According to Wovoka, the moment that changed his life took place on January 1, 1889, when a total eclipse of the sun occurred. It was a magical moment in time. Wovoka, who lay ill with a fever during the eclipse, had an out-of-body experience. "When the sun died," he said, "I went up to heaven and saw God and all the people who had died a long time ago. God told me to come back and tell my people that they must be good and love one another."

When Wovoka returned to the earth, he began preaching God's message and teaching the people a sacred dance, which the Lakotas called the "Spirit" or "Ghost Dance" because many who danced fell into a trance and saw the "ghosts" of their ancestors. Wovoka told Mooney that he was not the "messiah" but a "prophet who has received a divine revelation." But that was not what many Indian delegates understood. Listening to Wovoka's preaching, they saw him as the messiah, the Christ figure who bore the crucifixion marks and came to save the Indian people.

These delegates returned to their reservations with a joyous message: Indians should prepare for the return of the messiah by embracing the religious teachings of Wovoka, dancing the sacred Ghost Dance, and singing the sacred songs. The earth would very soon be renewed, the buffalo would return, dead Indians would reappear to join their living relatives in the new paradise, and, most important, whites would disappear from the earth. The Lakota delegates spoke of a cataclysmic event that would destroy whites, but consistent with Wovoka's teaching, this great moment would take place through supernatural, not military force.

By late summer 1890, thousands of Lakota Indians at Pine Ridge, Rosebud, Cheyenne River, and Standing Rock had taken up the new religion and the Ghost Dance. Rani-Henrik Andersson, in *The Lakota Ghost Dance of 1890*, estimated that some 4,200 Lakota were caught up in the movement.

The Lakotas danced with passion, dressed in their "ghost shirts" that would protect them from white men's bullets.

They were right to fear the whites, who misunderstood the peaceful nature of the Ghost Dance and saw only danger instead. On November 15, 1890, Daniel F. Royer, the inexperienced and frightened Indian agent at Pine Ridge, sent a fearful telegram to the commissioner of Indian Affairs calling for troops to protect the agency, claiming that the "Indians are dancing in the snow & are wild & crazy." Indian agent E. B. Reynolds, who witnessed the Ghost Dance at Pine Ridge and Rosebud, backed up Royer's exaggerated claim. President Harrison ordered the War Department in mid-November to intervene and restore order. The president's decision to send soldiers set in motion a horrific chain of events.

General Nelson Miles directed the army's response and by December had ringed the reservations with several thousand well-armed troops— enough to intimidate the ghost dancers into surrendering or destroy them if they chose to fight. The presence of soldiers frightened the ghost dancers. Some sought to avoid conflict by staying close to the agencies; others decided that they could find safety and freedom to continue the sacred dance by fleeing into the vastness of the Dakota Badlands. By mid-December both sides had avoided bloodshed, but the uneasy peace was shattered at Standing Rock.

James McLaughin, the autocratic Indian agent, had long feuded with the strong-willed Sitting Bull, and that conflict intensified when Sitting Bull encouraged his followers to take up the Ghost Dance. On December 15, 1890, the long-standing conflict came to an explosive end when McLaughlin sent Indian Police to arrest Sitting Bull and a deadly fight broke out between Sitting Bull's supporters and the Indian Police. When it was over, Sitting Bull lay dead and some of his followers fled to join Big Foot's ghost dancers at Cheyenne River.

Big Foot remained the only leader of the Ghost Dance movement outside the Badlands. Surrounded by soldiers, he feared for his people's safety. He had no desire to fight the soldiers. Best known as a diplomat, he had been asked by the chiefs at Pine Ridge to come and restore peace to their troubled reservation. So, in late December, Big Foot led his band of some four hundred Miniconjous and Hunkpapas to Pine Ridge. He never made it. Soldiers from the Seventh Cavalry intercepted his line of march and brought the sickly Big Foot (on Christmas day the old chief came down with pneumonia) and his followers to the army's base at Wounded Knee Creek, not far from Pine Ridge.

Colonel James W. Forsyth, who commanded the Seventh Cavalry at Wounded Knee, was authorized to disarm Big Foot's band and take every precaution to prevent their escape if they surrendered, but to destroy them if they fought. On the cold morning of December 29, 1890, the Indians woke, as feared, to the frightening reality that they were surrounded by five hundred well-armed soldiers, with four deadly Hotchkiss guns placed on a high hill, pointed down directly at their camp.

The warriors, men and boys, were summoned to meet in an open space next to Big Foot's tent. The soldiers set about to disarm the Indian men and in the process a gun accidently went off. Hell broke loose. The soldiers poured a withering round into the ghost dancers, who fought back with guns and knives in hand-to-hand fighting. Within ten minutes the field was littered with the dead and wounded. Big Foot had been shot dead.

The surviving warriors fought their way out of the circle and headed for their village, but the Hotchkiss guns on the hill opened deadly fire on the village, causing widespread death and destruction. Desperate survivors—warriors, old people, women, and children—fled for safety in every direction: toward the agency road, the banks of Wounded Knee Creek, and a nearby deep ravine. But wherever they went, soldiers fired on them. The historian Renée Sansom Flood, who wrote *Lost Bird of Wounded Knee*, believes that somewhere in this frenzied flight a woman carrying a little girl child wearing a buckskin cap decorated with an American flag was mortally wounded, the dying woman crawling to a cutbank where she dug in and wrapped the baby in a shawl under her body to save her. Other wounded women followed. The falling snow buried them. All died but the child.

The terrible fight finally came to an end with dead and dying Indians everywhere on the battlefield. The soldiers withdrew to Pine Ridge with their dead and wounded, leaving dead Indians on the battlefield. They did take back fifty-one badly wounded and frightened Indians, mostly women and children. The next day a blizzard struck the Northern Plains, covering the frozen Indian bodies with snow.

On New Year's Day search parties came from Pine Ridge to look for survivors and bury the dead. They found seven survivors. For two days they gathered the bloody, frozen bodies and buried them one on the other, "like so much cordwood," in an open trench on the very hill where the Hotchkiss guns had rained down so much destruction. There is no way to know with any certainty the number of Indians who died at Wounded Knee, but the lowest number would be 146, matching the names of the known dead men, women, and children etched on the monument at the present-day gravesite at Wounded Knee. William Peano, a member of the burial party, told Judge Eli S. Ricker, who collected stories from Indian and white participants in the Wounded Knee fight, that 146 bodies were buried in the trench. More importantly, he identifies the dead: 24 old men too feeble to fight; 7 very old women; 6 boys between five and eight; 7 babies under two years old; and 102 young men and women, which included boys and girls ten years and up. Even at the low number of 146, Wounded Knee was a murderous affair.

The number of dead and badly wounded women, children, and older people was indefensible. While some historians like Robert Utley called Wounded Knee a "regrettable tragic accident of war," the Lakota rightly call it a massacre. Many died at Wounded Knee—and so did the dream of a restored world.[1]

A few days after the Wounded Knee massacre, Brigadier General Leonard Wright Colby, the commander of the Nebraska National Guard, arrived at Pine Ridge. While there, Colby met the little girl, the Child of the Battlefield, at John Yellow Bird's trading post. Fascinated with this little girl's story, Colby decided to adopt her for his wife, Clara Colby. But Anne Yellow Bird had no intention of surrendering the little child to a white man. She fled with the child to a hostile camp of remaining ghost dancers.

Colby was determined to have the child. He enlisted the help of two sisters, Margaret and Elizabeth Asay, who ran a trading post at Pine Ridge. The sisters dressed Colby to look like a mixed-blood Indian. A reluctant John Yellow Bird, with an interpreter, led the party into the hostile camp. The sisters brought food for the hungry ghost dancers who, in turn, led them to Anne and the baby girl.

An old woman held the child. Speaking through an interpreter, Colby pleaded his case: "I am a Seneca Indian—my grandmother was a full-blood Seneca. . . . I rescued the child who survived the massacre at Wounded Knee. Take pity on me and my wife. We have no children of our own."

---

1   The literature on the Ghost Dance and Wounded Knee is immense. For a short but critical introduction to this chapter in Lakota history, one can consult Joseph Agonito, Chapter 8, "The Ghost Dancers: Hope and Death at Wounded Knee," in *Lakota Portraits: Lives of the Legendary Plains People*, Helena, MT: TwoDot Books, 2011.

The statement was a complete lie. Colby was not a Seneca Indian; he did not save the child at Wounded Knee; and he and his wife already had an adopted son.

Several Lakota men and women in the camp who did not want Colby to claim the full-blood child stepped forward to adopt her, but Colby's interpreter vouched for his good intentions. Colby reached for the child but the old woman holding her resisted and cried out, "Zintkala Nuni! Zintkala Nuni!" ("The Lost Bird! The Lost Bird!). Then, for unknown reasons, the woman released the child to the seemingly sincere "mixed-blood" Indian. With the child in hand, Colby and the others rode quickly out of camp back to the safety of John Yellow Bird's store.

Colby was not yet done. A Miniconjou couple, Felix Crane Pretty Voice and Rock Woman, claimed they had lost a daughter at Wounded Knee. They did not make a compelling case, and Colby was suspicious of their claim. Desperately poor, they accepted Colby's financial assistance and went on their way—to reappear some years later in Lost Bird's story.

It's not certain that present-day historians have resolved the issue of her parentage. Renée Sansom Flood, Lost Bird's biographer, asserted that the woman who died in the snow with a child wrapped in her embrace was most likely the real mother. Jerome A. Green, in his recent study on Wounded Knee, *American Carnage*, argued that Felix Crane Pretty Voice and Rock Woman were the real parents. But to accept this view one would have to believe that a Lakota woman would give up her child to a white stranger and that George Bartlett's story to Judge Eli Ricker that he found the mother and child buried in the snow was fabricated. What's more, Felix Crane Pretty Voice told the chief of Indian Police at Cheyenne River in 1925 that he was not the father.

Threatening Colby's claim to the girl even more, some Lakota women claimed the child was the daughter of Black Day Woman, the young wife of Sitting Bull who may have fled after her husband's death to Big Foot's camp. Fearful of losing his prized little girl, Colby left Pine Ridge and headed for his home in Beatrice, Nebraska, where on January 20, 1891, he formally adopted Zintkala Nuni, the Lost Bird. He named the child Margaret Elizabeth in honor of the two Asay sisters who had helped him win the child. Zintkala Nuni would be haunted the rest of her life as to the true identity of her mother.

Throughout this tumultuous period, Clara Colby was in Washington, D.C., with her adopted eleven-year-old son, Clarence—a young boy diagnosed with limited mental facility.

Clara was a nationally known suffrage leader and founding editor of the *Woman's Tribune*, the official voice of the National Women's Suffrage Association. She spent six months every year in Washington, editing the newspaper and lobbying Congress for women's suffrage.

Leonard did not notify his wife until January 23, 1891, that she was now the adoptive mother of a full-blood Lakota girl found on the bloody field at Wounded Knee. Leonard told her to come home and mother the child. At age forty-four, Clara must have been astonished by her husband's strange, impulsive action that would change her life forever.

After some soul-searching, Clara decided to accept the child. But, despite her husband's plea, Clara did not rush home. She remained in Washington for some months, celebrating Susan B. Anthony's birthday and working for women's suffrage. Fortunately for Clara, her sister, Dr. Mary White, assumed responsibility for the child. Dr. White hired a beautiful seventeen-year-old German girl, Marie Miller (better known as "Maud"), as the child's governess.

Clara arrived home in Beatrice on May 1, 1891. From the beginning she called the child by her Lakota name, shortening it to Zintkala or Zintka. For the next few years as she moved between Beatrice and Washington, Clara tried her best to look after Clarence and Zintkala while continuing her work on behalf of women's suffrage, editing the *Woman's Tribune*, lecturing on women's issues, and traveling with Susan B. Anthony. She depended on Maud to look after the children while away since Leonard was too busy for the responsibility of fatherhood. Inevitably, Zintkala suffered from Leonard's disinterest and Clara's long absences from home.

The lives of Clara and Zintkala took a decisive turn for the worse in December 1892 when Maud left, pregnant with child. After Maud gave birth to a son, Clara discovered that Leonard was the boy's father. Though devastated by this betrayal, Clara refused to divorce Leonard for fear of scandal. Leonard promised not to see Maud again, a promise he did not keep.

In the next few years, Leonard played less and less a role in the family, and Clara carried on as best she could in his absence. Despite a brief attempt at reconciliation in 1896, Leonard left Clara once again for Maud,

Brigadier General Leonard Wright Colby with Lost Bird, 1891 COURTESY OF DENVER
PUBLIC LIBRARY, WESTERN HISTORY COLLECTION, X31472

never to return. Having lost her mother at Wounded Knee, Zintkala now
lost her adoptive father. From her meager earnings as a lecturer and writer,
Clara struggled to support the family, which lived constantly on the edge
of poverty.

Washington, D.C., was not always kind to Clara or Zintkala. Susan B.
Anthony, her mentor, never approved of Clara's adoption of Zintkala and
some suffragists made hurtful remarks about the Indian child. Zintkala

attended school in the city, where she suffered the taunts of her white class-mates who called her derogatory names.

As she grew older, Zintkala became more aware of her difference from her classmates. Perhaps to ease her young daughter's plight, Clara told the girl about her real mother, who died protecting the child on the bloody field at Wounded Knee. Zintkala always cherished this image of a loving mother and treasured the beaded cap, which Clara had saved, becoming increasingly curious about her Indian past.

Zintkala's first contact with the Lakota world came in 1900 when Clara took her to the Pan-American Exposition in Buffalo, in which American Indians participated. By chance, the ten-year-old girl met the Lakota del-egation. The elders were fascinated to meet a surviving child of Wounded Knee, and Zintkala was excited to meet the long-lost members of her tribe.

Renée Sansom Flood saw this as a turning point for the young woman, who began a lifelong quest to reclaim her Lakota heritage. But the struggle took a toll on the young girl as "she became frustrated, morose, and often physically and emotionally out of control. She yearned for her mother and suffered terrible nightmares." Despite her care and love, Clara was at a loss.

Zintkala became more strong-willed and difficult as she grew older, and Clara found it increasingly hard to cope with her daughter's emotional problems. Seeking an alternative to Washington's public schools, Clara con-sidered sending Zintkala to Carlisle Indian Industrial School, but Captain Richard H. Pratt advised against such a move, thinking that Zintkala would best thrive in a white, Christian society, not among Indians. Clara unwisely agreed.

A series of white, Christian boarding schools followed, with Zintkala doing poorly and staying in each for a short time. Besides, Clara could no longer afford to pay the high tuition costs at private schools and finally adopted a course of action she had long resisted. In October 1904 she sent Zintkala to a federally funded Indian industrial boarding school in Chamberlain, South Dakota. Surrounded by Indian students, Zintkala did well at school until the winter of 1905 when she became ill and joined her mother in Portland, Oregon, where Clara was editing her newspaper and fighting for women's suffrage. Desperately poor (Leonard never contrib-uted to the support of his children) and caught up in divorce proceedings with Leonard, Clara found it difficult to handle her troubled teenage daughter, so she enrolled Zintkala in Chemawa, an Indian boarding school near Portland.

Zintkala did not stay long at Chemawa. Caught between two worlds—Indian and white—Zintkala decided to find her true place. She ran away and headed to the Dakotas to find out if she really was the daughter of Black Day Woman, Sitting Bull's younger wife. Just sixteen, penniless and foolish in expectation, she made it as far as Lemmon, South Dakota, where she joined a Wild West show as a cowgirl riding horses. After several months of working in the show, she had enough money to visit Standing Rock to find her lost relatives.

Zintkala arrived on the reservation dressed as a gaudy cowgirl, without any knowledge of Lakota culture or language. She was badly out of place. Bold with men, talking and laughing loudly, she did not act like a properly brought up Lakota woman. Suspicious of this strange woman who claimed to be Sitting Bull's daughter, the Hunkpapas shunned her as they did other Lakota students who came back from the boarding schools sounding "white." One of Ms. Flood's Lakota informants said that Zintkala ended up on a muddy road crying, "It's me, Lost Bird! Zintkala Nuni! Please help me."

Zintkala left Standing Rock and headed for Pine Ridge to continue her search for lost relatives. At Pine Ridge she met Neglicu, "Comes Out Alive," who had also survived the massacre at Wounded Knee. Unlike Zintkala, Comes Out Alive had been adopted by Lakota parents and lived her life on the reservation. The two girls became more than friends; they considered themselves twin sisters. Comes Out Alive took her new "sister" to the Wounded Knee cemetery, where it is said that Zintkala lay down on the grave site and cried.

After these emotional experiences, Zintkala returned to live with Clara in Portland but did not stay long. No longer able to care for her troubled daughter, Clara sent Zintkala to live with Leonard Colby in Beatrice, Nebraska, where Colby actually spent time with his adopted daughter and gave her nice presents, much to the displeasure of his wife, Maud.

Colby placed Zintkala in the public school, where she did not mix with the white children. By year's end Colby placed Zintkala at Haskell Institute, an Indian boarding school in Kansas. Clara was so pleased with the move that she embarked on a five-month European speaking tour on behalf of women's suffrage.

However, unknown to Clara, Zintkala was pregnant when she arrived at Haskell. Clearly something had happened in Beatrice. Who was the father? Could it have been Leonard? After all, he had seduced the young Maud. In any case, Haskell dismissed the pregnant girl.

Fearful of scandal, Leonard used his authority as the girl's father to place Zintkala in the Milford Industrial Home in Nebraska, a reform school for young girls. (The Milford Industrial Home was originally named the Nebraska Maternity Home.) Less than a month after she entered Milford, Zintkala gave birth to a stillborn baby boy (April 22, 1908). Still, she could not leave. Once committed to Milford, a resident had to remain one year—though it's not clear in Zintkala's case that she was ever formally sentenced by any judge, which was the normal procedure. Perhaps Colby had used his political influence in Nebraska to keep the whole affair private.

Clara did not find out the awful truth about Zintkala's plight until she returned from Europe. She rushed to Milford to see her troubled daughter. Clara could have possibly arranged an earlier release for Zintkala had Colby been willing to finance his daughter's education at a nearby nursing school, but he refused to pay the tuition. Colby left Zintkala at Milford for the entire year. When released in April of 1909, Zintkala returned to her mother's home in Portland.

Back in Portland, Zintkala met Albert Chalivat, an attractive young Frenchman. Though young and poor, they soon married. Clara hoped that her daughter would find happiness with Albert, but happiness once again eluded the Lost Bird of Wounded Knee. Within a few weeks of marriage, Zintkala contracted syphilis. Furious with her husband, she threw him out. For one year the disillusioned Zintkala remained in her mother's house under doctor's care, a syphilitic invalid. Clara, desperately poor, could no longer edit her beloved *Woman's Tribune*. Leonard refused to provide any financial aid for his beleaguered ex-wife and adopted daughter.

Sometime during this difficult year, Clara shared with Zintkala Elaine Goodale Eastman's novel, *Yellow Star*, a fictional version of Lost Bird's life. (Ms. Eastman had been a teacher at Pine Ridge during the Wounded Knee massacre.) Yellow Star, the novel's heroine, had survived the massacre at Wounded Knee, where her natural mother was killed by the soldiers. A kind missionary couple adopted the child, but when the missionary died, his wife took the child back east to her hometown in New England. Yellow Star grew up comfortably in the small town, where she made good friends and attended the Laurel Academy. After graduation Yellow Star returned to Pine Ridge, where she worked hard as a field matron, winning the respect and trust of her own people. What must Lost Bird have thought of this charming story that had so little to do with her own life as she lay in bed, a victim of syphilis, depressed, impoverished, abandoned by her adoptive father, struggling to find her place in the world?

When Zintkala felt better, she headed for the Cheyenne River Reservation, again to find her lost Miniconjou relatives. She met Olney Runs After, a young, attractive Lakota serving as agency interpreter. The young man took her to the home of Felix Crane Pretty Voice and Rock Woman, the same couple that claimed her as their daughter back in 1891. Zintkala lived with them for a year, during which Felix Crane Pretty Voice treated the young woman like his own daughter, though he admitted later to the chief of police at Cheyenne River she was not. But Rock Woman disliked Zintkala because she did not act like a proper Lakota woman.

After a year Zintkala became restless. Still caught between two worlds, she did not know where she belonged. She decided to head west to California and find work in the movies and Wild West shows. She begged Olney Runs After to run away with her, but he refused to leave the reservation. She went on alone.

Zintkala found work in Hollywood as a movie extra, mostly playing Indian roles. She earned seven dollars a week, barely enough to live. There she met a Texas cowboy, Robert J. Keith, who was working as a cowpuncher in the movies; they married in 1913. Zintkala gave birth to a boy she named Clyde. It was a short-lived affair, since Robert turned out to be an abusive drunk. Zintkala left him, taking the boy with her.

Zintkala then found work in Buffalo Bill's Wild West show, where she became attracted to Ernest Cornelius "Dick" Allen, a nineteen-year-old clown in the circus. Even though she never divorced Robert Keith, she married Dick in 1915 and soon gave birth to another baby boy.

The couple left the show in the spring and moved to San Francisco, where they started a vaudeville group, playing the theaters, saloons, and dance halls of San Francisco's Barbary Coast. Desperately poor, they often depended on private charities to make ends meet. Ever in need of help, Zintkala visited Dr. Valentine McGillycuddy, a onetime Indian agent at Pine Ridge, then living in San Francisco. McGillycuddy knew the remarkable story of Lost Bird and tried to help. He cashed a check for her for twenty-

Zintkala Nuni, the Lost Bird, at the 1915 Panama-Pacific Exposition in San Francisco REPRINTED FROM THE OCTOBER 1915 ISSUE OF *SUNSET* MAGAZINE. DIVISION OF RARE AND MANUSCRIPT COLLECTIONS, CORNELL UNIVERSITY LIBRARY

five dollars, which later bounced. And Zintkala borrowed a copy, which she never returned, of James Mooney's famous *The Ghost Dance Religion and the Sioux Outbreak of 1890*. What must have been her thoughts as she looked at the sketches and photos of the ghost dancers, including her own baby picture?

Throughout these difficult years Clara and Zintkala continued to correspond, but neither shared their true plight. Desperately poor and dependent on friends in the movement, Clara continued the struggle for women's suffrage. Becoming more radical with age, she fought alongside Emmeline Pankhurst's militant "suffragettes" in London and Alice Paul's combative feminists in Washington, D.C.

Mother and daughter finally met again in the spring of 1915 when Clara came to San Francisco to take part in the Federal Suffrage Association Convention. Dressed in an Indian outfit, Zintkala joined her mother at the convention. Clara "loaned" Zintkala ten dollars, her last small gesture of support for her adopted daughter. They would never meet again.

In her late sixties, exhausted from her hard life and extremely ill, Clara was taken in by her sister, Dr. Mary White (who had once looked after little Zintkala), in Palo Alto, California. Despite her sister's best care, Clara Colby died from pneumonia in 1916. Zintkala's reaction to her adoptive mother's death has not been recorded.

Meanwhile, Zintkala was engaged in her own losing battle with life and syphilis. She lived in a series of run-down hotels, caring for a sick husband and two children. The baby boy she had with Dick Allen died and she sent Clyde, the older boy, to live with an Indian woman in Los Angeles. Zintkala appealed to the commissioner of Indian Affairs for legal title on her allotted land at Cheyenne River (Clara Colby had enrolled Zintkala as a Miniconjou at Cheyenne River in 1902). Perhaps she intended to settle on her own piece of land on the reservation, but always desperate for money, Zintkala mortgaged the land for $1,500, and when she could not repay the loans, she lost the land.

Without money, evicted from their hotel, and sick from the lingering effects of syphilis (she went blind in one eye), Zintkala returned with Dick to his hometown in Hanford, California, to live with his father—her last stop on her troubled journey in this world. Weakened by syphilis, Zintkala came down with the Spanish influenza ravaging the country. On February 14, 1920, she suffered intense pain in her chest and died from an apparent heart attack. Zintkala Nuni, the Lost Bird, was buried in Hanford, a long way from the bloody field at Wounded Knee.

A life that began badly, ended badly. But there was one surprising endnote. On April 8, 1990, Renée Sansom Flood was invited to share her research about the life of Lost Bird with the members of the Pine Ridge Wounded Knee Survivors' Association. One of the Lakota elders suggested they should bring Lost Bird home and bury her with her relatives in the

Wounded Knee cemetery. The idea took hold, funds were raised, and a delegation led by Avrol Looking Horse, Keeper of the Sacred Pipe of the Lakota Nation, went to Hanford, California, to recover the remains of Lost Bird. Her body was taken to Pine Ridge and, in a moving ceremony, reburied in the Wounded Knee cemetery, just outside the gate that encloses the mass grave. As a gesture of respect for Lost Bird's adoptive mother, who did her best for the child, Avrol Looking Horse placed a picture of Clara Colby in the coffin. Lost Bird had at last come home to stay with her people.

CHAPTER 19

Mary Brave Bird: Defender of Her People

On the first day of 1891, a search party combing through the dead after the ordeal of the Wounded Knee massacre discovered a small baby girl alive in the snow. Her mother dead, the child's name was unknown, though she came to be remembered as Zintkala Nuni, the Lost Bird of Wounded Knee, a symbol of the bloody tragedy that cost the lives and dreams of hundreds of ghost dancers.

Many years later a young seventeen-year-old woman, a Brulé Lakota of mixed ancestry, gave birth to a baby boy during a second tumultuous time at Wounded Knee, when followers of the American Indian Movement (AIM) and Lakota traditionalists had taken over the sacred site, protesting the long suffering of their people at the hands of the BIA and reservation officials at Pine Ridge. This baby, named Pedro, became a symbol of rebirth among the Lakota Indians. The young woman's name was Mary Brave Bird, and her tumultuous life and writings gave voice to a new generation of American Indians fighting to regain their sovereignty and cultural heritage.[1]

Unlike Zintkala Nuni, Mary Brave Bird grew up on the Rosebud Reservation surrounded by members of her extended family, the "tiyospaye." She never knew her maternal grandfather, Robert Brave Bird, who died in a tragic accident many years before her birth. But she did know her maternal grandmother, Louise Flood, and her second husband, Grandpa Noble Moore, who raised Mary and her siblings while their mother was away from Rosebud studying to be a nurse and later a teacher.

Emily Brave Bird, Mary's mother, was a quiet source of strength for her children, though it took Mary some time to realize the constancy of her mother's love. Emily met Mary's father in a strange way. After Mary's grandfather, Robert Brave Bird, died in an accident sometime in the 1930s,

---

1   The primary sources for Mary's life remain the two autobiographies she wrote in collaboration with Richard Erdoes. The first book, *Lakota Woman*, was published under her married name, Mary Crow Dog, and covered the early years of her life, roughly from her birth up to 1977. In the early 1990s, Mary's publisher wanted a second book bringing her life up-to-date. The second book, *Ohitika Woman*, was published under her birth name, Mary Brave Bird.

Grandma Louise took her children to live with her sister at the Rosebud Agency. There Emily attended the St. Francis Mission School, where (according to Mary) "she chose the white man's road as her way." The well-known Jesuit priest Fr. Eugene Buechel baptized Emily, and, while life at the Catholic boarding school was difficult, Emily took her education seriously.

Some years later Grandma Louise married the widower Noble Moore, a kind man who Mary would later call "father." Noble Moore had a son named Bill Moore, who was part white (French and Spanish), part Indian, and the same age as Emily. Bill and Emily married. By all accounts a handsome man, he proved to be a bad husband who got drunk and chased other women. One year after Mary was born (the last of five children), Emily finally divorced her husband. Mary grew up without a father, remembering only a picture of him on the mantelpiece dressed in a navy suit. Although she later saw him for brief moments on three separate occasions, he barely acknowledged her as his daughter. Because of this parental background, Mary grew up as "iyeska," a mixed-blood. After the divorce Emily became the sole support of her family and went to Pierre, South Dakota, where she studied to become a nurse and found work.

While away, Emily left the children with Grandma Flood and Grandpa Moore. The family lived, at first, in the community of He Dog in a simple house without electricity, running water, or heat. Later, they moved to Parmelee, where they lived in government housing, residing close to the agency school where Grandpa Moore worked as a janitor. Mary loved her grandparents and was saddened when her grandfather died suddenly in 1972.

Living simple lives in the "Sioux way," the grandparents chose not to speak Sioux to the children lest it impede their entrance into the white educational system, which they considered necessary for their future. Fortunately, there were other members of Grandma Flood's extended family who exposed Mary to Sioux language and cultural traditions.

When Mary was six or seven, she went back to live with her mother. Emily raised Mary as a Catholic, sending her to St. Francis for an education, the school that claimed three generations of the Flood/Brave Bird family. Grandma Flood went there as a child and suffered the harsh discipline of the nuns. Emily attended as well, and though she experienced the hard time of a boarding school, she chose to dwell not on the discipline but on the good education she received. Barbara (Mary's older sister) was already at

St. Francis and now it was young Mary's turn to receive a good, Catholic education—at least that was Emily's hope.

Mary came of age at St. Francis during the 1960s, growing to dislike the nuns who ran the place like a "penal institution." Mary resented the daily, boring routine that went against the upbringing of Lakota children; she found the food dull and tasteless; she hated the physical abuse of the nuns who used the strap on "unruly" children, something a Lakota mother in the old days would not have done; and she disapproved of the forced prayer and worship.

As Mary grew into a teenager, she began to rebel against this harsh discipline. Sometime in 1969 or 1970, Mary and her friends Charlene Left Hand Bull and Gina One Star met a young, long-haired Anglo woman, the first "hippie" they had ever met, who told them that young people—white, black, and Indian—were fighting back against the system. Why didn't they do the same? Mary and her friends decided to put out an underground newspaper called the *Red Panther*, which blasted conditions at St. Francis, circulating it widely. They were caught and punished, but it was the beginning of Mary's revolt against white-run St. Francis.

Mary tolerated one more "spanking" for a minor infraction, and then she told Charlene, "We are getting too old to have our bare asses whipped this way. We are old enough to have babies. Enough of this shit. Next time we fight back." An opportunity came shortly after. When the girls took their evening showers, one little girl was too embarrassed to take off her panties. The supervising nun threated to spank the girl, but Mary stepped in and knocked the nun down.

Meanwhile Mary had found a "boyfriend" at school and was caught holding hands with him. Sister Bernard signaled Mary out in front of a class as being an "unchaste" woman. Taking offense, Mary told the Sister that "you people are a lot worse than us Indians." Based on stories told to her by her grandmother and mother, Mary accused the priests and nuns of illicit relations in the old days and noted that some priests at St. Francis were guilty of sexual harassment.

Mary's last run-in occurred when a Jesuit priest embarrassed a young boy in English class. Mary took the priest to task and the angry priest kept Mary after class. Grabbing Mary's arm, he pushed her against the blackboard. Mary hit him in the face, giving him a bloody nose, so the priest took Mary to the principal's office. Mary had had enough. She told Sister Bernard that she quit school and wanted her diploma, which she got.

After leaving St. Francis, Mary entered a wild period she referred to as "aimlessness." Along with her sister Barbara, Mary hung around the reservation towns of Parmelee and Mission, "drunk towns," she called them. She started drinking heavily in bars and getting into fights, calling it "the natural way of life" on the reservation. Mary and Barbara did not get along with their mother, who was disappointed in her children's conduct. Mary, with Barbara, left her mother's house. Drifting from place to place, drinking and smoking marijuana, the sisters supported themselves by shoplifting (which they called "liberating") groceries, clothes, and jewelry.

Sex, including casual sex, was part of the lifestyle of young Indian men and women on the reservations. Mary complained that most young Indian warriors "just wanted to hop in the sack with you." She had mixed feelings about Indian men: "They were incredibly brave in protecting us, they would literally die for us, and they always stood up for our rights—*against outsiders!*" But, while defending women against sexual advances by white men, they were not troubled by taking sexual advantage of Indian women.

Mary and Barbara, perhaps because of their Christian upbringing, took sexual relations more seriously, but even they became pregnant outside of wedlock. Mary first told the story of her pregnancy in *Lakota Woman*, but she provided more personal details later in *Ohitika Woman*. In the summer of 1972, when her mother, Emily, was taking college classes in Vermillion, South Dakota, Mary visited her. She met Pat Spears, a handsome young half-blood Indian hippie with long hair who smoked marijuana and partied in his trailer house by the Missouri River. Mary, not yet seventeen, was "fascinated" and "turned on" by this young man. After sleeping with Pat Spears, she became pregnant, shocking her mother and grandmother.

The wild period of her early teens ended, Mary said, when she encountered the American Indian Movement (AIM), which hit Rosebud in the early 1970s "like a tornado," loosening an "earthquake" inside her. She compared it to the Ghost Dance "fever" of 1890 that spread "like a prairie fire" among the Lakotas. In her enthusiasm for the coming of AIM, Mary recited the hopeful words found in an old Lakota Ghost Dance song:

> *A new world is coming,*
> *a nation is coming,*
> *the eagle brought the message*

Her first encounter with AIM and its followers took place at a powwow in 1971 at Henry Crow Dog's place after the Sun Dance. There she met Leonard Crow Dog, one of the spiritual leaders of the new movement. She was impressed with the very look of the young urban warriors, with their sense of purpose and their fiery speeches made in defense of American Indian rights.

Founded by young urban Indians in St. Paul, Minnesota, AIM sought to address the problems of Indians living in the city's ghetto. Many of AIM's leaders had been in prison and had lost ties with their tribal language, traditions, and ceremonies. According to Mary, who had great respect for the "real old folks who had spirit and wisdom to give us," AIM only became a national force when its young, urban founders met traditional reservation Indians. AIM's leaders learned the old ways from tribal elders, and in return these young radicals opened up the outside world to the reservation Indians. Mary joined the movement with passion and gave up drinking, proudly declaring that "we kids became AIM's spearheads and the Sioux set the style."[2]

In the summer of 1972, Mary attended the Sun Dance ceremony at Crow Dog's place, where many AIM leaders came to dance in the sacred ceremony. Afterwards they began to discuss the plight of American Indians in white society. Some older women engaged in the conversation, but Mary, young and shy, just listened. It was out of these feelings of anger and despair that the "Trail of Broken Treaties" was born. Bob Burnette, onetime tribal chairman at Rosebud, proposed that American Indians from around the country descend on the nation's capital during the height of the presidential campaign to make their case for Indian rights.

AIM took up Burnette's suggestion at its September meeting in Denver. The organization urged American Indians throughout the country to join the Trail of Broken Treaties Caravan and converge at St. Paul, Minnesota, where they drafted a twenty-point proposal stating their demands. From here they headed to the nation's capital. Bob Burnette went ahead to prepare crucial arrangements for lodging, food, and permits.

Mary Brave Bird, along with her sister Barbara and her brother, joined the march. Their car caravan started from the sacred site of Wounded Knee. After a period on the road, the travelers—men, women, and children—

---

2   For Mary Brave Bird's involvement with AIM, I follow her personal account in *Lakota Woman*; but for the larger story I rely on Paul Chaat Smith and Robert Allen Warrior's *Like a Hurricane: The Indian Movement from Alcatraz to Wounded Knee.*

arrived in Washington the first week in November. Cold, tired, and hungry, they expected to find food and a safe place to sleep. But they were sadly disappointed.

What had gone wrong? Bob Burnette's failure to prepare for their arrival, coupled with orders from the Interior Department that the BIA provide no assistance to the caravan, meant that the only shelter the Indians found was at St. Stephen's Church in the ghetto. The tired travelers, some seven hundred strong, slept that night in the cold basement of the church with broken toilets and rats and cockroaches. According to Mary, many Indians were disgusted with their treatment, declaring, "We ain't going to stand for this. Let's all go to the BIA."

Trail leaders urged everyone to gather at BIA headquarters. By now their numbers had grown to nearly one thousand. They settled in the BIA auditorium, bought lunch in the cafeteria, and greeted fellow Indians working for the BIA. By all accounts there was no intention to take over the building. Trail leaders had conferred with federal officials who promised to help them find food and shelter. Reason seemed to prevail, but the Indians did not know that some two hundred policemen were in the nearby Interior Department waiting for instructions.

Around five o'clock Dennis Banks, AIM leader and Trail spokesperson, held a news conference. They had accepted Washington's offer for temporary lodgings, but then police stormed in and ordered the Indians to leave the building. A fight broke out and the police were driven out by the young warriors. The Indians took control of the building, prepared for defense against further assault, and unfurled a new banner that read, "Native American Embassy."

Police surrounded the building and every day threatened to invade, which prompted a new round of frenzied defense. Barricades were set up at doors and windows, and young warriors prepared homemade weapons. Mary joined the men on the front line, having taped half of a pair of scissors to a broken-off wooden chair leg. Her brother, who had been a Marine, teased Mary about her weapon.

As the days dragged on, tensions rose among the besieged Indians. Years of rage against the BIA boiled over. In *Like a Hurricane*, Paul Chaat Smith and Robert Allen Warrior declared that the Indians who occupied the BIA "launched a wave of violence against the building. The earlier actions had been vandalism; this was war."

Still the police held back. President Nixon, facing reelection, wisely ruled against a deadly assault in favor of restraint. White House officials met with the weary occupiers and a compromise was reached. The president's men promised amnesty and money for the Indians to return to their homes. Federal officials promised, but never gave, any serious consideration to the twenty-point proposal, which they rejected out of hand.

Mary Brave Bird concluded her account of the Trail of Broken Treaties by saying that "from the practical point of view, nothing had been achieved." Still, she considered it a moral victory. "We had faced White America collectively, not as individual tribes. We had stood up to the government and gone through our baptism of fire. We had not run."

Mary returned with many AIM leaders to South Dakota to continue the struggle. January 1973 found her in Rapid City, South Dakota, which some Indian people called the "most racist town in the United States." AIM's followers were demonstrating against poor housing for Indians, police brutality, and general discrimination in all parts of city life.

Although Mary was far along in her pregnancy, she went there with his sister Barbara and her brother. One night some of her women friends decided to wreak havoc on the city bars that discriminated against Indians. Mary wanted to go, but the women decided it was not wise given her condition. Mary went anyway. Once there a "redneck" told Mary, "We're going to make good Injuns out of you!" Mary kicked him in the shin and he hit her hard in the chest. Mary charged the man and they both ended up on the floor. "It was sure," Mary admitted, "no way for a lady in my interesting condition to behave."

In the midst of this conflict, word came that Wesley Bad Heart Bull had been stabbed to death by a white man in Buffalo Gap, a small hamlet not far from Rapid City. A trial was scheduled in Custer City, well known for its racist attitudes toward Indians. AIM and traditionalists from Pine Ridge, Rosebud, and Cheyenne River converged on Custer City. Mary and her sister Barbara joined the caravan.

They gathered before the courthouse, where the district attorney promised justice for Wesley Bad Heart Bull. His killer was charged with second-degree manslaughter, which displeased the demonstrators. After trying to force their way into the courthouse, a fight broke out with state troopers, who used tear gas, smoke bombs, and fire hoses to drive the demonstrators away. Indians responded with rocks, fists, and clubs, and the angry crowd poured gasoline on the front door of the courthouse, setting it on fire. Fortunately, no shooting occurred on either side. Many were briefly arrested, including Russell Means, Dennis Banks, Sarah Bad Heart Bull (Wesley's mother), and Barbara. Mary was not arrested. She headed back to Rapid City in a car with an old sticker on its rear fender that read, CUSTER HAD IT COMING!

Members of AIM did not stay long in Rapid City. By late February they were called back to Pine Ridge to help the traditional full-bloods in their struggle with Dick Wilson, a mixed-blood elected tribal chairman in 1972. The opposition of traditionalists long predated Dick Wilson, going back to the Indian Reorganization Act (IRA) of 1934, which called for a written constitution and elected tribal council, destroying at Pine Ridge the old, traditional form of self-government that rested in the chiefs, tribal elders, and holy men. The IRA exacerbated the differences between full-blood traditionalists and the mixed-blood community.

Mary called Dick Wilson "the worst tribal president," since he ruled the reservation with an iron hand, backed by his private supporters, called "goons" by his enemies. Wilson and his mixed-blood supporters dominated the tribal council, and he filled most agency positions with friends and relatives, showing little support or respect for the traditional leaders, who tried unsuccessfully to impeach the hated tribal chairman.

Fearing for their safety and rights, the full-bloods organized the Oglala Sioux Civil Rights Organizations (OSCRO). Frank Fools Crow, speaking for the traditional chiefs and elders, invited AIM to a meeting that took place on February 27, 1973, at Calico, some five miles from Pine Ridge village. Russell Means, an Oglala born on Pine Ridge, and Dennis Banks, an Anishinaabe, represented AIM.

Some three hundred people, mostly women and old men, voiced their complaints against the Wilson regime. Banks and Means could not help but be moved by some of the older women, such as Gladys Bissonnette and Ellen Moves Camp, who spoke eloquently for action. The chiefs withdrew from the large gathering and met privately with Russell Means and Dennis Banks. Means suspected the chiefs would ask AIM to demonstrate before Wilson's heavily fortified headquarters at Pine Ridge, the seat of Wilson's power, but he was wrong. Chief Fools Crow told the two young men, "Go ahead and do it, go to Wounded Knee. You can't get in the BIA office and the Tribal council, so take your brothers from the American Indian Movement and go to

Wounded Knee and make your stand there." Mary Brave Bird remembered it differently. She said that it was Ellen Moves Camp and Gladys Bissonnette who told the AIM leaders to make their stand at Wounded Knee. The place was well chosen. Wounded Knee, where Big Foot's ghost dancers were slaughtered by soldiers in 1890, was a symbol to all American Indians of their long, painful struggle with whites.

A caravan of cars carrying AIM members and traditionalists, men, women, and children, old and young, left the meeting to take possession of the hamlet of Wounded Knee with its famous cemetery. When Mary Brave Bird realized they were going to take over Wounded Knee, she described it as "an excitement choking our throats." By that evening they controlled the hamlet, taking possession of the hated Gildersleeve Trading Post, the museum, and the Catholic church that overlooked the cemetery. There was a brief moment of quiet as everyone contemplated the significance of what they had done. Mary remembered hearing somebody on the phone in the trading post yelling proudly again and again, *"We hold the Knee!"* Then everyone got busy building a series of defenses for the onslaught they expected would follow.

Although surprised by the takeover of Wounded Knee, Wilson and the BIA reacted quickly. By the next day federal marshals (already stationed at Pine Ridge anticipating trouble from AIM), FBI agents, Indian Police, and Wilson's goons loosely surrounded the hamlet. The two armed camps faced each other, though none of the Indians who occupied Wounded Knee imagined that they would withstand a seventy-one-day siege that captured the country's attention. While there were some in the police force and in the country at large that favored storming the village, wiser heads prevailed in Washington. There was no desire, as Smith and Warrior stated in *Like a Hurricane*, for another "Wounded Knee" at Wounded Knee.

At first Mary settled in the crowded trading post. But since her pregnancy was so far along, she sought more privacy in a trailer house at the edge of the hamlet. Sometime in early March, both sides declared for a cease-fire so that women and children could leave. One of the Wounded Knee leaders ordered Mary to leave because she was pregnant. Mary refused: "No, I won't. If I'm going to die, I'm going to die here. All that means anything to me is right here. I have nothing to live for out there." Few women left. Most of the older women stayed; most of the younger women with children stayed; and the sweethearts of warriors stayed.

As the weeks passed, Mary pregnancy became increasingly visible. The men protected her from the firefights and heavy work, but Mary continued to do chores like all the women, cooking, sewing, and bringing coffee to the warriors at the bunkers. In fact, as the siege went on, Mary and the women grew stronger in the struggle. Mary was fond of quoting a Cheyenne saying: "A nation is not lost as long as the hearts of its women are not on the ground."

March 12 was a historic day at Wounded Knee. Though surrounded, outgunned in the firefights, and struggling to survive in the isolated hamlet called Wounded Knee, AIM and the elders issued a far-reaching manifesto, which proclaimed the rebirth of an independent Oglala Nation, the restoration of traditional Sioux government, the recognition of Sioux rights as guaranteed in the Fort Laramie Treaty of 1868, and the abolition of the IRA (Wilson's) tribal council. Like the twenty-point manifesto, it was an ambitious document.

Wounded Knee proved an unlikely place for a birth and a wedding, but both happened. On April 11, 1973, Mary Brave Bird gave birth to a baby boy. When those gathered outside heard the baby cry, all the "women gave the high-pitched, trembling brave-heart cry." Tough AIM warriors cried. Mary looked out the window and saw women and men with their fists raised in the air celebrating the new birth. She felt proud that she had accomplished something good for her people and named the boy Pedro, in honor of the respected elder and Wounded Knee defender Pedro Bissonnette.

The next day Mary's best friend, Annie Mae Pictou, a Micmac Indian from Novia Scotia and fighter for Indian rights, married Nogeeshik Aquash, an Ojibwa artist. Wallace Black Elk performed the ceremony.

Death visited Wounded Knee as well. On April 17 Frank Clearwater, a Cherokee, was killed in a firefight. A week later Buddy Lamont, a well-liked Oglala from Pine Ridge, was killed by sniper fire. Mary was related to Buddy, and the Lamont family asked Mary to escort his body out of Wounded Knee for the funeral. Buddy would be buried a few days later just outside the iron gates that enclosed the mass gravesite at Wounded Knee.

Mary took Pedro and left Wounded Knee. But despite promises, Mary was arrested and taken to a Pine Ridge jail. They held her for twenty-four hours before releasing her. Mary's mother was waiting outside, angry at Mary for being at Wounded Knee and angry at the police for jailing a mother with a child. Mary stopped her by saying, "Yes, I'm a mother now and made you a grandmother." Mary noted with some pleasure, "Suddenly we got along very well and could understand each other . . . and somehow things were better between us after this."

The siege ended a week later. By early March the occupation of Wounded Knee had worn thin and the two deaths, especially that of Buddy Lamont, cast a pall over everything. The burning of the trading post by an accidental fire and the constant struggle to get food past the blockade worsened conditions within the encampment. Frank Fools Crow, the elderly leader of the traditionalists, played an intermediary role in negotiations with White House officials, who promised to listen to the concerns of AIM and traditional leaders about Sioux rights under the Fort Laramie Treaty of 1868 and to investigate the conduct of Wilson's regime. Fools Crow presented the agreement to Wounded Knee leaders and federal marshals. Both accepted. On the eighth of May, after seventy-one long days, the siege at Wounded Knee ended.

Surprisingly, Mary Crow Dog expressed no final thoughts in *Lakota Woman* about the significance of Wounded Knee. But Gladys Bissonnette, who had been at Wounded Knee from the beginning, said, "This was one of the greatest things that ever happened in my life. I hope that Indians [at least throughout the Pine Ridge Reservation], unite and stand up together, hold hands, and never forget Wounded Knee. We didn't have anything here, we didn't have nothing to eat. But we had one thing—that was unity and friendship amongst sixty-four different tribes. . . . I have never seen anything like this."

Shortly after, White House officials met with traditional leaders and representatives from Wounded Knee at Fools Crow's place at Kyle on May 17, 1973. Indians complained about conditions at Pine Ridge, but the heart of their grievance was a call for restoration of Lakota sovereignty as it existed in 1868 at the time of the Fort Laramie Treaty. Taken aback by such a fundamental demand, the Washington delegation withdrew and promised to return in two weeks. But they did not. Instead, Washington sent a terse written statement that rejected any return to tribal sovereignty and never mentioned any investigation of Wilson's regime.

The takeover and siege at Wounded Knee intensified the grievances that traditionalists and AIM leaders had against Wilson's regime. Tensions flared a year later when Russell Means challenged Wilson for presidency of the tribal council but narrowly lost. Threats, beatings, and shootings spread across Pine Ridge, most of them perpetrated by Wilson's goons.

While Mary Brave Bird was aware of the political conflict taking place at Pine Ridge, she was not directly involved. Her life took a more personal turn when Leonard Crow Dog began to court her. Mary suspected that even at Wounded Knee he was attracted to her, but at first she was not attracted to him. He was thirty years old and a respected spiritual leader, while she was a young eighteen-year-old woman.

They first came together at the Rosebud fair and rodeo when Leonard took her for a ride in his old red convertible, extending his arm and kissing her. Mary implies that she slept with him, but she was not ready to marry. Next, after the Sun Dance ceremony at Crow Dog's place, Leonard took Mary up into the hills, supposedly looking for tipi poles. They stayed together for the night but, again, Mary turned down his offer of marriage. The third time was the charm. At Crow Dog's place, Leonard conducted a healing service for one of their AIM friends, after which he again asked Mary to be his wife. She agreed and they were married in a traditional Indian ceremony with a blanket wrapped around them, holding the sacred pipe, while being fanned with an eagle feather from the smoke of burnt cedar.

Mary Brave Bird became Mary Crow Dog, and she and little Pedro went to live with Leonard at old Henry Crow Dog's place. A sign at the entrance read "Crow Dog's Paradise." Indeed, Henry Crow Dog's allotted land was beautifully situated, but Mary found that it was not always "paradise."

Many members of the family lived on Henry's allotted land, but the immediate property contained two main buildings. Henry and Gertrude lived in the big, rambling house that Henry had thrown together in the 1930s. The kitchen had an old-fashioned iron cooking range, and beyond the kitchen was a large living room with a number of beds heated by a wood-burning stove. The ramshackle house had electricity but no running water or indoor toilet.

Next door was Leonard's house—built by the BIA —which people called a "transitional house" or "poverty house." The place was "jerry-built, flimsy, and resting on cinder-blocks without a basement." There was a kitchen with a gas stove, a living room, and two tiny bedrooms. The walls were thin and in winter it was hard to keep warm. The house had electricity (Leonard had connected a wire from Henry's place) and occasionally running water in the sink. There was a toilet and bathroom, but they had never been connected to the water line. All in all, it was too crowded for Mary, Pedro, Leonard, and his three children from a previous marriage.

The Crow Dogs were traditional full-bloods, but even among the full-bloods they were a "tribe" apart. As a mixed-blood, Mary felt out of place. Not raised in the traditional way, she could not speak Lakota. Leonard's parents, Henry and Gertrude, found it difficult at first to accept their new daughter-in-law. They still missed Francine, Leonard's first wife, who was full-blood and spoke Lakota and with whom Leonard had three children still living at Crow Dog's place. Mary also had trouble with her side of the family, who did not think Leonard the right kind of husband and feared she was going "back to the blanket."

Mary said she was in "no way prepared for my role as instant wife, mother and housekeeper." Visitors came at all times to see Leonard, a spiritual leader, asking for advice and for money, which Leonard generously shared, even though that money was needed for his own household. Mary complained that Leonard made his house into a dormitory and free hotel since some stayed a night, some a week, some a month, some a year. There was never any privacy. Mary spent considerable time feeding people at all hours and cleaning up after them. She was especially angry at the Sioux men who did nothing to clean up their mess. Although many called Leonard a holy man, Mary noted, "It can be hell on a woman to be married to such a holy one."

Mary broke down under the tension and hard work. Sick and losing weight, she thought she might die. Leonard held a peyote ceremony for her. The wise road man who conducted the ceremony said that Mary was suffering a sickness of the mind, not the body, that she was "sickening for want of love," that she felt unloved. During the ceremony everyone prayed for her, giving words of comfort. Even Old Henry patted her cheek and called her "daughter." Mary got well, determined to go on living.

The Crow Dogs were among the first families at Rosebud to take up with peyote. By the 1930s Henry Crow Dog became a leader in the Native American Church, which preached the peyote way. The Aztec word for the sacred herb was *peyotl*, meaning caterpillar, because the cactus plant from which the peyote button was harvested has fuzz at its top like the hairs of a caterpillar. Leonard followed in his father's footsteps as a peyote spiritual leader, a traditional medicine man, and a Sun Dance priest. He saw no incompatibility between peyote and traditional Lakota religious practices, nor did Mary Crow Dog, who found in peyote and the Sun Dance the way back to her Indian heritage, a way to get beyond her mixed-blood status.[3]

When Mary took part in peyote ceremonies at Crow Dog's place, she was surprised to find that Henry Crow Dog practiced the Cross-Fire version, which included the New Testament and references to Jesus. At first Mary accepted this version, but over time she came to prefer the Half-Moon version incorporating traditional Indian, not Christian, symbols in its ritual. Both versions of the Native American Church demanded a good life from its followers, who were encouraged to abstain from alcohol and drugs and stay faithful to their marriage partners and children.

Every summer at Crow Dog's place, Leonard would lead the Sun Dance, the most important religious ceremony among the Lakotas. The second year after marrying Leonard (Mary was only twenty-six), she participated in the ceremony by having her flesh pierced: Leonard cut a piece of flesh from Mary's arm as an offering to Wakan Tanka, the Great Mystery, on behalf of her Indian friends suffering in jail or sickness. Then Leonard inserted a pin in each arm. Mary felt no pain. She was transfixed. "Brightness," she said, "filled her mind." In the brilliance of the sun, Mary saw her lost friends who had suffered at Wounded Knee and its aftermath: Buddy Lamont, Pedro Bissonnette, and Annie Mae Aquash. "It was at that moment," Mary exclaimed, "that I, a white-educated half-blood, became wholly Indian."

It was good that Mary gained new strength from peyote and the Sun Dance because she would be tested when Leonard went to trial in the summer of 1975 on charges relating to Wounded Knee and its aftermath. Leonard was found guilty and taken into custody on the thirtieth day of November to begin serving his long prison sentence. After several prison stops, he ended up in a maximum-security prison in Lewisburg, Pennsylvania.

Mary took Pedro and headed to New York City so she could be closer to Leonard, staying for a year with Richard and Jean Erdoes, friends of the Crow Dog family and strong supporters of the Indian struggle. Richard was good at raising money and public sympathy, so he seemed a logical choice to serve as Leonard's defense coordinator.

---

3   Mary struggled with her mixed-blood heritage in *Lakota Woman*, but by the time she wrote *Ohitika Woman*, she came to acknowledge and accept her status as "a mixed-blood woman and a Lakota woman." I am indebted for this insight to Larissa Petrillo's master's thesis, "The Life Stories of a Woman from Rosebud: Names and Naming in *Lakota Woman* and *Ohitika Woman*."

Mary found comfort in the Erdoes' apartment and in the city, where she and Pedro enjoyed their own room and a private bathtub. The big city exposed Mary to the larger world outside of Rosebud. There she worked long days fighting for Leonard's freedom, conferring with lawyers, talking to newspaper reporters, and giving speeches at public gatherings to win support and raise funds for Leonard's defense. She met white and black people, including some celebrities, with whom she became friends.

Though distant at first, Mary became in time very close to Richard Erdoes, who was very different from her. From Vienna, Austria, he had emigrated to the United States at the age of twenty-eight. Richard was an artist, working as a book and magazine illustrator. In 1964 two national magazines sent him west to do a painting/photo essay on Indian reservations. He made friends with several Lakota families, including the Crow Dogs. Somewhere along the way he met the medicine man John Fire Lame Deer and they worked together on a book, *Lame Deer, Seeker of Visions,* which became a classic in Native American literature. Richard Erdoes had become a writer.

Richard Erdoes's publisher wanted another book on Native Americans, and Richard suggested that he write the story of Mary Crow Dog. His publisher agreed. So the two set time aside from their busy schedules, and Richard recorded on tape Mary's life story from birth to the takeover of Wounded Knee and its aftermath. At year's end Richard transcribed the tapes into a workable manuscript, but his editor turned the book down as "too radical." One year wasted and no money. Richard put the manuscript on the shelf, where it lay for ten years.

After a year and a half in prison, Leonard was finally released, with time served. Leonard and Mary returned in triumph to Crow Dog's place, where the assembled crowd sang the "chief-honoring song" for Leonard. Mary was not left out. Two holy men fastened an eagle plume in her hair and gave her a new name, Ohitika Win, "Brave Woman."

New York City had changed Mary's outlook. While not a feminist (she did not accept the white feminist position on contraception and abortion, which she saw as race suicide for the Indian), Mary had become a stronger person who questioned dominance by Indian men who drank too much, beat their wives, and failed to assume responsibility for their children. Even Leonard had become more open toward women and more understanding of Mary's difficulty in resuming the old life. But he did not fundamentally challenge the roles men and women played in traditional Indian life, and that would prove troublesome.

Mary Crow Dog would need all the bravery she could find in the years to come. After a year in New York City, she found Crow Dog's place more impoverished than ever, all the more since Henry and Gertrude's place burned down and they went to live in Leonard's crowded house. Fortunately, Roque Duanes, a longtime guest at Crow Dog's Paradise, helped Leonard build an upper addition to the house. In time Mary had three more children who came into the crowded Crow Dog house, two boys and one girl. Anwah, her first child with Leonard, was born in 1979 while Mary was in Washington demonstrating for the release of Leonard Peltier, who had been convicted for killing two FBI agents at Pine Ridge. Leonard Eldon (best known as "June Bug") was born July 30, 1981, during the Sun Dance ceremony, held annually at Crow Dog's place, which made him a special child. Finally, Mary gave birth to a girl named Jennifer Louise, who was born in the Indian hospital at Rosebud.

Life at Crow Dog's Paradise continued in some poverty as the family depended on the little money Leonard made by performing Indian rituals around the country. Visitors continued to arrive at Crow Dog's place seeking advice or money from Leonard. Many stayed, camping on the grounds, resulting in too little privacy and too much work. Mary longed for a quiet home life, but did not find it at Crow Dog's Paradise.

As a medicine man, Leonard traveled the country, lecturing and performing traditional ceremonies. Mary and the children joined Leonard on the road, as did many of his followers, resulting in Mary finding no more privacy on the road than at home. Leonard and his entourage traveled in caravans, living as best they could a life on the road that was exciting, but hard. In the end Mary grew tired of the "gypsy" life.

Once a year Leonard and Mary traveled to the Mexican border to gather peyote, the sacred button used in peyote ceremonies. On these trips south Mary encountered the Pueblo Indians. At first she was not impressed. She thought them "too peaceful and self-contented," not "committed to the struggle." In time, however, Mary came to recognize their inner strength to endure, "strength without macho." She came to admire them for quietly holding on to their old ways, living in comfortable homes, secure in their lifestyle and culture, and having fewer problems with alcohol. Mary especially admired the great role Pueblo women played in society. "They might be doing a better job," Mary concluded, "at [protecting their land] than we flamboyant Lakotas."

Their struggles for Indian rights throughout the late 1970s and 1980s took Mary and Leonard all over the country. In the latter part of 1979, they spent time in Washington, D.C., protesting the imprisonment of Leonard Peltier, who had been, in their minds, wrongfully convicted of murder.

The next year Leonard and Mary traveled to Big Mountain, Arizona, where the Navaho Indians faced relocation from lands that had been opened to mining companies. They had invited Leonard to perform the Sun Dance ceremony as a way to rally support from other tribes. While there, Leonard and Mary were arrested for obstructing mining operations.

Leonard and Mary returned to Big Mountain throughout the 1980s to support the Navahos in their struggles. Leonard continued to perform the Sun Dance ceremony. In 1987 Mary decided to take part once again in the Sun Dance—but this time she would pierce her flesh as an offering to Wakan Tanka on behalf of the suffering Navaho people. Mary was cut in two places on her upper back, wooden pegs were inserted between these cuts, and ropes were then attached to the pegs and thrown over the crotch in the sacred tree. They hoisted Mary seven feet off the ground. She hung there for some time until the weight of her body broke her free and she fell to the ground, bruised but triumphant. The elderly Navaho praised her courage and self-sacrifice for the people; the women made the "ululating, shrill, high-pitched 'brave heart cry'" for her. Mary proudly carried her Sun Dance scars for the rest of her life.

Leonard and Mary also held demonstrations at Attica prison in New York State to support the plight of Decajawiah Hill, who had been involved in the infamous prison uprising there. As they were engaged in ever more causes around the country, Mary became increasingly "weary of the everlasting gypsy life, with no real home to return to."

Crow Dog's Paradise was no longer the same place by the late 1980s. Old Henry had died at age eighty-six; Mary Gertrude died a year later while Mary and Leonard were away. Emily Brave Bird, childhood friend of Mary Gertrude, attended the funeral and reported that Henry and Mary Gertrude's marriage certificate was displayed. It surprised some that Henry and Mary Gertrude, strong traditionalists, had been married in a Catholic church. They were buried together at Ironwood Cemetery.

The two main buildings were now gone, so Leonard and Mary were forced to camp out. Mary slept in a little U-Haul trailer, while Leonard slept with the children in a tipi. They cooked outside on a propane gas stove, carried water from a well, and used an outhouse. When Mary complained of these primitive living arrangements, Leonard censured her: "This is my grandfather's way. I live in a tipi. But you lost the spiritual side of it."

Life with Leonard at home and on the road had taken its toll on Mary. She tired of the poverty, the lack of privacy, and the lack of a home life, and said that it affected Leonard, too: "We got short-tempered with each other. We exploded emotionally." The marriage broke down. Mary admitted that she "strayed," and so did Leonard. In the end they no longer shared the same bed. Finally, Mary could bear the life no more; she ran away from Leonard and Crow Dog's Paradise. "I was alone," she declared, "penniless, without a roof over my head, and with four children to take care of. I was vulnerable, without protection."

Mary's life entered a long, downward spiral. She lived for a time in a shack out in the "boondocks." She was "utterly depressed," drinking, wanting to die. As always, in desperate times, she went to live with her mother, but the house was already crowded with her two sisters and their babies. Next Mary moved in with a man who physically abused her. Her sister Barbara and Mary Ann Brave encouraged Mary to leave and go to the shelter for battered women in Mission, South Dakota. There Leonard tracked her down; he wanted her back. Mary then fled to a women's shelter in Marshall, Minnesota, where she lived, for a time, on the street. Her old friend from New York, Richard Erdoes, sent her some money to live until she received her federal check from the Aid to Families with Dependent Children program. Once again Leonard found out where she was, so she fled to Sioux Falls, South Dakota, and then to Omaha, Nebraska, arriving there at Christmastime. In Omaha she tracked down her father, who gave her thirty dollars, but nothing more. Next Mary went to Denver, then Tucson (where friends took her in), and finally to Phoenix, where Leonard finally caught up with her and the children.

They decided to live together, but not as man and wife, staying together mostly for the children. Each went their own way. Unfortunately for Mary, Leonard's friends followed him to Phoenix, and once again she lost her privacy. Somehow, Mary survived three years in Phoenix.

They lived mostly in poor sections of Phoenix, largely Mexican and Indian areas, rough neighborhoods with gangs, drugs, and prostitutes. Mary sheltered the children as best she could and sent them to school. Unfortunately, her oldest boy, Pedro, dropped out of school, got involved with drugs and gangs, and followed Leonard, who did not value a "white" education, even though his mother believed education essential to the children's survival in a white world. Mary herself took classes at Phoenix Community College.

As always, Leonard went on speaking tours for long periods of time while Mary stayed home with the children. As life in Phoenix got harder, Mary started to drink and party heavily in bars, leaving the kids for days with friends and family members. Mary called it "a long drunk," and after three sordid years she tired of her life in Phoenix and decided to go back to Rosebud.

Mary Crow Dog had left her husband for good, although she still cared for Leonard and appreciated that "he opened the door for me, a door that led me back into being Indian and not merely a half-breed." But there was no turning back. Crow Dog's Paradise was gone forever.

Mary Brave Bird (she was no longer a Crow Dog) suffered from "culture shock" on her return to Rosebud. "The whole reservation," she said, "stank of poverty." "Everybody" she added, "was on welfare." Unemployment, poverty, and despair led to drugs and alcohol.

Mary did not escape the devastation. She went "on a tear," a drinking binge that lasted for nine months, from the summer of 1990 to the spring of 1991. She drank heavily, got into bar fights, got arrested for disorderly conduct and drunken driving, landed in local or reservation jails, and totaled no fewer than five cars.

There was one bright moment during this dark time in her life. *Lakota Woman* finally came off the press. The manuscript she had worked on years before with Richard Erdoes had lain in the drawer, largely forgotten; but in 1989 Richard Erdoes's agent remembered the book and shared it with Grove Press. They loved the book, which appeared in 1990. *Lakota Woman* received rave reviews, became a bestseller, and received an American Book Award in 1991. Still drinking, Mary managed to stay sober long enough to go on a book tour with Richard and Jean Erdoes, doing interviews in New York City and Washington, D.C.

The success of *Lakota Woman* did not change Mary's lifestyle. Back at Rosebud she went on wild drunks, got into barroom fights, and landed in jail. Slowly, she exhausted her royalties from *Lakota Woman* and found herself again desperately poor. She found a temporary break when Richard Erdoes told her that they had a contract for a second book. Mary went to Santa Fe (where the Erdoes were living) and brought her life story up to date, leaving Richard to transcribe the tapes. With an advance from her publisher, Mary bought a fancy-looking second-hand car and with money in her pocket drove back to Rosebud.

Back at Rosebud old habits took hold. She continued to drink and drive. Finally, on March 25, 1991, she lost control of her car while driving drunk and hit a utility pole. She nearly died in the crash and medics flew her to a larger hospital in Sioux Falls where she underwent life-threatening surgeries and stayed for one month.

As always, Mary went home to stay with her loving mother. Despite everything that happened, Mary drifted back to drinking and trouble, but she was tired of her life. What changed it all was the suicide of a friend who had been a good person, but an incurable drunk. Mary feared that alcohol would destroy her own life.

Emily Brave Bird took Mary aside and spoke words of wisdom to her child, telling Mary that she was not alone, that she had family and children who loved her. "You have a life to live," she told her daughter. "Choose life over death." Mary took her mother's words to heart. "So," she said, "one morning I got up, smiled at myself in the mirror, and poured the last bottle of Jack [Daniels] down the drain." Mary Brave Bird was ready to live again and face the world.

Having left Leonard, her spiritual mentor, Mary felt uncertain about attending peyote services. But her uncle Leslie, a road man, told her, "This is your church, you are baptized in it, and so are your children. Come!" Mary rejoined the church.

In addition to returning to church, Mary found love again. On August 24, 1991, she married Rudi Olguin, a Mexican-American, in Santa Fe before a justice of the peace.

Rudi Olguin had been involved in the struggle for Mexican and Indian rights and called himself a Chicano, a proud descendant of the Zapotec Indians of Mexico. Growing up in the Denver barrio, he got involved in drugs and gangs at an early age and spent time in prison.

Friends with Barbara and her husband, Jim, Rudi visited them at Rose-bud, where he met Mary at Crow Dog's place during a Sun Dance ceremony.

He became attracted to Mary, but she was married to Leonard Crow Dog at that time. When Mary finally left Leonard, Rudi came to Rosebud to court her and they fell in love.

The marriage was mutually beneficial as Rudi kept Mary from drinking and she kept him from drugs. The couple moved to Rosebud, where they lived in a tiny government house in the country. The younger children, June Bug and Jennifer, went to school. Rudi proved a good father to Mary's children.

Then, to Mary's great surprise, she became pregnant again at age thirty-five. She said: "I felt old and worn out. I thought, 'Oh, no, not again.'" Years of a hard life, drinking, and injuries had taken their toll and she was already a grandmother, thanks to Pedro, who had a child with his girlfriend. Despite her doubts, Mary never considered an abortion—that was the white, not the Indian, way. Mary gave birth on May 31, 1992, to a beautiful baby girl named Summer Rose, later followed by a boy, Rudi.

The quiet of their lives at Rosebud was temporarily broken when Mary's second book, *Ohitika Woman*, came out in 1993, although it did not generate the same excitement as *Lakota Woman*. Then the next year TNT televised its film version of *Lakota Woman* in which Mary had a small part. The filmmakers were reasonably faithful to the story, although Mary later told an interviewer that the film was "romanticized here and there, [and] some stuff I didn't really do." The second book and the film (which reached a larger audience) gave Mary Brave Bird some attention and provided limited royalties for her to live on.

Sadly, her marriage with Rudi ended. Their two young children, Summer Rose and Rudi, stayed with Mary. They were in school and doing well.

In June of 1998, Christopher Wise and R. Todd Wise came to Rosebud to interview Mary Brave Bird. Christopher Wise was an associate professor of English at Western Washington University in Bellingham, Washington. He had a keen interest in Mary Brave Bird's *Lakota Woman*, which he shared with his students. Mary Brave Bird was scheduled to give the keynote address at the Sisters of Color Conference at Western Washington University in late May 1998, but, at the last moment, she had to cancel her talk. (She could not get a ride from the Rosebud Reservation to the airport at Rapid City, South Dakota.) Christopher was disappointed; he had many questions to ask Mary Brave Bird about *Lakota Woman* and her working relationship with Richard Erdoes. So Christopher decided to go to Rosebud and inter-

Mary Brave Bird, circa 1992 RICHARD ERDOES PAPERS. YALE COLLECTION
OF WESTERN AMERICANA, BEINECKE RARE BOOK AND MANUSCRIPT LIBRARY.
PHOTOGRAPHED BY RICHARD ERDOES

view Mary. He invited his brother, R. Todd Wise, who taught Native American Studies at the University of Sioux Falls in South Dakota. R. Todd shared his brother's interest in *Lakota Woman*. The brothers left Sioux Falls on June 19, 1998, for the five-hour drive to the Rosebud Reservation.

They found Mary just out of the hospital and on medication, living in a trailer on a three-acre spread. The house needed work, which Mary was doing herself, and however simple a homestead, she was proud to say she owned it.

Unhappy with life on the reservation, Mary saw nothing good happening at Rosebud, certainly not for the young caught up in drugs and gangs. Although tired of tribal politics and the failure of the tribal leaders to confront the BIA and to serve as role models for the young, she had lost none of her old fire. When the brothers asked if she was involved in the struggle to get the Black Hills back, Mary responded, "We never lost it. We never lost it, but we are still in the struggle. . . . We're holding on. We're holding on to our land, our treaty, our sovereignty. A lot of the young people want to stand up and occupy again. But there has to be another way."

Wounded Knee was past. When young people expressed to Mary that they wished they had been there, she encouraged them to go to school and "fight, fight. Fight in the courts, fight in the law." She had always encouraged her own children to attend school, though Pedro, like Leonard, saw no need for a white education. She told Pedro to get his GED. "You [can] help your tradition, your culture, but at the same time you can educate yourself, and you can make it in the world." In *Ohitika Woman*, Mary had stated, "We have enough medicine men and enough high school dropouts. What we need are Indian lawyers, doctors, teachers, and scientists. Illiteracy will get us nowhere." Mary was herself taking a course in art at Sinte Gleska University in Mission, South Dakota.

Although Mary expressed some hope for the future, keeping in contact with Richard Erdoes and tracking her books, especially the foreign editions, she did not see a long-term future for herself. When asked by the Wise brothers where she saw herself in twenty years, she replied "I don't think I will be alive twenty years from now." She was then asked if she would be alive ten years from now and she said simply, "No."

Mary Brave Bird did not live twenty more years, but she did live past ten, dying of natural causes on February 14, 2013, in Crystal Lake, Nevada, at age fifty-eight. Buried in Clear Water Cemetery on Grass Mountain on the Rosebud Reservation, she left behind six children and two revealing books, *Lakota Woman* and *Ohitika Woman*, which will all live on to remember her struggle on behalf of Indian rights.

CHAPTER 20

SuAnne Big Crow: Shooting Star

Many of the Plains Indian women who transitioned from the nineteenth century to the reservation lamented the changing morals of younger women, educated in white society, who were no longer schooled in the traditional ways. They believed that many of these young women did not behave properly. They drank, smoked too much, and were more sexually casual with men than their mothers and grandmothers. But these older women had never met SuAnne Big Crow.[1]

An Oglala Lakota from the Pine Ridge Reservation, SuAnne Big Crow was born on March 15, 1974. Her mother, Leatrice "Chick" Big Crow, was twenty-five at the time, with two other young children, Cecelia ("Cee Cee") and Frances ("Pigeon"). Everyone recognized Everett "Gabby" Brewer as father of the two older girls, but Leatrice Big Crow never named the father of her newborn girl. SuAnne would grow up without a father in a house run by her mother, with support from her mother's large Big Crow family. Supporting her family from the salary she earned as an administrative assistant for the tribal planning office, Leatrice supported tribal chairman Dick Wilson during his struggles with the traditionalists and their AIM supporters.

SuAnne and her sisters grew up comfortable and safe in their mother's three-bedroom house in Pine Ridge village. A strict mother, Leatrice allowed the children to take part in supervised activities after school, but did not allow them to roam around the village. When the evening streetlights came on, the children had to be in the yard or house, where the three sisters played well together, creating their own little world of play and games.

Since Leatrice Big Crow encouraged her girls to play sports, they engaged in volleyball, softball, basketball, cross-country running, and track, in addition to cheerleading. SuAnne followed her older sisters, acting older than her age. At the age of three, she joined her aunt's "Tiny Tots"

---

1   Eric Haase and Jerry Reynolds's "A Salute of Love," *Lakota Times*, February 19, 1992, B4–5 provides a rich, contemporary account of SuAnne Big Crow's life; but the richest introduction to SuAnne Big Crow's remarkable life story can be found in Ian Frazier's *On the Rez*.

SuAnne Big Crow, star basketball player, straight-A student, member of the
National Honor Society, PEER alcohol and drug abuse counselor, and a proud
young Oglala Lakota woman from Pine Ridge, South Dakota COURTESY OF LEATRICE
"CHICK" BIG CROW

cheerleading squad. SuAnne would later become a prominent figure in Pine
Ridge's all-girls cheerleading teams. She played on her big sisters' softball
team even though she was smaller than the bat. While in kindergarten, she
even managed to play some minutes in a girls' basketball game that was
designed for girls ages seven to eleven.

Although SuAnne played many sports, basketball became her passion.
At Pine Ridge and most Indian reservations, basketball is by far the most
loved sport, and SuAnne followed intensely the fortunes of Pine Ridge's

Lady Thorpes (named after the legendary Jim Thorpe). She idolized Lolly Steele, a young high school student who played for the Lady Thorpes, and at the NBA level, Earvin "Magic" Johnson was her favorite star. She spent endless hours practicing basketball. As early as the fifth grade, she would spend each day dribbling the ball a thousand times with each hand and shoot layups against the gutter and drainpipe.

Charles Zimiga, who coached the Pine Ridge Lady Thorpes, took note of SuAnne when she was in the seventh grade. He was working with the Pine Ridge High School boys' cross-country team when SuAnne, who practiced cross-country running each fall, came running by. Zimiga noticed how strong and graceful she ran. The young woman, ever bold, asked the coach what he was staring at, and he said simply, "A runner." SuAnne could have been a great cross-country runner, but it conflicted with the basketball season, her first love.

Coach Zimiga persuaded Leatrice Big Crow to enroll SuAnne at Pine Ridge High School, placing her on the junior varsity basketball team. By the eighth grade, SuAnne, long limbed, well-muscled, and quick, was five feet five inches although, as Zimiga explained, "she played six foot." During the playoffs Zimiga moved her up to the varsity team, which had many good players. Doni De Cory, SuAnne's cousin, at five feet ten inches, was the team's star and good rebounder. During play the cousins combined for many long-break baskets, with Doni throwing down-court passes to SuAnne. In the district playoff against Red Cloud, their arch rivals, SuAnne scored thirty-one points.

SuAnne became a star player on the Lady Thorpes' team in her freshman year, at just fourteen. The most memorable game she played in took place in Lead, South Dakota. Ian Frazier reported on the game in his book *On the Rez*. He had read about that game in a piece on SuAnne in the *Lakota Times* dated February 19, 1992, and he interviewed Doni De Cory, who also played in the game. Frazier tells a dramatic story, declaring that "for the Oglala, what SuAnne did that day took on the stature of myth."

Prior to the game the Lady Thorpe players could hear that the Lead fans were hostile, shouting mock Indian war cries and crude epithets, while the Lead band played mock Indian drum music. Doni De Cory did not want to lead the team out on the floor, so SuAnne took the lead, dribbling the ball as her teammates followed. The whooping increased. Instead of encircling the court, SuAnne stopped in center court, threw the ball to Doni, draped

SuAnne Big Crow, star Lady Thorpes' basketball player at Pine Ridge
High School, three-time all–South Dakota girls' basketball team,
and National American Indian Women's Basketball Team COURTESY OF
LEATRICE "CHICK" BIG CROW

her warm-up jacket over her shoulder, and began the Lakota Shawl Dance,
singing in Lakota. The crowd fell silent. SuAnne then grabbed the ball from
Doni, ran a lap dribbling the ball, and then put the ball through the hoop,
drawing cheers. Pine Ridge fans who were there described SuAnne's act with
"awe and disbelief." In the Lakota way she had counted coup on the Lead
fans.

However, Bill Harlan, a South Dakota reporter with relatives in Lead,
challenged Frazier's dramatic story in a letter to the editor of the *New York
Review of Books* dated May 11, 2000. Based on his own investigation, Harlan
argued that Frazier had seriously overstated the racial animosity of the Lead

fans and the center-court theatrics of SuAnne. In his reply Frazier admitted that he may have depended too heavily on his Pine Ridge sources, that he should have interviewed Lead fans, and that he may have overdramatized the antics of the fans and SuAnne's performance. But clearly something dramatic had happened at Lead. Frazier admitted that "the story of SuAnne at Lead had moved partly into the realm of myth." Still, Frazier reminded Harlan that Lead fans were not so innocent and that many people from Pine Ridge—coaches, parents, and players—encountered insults and racial taunts at Lead.[2]

Whatever the full truth about this game at Lead, the Lady Thorpes did not have a great year, finishing fourth in the state tournament. After the girls' basketball season ended in late November, SuAnne became a cheerleader for the boys' basketball team and played on the girls' volleyball team. In the spring she ran sprints and relays on the girls' track team and in the summer played on the Pine Ridge women's softball team. During the summer of her freshman year, SuAnne worked the cash register and deli counter at Big Bat's Convenience Store but still found time to run cross-country for endurance and to practice basketball. This was a routine she continued throughout her high school years.

Through it all SuAnne did not neglect her academics, becoming a straight-A student, active in student government, and a PEER alcohol and drug abuse counselor. Like her mother, she was strongly opposed to alcohol and drugs. As a nine-year-old girl, SuAnne had witnessed the destructive effects of alcohol while spending New Year's Eve with her godmother, whose teenage son came home drunk and shot himself in the chest. His mother was so distraught that SuAnne had to call the ambulance and police. As a high school student, she was active in the cause, speaking to her fellow students about the dangers of alcohol and drugs.

SuAnne delivered a graduation speech to the eighth-grade class at American Horse Day School; this speech captured her philosophy about education and life at Pine Ridge. A piece on SuAnne in the February 19, 1992, *Lakota Times* quoted parts of her speech:

> *High School can be the most fun time of your life but don't lose sight of the main purpose, an education. It is the key to a better life for our people.*

---

2   For this exchange, see http://www.nybooks.com/articles/archives/2000/may/11/the-game-at-lead/.

Many people believe that you must leave the reservation in order to have a better life, but I don't believe that. This is my home. I love it here. I don't want to leave.

I believe that we can have a good life here . . . we need to work together to make this a more prosperous place . . . we need to build on the positive.

Doni De Cory put it colorfully when she told Ian Frazier that her cousin was proud of Pine Ridge's Oglala community. "Wherever SuAnne went, she would tell people, 'We're from an Indian reservation. . . . We're from Pine Ridge, South Dakota.' Then, sometimes she'd throw back her head and yell, 'We're Oglala Siooooooooooux!'"

SuAnne had a great sophomore year at Pine Ridge High School. Doni De Cory had graduated, but there were still some very good basketball players on the Lady Thorpes. SuAnne and the team had a sensational season. She scored thirty-five points against their archrival, Red Cloud High School, and then seventy-six points against a team from Lemmon, South Dakota, creating a state record. She set another state record by scoring 761 points for the season.

The Lady Thorpes, with a record of sixteen wins and only four losses, continued their winning streak at the district and regional playoffs. It was around this time that NBC *Nightly News* (November 20, 1989) broadcast a devastating report called "Tragedy at Pine Ridge," detailing the harsh conditions on the reservation: high unemployment, poverty, and alcoholism. SuAnne was furious at the bleak coverage, which did not speak to the good things happening at Pine Ridge, like the Lady Thorpes playing in the state tournament at Sioux Falls for class A schools, those with an enrollment of less than four hundred students.

The Lady Thorpes beat the girls' basketball team from Flandreau, 70 to 55, with SuAnne scoring 36 points. They also beat the Parkston Trojans, 62 to 47, with SuAnne scoring 28 points. In the final game, the Lady Thorpes played the Lady Bulldogs from Milbank, South Dakota. It was a tough and close game, which everyone predicted would go down to the last shot—and it did. With only eleven seconds left in a tie game, SuAnne sank the winning shot, jumping in the air and sprinting down court in victory. The Pine Ridge Lady Thorpes had become the state champs. When SuAnne was interviewed by a reporter, she told him to call the story "Tragedy at Sioux Falls," a clear dig at NBC's use of that word.

The Lady Thorpes returned home in triumph. Everyone in Pine Ridge who was not at the game heard it on KILI, the local radio station serving the reservation. Fifty miles outside of Pine Ridge village, carloads of fans greeted the girls' bus as hundreds more waited at the Wounded Knee turnoff and more cars joined along the way. Coach Zimiga and SuAnne could see the long line of cars following the bus with their headlights blazing. SuAnne said to the coach with some amazement, "Oh Char[les]! Oh Char! Oh Char!"

Hundreds of people were waiting at Pine Ridge village, as a drum group welcomed them back. Some were singing a Lakota victory song while SuAnne and her teammates danced on the roof of the bus. Dennis Banks, the former AIM leader and a fan of the Lady Thorpes, joined in the celebration, proclaiming the obvious: "Those girls *owned* that town." People carried the girls on their shoulders. Everyone, even former enemies, joined in the round dance. Finally, the crowd gathered in Billy Mills Hall for speeches and a celebration of the Lady Thorpes. *USA Today* included SuAnne Big Crow on its list of All-American girls' basketball players.

After the celebration SuAnne tried to resume her everyday life. She continued her academic studies, participated as a cheerleader for the boys' basketball team, and played volleyball. In the spring she ran sprints and relays on the girls' track team. But after winning the state tournament and winning national recognition, life did not simply return to normal. Along with the fame, SuAnne encountered some rivalry and jealousy, especially from the fans at Holy Rosary High School. Pine Ridge village (and Pine Ridge Reservation, for that matter) was a small place with its own factions; there were always some people who resented one of their own rising above the crowd. It was a part of reservation life that SuAnne did not like.

SuAnne spent part of the summer traveling abroad. She had been invited to join the National American Indian Women's Basketball Team, which played in Finland and Lithuania. Unfortunately, she got sick in Europe with a stomach ailment and returned home in late summer, sickly and eleven pounds lighter. The illness lingered through the fall of her junior year, and as a result, SuAnne missed classes and basketball games. She returned to school and her team in late fall and played well in some games, but it was too late to salvage the season. The Lady Thorpes failed to play in any post-season competition. Somehow, SuAnne still made the all–South Dakota girls' basketball team.

Once again, SuAnne was invited to play on the National American Indian Women's Basketball Team, where they journeyed Down Under to play in Australia and New Zealand. This time SuAnne did not get sick.

SuAnne returned with great promise for her senior year at Pine Ridge, but it got off to a bad start. One night in front of Big Bat's, a fight broke out between Angie Big Crow (SuAnne's cousin) and a girl from Red Cloud High School. SuAnne and her mother stepped in to break up the fight, but as other Red Cloud kids jumped in, SuAnne and her mother somehow got involved in the fight. The Indian Police intervened and arrested everyone involved for disorderly conduct, although eventually the charges were dropped. It was SuAnne's first and last fight.

Two weeks later SuAnne appeared during halftime at the football game as Pine Ridge's Homecoming Queen. She looked very pretty in a ruffled red dress with black sequins and a tiara in her hair.

SuAnne had a good year in the classroom and on the basketball court, maintaining a 4.0 grade point average. Everyone assumed that she would be selected as class valedictorian. She also served as vice-president of her senior class and was a member of the National Honor Society.

SuAnne planned to go to college and play Division I basketball. Faraway Columbia University, evidently impressed by her academic and basketball skills, had already invited SuAnne and her mother to visit. The Air Force Academy, the University of Montana, Penn State, and the University of Colorado (along with other colleges) also called, but SuAnne was undecided about going far from home. She thought of attending college in South Dakota. But one thing was certain, as she told her cousin Wesley Bettelyoun: She planned to return to Pine Ridge after college and work among her people.

During her senior year, SuAnne continued to excel on the basketball court, averaging an astonishing thirty-nine points a game. Once again she was selected for the all–South Dakota girls' basketball team. The Lady Thorpes lost only two games that season, but they were the games that counted. Both times, in the all-Indian tournament and the district playoffs, they lost to their archrival, Red Cloud High School.

At Christmas the Pine Ridge cheerleading team was invited to participate in the half-time show during the Fiesta Bowl in Tempe, Arizona.

SuAnne did not enjoy it as much as the team's visit the previous Christmas to Hawaii, but it was a welcome break from Pine Ridge.

January started off on an ominous note. A popular teacher at school died young from a heart attack. Coming home on the bus from a volleyball game, the girls talked about the teacher's death and funeral. The conversation turned to each girl describing how they imagined their own funeral. SuAnne said that she expected that KILI radio would announce her death on the radio, everyone in town would come to the funeral, and hundreds of cars would follow the hearse to the burial site. Then, as if to lighten the conversation, she added that if "she died tomorrow she'd die a virgin and would be buried in a coffin of pure white."

The gloom of this conversation soon passed. February promised to be a good month. SuAnne had been nominated as a finalist for the South Dakota "Miss Basketball" title. SuAnne and her mother planned to drive to Huron, South Dakota, for the awards banquet.

The night before they planned to leave for Huron, SuAnne went on her first date with a young sophomore named Justin, the quarterback on the Pine Ridge football team. Justin picked SuAnne up at six o'clock. He took her to the Pizza Hut in Chadron and then to a movie.

SuAnne got home at eleven. Her mother was away, working the night shift at the police dispatch desk. SuAnne was excited. She couldn't sleep, so she called her mother. They talked until two in the morning and, even then, SuAnne had trouble getting to sleep. When her mother came home early in the morning, they had breakfast together and began their three-hundred-mile journey to Huron. It was Sunday, February 9, 1992.

Leatrice Big Crow drove the first leg of the trip, some ninety miles from Pine Ridge to Kadoka, where she stopped to buy SuAnne a snack. When Leatrice returned to the car, SuAnne decided to give her tired mom a break and took the wheel while Leatrice dozed in the passenger seat. Once or twice, Leatrice asked her daughter if she was tired, but SuAnne said she was fine. SuAnne was driving around sixty miles an hour on the highway. The interstate highway was straight but boring, the weather fair.

Some miles outside the small town of Murdo, on a long, gradual upgrade, SuAnne apparently fell asleep, the car drifting to the right, hitting a delineator post on the side of the road. The jolt must have awakened SuAnne who, sensing danger (there was a steep decline on her right), tried to get back on the pavement, but she must have turned the wheel sharply, because the car rolled over twice. SuAnne and her mother were not belted. As the front door flew open, SuAnne was flung with great force, landing on the highway; Leatrice, dazed and injured, lay in the car. The state police arrived within minutes, followed by two ambulances. SuAnne had suffered serious head injuries and was unconscious. The ambulances drove to St. Mary's Hospital in Pierre, some forty-five miles away, where doctors determined that SuAnne was so severely injured that they would fly her by helicopter to a larger hospital in Sioux Falls. But before they could do so, SuAnne died. Someone noted the time: It was 3:35 in the afternoon.

The residents of Pine Ridge were stunned when they heard the news that SuAnne had died in a tragic car accident. Crowds gathered on Monday as her body was brought to the Sioux Funeral Home of Pine Ridge. Two thousand mourners packed the Pine Ridge High School gym on Wednesday morning for the funeral services. As the reporters for the *Lakota Times* noted, the gym was decorated "with the trappings of SuAnne Big Crow's success." Four tables held her many trophies, medals, and plaques. A large bulletin board contained a photographic collage of scenes from her life. Flowers from relatives, friends, and admirers from across the state filled several tables. In the center of it all lay SuAnne Big Crow, slightly disfigured from the accident, in a white coffin partially covered by a flag of the Oglala Nation. After the service Coach Zimiga and members of the 1989 championship team each took a turn and cut down the basketball net, which the coach then placed in the casket.

The coffin closed, the hearse made its way to St. Ann's Catholic Cemetery at Wolf Creek, followed by a long line of cars stretching for six miles on the highway. At the gravesite a contingent of Pine Ridge military veterans fired a farewell salute in her honor. Loved ones covered her burial mound with dozens of flower bouquets.

After the funeral Leatrice Big Cow left her job at the Department of Public Safety and never went back. She stayed home the first weeks, severely depressed, and thought of leaving Pine Ridge. She had no idea how she could survive the loss of her daughter.

She found some comfort in Chauncey Yellow Horse, a medicine man who lived out in the country. He took her to a Wiping of Tears ceremony in the small community of Cherry Creek where well-wishers sang honor songs for her and SuAnne, gave her gifts, and whispered words of comfort.

Then, roughly a week after the funeral, something strange happened. She later told her story to Ian Frazier. She was home all alone and had been just sitting in grief for hours at her table. It turned dark. There was a knock at the door. Two girls—perfect strangers—entered and gave her a hug. They put something in her hand. When they left, she turned on the light. The two girls had left a card, a Valentine card, which simply read: "SuAnne was our hero. We loved her and we love you too."

By the next day, Leatrice Big Crow knew what to do! SuAnne had often talked of an ideal place, which she called "Happytown"—a safe place where young kids could go and have fun, play, and not get in trouble. SuAnne had said that one day she would build it, but since she could not, her mother would do it for her. With the help of the tribe, relatives, friends, and strangers, Leatrice Big Crow built the Big Crow Center, which opened in September 1992. Sometime later a representative from the Boys and Girls' Club of America, which provides sports and recreational activities for young people, approached Leatrice Big Crow, and from their discussion emerged the SuAnne Big Crow Boys and Girls' Club of America, the first in the country to open in a Native American community.

In 2012 the SuAnne Big Crow Boys and Girls' Club in Pine Ridge celebrated its twentieth year, a fitting tribute to a remarkable young woman whose dream for herself and her people, the Oglala of Pine Ridge, was tragically cut short, and to a mother who loved her so.

SuAnne lives on in the collective members of her family and in the Oglala community at Pine Ridge. There's a short story in Sherman Alexie's *The Lone Ranger and Tonto Fistfight in Heaven* that deals with the young men and women playing basketball on reservation teams. In reflecting on the legendary status of one fictional reservation basketball player, Sherman Alexie exclaimed, "In the outside world a person can be a hero one second and a nobody the next. . . . But a reservation hero is remembered. A reservation hero is a hero forever. In fact, their status grows over the years as the stories are told and retold." It's as if Sherman Alexie wrote this line as a fitting epitaph for the real-life heroics of SuAnne Big Crow on and off the basketball court.[3]

---

3   Sherman Alexie, "The Only Traffic Signal on the Reservation Doesn't Flash Red Anymore," in *The Lone Ranger and Tonto Fist Fight in Heaven*, New York: Harper Perennial, 1994. For this poignant quote by Sherman Alexie, I am indebted to Ellen J. Staurowsky's fine essay, "SuAnne Big Crow: Her Legend and Legacy," in *Native Athletes in Sport and Society*, edited by C. Richard King, Lincoln: University of Nebraska Press, 2005.

CHAPTER 21

Rosebud Yellow Robe:
Living in the Big City

Rosebud Yellow Robe had the unique distinction of being named after one of the six Lakota Reservations: Rosebud, the home of the Brulé Lakota. But Rosebud Yellow Robe never lived on the Rosebud Reservation. She was born and raised in Rapid City, South Dakota, where her father, Chauncey Yellow Robe, taught at the Rapid City Indian Industrial School.[1]

Rosebud's father was a remarkable man who greatly influenced his three daughters. Born in 1867 somewhere in southern Montana near Rosebud Creek where his people hunted buffalo, his parents named him Kills in the Woods. Spending his early years with his parents and grandparents living freely on the plains, the young boy dreamed of becoming a warrior/hunter in the Lakota tradition. But he was born too late for the life of a warrior, although he did take part in one hunt and killed his first buffalo.

By the late 1870s, as the old nomadic lifestyle had come to an end, his people began a painful transition to the reservation. Kills in the Woods followed his family as they relocated to Spotted Tail's Agency, which, in time, became Rosebud, the home of the Brulé Lakotas. His life changed dramatically when his father decided to send the fifteen-year-old boy and his younger brother to Carlisle Indian Industrial School in Carlisle, Pennsylvania, where he would receive an education allowing him to survive in the white world. Captain Richard Henry Pratt, Carlisle's founder, believed that an English-language, Euro-American-based education was the key to assimilate Indians into white society.

His time at Carlisle transformed Kills in the Woods. He went there with an Indian name, dressed in Indian regalia, with little knowledge of the white world. He emerged twelve years later as Chauncey Yellow Robe, a hand-

---

1   The indispensable book for an understanding of Rosebud Yellow Robe's life is Marjorie Weinberg's *The Real Rosebud: The Triumph of a Lakota Woman*. Mildred Fielder's "Chauncey Yellow Robe, Bridge Between Two Cultures," in *Sioux Indian Leaders*, is a good introduction to her father's life.

some, well-dressed young man of twenty-eight with a perfect command of English and Euro-American ways. Chauncey left Carlisle with a lifelong admiration for General Pratt, both the man and his work.

Having decided that he could best help his people as a teacher, Chauncey spent ten years teaching at various off-reservation boarding schools in the West. Then in 1905 Chauncey received an appointment as an industrial arts instructor at the Rapid City Indian Industrial School, close to the Lakota heartland, remaining there for the next twenty-three years as teacher, disciplinarian, and boys' basketball coach.

The year Chauncey took up his new position at Rapid City Indian Industrial School, he fell in love with Lillian Belle Springer, a nurse at the school. Chauncey and Lillian, who courted and fell in love, made a striking couple: Chauncey was tall and handsome, with attractive Lakota features, and Lillian was a beautiful "Germanic" woman, with blonde hair and an attractive figure. They married in a private ceremony on May 22, 1906, surrounded by a small group of friends. No member of their families attended the interracial wedding, although in time the Springer and Yellow Robe families accepted the couple. By and large the residents of Rapid City also accepted the couple since Chauncey Yellow Robe was well liked and well respected.

A year after the marriage, Lillian gave birth (February 26, 1907) in Rapid City to a daughter they named Rosebud, after the Brulé Reservation where Chauncey's family resided. Chauncey enrolled his daughter at the Brulé Reservation, which allotted her 160 acres of land. Two years later Lillian gave birth to a second daughter, named Chauncina, in honor of her father; and after a ten-year lapse, Lillian gave birth to a third daughter, Evelyn. The couple provided a loving and secure home for their children.

Wanting his daughters to receive an academic education, not the vocational training provided at the Indian School where he taught, Chauncey sent his daughters to public schools in Rapid City. It was perhaps a tacit admission that the boarding schools provided a limited education for Indian students. Outside of school, Chauncey exposed the girls to family and Lakota elders who visited the school and his home, instructing them in Lakota history and tradition.

At the Rapid City High School, Rosebud excelled in her studies, developed a talent for piano, and was elected class treasurer in her senior year. During high school the popular Rosebud was recognized as a great beauty.

Rosebud Yellow Robe in traditional dress, circa 1927 COURTESY OF
DENVER PUBLIC LIBRARY, WESTERN HISTORY COLLECTIONS, X-31841A. PHOTOGRAPHED
BY DELLA B. VIK, OLE ANDERS VIK STUDIO, RAPID CITY, SOUTH DAKOTA

Della B. Vik, a local photographer who took many pictures of Rosebud, said that she was "exceptionally beautiful. . . . Rosebud had all the full Sioux looks and in a very refined way. She was exceedingly graceful and naturally gracious."

As one of only two Indian students, Rosebud entered the University of South Dakota at Vermillion in 1925, where she excelled in her studies and enjoyed the school's social life. Throughout their school years, Chauncey instilled in his daughters a desire for excellence, expecting they would, by example, prove to whites that Indians had the ability and right to participate in all aspects of American life.

Pretty and talented, Rosebud was chosen by students in Dakota Hall (where she lived on campus) to represent them in the college's beauty contest. Since contest organizers wanted a Hollywood figure to select the winner, sixteen pictures were sent to Cecil B. DeMille, film producer and director. Rosebud did not win first place, but when DeMille realized she was Indian, he offered her the leading role in the film *Ramona*. Although her father would not let her go—Chauncey disliked Hollywood films and Wild West shows, which he believed exploited American Indians and perpetuated images of Indian "barbarism"—Rosebud gained national publicity.

Rosebud gained further attention when she entered a college-wide entertainment competition. With the help of a woman student from Dakota Hall, Rosebud put on a program of Lakota dances, performing the Hoop Dance, Rabbit Dance, and War Dance. She won first prize, fifty dollars, and more publicity. Ed Morrow, a college student and friend, admired Rosebud Yellow Robe, and many years later he told Marjorie Weinberg, Rosebud's biographer, that he regarded Rosebud Yellow Robe as a cultured, charming, bright, slightly distant young woman with a "royal attitude." Ed Morrow wrote for the student newspaper and the *Sioux Falls Press*, making sure that the talent and beauty of Rosebud Yellow Robe—whom he called "the most beautiful Indian girl in America"—became known to a larger audience.

While still in college, Rosebud took a temporary leave to return home and assist her mother, who had become seriously ill with rheumatoid arthritis. Lillian died on April 6, 1927, at age forty-two, leaving Chauncey to look after his daughters as he mourned the death of his beloved wife and companion.

Shortly after Lillian's death, Chauncey was asked by his fellow Lakotas to help organize an event to welcome President Calvin Coolidge, who spent the summer of 1927 in the Black Hills. On August 4, 1927, the president and his wife visited Deadwood, South Dakota, to take part in the city's Days of '76 Celebration. The Lakotas used the occasion to make President Coolidge an honorary member of their nation in recognition of the role he played in passing the Indian Citizenship Act of 1924. Several hundred Lakotas, dressed in costume, were present at the ceremony where Henry Standing Bear, a Carlisle graduate, greeted the president on behalf of his people. Chauncey Yellow Robe conferred on President Coolidge his new Lakota name, Leading Eagle, saying, "Today, Mr. President, you are a one-hundred percent American by adoption into an aboriginal tribe. Good White Father, we welcome you into our tribe." Rosebud Yellow Robe, dressed in full Indian regalia, presented the president a magnificent war bonnet. An observer at the event wrote that Rosebud was "a beautiful Indian maiden of rare talent."

In 1927 the "beautiful Indian maiden of rare talent" left for New York City after only two years in college, determined to pursue a career in theater. One of her female teachers at the University of South Dakota introduced Rosebud to Arthur de Cinq Mars, a theatrical manager who went by the professional name of Arthur Seymour. He agreed to manage her career. Given her love and knowledge of Lakota dance, Rosebud developed an Indian dance act that she performed in theaters and nightclubs.

Later, Rosebud received an invitation to speak at the American Museum of Natural History, where she told stories about Lakota legend and myth. She later added to her repertoire stories pertaining to the Eastern Woodland tribes, the original inhabitants of the East Coast, gathered from books in the museum library. Wearing a beautiful beaded deerskin dress, Rosebud captivated her audience.

Although Arthur Seymour was twenty-five years older than Rosebud, the two fell in love and married. Rosebud gave birth to a daughter in 1929, naming the girl Rosebud Tachcawin de Cinq Mars.

Meanwhile, Chauncey Yellow Robe, with his two other daughters, Chauncina and Evelyn, came to visit Rosebud and Arthur in New York City. While visiting the American Museum of Natural History, Chauncey met Molly Spotted Elk, a beautiful Penobscot Indian who, like Rosebud, had come to New York City for a career in theater. Molly Spotted Elk had just signed a contract to star in a film about the Ojibwa called *The Silent Enemy*. She introduced Chauncey to the directors, William Chandler and Douglas Burden, who were so impressed with the strikingly handsome Chauncey that they offered him the part of Chetoga, one of the leading figures in the film. Marjorie Weinberg, Rosebud's biographer, said that Chauncey at first turned the offer down given his dislike of Hollywood's depiction of the American Indian, but that Rosebud convinced her father that the film would present an honest depiction of Indian life.

Chauncey Yellow Robe spent nearly a year in the frigid wilderness of Ontario, Canada, working on the film with a creditable performance. Although a silent film, the directors inserted a spoken prologue, written and narrated by Chauncey. *The Silent Enemy* opened at the Criterion Theatre in New York City on May 5, 1930, to good reviews, although the film did poorly at the box office, perhaps because it could not compete in the era of sound movies.

Sadly, Chauncey never got to see the film's premier; he came down with pneumonia and died in a New York hospital on April 6, 1930. The family shipped the body back to Rapid City, where he was buried beside his wife in the Mountain View Cemetery. Former president Calvin Coolidge praised Chauncey for his role in serving as a peaceful mediator between the Indian and white world.

With the death of their father, Chauncina and Evelyn remained in the care of their older sister. Financially pressed, like many Americans, Rosebud (whose husband had lost his wealth in the Great Depression) had to make her way in the big city. An opportunity came when the Long Island State Park Commission opened Jones Beach State Park and sponsored a series of public lectures to promote the park. Rosebud Yellow Robe was invited to speak and so impressed park officials that they offered her a job as an instructor at the archery range. They assumed that, as an Indian, Rosebud knew something about bows and arrows; but she did not, and had to learn on the job.

Dressed in Indian costume, with her long hair braided, Rosebud began to share Lakota stories, which she had learned from her father, in her archery lessons. She broadened her appeal by incorporating into her repertoire tales about native peoples of Long Island. Rosebud's program became so popular that park authorities created a Plains Indian village on the park grounds with three tipis, one housing artifacts from the American Museum of Natural History and two serving as clubhouses where children engaged in various crafts and played Indian games. Rosebud wanted the children to simply call her Rosebud and not "Princess Rosebud," a title she did not think appropriate for a Native American. Rosebud's programs, storytelling, crafts, and games were mainly designed for young children, many of whom (like Marjorie Weinberg) became lifelong admirers. Always, Rosebud's programs were designed to educate the children and their parents in positive ways about American Indians.

In the winter months, Rosebud visited public schools to tell Indian stories dealing with the Lakota and Eastern Woodland tribes, wearing her famous beaded deerskin dress, with leggings and moccasins. Rosebud said

Rosebud Yellow Robe with children around campfire at Jones Beach Indian Village, July 6, 1934
COURTESY OF NEW YORK STATE OFFICE OF PARKS, RECREATION AND HISTORIC PRESERVATION

that when she was first introduced to schoolchildren in New York City, some children in the classrooms, frightened by the image of Indians that they had seen in the movies, tried to hide under their desks.

While working at Jones Beach, Rosebud also worked at CBS radio. Once a week, from 1935 to 1939, Rosebud appeared on *Sunday Mornings at Aunt Susan's*, where she told Lakota stories. Rosebud worked there at the same time as Orson Wells, who performed on *The Columbia Workshop* and *The Mercury Theater of the Air.* Edward Castle, a reporter for the *Las Vegas Sun*, argued in a piece that even though Wells never met Rosebud, he must have seen her name on the CBS ledger books or heard her on the radio, and that he named his famous sled in *Citizen Kane* after her. Why did Wells attach the name "Rosebud" to a sled? Wells never revealed the reason. Did it have something to do with his childhood, or did he hear Rosebud mention her father's famous boyhood sled on her radio program? People who knew Rosebud asked if she had been named after the sled and she teasingly replied, "No, the sled was named after me." (Owen Edwards, a freelance writer, reported in the *Smithsonian Magazine* that Rosebud donated to the National Museum of the American Indian a late-nineteenth-century sled fashioned from eight buffalo ribs. Edwards said that it was most likely the childhood sled of Rosebud's father, Chauncey Yellow Robe, which he wrote about in his autobiography, "My Boyhood Days.")

Jones Beach closed down the Indian village during the Second World War. Like so many women, Rosebud went to work in a military factory. After the war she returned to Jones Beach to direct activities at her beloved Indian village, where she remained until 1950. In 1951 Rosebud's husband died and sometime later she married Alfred Frantz, a close family friend. While Rosebud worked part-time as a receptionist in a doctor's office in her hometown, Forest Hills, New York, she remained active in Indian affairs.

Like her father, Rosebud was proud of her Indian heritage and her accomplishments as an educated Indian in the modern world. She continued to lecture for some years on Native American issues in the area at public libraries, schools, civic organizations, and the American Museum of Natural History.

As late as 1987, when Rosebud was eighty years old, she offered to make a special presentation in honor of Native American Heritage Month for the New York City Public Library. Everyone at the library who knew of Rosebud's illustrious background as a performer, lecturer, and writer recognized that it was a special treat, since Rosebud made few public presentations as she grew older. Rebekah Tanner, a young woman who worked in the Office of Children's Services, arranged the meeting, which she remembered took place in the Children's Room at the Lincoln Center for the Performing Arts.

Rebekah met Rosebud in the lobby. "She was," Rebekah said, "elegantly dressed, in flowing colors—not in her Lakota clothing; she no longer dressed 'like an Indian' as she had at Jones Beach in the 1950s." Rosebud carried her "beautifully, fully-beaded dress." Rebekah was also well dressed, wearing dangling earrings that she had made in the "Kansas Wyandot pattern, with porcupine quill drops, like spider legs." The two women connected. Perhaps Rosebud recognized a kindred soul. Rebekah, like Rosebud, celebrated an Indian father and a Euro-American mother for her parents. Though fifty years separated the older from the younger woman, their birthdays were only a day apart.

Rosebud gave one of her famous lectures, sharing with her audience stories about her father and the Lakotas, her work at the Indian village, and her life as a performer. She also regaled her audience with traditional Lakota tales. Towards the end of her performance, Rosebud showed the audience a small, beaded medicine bundle shaped like a turtle. On the day that she had been born, a female relative made the traditional Lakota gift: Rosebud's umbilical cord was placed inside the turtle—a sign of long life. She had carried the turtle with her all these years. Rosebud shared with the audience her beaded dress, which weighed some eighteen pounds—too much for her "old bones" to wear. Then to Rebekah's surprise, Rosebud placed the dress on her young host to model, so that everyone in the room could see and appreciate its historic beauty. It was a singular honor and one that Rebekah proudly remembers to this day.[2]

During these years Rosebud continued to complain about the negative portrayal of Native Americans in film and television, although she did make one exception for Delmer Daves's *Broken Arrow*. In fact, she so liked the film, which presented a sympathetic and reasonably authentic portrait of Cochise and the Apaches, that she worked as a publicist to promote the film for Twentieth Century Fox.

Rosebud wrote two books on Native Americans for children during this period. The first, *An Album of the American Indians* (1969), presented an overview of Native American life and history in the United States, including a photo and write-up of her father's life. The second book, *Tonweya and the Eagles* (1979), was a collection of Lakota tales about a boy named Chano (based on her father's Indian name)—stories that she heard from her father when she was a little girl. *Tonweya and the Eagles* has been translated into several languages and was selected as an American Library Association Notable Book.

As the years passed, Rosebud desired to reconnect with her Lakota roots. She had long gathered information from family members and friends about her parents and grandparents. She desired now to expand the research about her family and, at the same time, revisit familiar places from her early years in South Dakota. Marjorie Weinberg, her longtime friend and future biographer, accompanied Rosebud on the journey. They explored the National Archives in Washington, D.C., and the South Dakota Archives in Pierre to

---

2 Personal communication from Rebekah Tanner to Joseph Agonito, dated June 9, 2015.

learn more about the Yellow Robe family. The two women took a sentimental journey back to Rapid City in 1983, where they visited what had once been the Rapid City Indian Industrial School. They saw the River Ridge High Rise for the Elderly, which had been dedicated to Rosebud's father, and they paid their respects at the grave site of her parents at the Mountain View Cemetery. Family and friends came from the Pine Ridge and Rosebud Reservations to see Rosebud.

Rosebud took time during this visit to return to Vermillion, where she had attended college in the 1920s. She was greeted warmly by old friends. In May 1989 the University of South Dakota at Vermillion awarded Rosebud Yellow Robe the honorary Doctor of Humane Letters in recognition of her work "to preserve tradition and promote understanding between Indians and whites."

Accepting the honor, Rosebud spoke at a public gathering. She praised her father for his love of education and the respect he showed to all people. "He always said to listen to the stories of all peoples. Accept the best they have to offer. After all, we are one family. We are all relatives." Rosebud said she accepted this "great honor for the Lakota people, particularly for the Lakota women." She closed her remarks in a classic line that illustrated her philosophy by extending the Lakota notion of "relatives" to all those gathered: "With all things and all beings we shall be as relatives. I greet the highest in you."

Rosebud's last public performance was at the New York University Graduate Film Forum, where she was invited to speak at a showing of the restored film version of *The Silent Enemy*. Then eighty-five years old, she introduced the film and her father's role in the production. Students received her well.

Shortly after this presentation, Rosebud was diagnosed with pancreatic cancer. She spent six months in hospice care at the Calvary Hospital in the Bronx. Rosebud was a religious person. A short time before her death, she asked Marjorie Weinberg for an Indian version of the Twenty-third Psalm, the comforting psalm that begins with the words, "The Lord is my shepherd." Rosebud died on October 5, 1992, surrounded by her daughter Buddy, her granddaughter Karen, and her dear friend, Marjorie Weinberg.

Marjorie Weinberg accompanied Rosebud's ashes back to Rapid City, where a memorial service was held in the Lakota Episcopalian Church. Then her ashes were buried near her beloved parents who had died so long ago. At long last, Rosebud Yellow Robe had come home.

CHAPTER 22

Lillian Bullshows Hogan:
"A Plain Crow Indian Woman"

Loves Mankind/Lillian Bullshows's life spanned the whole of the twentieth century—and then some. Born at the turn of the twentieth century, her ties reached back to the nomadic past and well into the future. Her family was close to Plenty Coup, the last traditional Crow chief, and she probably purchased groceries as a young woman at his general store in Pryor, Montana. She remembered fondly Osh Tisch (Finds Them and Kills Them), the last batée among the Crows who, though born male, lived most of his life as a woman. She translated for William Wildschut, a Billings businessman who collected Crow artifacts and went on in the early 1920s to record the life of a Crow warrior that became the basis of Peter Nabokov's *Two Leggings: The Making of a Crow Warrior*. In the 1920s she married Robert Yellowtail, a rising star in Crow politics who became the first Indian superintendent at Crow Agency in 1934. Despite her Christian beliefs, she supported her brother's efforts in 1941 to bring back the ancient Sun Dance to the Crow Reservation.

Lillian Bullshows was not a major figure in Crow life—that is, she was not a warrior/hunter, a tribal leader, or a religious figure. However, she led a long and remarkable life. She once described herself to her daughter Mardell Hogan Plainfeather as just "a plain Crow Indian woman." That description does not do justice to her rich life.

Born in a tent in 1905 during the horse and buggy days, Lillian spoke only Apsáalooke (Crow) and learned the traditional ways of her people from her mother, who had been born during the last days of the nomadic era. By the time she died in 2003, she had the distinction of being one of the oldest Crows living on the reservation, where she had spent most of her life. Along the way she studied English and learned how to drive a car, speak on the telephone, write letters, manage a bank account with money from her leased land, shop in supermarkets, and watch television. On a more intimate note, she married four times, bore nine children, and lived to be surrounded by grandchildren and great-grandchildren too numerous to mention. She grew up in one world, transitioned to another, and always remained a Crow woman beloved by all.

Lillian came by her names in an interesting way. She believes that the priest who baptized her gave her the name Lillian. She is best known to the outside world by her English name, Lillian Bullshows, which is the last name of her father, though she added the last names of her husbands as she married. By the time Barbara Loeb and Mardell Hogan Plainfeather recorded her life story, she was known as Lillian Bullshows Hogan, the Hogan being her last husband's name. For reasons that are not entirely clear, the BIA called her "Effie," a name used only in select official documents.

Her father desired an Indian name for his daughter, so he made the unusual move of asking a well-respected and well-liked white man to give her an Indian name. This man did give her a name, but it created a problem: The family had difficulty interpreting the name, which came out as "Loves Man" or "Loves the Man." Members of the family thought the name too flirtatious and called her "Likes Men," which really did not make it any less suggestive. Her girlfriends, in a good-natured way, often teased her about the name—a name that Lillian never liked. Barbara Loeb, who later helped record Lillian's stories, suggested that the kindly white man really meant "Loves Mankind" or "Loves All Humanity." Mardell Hogan Plainfeather, Lillian's daughter, who worked with Barbara Loeb collecting the stories, liked the idea and suggested the lead title for the magnificent book that captures Lillian Bullshows Hogan's remarkable life: *The Woman Who Loved Mankind: The Life of a Twentieth-Century Crow Elder.*

Lillian received a new Indian name when she was six years old. She was a sickly child, so her father believed it was time to change her name. He believed, as did most Crow people, that sickness can come from a name that ill suits the person, and that changing their name will cause the person's health to improve. Her father called Ellen Cashen, a clan relative, to perform the ritual. Ellen herself had two Indian names, Loud Speaker and Ties the Bundle Woman. During a Sun Dance ceremony, Ellen proclaimed to the assembled crowd that she was giving away her name, Ties the Bundle Woman, to the young girl. Lillian said, "When my name was changed I became whole and well." It turned out, however, that Lillian's new name never quite stuck.

Little Horse, Lillian's mother, gave birth to many children. Unfortunately, most died young. Only Lillian and her older brother Caleb lived long lives. Horse (as she was mostly called) was born around 1872, during the last days of the nomadic life and the early days of the reservation. Having never attended school, Horse spoke only the Crow language. A good mother and a hardworking woman, Horse was a Christian who liked to sing hymns, especially her favorite, "Jesus loves me, this I know."

Lillian loved her mother. Everything Lillian learned about being a Crow woman, she learned from her mother, who instructed her in the art of domesticity. "You're going to gro-ow to be a woman," she would always tell Lillian, "and you're going to have a family some time." Horse taught Lillian how to collect and prepare wild foods—chokecherries, turnips, bitterroot— how to cook fry bread and pemmican, how to sew clothes, how to bead, how to make buckskin and moccasins, and even how to make a woman's saddle, which few could do.

Lillian had time to play as a child, although play was always instructive. Her mother made a little tipi for Lillian, a place where Lillian and her little girlfriends played with their dolls. Lillian had a gentle horse, which transported their little tipi to different locations where the girls cooked bread in a pan over the fire. They were keeping a lodge like their parents. But as Lillian grew older, she spent more time around the house with her mother doing simple chores like hauling wood for the fire or carrying in water for cooking and cleaning—all in preparation for the day when she too would become a wife and mother.

Like most Crow men, Lillian's father went by different names in his lifetime, but the name that stuck, "Bull that Shows," became the family name. When he was a young boy, his family sent him to the agency school, but before the officials could cut his hair and change his name, Bull Shows ran away. Like his wife, Bull Shows had no schooling. Around twenty years of age, Bull Shows found work punching cows on Montana ranches, and while working alongside American cowboys, he learned a little English.

Lillian had little affection for her father since he loved to gamble, drink, and chase women. Sometimes when he drank too much, he beat her mother. Lillian was afraid of him and begged her father to stop drinking, but to no avail. Her father gambled away money that Horse could have used for the family.[1] Sometimes, Lillian said, they were too poor to buy new clothing. Lillian felt bad for her "poor little old mother." But this "poor little old woman" loved her children and would not leave her husband despite his faults. "I'll never quit him," she said. "I'll ne-ever quit him because for my children's sake. I don't want my children to have a stepfather or a step-mother." Lillian's brother Caleb followed in his father's footsteps and became a heavy drinker, neglecting his familial obligations. As a result of her own experiences, Lillian strongly opposed drinking among the Crows.

When Lillian was six years old, her parents sent her to the agency board-ing school in Pryor. School was compulsory and the Indian Police harshly enforced the law. Lillian cried when separated from her dear mother, and while she did not miss her "cranky" and often "absent" father, he came to her side in a crisis when she needed him most. During her first year at the school when Lillian got deathly ill, the white doctor could not help her. Her father came to the school and literally carried her out, threatening to fight any person who tried to stop him. Bull Shows believed an Indian doctor could save his child. But three medicine men came and said the child was so sick their medicine could not help. In desperation, Bull Shows called a clan uncle, Kicking Bear, and the medicine man Shows Plenty, whose "medicine" finally saved the child. Bull Shows promised Kicking Bear that if his daugh-ter lived, he would have the honor of "adopting" her into the sacred Tobacco Society, which Kicking Bear did some years later.

After she recovered, Lillian returned to the boarding school, which she found a difficult place. For the first four years, Lillian spent Monday through Friday at school, but she could go home for the weekend, which eased some of the loneliness she felt in being separated from her family. When Lillian turned ten, the school changed its leave policy and students could no longer go home on weekends. However, their families could visit them on Sunday, and after religious service at the Catholic church, the children could picnic with their parents.

Lillian did not care for the program or the teachers. She spent part of her day in the classroom, where English was the only language of instruction. Once Lillian was caught speaking in Apsáalooke and the teacher punished

---

1   Mardell Hogan Plainfeather was "surprised and shocked" when she first heard her mother describe Bull Shows's bad behavior. By the time Mardell was born, her grandfather was an elderly man who no longer drank. Mardell had fond memories of her grandfather taking her and her cousin Iva almost every day to Crow Agency, where he bought them candy and soda.

her by washing her mouth with soap. Lillian also performed manual chores, like washing dishes and working in the laundry.

School employees treated the children harshly, seeing corporal punishment as a way to keep the children in line. Lillian said the children were scared of being slapped or scolded by the teachers or dormitory matrons. She thought all the employees were "mean."

Lillian suffered her own share of punishment. On one Sunday after visiting with their parents, Lillian (then age eleven) and some of her friends brought sweets back to the dormitory even though that was forbidden. The girls were caught, lined up, and struck hard on the backside with a rubber hose. Lillian screamed from the blow and her back turned "purple." By good fortune, her family was still nearby. At the sound of her screams, Red Star, one of her relatives, broke through a window to get to her. The matron ran away. Lillian's mother was so enraged that she found the matron and dragged her by the hair outside for a beating, but the Indian Police intervened, threatening Lillian's mother with court and jail for roughing up the matron. But Horse was not afraid to go to jail for protecting her daughter from abuse. In the end, all charges were dropped.

Lillian stayed at the boarding school a few more years. Conditions likely improved after Chief Plenty Coup complained to Washington about how badly the schoolchildren were treated. When the Pryor boarding school closed in 1920, the teenaged Lillian attended the agency day school for at least six months, riding to school and back home on her horse. Since Lillian was one of the oldest students at school, her teacher asked her to help prepare lunch for the younger children.

Lillian wanted to continue her education at the Chemawa Indian School in Salem, Oregon, but her parents would not let her go. A disappointed Lillian later told her children, "That's why I have no education today. . . . I could've made better than this." Lillian did not return to the day school; she was all of sixteen.

A short time later, Lillian began to date a young man named Alex Plainfeather. They went together for only a short time before Alex proposed marriage the Crow way by telling Lillian, "I'm going to take you home tonight." Lillian's parents told her that she should not rush to get married since they were both too young. But Lillian, with the support of her older brother Caleb, decided to marry anyway. Alex's family "outfitted" Lillian in a beautiful elk-tooth dress and showered her with gifts, which was a public

Lillian Bullshows (Loves Mankind), approximately fifteen years old, in dress with beaded flowers, circa 1920 COURTESY OF MARDELL HOGAN PLAINFEATHER (LILLIAN BULLSHOWS HOGAN'S DAUGHTER)

recognition of the marriage. That would have been sufficient recognition of the marriage in the old days, but in the twentieth century, under the influence of the agent and missionaries, Alex and Lillian married in church on Sunday and then, the next day, went to Red Lodge, Montana, to obtain a marriage license.

Lillian should have listened to her parents. She stayed with Alex for less than a year, time enough to get pregnant. Her first child, Samuel, was born in July 1922. Lillian's mother decided to raise Sammy since in Crow culture, grandparents often took the firstborn grandchild. The boy was all the more precious to Horse and Bull Shows since they lost their youngest son that very year to polio. In time Alex and Lillian went to Hardin, Montana, to finalize their divorce.

The year before Sammy's birth, Lillian was formally adopted into the Tobacco Society/Medicine Dance. Once adopted, Lillian was given sacred tobacco medicine and special songs, which she remembered and sang throughout her life. Lillian had witnessed the tobacco-planting ceremony, which took place in the spring, when she was seven or eight years old. During the ceremony society members prepared a garden with the elders opening the sacred tobacco bags, taking out the seeds, and placing them in the ground, while being accompanied by drumming, dancing, and the singing of tobacco songs. As a child, Lillian had played a small part in the ceremony by collecting sticks for a fence protecting the garden.

Lillian remained single for four years. At Christmastime in 1924, Lillian went with friends to a dance at St. Xavier, one of the districts on the Crow Reservation. Lillian drove her friends in a borrowed car to the dance, where she met Robert Yellowtail, one of the drummers. It was not their first meeting. Robert Yellowtail was one of the rising stars in Crow politics and Lillian knew him from earlier meetings. After the dance they talked, and Robert proposed to "take her home," and she agreed. Once again her parents objected, reminding Lillian that Robert Yellowtail was fifteen years older, a widower with four daughters. Neither Lillian nor Robert listened to her parents' objections. The next day the couple went to Hardin, Montana, for a wedding license. Robert Yellowtail's family welcomed Lillian into their circle with traditional wedding presents, and they were married in the early winter of 1925.

The couple was good together in the early years. While Robert was away on tribal business, Lillian managed his lands and was praised by her husband for her hard work. Lorena Mae was born in 1927 and Robert was happy to have another girl. But four years later the marriage ended. It seemed that the often-absent Robert Yellowtail spent intimate time with other women. Some men told Lillian about Robert's affairs and one man said, "Don't let him be mean to you, leave him." Lillian did, saying, "I just took off." She left Lorena Mae with her mother and went to Billings to file for divorce.

Lillian was single again, but not for long. Her marriage to Paul Singer came about in a strange way. The marriage proposal came from Paul's father, who asked Lillian to marry his son, who was in the midst of a divorce. Paul was not a stranger; she had danced with him on several occasions. Lillian decided to marry again.

On March 12, 1930, Lillian and Paul married, starting out with very little, though Paul owned his own house. They worked hard together. Paul managed their farm, raising wheat, barley, alfalfa, hay, and sugar beets for market. Lillian cultivated a big garden where she raised tomatoes, carrots, beans, squash, and watermelons, preserving what she needed for the family and selling the rest. In addition, Lillian also raised chickens and milk cows, selling eggs, cream, and butter to her neighbors.

In the course of four years, Lillian gave birth to four children, though she lost her first child, Louis Charles, to whooping cough and her second child, Rose Marie, to whooping cough and pneumonia. Fortunately, Nellie and Adam were healthy and survived into adulthood.

Lillian called Paul Singer a hard worker, but he had one serious flaw: He drank heavily. When Paul drank, he became mean and Lillian would flee the house until he sobered up. The drinking eventually killed him. Paul had taken a load of agency cattle to Billings with his new truck. After unloading the cattle, Paul started drinking so heavily that he passed out in the snow and "chilled his whole body." Although Paul reached home, he was so sick with double pneumonia that they took him to the hospital in Hardin, where he died on February 19, 1936, at the age of thirty-two. He died, as Lillian said, "From whiskey, from drinking."

Lillian stayed single for four years. With young children to support, she took a job in a sewing project at Crow Agency, a project started by the government to provide income for poor women, including widows. Cordelia Big Man supervised the program. Lillian and the women sewed jackets, pants, shirts, and dresses that were distributed to needy Crow people throughout the reservation. For her work Lillian received forty-eight dollars every two weeks. She had sent four-year-old Adam to live with her mother at Pryor. On Saturdays she would buy bags of groceries to take to her mother's house. Six-year-old Nellie stayed with Lillian, who sent the young girl to school at Crow Agency. The sewing project got caught up in tribal politics. According to Lillian, Robert Yellowtail, her former husband

and now superintendent of Crow Agency, did not like the Big Man family, so he closed the program down.

Lillian was sheltered from that blow when she married George Washington Hogan in 1940. George grew up in the Lodge Grass district, attended the boarding school at Crow Agency, and spent thirteen years at Carlisle, where he got his English name. At least twenty years older than Lillian, George had been married twice before, but both wives had died. George Hogan was a good man, a good provider, and a good Christian. Despite the age difference, Lillian's father encouraged her to marry once again. Bull Shows was sure that George (who held a series of positions in the BIA) would look after Lillian and the children. In the course of the marriage, Lillian and George did well. They owned a home at Crow Agency, a car, and land. Lillian gave birth to twins in 1941—though only one child, Mary, survived—and in 1945 gave birth to her last child, Mardell.

George Hogan impacted Lillian's life in significant ways. Well-educated and worldly, George knew how to survive in the white world. Lillian owned land, having received 160 acres of allotted land under the Dawes Act of 1887, 160 acres of grazing land under the Crow Act of 1920, and a smaller parcel of land from her parents. Lillian leased this land, but after the marriage George renegotiated the leases so that Lillian received roughly $10,000 yearly, enough for her to live comfortably for the rest of her life.

George Hogan was a devout Christian and a deacon in the Baptist Church. He made Lillian promise that when married she would no longer attend the Sun Dance, the Medicine Dance/Tobacco Society, or other sacred Apsáalooke rituals. When it came to religion, Lillian was conflicted between the Christian and Apsáalooke way. The Christian side of the equation was not difficult. Lillian had long professed a belief in the Catholic faith—in God and the Bible. Lillian's daughter Mardell said that Lillian, like her mother, was a "devout" Catholic who fasted and prayed in a lonely place reading the New Testament.

In a radio interview on Montana Public Radio on March 21, 2013, Mardell said that her mother was a deeply religious person. She worshipped in the Catholic Church, the Baptist Church, the Pentecostal Church, and the nondenominational Church of God, which she helped to establish. As Lillian said, "Anywhere they have prayer, that's where I'll be." Lillian could pray to Jesus in any Christian church.

Lillian's story does not always have a fixed chronology, but it's likely that as a Christian, Lillian had already stopped participating in Crow rituals before she married George. Speaking of the Medicine Dance/Tobacco Society ceremony, Lillian said, "When I went to this [Christian] religion . . . go to church and kind of be religious, I quit that stuff, so I don't go to them dances anymore." Lillian noted, with some regret (perhaps at her own decision), that many Crows stopped participating in the Tobacco Society ceremony with the coming of the missionaries. "They say," she explained, "that you mustn't worship any plant or any image. We have to read the Bible, live for God, so all that medicine all gone now." But for someone who supposedly gave up the Medicine Dance, Lillian was concerned that the new generation of Crows knew little of the Tobacco Society. She noted, with sadness or hope, that one Crow woman, Winona Plenty Hoops, still possessed the sacred tobacco seeds. Mardell Hogan Plainfeather witnessed Winona planting the tobacco seeds. She noted in the faces of those attending the ceremony the hope that the tobacco would grow, while repeating a long-standing belief: The Crows would continue to exist as a people as long as they possessed the sacred seeds.

Lillian told George that she would not attend the sacred ceremonies, but what she must have really meant to say was that she would not participate, because she continued to attend as an observer the Medicine Dance/Tobacco Society ceremonies. Lillian remembered and sang the tobacco songs into old age, and after George died she allowed Mary and Mardell to join the Tobacco Society.

In 1941, a year after Lillian married George, the Sun Dance ceremony returned to Crow Agency—the first time since the 1870s. The performance of the Sun Dance, like the Medicine Dance ceremony, had long been opposed by Indian agents and Christian missionaries. As early as 1935, Caleb Bullshows, Lillian's older brother, had taken part in the Shoshone Sun Dance ceremony at Fort Washakie on the Wind River Indian Reservation. During the Sun Dance ceremony at Fort Washakie in 1940, Caleb asked the Shoshone spiritual leader to stage the ceremony the following year at Pryor on the Crow Reservation. Lillian had not been well, and Caleb wanted to dance and pray for Lillian's good health.

As a Christian, Lillian did not feel that she could take part in the dance, but she was proud of Caleb for bringing the ceremony back to the Crows.

Lillian supported her brother. She attended the event and prepared food for the dancers. The dancers thought the ceremony holy, and Lillian was willing to grant the possibility that the Sun Dance was indeed a holy ritual.

The 1940s and 1950s were years of happiness and sorrow. In 1945 Lillian's oldest daughter, Lorena May—the only child she had with Robert Yellowtail—married Cedric Walks Over Ice. Robert was opposed to the marriage, but Lillian liked the young man. She gave the couple twenty-five dollars for a marriage license and loaned them her car so they could go get the license. A year later Lorena May gave birth to her first son, Carson. Even though Samuel, Lillian's firstborn, had already made her a grandmother, Lillian was excited because she was there when her oldest daughter gave birth.

Lillian's great sorrow came with the death of her beloved mother, Horse, who died of cancer in 1948. In the last days, Lillian went to Pryor to nurse her mother while her husband looked after the girls—Nellie, Mary, and Mardell—who attended school in Crow Agency. Caleb, her older brother, was drinking in Billings with little thought that his mother was dying. Horse was buried in the cemetery at Pryor, and every year Lillian decorated the grave site.

Lillian returned home to Crow Agency, but she spent every summer in Pryor looking after her aging father, Bull Shows. When Bull Shows turned ninety, he became very ill. Sensing his death, Bull Shows expressed his desire to die in Lillian's home at Crow Agency rather than the hospital. So Lillian was there at the very end when her father died in his sleep. At his request Bull Shows was buried in "white," not Indian, clothes as he prepared to meet his Christian God. They took Bull Shows's body to a mortuary in Hardin for the wake service. Caleb was in Billings drinking when someone told him that his father had died. He walked and hitchhiked from Billings to Hardin to see his father for the last time. The family buried Bull Shows alongside his wife.

In the early 1950s, tragedy struck Lillian and George. While Lillian was driving her pickup with George in the passenger seat, a car struck them with such force that it turned the pickup around. Both suffered a jolt to their necks, arms, and shoulders and were taken to the hospital. In time Lillian recovered; George's injuries were more serious. He suffered pinched nerves in his spine, but the doctor could not operate because of his advanced age. George never fully recovered, and for the remainder of his years, his hands and neck troubled him.

It was probably around this time that George retired from the BIA and they moved to Lillian's home in the small community of Dunmore. George lived for a few more years and died in the hospital at Crow Agency on April 27, 1958, in his late seventies. Lillian was fifty-three.

Lillian never remarried and lived the remainder of her long life as a widow. She was never lonely for company since her house in Dunmore was always full, not only with her own children—Nellie, Mary, and Mardell—but with the children of relatives, foster children, and even white youths who worked as Vista volunteers on the reservation.

In the early 1960s, Lillian decided to build a new house, paying for most of it herself and securing a small loan from the Indian Office. Nellie supervised the operation, ordering the plans for the house through a catalog from a company in Minneapolis. Adam, who worked in construction, put in the basement. When the lumber arrived, Nellie arranged for Indian carpenters to build the house.

Lillian was proud of her new house and so were tribal officials. In August 1964 Lady Bird Johnson visited the Crow Reservation. The tribal chairman wanted Lillian to host the First Lady at her new house, a sign of their respect for Lillian. When word arrived that Lady Bird Johnson would visit her home, Lillian was at the Billings Fair. She rushed home to make the house presentable. Mary and Mardell were at college in Butte, Montana, with Nellie looking after Mary's children, when they heard the news. They rushed home in the new car Lillian had bought for them, but not before a reporter took their picture for the local newspaper with the caption that read: "The three sisters are going back to their mother for the visit of Lady Bird Johnson." The First Lady came with Secret Service agents and a full entourage that included the secretary of the Interior, whom Mardell enjoyed meeting. Lady Bird shook hands with Lillian and they enjoyed fry bread together. It was a brief but happy visit that Lillian long remembered.

Except for a six-month stay with her daughter Lorena Mae in Phoenix, a brief visit to see Lorena Mae and Cedric in Nespelem, Washington, where they accepted a new assignment for the BIA at the Colville Reservation, and a trip to see Mardell in Arkansas where she worked for the National Park Service, Lillian remained at Crow Agency for the rest of her life. She lived comfortably there, receiving good money from her leases and from George's pension. Lillian had money in the bank, but she did not like to write checks. Instead, she kept good sums of money with her, some she stashed in a jar and some she carried in her purse, using the money to meet everyday expenses and help her children and grandchildren. The money gave Lillian a measure of independence and she did not receive welfare or help from the tribe. Even when her furnace broke, the tribe did not help her fix it, since Lillian paid for it herself. She said proudly, "I like to be my own boss."

The years passed as Lillian lived an active life well into her eighties. She continued to drive, but with poor eyesight she drove only on the reservation. Nellie drove when Lillian had to go to Billings or Hardin. Lillian continued to enjoy going to the mountains for new poles for the family's tipi encampment at the annual Crow Fair, one of the most exciting events of the year. She loved to attend the fair with her family; and though she could no longer ride in the procession or race her horse as she did when young, she provided horses and beautiful buckskin outfits for her grandchildren and great-grandchildren who took part in the event. She enjoyed digging bitterroots in the mountains like the old days when she went there with her mother, and she expressed some regret that there were women who no longer went digging for this delicious plant and young people who never experienced the taste of prepared bitterroot. She gathered chokecherries and relished the taste of deer meat. "I guess I'm an old timer," she said. "I like all the Indian food."

Lillian experienced some nostalgia for the old days. When she remembered racing her horse at the Crow Fair, Lillian looked back with some sadness, "Oh dear / I'll never go back to the young times / have those times again." Although sometimes conflicted between the old ways and the modern world, she did not dwell on the past as did some older women. She was comfortable with modern society, and she looked forward to the future for her children and their families.

Understanding that her children's generation was different from that of her parents, she encouraged them to get an education so they could lead self-sufficient, independent, and productive lives. Her six children who survived into adulthood—Samuel, Lorena Mae, Adam, Nellie, Mary, and Mardell—eventually settled on the Crow Reservation or in nearby towns such as Billings or Hardin. Her daughters were especially close to their mother, calling and visiting frequently. She was simply proud of her children: "My children all growed up—grown up nice. They have their own family, and I love them all." While Lillian loved all her children, she was especially proud of Lorena Mae, who went to school, worked for the BIA, and returned to the Crow Reservation to buy land and managed a ranch; Mardell, who went to college and ended up working as an interpreter and historian for the National Park Service; and Adam, who enlisted in the army and returned home a hard worker.

As Lillian grew older—she was well into her late eighties when Barbara Loeb and Mardell Hogan Plainfeather recorded her life story—she became a respected elder among her people. A Crow father who wanted Lillian to name his child explained why he chose her: "You're an old woman now and you're a good woman." Lillian gave the boy a positive name: "Will Go Far." Family members turned to Lillian for the same reason. In naming a child, Lillian did what many Crow people did and that was to draw from her own experiences. She named one great-granddaughter "Lady Bird," in honor of the First Lady who had visited her. She named her great-grandson Calvin, "Good Dancer." Lillian had been a good dancer in her youth and she saw that quality in the young boy, who turned out to be a graceful fancy-dancer, which the Crows admired.

Lillian inherited her mother's special knowledge of medicinal roots, and family members turned to her for help. Her nephew caught a bad case of poison ivy that no white doctor or Indian medicine man could cure. Lillian applied her "medicine" and cured the boy. She did the same for her daughter Nellie, whose legs swelled up.

The Crows also recognized Lillian's religious faith, and parishioners asked her to say prayers in church for her people's well-being. Some said that they felt good when Lillian prayed for them since it seemed that Lillian had a special gift with prayers. Once she visited a sick relative named Yellow Bull. Doctors had given up all hope for his recovery. But when Lillian touched his body and prayed, Yellow Bull was cured. He confessed that there was something "special" about Lillian's prayer, but Lillian said that it was not her but the Lord who cured him.

As old age came on, Lillian suffered some misfortune in her life. Caleb, her older, hard-drinking brother, ended up in a nursing home where he lived for four or five years before he died in 1991. Caleb, her long-suffering brother, was the last of her siblings. When Lillian fell and broke her hip, they rushed her to Billings for surgery, which went well. She spent several weeks recovering at St. Vincent's Hospital in Billings and then was transferred to the hospital at Crow Agency for a few weeks. Lillian made a good recovery, which she attributed to prayer. "I walk just fine," she said, but in reality she could no longer go to the mountains and pick bitterroot and chokecherries with other women.

As she moved into her nineties, Lillian started to take her dinners at the senior center in Crow Agency, but she turned down an offer to have an apartment in the complex. Lillian told them that she preferred to stay in her own home, which she did for some years. However, finally age caught up with her, and she took an apartment in the senior center. Her children often called and visited.

In the last days of her life, Lillian lived in the Awe Kuualawache Rest Home, where her children visited daily. Mardell tried to encourage her mother to attend church service, but she would not go even when Mardell requested they sing some of her favorite hymns, such as "What a Friend We Have in Jesus." Mardell explained that her mother had gone back to the days of her youth. She sang her beloved tobacco songs, and as she approached death, Mardell said "she did the hand gestures we use in the Tobacco Society dance, and I felt that she was already in the afterlife the Crow knew as 'the Other Side Camp.'"

Lillian died on July 2, 2003, almost one hundred years old. Her life spanned nearly the whole of twentieth-century reservation life. It had been a remarkable journey from the early reservation years to the modern world, and Lillian made the transition better than most. Mardell said that Lillian once called herself just "a plain Crow Indian woman," and in some ways she was. But in other ways, she was a remarkable woman who blended the best of both worlds: Crow and white, old and new. Born in a tipi, by the time Lillian died in 2003, she had the distinction of being one of the oldest Crows living on the reservation.

ACKNOWLEDGMENTS

Writing is sometime perceived as a lonely profession—but, in reality, there are countless individuals you meet along the way. Sometimes it's a brief exchange; sometimes it's an extended conversation, but all the individuals I met in my research helped in various ways, large or small, to shape this book.

One day in a class on the Plains Indians, I made reference to Rosebud Yellow Robe, whom I had written about in *Lakota Portraits*. To my great surprise, Rebekah Tanner, one of my older, nontraditional students, exclaimed that she had met Rosebud some years before in New York City. So when I started to write the chapter on Rosebud Yellow Robe for *Brave Hearts: Indian Women of the Plains*, I asked Rebekah to share her recollection of meeting Rosebud. It's a wonderful story. Thanks, Rebekah.

My decision to include Josephine Crowfeather/Sister Mary Catharine in this book came from reading an entry in Gretchen Bataille's *Native American Women: A Biographical Dictionary*. That brief but well-written piece by Mark G. Thiel got me started on the topic. Sometime later I contacted Marquette University for a photograph of Sister Mary Catharine, and the friendly and helpful librarian at the other end turned out to be none other than Mark G. Thiel. Mark guided me through the Marquette photo archives, where I obtained my picture of Sister Mary Catharine. Mark also shared with me some letters that Gertrude Simmons Bonnin/Zitkala-Ša had written to Catholic priests that were in the Bureau of Catholic Indian Missions files. I've made use of these letters in my chapter on Zitkala-Ša.

Early in my research as I struggled to understand the relationship between Lieutenant Colonel George Armstrong Custer and Monahsetah, Rev. Vincent Heier, a longtime member of the Little Big Horn Associates, kindly sent me a difficult-to-find copy of Barbara Zimmerman's article "Monahsetah—Fact or Fiction." Later he shared with me a talk that Gail Kelly-Custer gave before the Western History Association in which she claimed that she was a descendant of Yellow Swallow, the supposed child of Custer and Monahsetah. Fr. Heier professed his serious doubts about this claim.

In 1919 General Hugh L. Scott interviewed a Crow batée whom whites called "Squaw Jim," but who was better known to his fellow Crows as Osh Tisch/Finds Them and Kills Them. Adam Minakowski, reference archivist at the National Anthropological Archives, Smithsonian, kindly sent me both the typed and handwritten versions of this interview, a rich source for our understanding of Osh Tisch.

I tried to include a photographic image for each of the women in the book, but it was not always easy and in some cases downright difficult to find a good photograph for each individual since Native American women tended to be more invisible than their male counterparts. If you want a photograph of Red Cloud, the famous Oglala Lakota war leader, you can easily find it in the Library of Congress, the National Archives, the Smithsonian, and the Nebraska State Historical Society, to mention a few places. But for some women in the book, such as Woman Chief and Running Eagle, there are no known photographs. Perhaps they simply lived too early in the nineteenth century for a wandering photographer to capture their image. But why didn't some wandering painter capture their images on canvas? One can only express some dismay that Rudolph F. Kurz, the Swiss painter, was so impressed with the scalp presented to him by Edward Denig—a scalp that Woman Chief took from a fallen Blackfoot warrior—that he forgot to paint a portrait of the famous warrior woman who stood before him! We don't have a photograph of Buffalo Calf Road, the famous warrior woman who fought at the Rosebud and the Little Bighorn in the 1870s, but we are fortunate that a Cheyenne artist later sketched her exploits.

For many other women in this book—especially those who lived in the nineteenth century—there are, at best, one or two pictures. But with the help of many individuals—family members, scholars, and photo-archivists—I was able to track them down. Each picture had its own story.

Some of the photographs were in private collections, and so I was dependent on the generosity of family members to share photographs of their relatives. A photograph of Josephine Waggoner, another of Susan Bordeaux and Josephine Waggoner at the Crazy Horse memorial at Fort Robinson, and a third of Josephine Crowfeather with her spiritual mentor Fr. Francis Craft came courtesy of Lynne Allen, Josephine Waggoner's great-granddaughter, and Emily Levine, editor of *Witness: A Húnkpapha Historian's Strong-Heart Song of the Lakotas.*

ACKNOWLEDGMENTS

Barbara Loeb and Mardell Hogan Plainfeather, who collaborated on *The Woman Who Loved Mankind: The Life of a Twentieth-Century Crow Elder*, were next to share a family photo. Mardell Hogan Plainfeather, Lillian Bullshows's daughter, sent me a beautiful portrait of her mother dressed in a splendid Crow outfit.

Leatrice "Chick" Big Crow from Pine Ridge, South Dakota, most graciously sent me some photographs of her beautiful daughter SuAnne Big Crow. I am honored to include two pictures of SuAnne Big Crow in the book.

I am grateful to all these family members for sharing such personal photographs, which enriched *Brave Hearts: Indian Women of the Plains*.

Finally, Dr. James S. Brust sent me a long-sought-after portrait of a young Osh Tisch, the Crow batée, with a companion, taken by John H. Fouch, frontier photographer. Dr. Brust, a collector and scholar on the photographer John H. Fouch, was most generous to share with me this rare photograph from his private collection.

Photo-archivists at state and federal public archives proved equally generous of their time and talent in locating and sharing pictures in their collections. Cindy Hagan, cultural resource specialist at the Little Bighorn Battlefield National Monument (LBBNM), was most helpful in locating a photograph by W. S. Soule of the captive Cheyenne women and children from the Washita fight. Unfortunately, Monahsetah was not in that picture; she was on the trail "scouting" for Custer. Cindy suggested that Peter Harrison's recently published book, *Monahsetah: The Life of a Custer Captive* (Chetwynd Press, 2015)—a book that I had been anticipating for some time—might prove helpful in the search. Indeed, it was. Harrison located the only known photograph of Monahsetah, in the Chisholm Trail Museum in Lawton, Oklahoma. Adam Lynn, the director of the museum, granted me permission to use the long-lost photograph. I continued my work with the LBBNM with Sorn Jessen, a young man interested in the role of Plains Indian women in warfare, who helped me locate a rare photograph of Susan Iron Teeth, taken by Dr. Thomas Marquis when she was ninety-three. Dr. Marquis also photographed Kate Bighead in old age. Sean Campbell, imaging manager at the Buffalo Bill Center of the West, kindly located her photograph for me.

Sanapia proved elusive. I could not locate Dr. David E. Jones, who included old and contemporary photographs of Sanapia (born Mary Poafpybitty) in his book *Sanapia: Comanche Medicine Woman*. Nor could I locate any archives where he may have deposited his pictures. I canvassed various archives in Oklahoma (where Sanapia had lived) until finally Deborah Anna Baroff, head curator at the Museum of Great Plains, notified me that she had found a photograph of Sanapia in a family portrait.

I had long held the famous picture of General Colby holding baby Lost Bird, but for a long time I searched for a grown-up picture of Zintkala Nuni/ Lost Bird taken at the San Francisco Panama-Pacific Exposition in 1915 when she was a twenty-five-year-old woman. It emerged after a strange, circuitous route. Renée Samson Flood, in her study of Lost Bird, listed the photo in the New York City Public Library (NYCPL). Zulay C. and Billy Parrott, photography collection specialists, conducted an extensive search in the various branches of the NYCPL. They did not find the print/image, but they did find the source of the Zintkala-Nuni photograph: the October 1915 issue of *Sunset* magazine. Marcie Farwell at Cornell University's Division of Rare and Manuscript Collections helped me locate the magazine and the image.

Fortunately, many of the photographs proved easier to find. My thanks to the following individuals and institutions for helping me locate the following images: Adrienne Leigh Sharpe, Stephen R. Young, and Lisa Conathan, all from Yale's Rare Book & Manuscript Library, for the picture of Mary Brave Bird; Rebecca Kohl, photograph assistant, Montana Historical Society, for Medicine Snake Woman; Benna Vaughan, special collections and manuscript archivist, and Geoff Hunt, audio and visual curator, at Baylor University, for Cynthia Ann Parker with her daughter Prairie Flower; John R. Waggener, associate archivist, and Charles E. Anderson, photographic assistant, at the University of Wyoming, for Pretty Shield; Jenny McElroy and Brigid Shields, reference librarians at the Minnesota Historical Society, for Buffalo Bird Woman; Kay Peterson at the National Museum of American History, Smithsonian, and Cindy Brightenburg, reference specialist at Brigham Young University, for the photographs of Zitkala-Ša; and finally, Mary-Jo Miller and Vonnda Shaw at the Nebraska State Historical Society for sending portraits of the four La Flesche sisters: Susette, Rosalie, Susan, and Marguerite.

I could not have written this book without the support of many people at Onondaga Community College (OCC), where I have taught American History for many years. The OCC Library is the heart of the institution. We hold a rich collection of Plains Indian material, far larger and more complete than many larger libraries. I am grateful to my friends and colleagues in the library—past and present—who made possible my work as a teacher and a writer. They have generously supported my requests over the years for important works on the Plains Indians.

My special thanks to Cheri Henderson and Kelly Nolan, inter-library loan specialists at the college, who searched diligently for the many books and articles that I needed for this study. I am constantly amazed by the willingness of the many unnamed librarians across the country who provided historical material, sometimes rare pieces, for my research. I could not have completed the book without them.

I want to thank Rick Boysen Jr., a technical specialist in the Photography Department, for his technical assistance in preparing some of the images for this book. Likewise, I want to thank Laura J. Matechak, academic technology specialist, who helped me navigate the more technical aspects of the computer.

Once again it's been a pleasure to work with Erin Turner, editorial director at TwoDot Books, for accepting the idea for this book and for guiding me through the difficult task of securing digital images for the many photos that grace the book's chapters. My thanks to Courtney Oppel, an editor at TwoDot, and copy editor Kate Hertzog for their careful reading of the manuscript, and to Caroline McManus, assistant production editor at Globe Pequot, for bringing this book to fruition.

Above all, I must thank Rosemary Agonito, the one constant force in my life and work. Despite her own writings, she has given of her time freely, reading the manuscript with a critical eye. Whenever I felt overwhelmed by the nature of the work, she encouraged me to go on and, for that, I am grateful. It's a far better book for her involvement.

BIBLIOGRAPHY

Woman Chief: Leader of Her People

Capps, Benjamin. *Woman Chief.* New York: Ace Books, 1979.

Denig, Edwin Thompson. *Five Indian Tribes of the Upper Missouri.* Edited by John C. Ewers. Norman: University of Oklahoma Press, 1961.

Ewers, John. "Deadlier than the Male." *American Heritage,* XVI (June 1965), 10–13.

Jenkins, Jennifer L. "Woman Chief," in *Native American Women: A Biographical Dictionary.* New York: Garland Publishing, 1993.

Kurz, Rudolph Friedrich. *Journal of Rudolph Friederich Kurz: An Account of His Experiences Among Fur Traders and American Indians on the Mississippi and the Upper Missouri Rivers During the Years 1846–1852.* Translated by Myrtis Jarrell. Edited by J. N. B. Hewitt. Bulletin 115 Bureau of American Ethnology Smithsonian Institution, Washington, D.C.: U.S. Government Printing Office, 1937.

Lang, Sabine. *Men as Women, Women as Men: Changing Gender in Native American Cultures.* Translated from the German by John L. Vantine. Austin: University of Texas Press, 1998.

Williams, Walter L. *The Spirit and the Flesh: Sexual Diversity in American Indian Culture.* Boston: Beacon Press, 1986.

Osh Tisch: Becoming a Woman

Agonito, Joseph. "Half-Man, Half-Woman: The Native American Berdache." *True West* (March 1989), 22–29.

Brust, James S. "John H. Fouch: First Photographer of Fort Keogh." *Montana, The Magazine of Western History,* 44 (Spring 1994), 2–17.

Hogan, Lillian Bullshows. *The Woman Who Loved Mankind: The Life of a Twentieth-Century Crow Elder.* As told to Barbara Loeb and Mardell Hogan Plainfeather. Lincoln: University of Nebraska Press, 2012.

Holder, A. B. "The Boté: Description of a Peculiar Sexual Perversion Found Among North American Indians." *New York Medical Journal* 50 (December 7, 1889), 623–25.

Lang, Sabine. *Men as Women, Women as Men: Changing Gender in Native American Cultures.* Translated from the German by John L. Vantine. Austin: University of Texas Press, 1998.

Linderman, Frank B. *Pretty Shield: Medicine Woman of the Crows.* New York: John Day Company, 1972.

Medicine Horse, Mary Helen. *A Dictionary of Everyday Crow.* Crow Agency, MT: Bilingual Materials Development Center, 1987.

Riebeth, Carolyn Reynolds. *J. H. Sharp Among the Crow Indians 1902–1910.* El Segundo, CA: Upton and Sons, 1985.

Roscoe, Will. "That Is My Road: The Life and Times of a Crow Berdache." *Montana, The Magazine of Western History,* 40 (Winter 1990), 46–55.

Scott, Hugh L. "Notes on Sign Language and Miscellaneous Ethnographic Notes on Plains Indians." National Anthropological Archives, Smithsonian. MS 2392. Box 3, "Marriage and Family, Berdache."

Simms, S. C. "Crow Indian Hermaphrodites." *American Anthropologist,* New Series, 5 (July–September 1903), 579–84.

Williams, Walter L. *The Spirit and the Flesh: Sexual Diversity in American Indian Culture.* Boston: Beacon Press, 1986.

Running Eagle: Brave-Hearted Woman

Ewers, John C. "Deadlier Than the Male." *American Heritage,* XVI (June 1965), 10–13.

Godfrey, Audrey M. "Running Eagle," in *Native American Women: A Biographical Dictionary.* New York: Garland Publishing, 1993.

Hungry Wolf, Beverly. *The Ways of My Grandmothers.* New York: Quill, 1982.

Lang, Sabine. *Men as Women, Women as Men: Changing Gender in Native American Cultures.* Translated from the German by John L. Vantine. Austin: University of Texas Press, 1998.

Schultz, James Willard. *Blackfeet and Buffalo: Memories of Life among the Indians.* Edited and with an introduction by Keith C. Seele. Noman: University of Oklahoma Press, 1962.

———. *Running Eagle: The Warrior Girl.* New York: Houghton Mifflin, 1919.

Buffalo Calf Road: Warrior Woman

Agonito, Rosemary, and Joseph Agonito. "Resurrecting History's Forgotten Women: A Case Study from the Cheyenne Indians." *Frontiers, A Journal of Women Studies*, VI (Fall 1981), 8–16.

———. *Buffalo Calf Road Woman: The Story of a Warrior of the Little Bighorn*. Helena, MT: TwoDot Books, 2005.

Bighead, Kate [Antelope Woman]. "She Watched Custer's Last Battle," in *Custer on the Little Bighorn*. Compiled and recorded by Thomas B. Marquis. Lodi, CA: Dr. Marquis Custer Publications, 1967.

Iron Teeth, Susan. "Iron Teeth, A Cheyenne Old Woman," in *Cheyenne and Sioux: The Reminiscences of Four Indians and a White Soldier*. Compiled and recorded by Thomas B. Marquis. Stockton, CA: Pacific Center for Western Historical Studies, 1973.

Monnett, John H. *Tell Them We Are Going Home: The Odyssey of the Northern Cheyennes*. Norman: University of Oklahoma Press, 2001.

Powell, Peter. *People of the Sacred Mountain*. 2 volumes. San Francisco: Harper & Row, 1981.

Sandoz, Mari. *Cheyenne Autumn*. New York: McGraw-Hill, 1953.

Stands in Timber, John, and Margot Liberty. *Cheyenne Memories*. Lincoln: University of Nebraska Press/Bison Books, 1972.

Wooden Leg. *Wooden Leg: A Warrior Who Fought Custer*. Interpreted by Thomas B. Marquis. Lincoln: University of Nebraska Press/Bison Books, n.d.

Kate Bighead: Wartime Reporter

Bighead, Kate. "She Watched Custer's Last Battle," in *Custer on the Little Bighorn*. Compiled and edited by Thomas B. Marquis. Lodi, CA: Dr. Marquis Custer Publications, 1967.

Hardorff, Richard G., editor and compiler. *Cheyenne Memories of the Custer Fight*. Lincoln: University of Nebraska Press/Bison Books, 1998.

———, editor and compiler. *Lakota Recollections of the Custer Fight*. Lincoln: University of Nebraska Press/Bison Books, 1997.

Iron Teeth, Susan. "Iron Teeth, A Cheyenne Old Woman," in *Cheyenne and Sioux: The Reminiscences of Four Indians and a White Soldier*. Compiled and recorded by Thomas B. Marquis. Stockton, CA: Pacific Center for Western Historical Studies, 1973.

Marquis, Thomas B. *The Cheyennes of Montana*. Edited with an introduction by Thomas D. Weist. Algonac, MI: Reference Publications, 1978.

———. *A Northern Cheyenne Album*. Edited by Margot Liberty. Norman: University of Oklahoma Press, 2006.

Michno, Gregory F. *Lakota Noon: The Indian Narrative of Custer's Defeat*. Missoula, MT: Mountain Press Publishing Company, 1997.

Stands in Timber, John, and Margot Liberty. *Cheyenne Memories*. Lincoln: University of Nebraska Press/Bison Books, 1972.

———. *A Cheyenne Voice: The Complete John Stands in Timber Interviews*. Norman: University of Oklahoma Press, 2013.

Wooden Leg. *Wooden Leg: A Warrior Who Fought Custer*. Interpreted by Thomas B. Marquis. Lincoln: University of Nebraska Press/Bison Books, n.d.

Iron Teeth: Strong-Willed Survivor

Iron Teeth, Susan. "Iron Teeth, A Cheyenne Old Woman," in *Cheyenne and Sioux: The Reminiscences of Four Indians and a White Soldier*. Compiled and recorded by Thomas B. Marquis. Stockton, CA: Pacific Center for Western Historical Studies, 1973.

Marquis, Thomas B. *The Cheyennes of Montana*. Edited with an introduction by Thomas D. Weist. Algoncac, MI: Reference Publications, 1978.

———. *A Northern Cheyenne Album*. Edited by Margot Liberty. Norman: University of Oklahoma Press, 2006.

Monnett, John H. *Tell Them We Are Going Home: The Odyssey of the Northern Cheyenne*. Norman: University of Oklahoma Press, 2001.

———. "'My heart now has become changed to softer feelings': A Northern Cheyenne Woman and Her Family Remember the Long Journey Home." *Montana, The Magazine of Western History*, 59 (Summer 2009), 45–61.

Medicine Snake Woman: Embracing the White World

Audubon, Maria R., editor. *Audubon and His Journals*. 2 volumes. New York: Dover Publications, 1960. A Reprint of the original published by Charles Scribner's Sons, 1897.

Ewers, John C. *Indian Life on the Upper Missouri*. Chapter 5, "Mothers of the Mixed Bloods." Norman: University of Oklahoma Press, 1968.

——. *The Blackfeet: Raiders on the Northwestern Plains*. Norman: University of Oklahoma Press, 1958.

Kurz, Rudolph Friederich. *Journal of Rudolph Friederich Kurz: An Account of His Experiences Among Fur Traders and American Indians on the Mississippi and the Upper Missouri Rivers During the Years 1846–1852*. Translated by Myrtis Jarrell. Edited by J. N. B. Hewitt. Bulletin 115. Smithsonian Institution, Bureau of American Ethnology. Washington, D.C.: U.S. Government Printing Office, 1937.

Mattison, Ray H. "Alexander Culbertson," in Volume 1, *The Mountain Men and the Fur Trade of the Far West*. Edited by LeRoy R. Hafen. Glendale, CA: The Arthur H. Clark Company, 1965.

McDonald, Anne. "Mrs. Alexander Culbertson." *Contributions to the Historical Society of Montana*, 10 (1941), 243–46.

Morgan, Lewis Henry. *The Indian Journals 1859–62*. Edited by Leslie A. White. New York: Dover Publications, 1993.

Schemm, Mildred Walker. "The Major's Lady: Natawista." *Montana, The Magazine of Western History*, 2 (January 1952), 5–15.

Stevens, Isaac I. *Annual Reports*. Commissioner of Indian Affairs, 1854.

Eagle Woman: Peace Emissary

Chittenden, Hiram M., and Alfred T. Richardson, editors and compilers. *Life, Letters and Travels of Father Pierre Jean De Smet, S. J.* 2 volumes. New York: Kraus Reprint Company, 1969.

Gray, John S. "The Story of Mrs. Picotte-Galpin, a Sioux Heroine: Eagle Woman Learns about White Ways and Racial Conflict, 1820–1868." *Montana, The Magazine of Western History*, 36 (Spring 1986), 2–21.

——. "The Story of Mrs. Picotte-Galpin, a Sioux Heroine: Eagle Woman Become a Trader and Counsels for Peace, 1868–1888." *Montana, The Magazine of Western History*, 36 (Summer 1986), 2–21.

Holley, Frances C. *Once Their Home: or, Our Legacy from the Dakotahs*. Chicago: Donohue & Henneberry, 1892.

Phaller, Louis. "The Galpin Journal: Dramatic Record of an Odyssey of Peace." Rev. ed. *Montana, The Magazine of Western History*, 18 (April 1968), 2–23.

Waggoner, Josephine. *Witness: A Húnkpapha Historian's Strong-Heart Song of the Lakotas.* Edited and with an introduction by Emily Levine. Lincoln: University of Nebraska Press, 2013.

Cynthia Ann Parker: White Comanche

Brown, Marion T. *Marion T. Brown: Letters from Fort Sill, 1887–1888.* Edited by C. Richard King. Austin, TX: Encino Press, 1970.

Carlson, Paul H., and Tom Crum. *Myth, Memory and Massacre: The Pease River Capture of Cynthia Ann Parker.* Lubbock: Texas Tech University Press, 2010.

Exley, Jo Ella Powell. *Frontier Blood: The Saga of the Parker Family.* College Station: Texas A&M University Press, 2001.

Frankel, Glenn. *The Searchers: The Making of an American Legend.* New York: Bloomsbury, 2013.

Gelo, Daniel J., and Scott Zesch. "'Every Day Seemed to Be a Holiday': The Captivity of Bianca Babb." *Southwestern Historical Quarterly*, CVII (July 2003), 35–67.

Hacker, Margaret Schmidt. *Cynthia Ann Parker: The Life and the Legend.* El Paso: The University of Texas Press, 1990.

Gwynne, S. C. *Empire of the Summer Moon: Quanah Parker and the Rise and Fall of the Comanches.* New York: Scribner, 2010.

Marcy, Captain Randolph B., and Captain G. B. McClellan. *Adventure on Red River: Report of the Exploration of the Headwaters of the Red River.* Edited and annotated by Grant Foreman. Norman: University of Oklahoma Press, 1937. (Reprint of the 1853 edition.)

Plummer, Rachel. *Narrative of the Capture and Subsequent Sufferings of Mrs. Rachel Plummer.* Houston: 1839.

Zesch, Scott. *Captured: A True Story of Abduction by Indians on the Texas Frontier.* New York: St. Martin's Press, 2004.

Wellman, Paul I. "Cynthia Ann Parker." *Chronicles of Oklahoma*, 12 (June 1934), 163–70.

Monahsetah: Custer's Captive "Wife"

Barnett, Louise. *Touched by Fire: The Life, Death, and Mythic Afterlife of George Armstrong Custer.* New York: Henry Holt and Company, 1996.

Bighead, Kate. "She Watched Custer's Last Battle," in *Custer on the Little Bighorn*. Compiled and edited by Thomas B. Marquis. Lodi, CA: Dr. Marquis Custer Publications, 1967.

Brill, Charles J. *Conquest of the Southern Plains*. Oklahoma City: Golden Saga Publishers, 1938.

———. *Custer, Black Kettle, and the Fight on the Washita*. Norman: University of Oklahoma Press/Red River Books, 2002. (Reprint of Brill's *Conquest of the Southern Plains*.)

Carroll, John M., editor. *The Benteen-Goldin Letters on Custer and His Last Battle*. New York: Liveright, 1974.

Crow Dog, Mary, and Richard Erdoes. *Lakota Woman*. New York: Harper Perennial, 1991.

Custer, Elizabeth Bacon. *Following the Guidon*. Norman: University of Oklahoma Press, 1966.

Custer, George A. *My Life on the Plains*. Lincoln: University of Nebraska Press/Bison Books, 1966.

Elliott, Michael A. *Custerology: The Enduring Legacy of the Indian Wars and George Armstrong Custer*. Chicago: University of Chicago Press, 2007.

Hardorff, Richard G., compiler and editor. *Washita Memories: Eyewitness Views of Custer's Attack on Black Kettle's Village*. Norman: University of Oklahoma Press, 2006.

Harrison, Peter. *Monahsetah: The Life of a Custer Captive*. Edited by Gary Leonard. Southampton, United Kingdom: Chetwynd Press, 2015.

Kelly-Custer, Gail. *Princess Monahsetah, the Concealed Wife of General Custer*. Victoria, British Columbia: Trafford Publishing, 2007.

Koster, John. "Squaring Custer's Triangle." *Wild West* (June 2009), 26–31.

Leckie, Shirley A. *Elizabeth Bacon Custer and the Making of a Myth*. Norman: University of Oklahoma Press, 1993.

Michno, Gregory F. *Lakota Noon: The Indian Narrative of Custer's Defeat*. Missoula, MT: Mountain Press Publishing Company, 1997.

Miller, David Humphreys. *Custer's Fall: The Native American Side of the Story*. New York: Pengun/Meridian, 1992.

Monaghan, Jay. *Custer: The Life of General George Armstrong Custer*. Lincoln: University of Nebraska Press/Bison Books, 1971.

Sandoz, Mari. *Cheyenne Autumn*. New York: McGraw-Hill, 1953.

Stands in Timber, John, and Margot Liberty. *Cheyenne Memories.* Lincoln: University of Nebraska Press/Bison Books, 1972.

Utley, Robert M. *Cavalier in Buckskin: George Armstrong Custer and the Western Military Frontier.* Norman: University of Oklahoma Press, 1988.

Wert, Jeffry D. *Custer: The Controversial Life of George Armstrong Custer.* New York: Simon & Schuster, 1996.

Pretty Shield: Remembering the Old Days

Harcey, Dennis W., and Brian R. Croone, with Joe Medicine Crow. *White Man Runs Him: Crow Scout with Custer.* Evanston, IL: Evanston Publishing, 1995.

Hoxie, Frederick E. *Parading Through History: The Making of the Crow Nation in America 1805–1935.* Cambridge: Cambridge University Press, 1995.

Linderman, Frank B. *Pretty Shield: Medicine Woman of the Crows.* New York: The John Day Company, 1972. (Reprint of the original edition published in 1932 under the title *Red Mother.*)

Snell, Alma Hogan. *Grandmother's Grandchild: My Crow Indian Life.* Edited by Becky Mathews. Lincoln: University of Nebraska Press/Bison Books, 2001.

Stevenson, Elizabeth. *Figures on a Western Landscape: Men and Women of the Northern Rockies.* Baltimore: Johns Hopkins University Press, 1994.

Buffalo Bird Woman: Keeping the Traditions Alive

Buffalo Bird Woman. *Waheenee: An Indian Girl's Story.* Edited by Gilbert L. Wilson. Lincoln: University of Nebraska Press/Bison Books, 1981.

Fenn, Elizabeth A. *Encounters at the Heart of the World: A History of the Mandan People.* New York: Hill and Wang, 2014.

Gilman, Carolyn, and Mary Jane Schneider. *The Way to Independence: Memories of a Hidatsa Indian Family, 1840–1920.* St. Paul: Minnesota Historical Society Press, 1987.

Goodbird, Edward. *Goodbird the Indian: His Story.* Edited by Gilbert L. Wilson. New York: Fleming H. Revell Company, 1914.

Meyer, Roy W. *The Village Indians of the Upper Missouri: The Mandans, Hidatsas, and Arikaras.* Lincoln: University of Nebraska Press, 1977.

Nabokov, Peter, and Robert Easton. *Native American Architecture*. New York: Oxford University Press, 1989.

Peters, Virginia Bergman. *Women of the Earth Lodges: Tribal Life on the Plains*. Norman: University of Oklahoma Press, 1995.

Wilson, Norma C. "Buffalo Bird Woman," in *Native American Women: A Biographical Dictionary*. Edited by Gretchen M. Bataille. New York: Garland Publishing, 1993.

Josephine Crowfeather: Catholic Nun

Craft, Father Francis M. *At Standing Rock: The Journals and Papers of Father Francis M. Craft, 1888–1890*. Edited and annotated by Thomas W. Foley. Norman, OK: The Arthur H. Clark Company, 2009.

Duratschek, Sister Mary Claudia. *Crusading Along Sioux Trails: A History of the Catholic Church Indian Missions Among the South Dakota Sioux*. St. Meinrad, IN: The Grail Press, 1947.

Ewens, Sister Mary. "The Native Order: A Brief and Strange History," in *Scattered Steeples—The Fargo Diocese: A Written Celebration of Its Centennial*. Edited by Jerome D. Lamb, Jerry Ruff, and William C. Sherman. Fargo, ND: Burch, Londergan and Lynch, Publishers, 1988.

Foley, Thomas W. *Father Francis M. Craft: Missionary to the Sioux*. Lincoln: University of Nebraska Press, 2002.

———. *Faces of Faith: A History of the First Order of Indian Sisters*. Baltimore: Cathedral Foundation Press, 2008.

Thiel, Mark G. "Sacred White Buffalo, Mother Mary Catherine," in *Native American Woman: A Biographical Dictionary*. Edited by Gretchen M. Bataille. New York: Garland Publishing, 1993.

Sanapia: Comanche Medicine Woman

Bannan, Helen M. "Sanapia," in *Native American Women: A Biographical Dictionary*. Edited by Gretchen M. Bataille. New York: Garland Publishing, 1993.

Hoebel, E. Adamson. *The Political Organization and Law-Ways of the Comanche Indians*, Memoir No. 54. Menasha, WI: American Anthropological Association, 1940.

Jones, David E. *Sanapia: Comanche Medicine Woman*. New York: Holt, Rinehart and Winston, 1972.

Kardiner, Abram. "The Comanche," in *The Psychological Frontiers of Society*. New York: Columbia University Press, 1945.

Wallace, Ernest, and E. Adamson Hoebel. *The Comanches: Lords of the South Plains*. Norman: University of Oklahoma Press, 1952.

The La Flesche Sisters: Walking in Two Worlds

Diffendal, Anne P. "The LaFlesche Sisters: Victorian Reformers in the Omaha Tribe." *Journal of the West*, 33, no. 1 (1994), 37–44.

Emmerich, Lisa E. "Marguerite Laflesche Diddock: Office of Indian Affairs Field Matron." *Great Plains Quarterly*, 13 (Summer 1993), 162–71.

Fletcher, Alice C., and Francis La Flesche. *The Omaha Tribe*. 2 volumes. Lincoln: University of Nebraska Press/Bison Books, 1972.

Green, Norma Kidd. *Iron Eye's Family: The Children of Joseph La Flesche*. Lincoln, NE: Johnsen Publishing Company, 1969.

Mathes, Valerie Sherer. "Susan LaFlesche Picotte, M.D.: Nineteenth-Century Physician and Reformer." *Great Plains Quarterly*, 13 (Summer 1993), 172–86.

O'Shea, John M., and John Ludwickson. "Omaha Chieftainship in the Nineteenth Century." *Ethnohistory*, 39 (Summer 1992), 316–52.

Peterson, Nancy M. *Walking in Two Worlds: Mixed-Blood Indian Women Seeking Their Path*. Caldwell, ID: Caxton Press, 2006.

Street, Douglas. "La Flesche Sisters Write to St. Nicholas Magazine." *Nebraska History*, 62 (1981), 515–23.

Tibbles, Thomas Henry. *Buckskin and Blanket Days: Memoirs of a Friend of the Indians*. New York: Doubleday & Company, 1957.

Tong, Benson. *Susan La Flesche Picotte, M.D.: Omaha Indian Leader and Reformer*. Norman: University of Oklahoma Press, 1999.

Wilson, Dorothy Clarke. *Bright Eyes: The Story of Susette La Flesche, an Omaha Indian*. New York: McGraw-Hill, 1974.

Josephine Waggoner: Lakota Historian

Agonito, Joseph. *Lakota Portraits: Lives of the Legendary Plains People*. Helena, MT: TwoDot Books, 2011.

Bordeaux Bettelyoun, Susan, and Josephine Waggoner. *With My Own Eyes: A Lakota Woman Tells Her People's History*. Edited and introduced by Emily Levine. Lincoln: University of Nebraska Press/Bison Books, 1998.

Crawford, Lewis F., and Josephine Waggoner. *The Exploits of Ben Arnold*. Foreword by Paul L. Hedren. Norman: University of Oklahoma Press, 1999.

Hultgren, Mary Lou. "'To Be Examples to . . . Their People': Standing Rock Sioux Students at Hampton Institute, 1878–1923" (Part Two). *North Dakota History*, 68, No. 3 (2001), 20–42.

Molin, Paulette F. "'To be Examples to . . . Their People': Standing Rock Sioux Students at Hampton Institute, 1878–1923 (Part One)." *North Dakota History*, 68, No. 2 (2001), 1–23.

Peterson, Nancy M. *Walking in Two Worlds: Mixed-Blood Indian Women Seeking Their Path*. Caldwell, ID: Caxton Press, 2006.

Waggoner, Josephine. *Witness: A Húnkpapha Historian's Strong-Heart Song of the Lakotas*. Edited and introduced by Emily Levine. Lincoln: University of Nebraska Press, 2013.

Zitkala-Ša: Woman of the World

Fisher, Dexter. "Zitkala-Ša: The Evolution of a Writer." *American Indian Quarterly*, 5 (August 1979) 229–38.

Hafen, P. Jane. "A Cultural Duet: Zitkala-Ša and the Sun Dance Opera." *Great Plains Quarterly*, 18 (Spring 1998), 102–11.

———. "'Help Indians Help Themselves': Gertrude Bonnin, the SAI, and the NCAI." *American Indian Quarterly*, 37 (Summer 2013), 199–218.

Lisa, Laurie. "Bonnin, Gertrude Simmons [Zitkala-Ša, Red Bird]," in *Native American Women: A Biographical Dictionary*. Second Edition. Edited by Gretchen M. Bataille and Laurie Lisa. New York: Routledge, 2001.

Parker, John W., and Ruth Ann Parker. *Josiah White's Institute: The Interpretation and Implementation of His Vision*. Dublin, IN: Prinit Press, 1983.

Peterson, Nancy M. *Walking in Two Worlds: Mixed-Blood Indian Women Seeking Their Path*. Caldwell, ID: Caxton Press, 2006.

Spack, Ruth. "Dis/engagement: Zitkala-Ša's Letters to Carlos Montezuma, 1901–1902." *Melus*, 26 (Spring 2001), 172–204.

Stewart, Omer S. *Peyote Religion: A History*. Norman: University of Oklahoma Press, 1987.

Welch, Deborah Sue. *Zitkala-Ša: An American Indian Leader, 1876–1938*. University of Wyoming, 1985. PhD Dissertation.

———. "Gertrude Simmons Bonnin (Zitkala-Ša) Dakota," in *The New Warriors: Native American Leaders Since 1900*. Edited by R. David Edmunds. Lincoln: University of Nebraska Press, 2001.

Zitkala-Ša. *American Indian Stories*. Lincoln: University of Nebraska Press/Bison Books, 1985. Foreword by Dexter Fisher. (Reprint of the original published by Hayworth Publishing House, 1921.)

———. *Zitkala-Ša: American Indian Stories, Legends, and Other Writings*. Edited with an introduction and notes by Cathy N. Davidson and Ada Norris. New York: Penguin Books, 2003.

———. *Dreams and Thunder: Stories, Poems, and the Sun Dance Opera*: *Zitkala-Ša*. Edited by P. Jane Hafen. Lincoln: University of Nebraska Press, 2001.

———. *Old Indian Legends*. Foreword by Agnes M. Picotte. Lincoln: University of Nebraska Press/Bison Books, 1985. (Reprint of the original published by Ginn and Company, 1901.)

Lost Bird: Sacred Child of the Wounded Knee Battlefield

Eastman, Elaine Goodale. *Yellow Star: A Story of East and West*. Boston: Little, Brown and Company, 1911.

Flood, Renée Sansom. *Lost Bird of Wounded Knee: Spirit of the Lakota*. New York: Scribner, 1995.

Jensen, Richard E., ed. *Voices of the American West*. Volume 1, *The Indian Interviews of Eli S. Ricker 1903–1919*. Interviews: Joseph Horn Cloud; William Peano; Paddy Starr. Lincoln: University of Nebraska Press, 2005.

———. *Voices of the American West*. Volume 2, *The Settler and Soldier Interviews of Eli S. Ricker 1903–1919*. George Bartlett interview. Lincoln: University of Nebraska Press, 2005.

Mooney, James. *The Ghost Dance Religion and the Sioux Outbreak of 1890*. Abridged edition. Chicago: University of Chicago Press, 1965.

Mary Brave Bird: Defender of Her People

Brave Bird, Mary, with Richard Erdoes. *Ohitika Woman*. New York: Grove Press, 1993.

Crow Dog, Mary, with Richard Erdoes. *Lakota Woman*. New York: Grove Press, 1990.

Crow Dog, Leonard, and Richard Erdoes. *Crow Dog: Four Generations of Sioux Medicine Men.* New York: Harper Collins, 1995.

Matthiessen, Peter. *In The Spirit of Crazy Horse.* New York: Viking Penguin, 1991.

Means, Russell, with Marvin J.Wolf. *Where White Men Fear to Tread: The Autobiography of Russell Means.* New York: St. Martin's Press, 1995.

Petrillo, Larissa. "The Life Stories of a Woman from Rosebud: Names and Naming in *Lakota Woman* and *Ohitika Woman*." MA Thesis. Wilfrid Laurier University, 1996.

Smith, Paul Chaat, and Robert Allen Warrior. *Like a Hurricane: The Indian Movement from Alcatraz to Wounded Knee.* New York: The New Press, 1996.

Wise, Christopher, and R. Todd Wise. "A Conversation with Mary Brave Bird." *American Indian Quarterly*, 24 (Summer 2000).

Yardley, William. "Mary Ellen Moore-Richard, 58, American Indian Memoirist." *New York Times*, March 5, 2013.

SuAnne Big Crow: Shooting Star

Frazier, Ian. *On the Rez.* New York: Farrar, Straus, and Giroux, 2000.

Haase, Eric, and Jerry Reynolds. "A Salute of Love." *Lakota Times*, February 19, 1992, B4–5. SuAnne's obituary notice is in the *Lakota Times*, February 19, 1992, C7.

Stillman, Pamela. "Goals and Dreams." *Lakota Times*, February 26, 1992, B1.

Staurowsky, Ellen J. "SuAnne Big Crow: Her Legend and Legacy," in *Native Athletes in Sport and Society*. Edited by C. Richard King. Lincoln: University of Nebraska Press, 2005.

Rosebud Yellow Robe: Living in the Big City

Brownlow, Kevin. *The War, the West, and the Wilderness.* New York: Alfred A. Knopf, 1979.

Castle, Edward. "Rosebud: Solution to Mystery Offered." *Las Vegas Sun*, August 11, 1991, 1A.

Edwards, Oren. "Gathering Rosebuds." *Smithsonian Magazine*, January 2007.

Fielder, Mildred. *Sioux Indian Leaders.* Chapter 7, "Chauncey Yellow Robe, Bridge Between Two Cultures." New York: Bonanza Books, 1981.

McBride, Bunny. *Molly Spotted Elk: A Penobscot in Paris*. Norman: University of Oklahoma Press, 1995.

O'Harra, C. C. "President Coolidge in the Black Hills." *Black Hills Engineer*, XV, No. 4 (November 1927), 205–48.

Riney, Scott. *The Rapid City Indian School, 1898–1933*. Norman: University of Oklahoma Press, 1999.

The Silent Enemy. 1930. Producers, Douglas Burden and William Chandler.

Weinberg, Marjorie. *The Real Rosebud: The Triumph of a Lakota Woman*. Lincoln: University of Nebraska Press, 2004.

Yellow Robe, Chauncey. "My Boyhood Days." *Indian Leader*, October 30, 1925, 12–15.

Yellow Robe, Rosebud. *An Album of the American Indian*. New York: Franklin Watts, 1969.

Lillian Bullshows Hogan: "A Plain Crow Indian Woman"

Hogan, Lillian Bullshows. *The Woman Who Loved Mankind: The Life of a Twentieth-Century Crow Elder*. As told to Barbara Loeb and Mardell Hogan Plainfeather. Lincoln: University of Nebraska Press, 2012.

Plainfeather, Mardell Hogan. Radio interview with Cherie Newman. The Write Question Radio, Montana Public Radio, March 21, 2013.

Snell, Alma Hogan. *Grandmother's Grandchild: My Crow Indian Life*. Edited by Becky Matthews. Lincoln: University of Nebraska Press, 2000.

INDEX

Note: Italicized page numbers indicate illustrations. Footnotes are indicated with "n."

330

Greater Federation of Women's
  Clubs, 232
Great Sioux Reservation, 20,
  42, 64–65, 236–37
Great Sioux War
  Lakota history and official
    end of, 211
  Little Bighorn battle, 22–24,
    32–36, 42, 68, 112–13,
    195
  Powder River battle, 32
  Rosebud battle, 9–10,
    20–23, 22, 32, 112
Great Spirit, 208
Green, Jerome A., 242
Green, Nathanael, 136
Green, Norma Kidd, 160, 175
Gregory, Sister, 141n
Griffin, Fannie Reed, 171
Grinnell, George Bird, 45–46,
  211
Gros Ventre of the Prairie, 1, 4
Gwynne, S. C., 71, 78

hair, 8, 55, 83, 134, 216
Hall, Charles L., 120, 131,
  132, 134
Hampton Minstrels, 198
Hampton Normal and
  Agriculture Institute,
  178–79, 187, 197, 198
Hanging Stone, 128–29
Hanson, William F., 225–26,
  234–35
Hardorff, Richard G., 35n
Harmon, William, 66
Harrison, Benjamin, 239
Harrison, Peter, 87, 91, 93–94,
  96, 97, 98, 99
Haskell Institute, 148, 201,
  246–47
Hawk, 89
Hayden, Ferdinand V., 60
Hayes, Rutherford B., 168
Heritage, Marian, 174–75,
  180, 181
Herriott, Frank I., 203, 206
Hiawatha (Longfellow), 168,
  220

Hidatsas/Mandans
  agencies for, 131, 139
  bravery symbols, 130
  childhood descriptions,
    122–25
  courtship rituals, 126–29
  disease decimation, 122,
    123
  housing traditions, 124
  marriage traditions and
    rituals, 122, 129–30
  mourning rituals, 134
  naming ceremonies,
    122–23
  religious beliefs and
    practices, 123, 124, 133
  sacred crafts and knowledge
    rights, 129–30
  traditional lifestyle
    descriptions, 122,
    123–27, 135
  tribal conflicts, 128
  white society and lifestyle
    influences, 131–33
  womanhood preparation,
    125–28
hide scrapers, 44, 46, 49–50
Hill, Decajawiah, 268
Hinman, Samuel D., 68
History of the Dakota or Sioux
  Indians, A (Robinson),
  207
Hogan, George Washington,
  304, 305, 306–7
Hogan, Mary, 304, 305, 307,
  308
Holder, A. B., 7–8
Holley, Frances Chamberlain,
  59n, 60, 63, 65, 69
homosexuality, 3, 8
hospitals, 185–86
Houston, Sam, 74
Hungry Wolf, Beverly, 16, 17n
Hunkpapas (Lakota tribe)
  Catholic missionary work
    and nun recruitments,
    136–45
  chiefs of, histories, 212–13
  land allotments, 201

land conflicts and
  commissioner protection,
  68
  murders and arrests, 66–67
  peace envoys and
    negotiations, 59, 63–65,
    68
  religious practices and
    beliefs, 137
  reservation dissatisfaction
    and relocation, 25, 65,
    68, 194–95, 196–97
  reservation lifestyle
    descriptions, 211–12
  US Army conflicts, 22–24,
    32, 33, 62

Ikinicapi, Thomas, 178, 179,
  181
Indian Citizen Act, 233
Indian Reorganization Act
  (IRA), 233–34, 259, 261
Indian rights advocacy
  cross-country protests,
    256–58
  land allotment protests, 170,
    184–85
  land theft issues, 232, 233
  legal system corruption,
    232–33, 267, 268
  legal system protests,
    258–59
  literary themes of, 169
  mining protests, 268
  missionary society speeches
    on, 180
  organizations for, 229–30,
    232, 233, 255–56
  religious practices and
    debate, 230–32
  reservation system criticism,
    230
  self-determination issues,
    233–34
  siege protests for, 98, 252,
    259–63
  treaty negotiations and
    forced migrations,
    164–69

ABOUT THE AUTHOR

Joseph Agonito, PhD, an award-winning author, has published three books, as well as numerous popular and scholarly articles, and produced three film documentaries. He is the coauthor of *Buffalo Calf Road Woman: The Story of a Warrior of the Little Bighorn*, based on a true story, which won the 2006 Western Heritage Award for Outstanding Novel. He also won the Nebraska State Historical Society's Sellers Memorial Award for an Outstanding Original Contribution published in *Nebraska History*, "Young Man Afraid of His Horses: The Reservation Years," and three film awards for his documentary work. His most recent book was *Lakota Portraits: Lives of the Legendary Plains People*. Professor emeritus of American History, he specializes in the Plains Indians and the American West. Agonito has lectured widely on these and other topics.

CPSIA information can be obtained
at www.ICGtesting.com
Printed in the USA
BVHW071348020821
613134BV00002B/6